Teachings of Lord Caitanya

BOOKS BY HIS DIVINE GRACE A. C. BHAKTIVEDANTA SWAMI PRABHUPĀDA

Bhagavad-gītā As It Is
Śrīmad-Bhāgavatam (completed by disciples)
Śrī Caitanya-caritāmṛta
Kṛṣṇa, the Supreme Personality of Godhead
Teachings of Lord Caitanya
The Nectar of Devotion
The Nectar of Instruction
Śrī Īśopaniṣad
Light of the Bhāgavata
Easy Journey to Other Planets
Teachings of Lord Kapila, the Son of Devahūti
Teachings of Queen Kuntī
Message of Godhead
The Science of Self-Realization
The Perfection of Yoga
Beyond Birth and Death
On the Way to Kṛṣṇa
Rāja-vidyā: The King of Knowledge
Elevation to Kṛṣṇa Consciousness
Kṛṣṇa Consciousness: The Matchless Gift
Kṛṣṇa Consciousness: The Topmost Yoga System
Perfect Questions, Perfect Answers
Life Comes from Life
The Nārada-bhakti-sūtra (completed by disciples)
The Mukunda-mālā-stotra (completed by disciples)
Geetār-gān (Bengali)
Vairāgya-vidyā (Bengali)
Buddhi-yoga (Bengali)
Bhakti-ratna-boli (Bengali)
Back to Godhead magazine (founder)

BOOKS COMPILED FROM THE TEACHINGS OF HIS DIVINE GRACE A. C. BHAKTIVEDANTA SWAMI PRABHUPĀDA AFTER HIS LIFETIME

Search for Liberation
A Second Chance
The Journey of Self-Discovery
Civilization and Transcendence
The Laws of Nature
Renunciation Through Wisdom
The Quest for Enlightenment
Dharma, the Way of Transcendence
Spiritual Yoga
Bhakti-yoga, the Art of Eternal Love
Beyond Illusion and Doubt
The Hare Kṛṣṇa Challenge

Teachings of Lord Caitanya

The Golden Avatāra

A Treatise on Factual Spiritual Life

BY

HIS DIVINE GRACE
A. C. BHAKTIVEDANTA SWAMI PRABHUPĀDA

FOUNDER-*ĀCĀRYA* OF THE
INTERNATIONAL SOCIETY FOR KRISHNA CONSCIOUSNESS

THE BHAKTIVEDANTA BOOK TRUST
LOS ANGELES • STOCKHOLM • MUMBAI • SYDNEY

Readers interested in the subject matter of this book
are invited by the International Society
for Krishna Consciousness to correspond with
its secretary at the following address:

The Bhaktivedanta Book Trust
P.O. Box 341445, Los Angeles, California 90034, USA
Phone: +1-800-927-4152 • Fax: +1-310-837-1056
e-mail: bbt.usa@krishna.com

The Bhaktivedanta Book Trust
P. O. Box 380, Riverstone, NSW 2765, Australia
Phone: +61-2-96276306 • Fax: +61-2-96276052
e-mail: bbt.wp@krishna.com

Printed in China

Previous printings: 46,000
Current printing, 2019: 3,000

Library of Congress Cataloging in Publication Data

Bhaktivedanta Swami, A. C. 1896–1977
Teachings of Lord Caitanya
by A.C. Bhaktivedanta Swami Prabhupāda.
Los Angeles. Bhaktivedanta Book Trust

BL1215.B5B45 294.5'4 79-21183
ISBN 0-912776-08-0 MARC

Library of Congress 73 [4]

nama oṁ viṣṇu-pādāya kṛṣṇa-preṣṭhāya bhū-tale
śrīmate bhaktivedānta-svāminn iti nāmine

namas te sārasvate deve gaura-vāṇī-pracāriṇe
nirviśeṣa-śūnyavādi-pāścātya-deśa-tāriṇe

We offer our respectful obeisances unto His Divine Grace A.C. Bhaktivedanta Swami Prabhupāda, who is very dear to Lord Kṛṣṇa on this earth, having taken shelter at His lotus feet.

Our respectful obeisances are unto you, O spiritual master, servant of Sarasvatī Gosvāmī. You are kindly preaching the message of Lord Caitanyadeva and delivering the Western countries, which are filled with impersonalism and voidism.

We prostrate ourselves at the lotus feet of our beloved spiritual master and offer this treasured book to His Divine Grace on our bowed heads. We came to him looking for broken pieces of glass, and he has bestowed upon us a priceless gem. He has opened our eyes, which were blinded by the darkness of atheism, mental speculation, and sense gratification, to the glorious light of Lord Caitanya Mahāprabhu. His transcendental words are seeds which in our hearts have bloomed into the perfection of human life: the discovery that God lives and that we can live with Him—Kṛṣṇa consciousness.

The Publishers

DEDICATED TO

the sacred service

of

Śrīla Saccidānanda Bhaktivinoda Ṭhākura,

who initiated the teachings of Lord Caitanya

in

the Western world

(McGill University, Canada)

in 1896,

the year of my birth

A. C. Bhaktivedanta Swami

Acknowledgements

My thankful acknowledgements are due to Śrīmān Brahmānanda Brahmacārī (Mr. Bruce Scharf), Śrīmān Gargamuni Brahmacārī (Mr. Gregory Scharf) and Śrīmān Satyavrata Brahmacārī (Mr. Stanley Moskowitz) for their financial help for this publication, and I beg to thank Śrīmān Rāyarāma Brahmacārī (Mr. Raymond Marais), Śrīmān Satsvarūpa Brahmacārī (Mr. Stephen Guarino) and Śrīmān Madhusūdana Brahmacārī (Mr. Michael Blumert) for editing and typing the manuscript, and Śrīmān Goursundara Dāsa Adhikārī (Mr. Gary McElroy) and his good wife Śrīmatī Govinda Dāsī (Mrs. Bonnie McElroy), who are always engaged to see to my personal comforts, and I am so much obliged to them for their drawing all the nice pictures contained in this great publication.

All glories to the devotees engaged in the matter of Kṛṣṇa consciousness. I am sure that Lord Śrī Kṛṣṇa Caitanya Mahāprabhu will bestow His causeless mercy upon everyone who is engaged in pushing on the cause of Kṛṣṇa consciousness.

A.C.B.

Contents

Part II

Preface

There is no difference between the teachings of Lord Caitanya presented here and the teachings of Lord Kṛṣṇa in the *Bhagavad-gītā*. The teachings of Lord Caitanya are practical demonstrations of Lord Kṛṣṇa's teachings. Lord Kṛṣṇa's ultimate instruction in the *Bhagavad-gītā* is that everyone should surrender unto Him, Lord Kṛṣṇa. Kṛṣṇa promises to take immediate charge of such a surrendered soul. The Lord, the Supreme Personality of Godhead, is already in charge of the maintenance of this creation by virtue of His plenary expansion, Kṣīrodakaśāyī Viṣṇu, but this maintenance is not direct. However, when the Lord says that He takes charge of His pure devotee, He actually takes direct charge. A pure devotee is a soul who is forever surrendered to the Lord, just as a child is surrendered to his parents or an animal to its master. In the surrendering process, one should (1) accept things favorable for discharging devotional service, (2) reject things unfavorable, (3) firmly believe that the Lord will always protect His devotee, (4) feel exclusively dependent on the mercy of the Lord, (5) have no interest separate from the interest of the Lord, and (6) always feel meek and humble.

The Lord demands that one surrender unto Him by following these six guidelines, but the unintelligent so-called scholars of the world misunderstand these demands and urge the general mass of people to reject them. At the conclusion of the Ninth Chapter of the *Bhagavad-gītā,* Lord Kṛṣṇa directly orders, "Always think of Me, become My devotee, worship Me alone, and offer obeisances unto Me alone." By so doing, the Lord says, one is sure to go to Him in His transcendental abode. But the scholarly demons misguide the masses of people by directing them to surrender not to the Personality of Godhead but rather to the impersonal, unmanifested, eternal, unborn truth. The impersonalist Māyāvādī philosophers do not accept that the ultimate aspect of the Absolute Truth is the Supreme Personality of Godhead. If one desires to understand the sun as it is, one must first face the sunshine and then the sun globe, and then, if one is able to enter into that globe, one may come face to face with the predominating deity of the sun. Due to a poor fund of knowledge, the Māyāvādī philosophers cannot go beyond the Brahman effulgence, which may be compared to the sunshine. The *Upaniṣads* confirm that one has to penetrate the dazzling effulgence of Brahman before one can see the real face of the Personality of Godhead.

Lord Caitanya therefore taught direct worship of Lord Kṛṣṇa, who appeared as the foster child of the King of Vraja. Lord Caitanya also taught that the place known as Vṛndāvana is as good as Lord Kṛṣṇa because, Lord Kṛṣṇa being the Absolute Truth, the Personality of Godhead, there is no difference between Him and His name, qualities, form, pastimes, entourage and paraphernalia. Lord Caitanya also taught that the mode of worshiping the Lord in the highest perfectional stage is the method practiced by the damsels of Vraja. These damsels (*gopīs,* or cowherd girls) simply loved Kṛṣṇa without any motive for material or spiritual gain. Lord Caitanya also taught that *Śrīmad-Bhāgavatam* is the spotless narration of transcendental knowledge and that the highest goal in human life is to develop unalloyed love for Kṛṣṇa, the Supreme Personality of Godhead.

Lord Caitanya's teachings are identical to those given by Lord Kapila, the original propounder of *sāṅkhya-yoga,* the *sāṅkhya* system of philosophy. This authorized system of *yoga* teaches meditation on the transcendental form of the Lord. There is no question of meditating on something void or impersonal. When one can meditate on the transcendental form of Lord Viṣṇu even without practicing involved sitting postures in a secluded place, such meditation is called perfect *samādhi*. That this kind of meditation is perfect *samādhi* is confirmed at the end of the Sixth Chapter of the *Bhagavad-gītā*, where Lord Kṛṣṇa says that of all *yogīs*, the greatest is the one who constantly thinks of the Lord within the core of his heart with love and devotion.

On the basis of the *sāṅkhya* philosophy of *acintya-bhedābheda-tattva*, which maintains that the Supreme Lord is simultaneously one with and different from His creation, Lord Caitanya taught that the most practical way for the mass of people to practice *sāṅkhya-yoga* meditation is simply to chant the holy name of the Lord. He taught that the holy name of the Lord is the sound incarnation of the Lord and that since the Lord is the absolute whole, there is no difference between His holy name and His transcendental form. Thus by chanting the holy name of the Lord one can directly associate with the Supreme Lord by sound vibration. As one practices chanting this sound vibration, one passes through three stages of development: the offensive stage, the clearing stage and the transcendental stage. In the offensive stage of chanting one may desire all kinds of material happiness, but in the second stage one becomes clear of all material contamination. When one is situated on the transcendental stage, one attains the most coveted position—the stage of loving God. Lord Caitanya taught that this is the highest stage of perfection for human beings.

Yoga practice is essentially meant for controlling the senses. The central controlling factor of all the senses is the mind; therefore one first has to practice controlling the mind by engaging it in Kṛṣṇa consciousness. The gross activities of the mind are expressed through the external senses, either for the acquisition of knowledge or for the functioning of the senses in accordance with the will. The subtle activities of the mind are thinking, feeling and willing, which are carried out according to one's consciousness, either polluted or clear. If one's mind is fixed on Kṛṣṇa (His name, qualities, form, pastimes, entourage and paraphernalia), all one's activities—both subtle and gross—become favorable. The *Bhagavad-gītā's* process of purifying consciousness is the process of fixing one's mind on Kṛṣṇa by talking of His transcendental activities, cleansing His temple, going to His temple, seeing the beautiful transcendental form of the Lord nicely decorated, hearing His transcendental glories, tasting food offered to Him, associating with His devotees, smelling the flowers and *tulasī* leaves offered to Him, engaging in activities for the Lord's interest, becoming angry at those who are malicious toward devotees, etc. No one can bring the activities of the mind and senses to a stop, but one can purify these activities through a change in consciousness. This change is indicated in the *Bhagavad-gītā* (2.39), where Kṛṣṇa tells Arjuna of the knowledge of *yoga* whereby one can work without fruitive results: "O son of Pṛthā, when you act in such knowledge you can free yourself from the bondage of works." A human being is sometimes restricted in sense gratification due to certain circumstances, such as disease, but such proscriptions are for the less intelligent. Without knowing the actual process by which the mind and senses can be controlled, less intelligent men may try to stop the mind and senses by force, but ultimately they give in to them and are carried away by the waves of sense gratification.

The eight principles of *sāṅkhya-yoga*—observing the regulative principles, following the rules, practicing the various sitting postures, performing the breathing exercises, withdrawing one's senses from the sense objects, etc.—are meant for those who are too much engrossed in the bodily conception of life. The intelligent man situated in Kṛṣṇa consciousness does not try to forcibly stop his senses from acting. Rather, he engages his senses in the service of Kṛṣṇa. No one can stop a child from playing by leaving him inactive; rather, one can stop the child from engaging in nonsense by engaging him in superior activities. Similarly, the forceful restraint of sense activities by the eight principles of *yoga* is recommended for inferior men; superior men, being engaged in the superior activities of Kṛṣṇa consciousness, naturally retire from the inferior activities of material existence.

In this way Lord Caitanya teaches the science of Kṛṣṇa consciousness. That science is absolute. Dry mental speculators try to restrain themselves from material attachment, but it is generally found that the mind is too strong to be controlled and that it drags them down to sensual activities. A person in Kṛṣṇa consciousness does not run this risk. One therefore has to engage one's mind and senses in Kṛṣṇa conscious activities, and Lord Caitanya teaches one how to do this in practice.

Before accepting *sannyāsa* (the renounced order), Lord Caitanya was known as Viśvambhara. The word *viśvambhara* refers to one who maintains the entire universe and who leads all living entities. This very same maintainer and leader appeared as Lord Śrī Kṛṣṇa Caitanya to give humanity these sublime teachings. Lord Caitanya is the ideal teacher of life's prime necessities. He is the most munificent bestower of love of Kṛṣṇa. He is the complete reservoir of all mercies and good fortune. As confirmed in *Śrīmad-Bhāgavatam*, the *Bhagavad-gītā*, the *Mahābhārata* and the *Upaniṣads*, He is the Supreme Personality of Godhead, Kṛṣṇa Himself, and He is worshipable by everyone in this age of disagreement. Everyone can join in His *saṅkīrtana* movement. No previous qualification is necessary. Just by following His teachings, anyone can become a perfect human being. Anyone who is fortunate enough to be attracted by Lord Caitanya is sure to be successful in his life's mission. In other words, those who are interested in attaining spiritual existence can easily be released from the clutches of *māyā* by Lord Caitanya's grace, now presented in book form as *Teachings of Lord Caitanya*, which is nondifferent from the Lord.

The conditioned soul, engrossed in the material body, increases the pages of history by all kinds of material activities. *Teachings of Lord Caitanya* can help the members of human society stop such unnecessary and temporary activities and be elevated to the topmost platform of spiritual activities, which begin after liberation from material bondage. Such liberated activities in Kṛṣṇa consciousness constitute the goal of human perfection. The false prestige one acquires by attempting to dominate material nature is illusory. Illuminating knowledge can be acquired from *Teachings of Lord Caitanya*, and by such knowledge one can advance in spiritual existence.

Everyone has to suffer or enjoy the fruits of his activity; no one can check the laws of material nature that govern such things. As long as one is engaged in fruitive activity, one is sure to be baffled in the attempt to attain the ultimate goal of life. I sincerely hope that by understanding *Teachings of Lord Caitanya*, human society will experience a new light of spiritual life, which will open the field of activity for the pure soul.

oṁ tat sat

A. C. Bhaktivedanta Swami

14 March 1968
(The Birthday of Lord Caitanya)
Śrī Śrī Rādhā-Kṛṣṇa Temple
New York, N.Y.

PROLOGUE

The Life of Caitanya Mahāprabhu

by Śrīla Bhaktivinoda Ṭhākura

[This account originally appeared in a short work by Śrīla Bhaktivinoda Ṭhākura entitled "Śrī Caitanya Mahāprabhu: His Life and Precepts." (August 20, 1896)]

Caitanya Mahāprabhu was born in Māyāpur, in the town of Nadia, just after sunset on the evening of the 23rd Phālguna, 1407 Śakābda, answering to the 18th of February, 1486, of the Christian Era. The moon was eclipsed at the time of His birth, and the people of Nadia were then engaged, as was usual on such occasions, in bathing in the Bhāgīrathī with loud cheers of "Haribol!" His father, Jagannātha Miśra, a poor *brāhmaṇa* of the Vedic order, and His mother, Śacī-devī, a model good woman, both descended from *brāhmaṇa* stock originally residing in Sylhet. Mahāprabhu was a beautiful child, and the ladies of the town came to see Him with presents. His mother's father, Paṇḍita Nīlāmbara Cakravartī, a renowned astrologer, foretold that the child would be a great personage in time, and he therefore gave Him the name Viśvambhara. The ladies of the neighborhood styled Him Gaurahari on account of His golden complexion, and His mother called Him Nimāi on account of the *nima* tree near which He was born. Beautiful as the lad was, everyone heartily loved to see Him every day. As He grew up He became a whimsical and frolicsome lad. After His fifth year, He was admitted into a *pāṭhaśālā* [school], where He picked up Bengali in a very short time.

Most of His contemporary biographers have mentioned certain anecdotes regarding Caitanya, which are simple records of His early miracles. It is said that when He was an infant in His mother's arms He wept continually and when the neighboring ladies cried "Haribol!" He used to stop. Thus there was continuation of the utterance of "Haribol!" in the house, foreshowing the future mission of the hero. It has also been stated that when His mother once gave Him sweetmeats to eat He ate clay instead of the food. His mother asking for the reason, He stated that as every sweetmeat was nothing but clay transformed He could eat clay as well. His mother, who was the consort of a *paṇḍita,* explained that every article in a special state was adapted to a special use. Earth while in the state of a jug could be used as a waterpot, but in the state of a brick such a use was not possible. Clay, therefore, in the form of sweetmeats was usable as food, but not clay in its other states. The lad was convinced and admitted His stupidity in eating clay and agreed to avoid the mistake in the future.

Another miraculous act has been related. It is said that a *brāhmaṇa* on pilgrimage became a guest in His house, cooked his food and read his grace with meditation on Kṛṣṇa. In the meantime the lad came and ate up the cooked rice. The *brāhmaṇa,* astonished at the lad's act, cooked again at the request of Jagannātha Miśra. The lad again ate up the cooked rice while the *brāhmaṇa* was offering the rice to Kṛṣṇa with meditation. The *brāhmaṇa* was persuaded to cook for the third time. This time all the inmates of the house had fallen asleep, and the lad showed himself as Kṛṣṇa to the traveler and blessed Him. The *brāhmaṇa* was then lost in ecstasy at the appearance of the object of his worship.

It has also been stated that two thieves stole away the lad from His father's door with a view to purloin His jewels and gave Him sweetmeats on the way. The lad exercised His illusory energy and deceived the thieves back toward His own house. The thieves, for fear of detection, left the boy there and fled.

Another miraculous act has been described of the lad's demanding and getting from Hiraṇya and Jagadīśa all the offerings they had collected for worshiping Kṛṣṇa on the day of Ekādaśī. When only four years of age, He sat on rejected cooking pots, which were considered unholy by His mother. He explained to His mother that there was no question of holiness and unholiness as regards earthen pots thrown away after the cooking was over. These anecdotes relate to His tender age up to the fifth year.

In His eighth year, He was admitted into the *tola* [school] of Gaṅgādāsa Paṇḍita, in Gaṅgānagara, close by the village of Māyāpur. In two years He became well read in Sanskrit grammar and rhetoric. His readings after that were of the nature of self-study in His own house, where He had found all important books belonging to His father, who was a *paṇḍita* himself. It appears that He read the *smṛti* in His own study, and the *nyāya* also, in competition with His friends, who were then studying under the celebrated Paṇḍita Raghunātha Śiromaṇi.

After His tenth year, Caitanya became a passable scholar in grammar, rhetoric, the *smṛti* and *nyāya*. It was after this that His elder brother Viśvarūpa left His house and accepted the *āśrama* (status) of a *sannyāsī* (ascetic). Caitanya, though a very young boy, consoled His parents, saying that He would serve them with a view to please God. Just after that, His father left this world. His mother was exceedingly sorry, and Mahāprabhu, with His usual contented appearance, consoled His widowed mother.

It was at the age of fourteen or fifteen that Mahāprabhu was married to Lakṣmīdevī, the daughter of Vallabhācārya, also of Nadia. He was at this age considered one of the best scholars of Nadia, the renowned seat of *nyāya* philosophy and Sanskrit learning. Not to speak of the *smārta paṇḍitas,* the *naiyāyikas* were all afraid of confronting Him in literary discussions. Being a married man, He went to eastern Bengal on the banks of the Padma to acquire wealth. There He displayed His learning and obtained a good sum of money.

It was at this time that He preached Vaiṣṇavism at intervals. After teaching him the principles of Vaiṣṇavism, He ordered Tapana Miśra to go to and live in Benares. During His residence in eastern Bengal, His wife Lakṣmīdevī left this world from the effects of snakebite. On returning home, He found His mother in a mourning state. He consoled her with a lecture on the uncertainty of human affairs. It was at His mother's request that He married Viṣṇupriyā, the daughter of Rāja Paṇḍita Sanātana Miśra. His comrades joined Him on His return from *pravāsa,* or sojourn.

He was now so renowned that He was considered to be the best *paṇḍita* in Nadia. Keśava Miśra of Kashmir, who called himself the Great Digvijayī [world conqueror], came to Nadia with a view to debate the *paṇḍitas* of that place. Afraid of the so-called conquering *paṇḍita,* the *tola* professors of Nadia left their town on the pretense of invitation. Keśava met Mahāprabhu at the Barokonaghāṭā in Māyāpur, and after a very short discussion with Him he got defeated by the boy, and mortification obliged him to decamp. Nimāi Paṇḍita was now the most important *paṇḍita* of the times.

It was at the age of sixteen or seventeen that He traveled to Gayā with a host of His students and there took His spiritual initiation from Īśvara Purī, a Vaiṣṇava *sannyāsī* and a disciple of the renowned Mādhavendra Purī. Upon His return to Nadia, Nimāi Paṇḍita turned religious preacher, and His religious nature became so strongly represented that Advaita Prabhu, Śrīvāsa and others who had before the birth of Caitanya already accepted the Vaiṣṇava faith were astonished at the change in the young man. He was then no more a contending *naiyāyika,* a wrangling *smārta* and a criticizing rhetorician. He swooned at the name of Kṛṣṇa and behaved as an inspired man under the influence of His religious sentiment. It has been described by Murāri Gupta, an eyewitness, that He showed His heavenly powers in the house of Śrīvāsa Paṇḍita in the presence of hundreds of His followers, who were mostly well-read scholars.

It was at this time that He opened a nocturnal school of *kīrtana* in the compound of Śrīvāsa Paṇḍita with His sincere followers. There He preached, there He sang, there He danced, and there He expressed all sorts of religious feelings. Nityānanda Prabhu, who was then a preacher of Vaiṣṇavism and who had completed His travels all over India, joined Him at that time. In fact, a host of *paṇḍita* preachers of Vaiṣṇavism, all sincere at heart, came and joined Him from different parts of Bengal. Nadia now became the regular seat of a host of Vaiṣṇava *ācāryas* whose mission it was to spiritualize mankind with the highest influence of the Vaiṣṇava creed.

The first mandate that Caitanya issued to Prabhu Nityānanda and Haridāsa was this: "Go, friends, go through the streets of the town, meet every man at his door and ask him to sing the name of Hari and lead a holy life, and then come and report to Me every evening the result of your preaching." Thus ordered, the two preachers went out and met Jagāi and Mādhāi, the two most abominable characters in Nadia. These two insulted the preachers on hearing Mahāprabhu's mandate, but were soon converted by the influence of *bhakti* inculcated by their Lord.

The people of Nadia were now surprised. They said, "Nimāi Paṇḍita is not only a gigantic genius but is certainly a missionary from God Almighty." From this time to His twenty-third year, Mahāprabhu preached His principles not only in Nadia but in all the important towns and villages around His city. In the houses of His followers He showed miracles, taught the esoteric principles of *bhakti* and sang His *saṅkīrtana* with other *bhaktas*. His followers in the town of Nadia commenced to sing the holy name of Hari in the streets and bazaars. This created a sensation and roused different feelings in different quarters. The *bhaktas* were highly pleased. The *smārta brāhmaṇas* became jealous of Nimāi Paṇḍita's success and complained to Chand Kazi against the character of Caitanya, claiming it was un-Hindu. The Kazi came to Śrīvāsa Paṇḍita's house and broke a *mṛdaṅga* (*khola* drum) there and declared that unless Nimāi Paṇḍita ceased to make noise about His queer religion he would be obliged to enforce Mohammedanism on Him and His followers.

This was brought to Mahāprabhu's notice. He ordered the townspeople to appear in the evening, each with a torch in his hand. This they did, and Nimāi marched out with His *saṅkīrtana* divided into fourteen groups. On His arrival in the Kazi's house, He held a long conversation with the Kazi and in the end communicated into his heart His Vaiṣṇava influence by touching his body. The Kazi then wept and admitted that he had felt a keen spiritual influence which had cleared up his doubts and produced in him a religious sentiment which gave him the highest ecstasy. The Kazi then joined the *saṅkīrtana* party. The world was astonished at the spiritual power of the Great Lord, and hundreds and hundreds of heretics converted and joined the banner of Viśvambhara after this affair.

It was after this that some of the jealous and low-minded *brāhmaṇas* of Kulia picked a quarrel with Mahāprabhu and collected a party to oppose Him. Nimāi Paṇḍita was naturally a soft-hearted person, though strong in His principles. He declared that party feelings and sectarianism were the two great enemies of progress, and He saw that as long as He should continue to be an inhabitant of Nadia belonging to a certain family, His mission would not meet with complete success. He then resolved to be a citizen of the world by cutting off His connection with His particular family, caste and creed, and with this resolution He embraced the position of a *sannyāsī* at Katwa under the guidance of Keśava Bhāratī of that town, in the twenty-fourth year of His life. His mother and wife wept bitterly for His separation, but our hero, though soft in heart, was strong in His principles. He left His little world in His house for the unlimited spiritual world of Kṛṣṇa with man in general.

After Mahāprabhu took *sannyāsa,* He was induced to visit the house of Advaita Prabhu in Śāntipura. Advaita managed to invite all Mahāprabhu's friends and admirers from Nadia and brought Śacī Devī to see her son. Both pleasure and pain invaded her heart when she saw her son in the attire of a *sannyāsī*. As a *sannyāsī*, Kṛṣṇa Caitanya put on nothing but a *kaupīna* and a *bahirvāsa* (outer covering). His head was without hair, and His hands bore a *daṇḍa* (stick) and a *kamaṇḍalu* (hermit's waterpot).

The holy son fell at the feet of His beloved mother and said, "Mother! This body is yours, and I must obey your orders. Permit Me to go to Vṛndāvana for My spiritual attainments." The mother, in consultation with Advaita and others, asked her son to reside in Purī (the town of Jagannātha) so that she might obtain news of Him now and then. Mahāprabhu agreed to that proposal and in a few days left Śāntipura for Orissa.

His biographers have described the journey of Kṛṣṇa Caitanya (that was the name He got after His *sannyāsa*) from Śāntipura to Purī in great detail. He traveled along the side of the Bhāgīrathī as far as Chatrabhoga, situated now in Thānā Mathurāpura, Diamond Harbor, Twenty-four Parganas. There He took a boat and went as far as Prayāga-ghāṭa, in the Midnapura District. Thence He walked through Balasore and Cuttack to Purī, seeing the temple of Bhūvaneśvara on His way. Upon His arrival at Purī He saw Jagannātha in the temple and resided with Sārvabhauma at the request of the latter.

Sārvabhauma was a gigantic *paṇḍita* of the day. His readings knew no bounds. He was the best *naiyāyika* of the times and was known as the most erudite scholar in the Vedānta philosophy of the school of Śaṅkarācārya. He was born in Nadia (Vidyānagara) and taught innumerable pupils in the *nyāya* philosophy in his *tola* there. He had left for Purī some time before the birth of Nimāi Paṇḍita. His brother-in-law Gopīnātha Miśra introduced our new *sannyāsī* to Sārvabhauma, who was astonished at His personal beauty and feared that it would be difficult for the young man to maintain *sannyāsa-dharma* during the long run of His life. Gopīnātha, who had known Mahāprabhu from Nadia, had a great reverence for Him and declared that the *sannyāsī* was not a common human being. On this point Gopīnātha and Sārvabhauma had a hot discussion. Sārvabhauma then requested Mahāprabhu to hear his recitation of the *Vedānta-sūtras,* to which the latter tacitly submitted.

Caitanya heard with silence what the great Sārvabhauma uttered with gravity for seven days, at the end of which the latter said, "Kṛṣṇa Caitanya! I think You do not understand the *Vedānta,* as You do not say anything after hearing my recitation and explanations."

The reply of Caitanya was that He understood the *sūtras* very well but could not make out what Śaṅkarācārya meant by his commentaries.

Astonished at this, Sārvabhauma said, "How is it that You understand the meanings of the *sūtras* but do not understand the commentaries which explain the *sūtras*? All well! If You understand the *sūtras,* please let me have Your interpretations."

Mahāprabhu thereupon explained all the *sūtras* in His own way, without touching the pantheistic commentary of Śaṅkara.

The keen understanding of Sārvabhauma saw the truth, beauty and harmony of the arguments in the explanations given by Caitanya and obliged him to utter that it was the first time he had found one who could explain the *Brahma-sūtras* in such a simple manner. He also admitted that the commentaries of Śaṅkara never gave such natural explanations of the *Vedānta-sūtras* as those he had obtained from Mahāprabhu. Sārvabhauma then submitted himself as an advocate and follower. In a few days he turned out to be one of the best Vaiṣṇavas of the time. When reports of this came out, the whole of Orissa sang the praise of Kṛṣṇa Caitanya, and hundreds and hundreds came to Him and became His followers. In the meantime Mahāprabhu thought of visiting southern India, and He started with one Kṛṣṇadāsa Brāhmaṇa for the journey.

His biographers have given us details of the journey. He first went to Kūrmakṣetra, where He did a miracle by curing a leper named Vāsudeva. He met Rāmānanda Rāya, the governor of Vidyānagara, on the banks of the Godāvarī and had a philosophical conversation with him on the subject of *prema-bhakti*. He worked another miracle by touching (making them immediately disappear) the seven *tāla* trees from behind which Rāmacandra, the son of Daśaratha, had shot His arrow and killed the great Vāli Rāja. Mahāprabhu preached Vaiṣṇavism and *nāma-saṅkīrtana* throughout His journey. At Raṅgakṣetra He stayed for four months in the house of one Veṅkata Bhaṭṭa in order to spend the rainy season. There He converted the whole family of Veṅkata from Rāmānuja Vaiṣṇavism to *kṛṣṇa-bhakti*, including the son of Veṅkata, a boy of ten years named Gopāla, who afterwards came to Vṛndāvana and became one of the Six Gosvāmīs, prophets serving under their leader Śrī Kṛṣṇa Caitanya. Trained up in Sanskrit by his uncle Prabodhānanda Sarasvatī, Gopāla wrote several books on Vaiṣṇavism.

Caitanya visited numerous places in southern India as far as Cape Comorin and returned to Purī in two years by Pāṇḍarapura on the Bhīmā. In this latter place He spiritualized one Tukārāma, who became from that time a religious preacher himself. This fact has been admitted in his *abhaṅgas,* which have been collected in a volume by Mr. Satyendranath Tagore of the Bombay Civil Service. During His journey He had discussions with the Buddhists, the

Jains and the Māyāvādīs in several places and converted His opponents to Vaiṣṇavism.

Upon His return to Purī, Rāja Pratāparudra-deva and several *paṇḍita brāhmaṇas* joined the banner of Caitanya Mahāprabhu. He was now twenty-seven years of age. In His twenty-eighth year He went to Bengal as far as Gauḍa in Malda. There He picked up two great personages named Rūpa and Sanātana. Though descended from the lines of the Karṇātic *brāhmaṇas,* these two brothers had turned demi-Mohammedans by their continual contact with Hussain Shah, the then emperor of Gauḍa. Their names had been changed by the emperor into Dabira Khāsa and Sākara Mallika, and their master loved them heartily as they were both learned in Persian, Arabic and Sanskrit and were loyal servants of the state. The two gentlemen had found no way to come back as regular Hindus and had written to Mahāprabhu while He was at Purī, for spiritual help. Mahāprabhu had written in reply that He would come to them and extricate them out of their spiritual difficulties. Now that He had come to Gauḍa, both the brothers appeared before Him with their long-standing prayer. Mahāprabhu ordered them to go to Vṛndāvana and meet Him there.

Caitanya returned to Purī through Śāntipura, where He again met His dear mother. After a short stay at Purī He left for Vṛndāvana. This time He was accompanied by one Balabhadra Bhaṭṭācārya. He visited Vṛndāvana and came down to Prayāga (Allahabad), converting a large number of Mohammedans to Vaiṣṇavism by argument from the Koran. The descendants of those converts are still known as Pāṭhāna Vaiṣṇavas. Rūpa Gosvāmī met Him at Allahabad. Caitanya trained him up in spirituality in ten days and directed him to go to Vṛndāvana on two missions. His first mission was to write theological works scientifically explaining pure *bhakti* and *prema.* The second mission was to revive the places where Kṛṣṇacandra had at the end of Dvāpara-yuga exhibited His spiritual *līlā* for the benefit of the religious world. Rūpa Gosvāmī left Allahabad for Vṛndāvana, and Mahāprabhu came down to Benares. There He resided in the house of Candraśekhara and accepted His daily *bhikṣā* (meal) in the house of Tapana Miśra. Here it was that Sanātana Gosvāmī joined Him and took instruction for two months in spiritual matters. The biographers, especially Kṛṣṇadāsa Kavirāja, have given us details of Caitanya's teachings to Rūpa and Sanātana. Kṛṣṇadāsa was not a contemporary writer, but he gathered his information from the Six Gosvāmīs themselves, the direct disciples of Mahāprabhu. Jīva Gosvāmī, who was a nephew of Sanātana and Rūpa and who has left us his invaluable work the *Ṣaṭ-sandarbhas,* has philosophized on the precepts of his great leader. We have gathered and summarized the precepts of Caitanya from the books of those great writers.

While at Benares, Caitanya had an interview with the learned *sannyāsīs* of that town in the house of a Maratha *brāhmaṇa* who had invited all the *sannyāsīs* for an entertainment. At this interview, Caitanya showed a miracle which attracted all the *sannyāsīs* to Him. Then ensued reciprocal conversations. The *sannyāsīs* were headed by their most learned leader, Prakāśānanda Sarasvatī. After a short controversy they submitted to Mahāprabhu and admitted that they had been misled by the commentaries of Śaṅkarācārya. It was impossible even for learned scholars to oppose Caitanya for a long time, as there was some spell in Him which touched their hearts and made them weep for their spiritual improvement. The *sannyāsīs* of Benares soon fell at the feet of Caitanya and asked for His grace (*kṛpā*). Caitanya then preached pure *bhakti* and instilled into their hearts a spiritual love for Kṛṣṇa, which obliged them to give up sectarian feelings. The whole population of Benares, on this wonderful conversion of the *sannyāsīs,* turned Vaiṣṇava, and they made a massive *saṅkīrtana* with their new Lord.

After sending Sanātana to Vṛndāvana, Mahāprabhu went to Purī again through the jungles with His comrade Balabhadra. Balabhadra reported that Mahāprabhu showed a good many miracles on His way to Purī, such as making tigers and elephants dance on hearing the name of Kṛṣṇa.

From this time, that is, from His thirty-first year, Mahāprabhu continually lived in Purī, in the house of Kāśi Miśra, until His disappearance in His forty-eighth year at the time of *saṅkīrtana* in the temple of Ṭoṭā-gopīnātha. During these eighteen years, His life was one of settled love and piety. He was surrounded by numerous followers, all of whom were of the highest order of the Vaiṣṇavas and who were distinguished from the common people by their purest character and learning, firm religious principles and spiritual love of Rādhā-Kṛṣṇa.

Svarūpa Dāmodara, who had been known by the name of Puruṣottamācārya while Mahāprabhu was in Nadia, joined Him from Benares and accepted service as His secretary. No production of any poet or philosopher could be laid before Mahāprabhu unless Svarūpa had passed it as pure and useful. Rāya Rāmānanda was His second mate. Both he and Svarūpa would sing while Mahāprabhu expressed His sentiment on a certain point of worship. Paramānanda Purī was His minister in matters of religion. There are hundreds of anecdotes described by His biographers which we do not think it meet here to reproduce. Mahāprabhu slept short. His sentiments carried Him far and wide in the firmament of spirituality every day and night, and all His admirers and followers watched Him throughout. He worshiped, communicated with His missionaries in Vṛndāvana, and conversed with those religious men who newly came to visit Him. He sang and danced, took no care of Himself and ofttimes lost Himself in religious beatitude. All who came to Him believed in Him as the all-beautiful God appearing in the nether world for the benefit of mankind. He loved His mother all along and sent her *mahā-prasāda* now and then with those who went to Nadia. He was most amiable in nature. Humility was personified in Him. His sweet appearance gave cheer to all who came in contact with Him. He appointed Prabhu Nityānanda as the missionary in charge of Bengal. He dispatched six disciples (Gosvāmīs) to Vṛndāvana to preach love in the upcountry. He punished all of His disciples who deviated from a holy life. This He markedly did in the case of Junior Haridāsa. He never lacked in giving proper instructions in life to those who solicited them. This was seen in His teachings to Raghunātha Dāsa Gosvāmī. His treatment of Haridāsa (senior) showed how He loved spiritual men and how He defied caste distinction in the cause of spiritual brotherhood.

Lord Caitanya's Mission

Lord Caitanya Mahāprabhu instructed His disciples to write books on the science of Kṛṣṇa, a task which those who follow Him have continued to carry out down to the present day. Due to the unbreakable system of disciplic succession, the elaborations and expositions on the philosophy taught by Lord Caitanya are in fact the most voluminous, exacting and consistent of any religious culture in the world. Although Lord Caitanya was widely renowned as a scholar in His youth, He left only eight verses, called *Śikṣāṣṭaka*. These eight verses clearly reveal His mission and precepts. These supremely valuable prayers are translated herein.

1

Glory to the Śrī Kṛṣṇa *saṅkīrtana,* which cleanses the heart of all the dust accumulated for years together and thus extinguishes the fire of conditioned life, of repeated birth and death. This *saṅkīrtana* movement is the prime benediction for humanity at large because it spreads the rays of the benediction moon. It is the life of all transcendental knowledge, it increases the ocean of transcendental bliss, and it enables us to taste the full nectar for which we are always anxious.

2

O my Lord, Your holy name alone can render all benedictions to living beings, and thus You have hundreds and millions of names, like Kṛṣṇa and Govinda. In these transcendental names You have invested all Your transcendental energies, and there are no hard and fast rules for chanting these holy names. O my Lord, You have so kindly made it easy to approach You by Your holy names, but I am so unfortunate that I have no attraction for them.

3

One should chant the holy name of the Lord in a humble state of mind, thinking oneself lower than the straw in the street; one should be more tolerant than a tree, devoid of all sense of false prestige, and ready to offer all respect to others. In such a state of mind one can chant the holy name of the Lord constantly.

4

O almighty Lord, I have no desire to accumulate wealth, nor do I desire beautiful women, nor do I want any number of followers. I only want Your causeless devotional service in my life, birth after birth.

5

O son of Mahārāja Nanda, I am Your eternal servitor, yet somehow or other I have fallen into the ocean of birth and death. Please pick me up from this ocean of death and place me as one of the atoms at Your lotus feet.

6

O my Lord, when will my eyes be decorated with tears of love flowing constantly when I chant Your holy name? When will my voice choke up, and when will the hairs on my body stand on end at the recitation of Your name?

7

O Govinda! Feeling Your separation, I am considering a moment to be like twelve years or more. Tears are flowing from My eyes like torrents of rain, and I am feeling all vacant in the world in Your absence.

8

I know no one but Kṛṣṇa as My Lord, and He shall always remain so, even if He handles Me roughly by His embrace or makes Me brokenhearted by not being present before Me. He is completely free to do anything and everything, yet He is always My worshipable Lord, unconditionally.

Introduction

(Originally delivered as five morning lectures on the Caitanya-caritāmṛta*—the authoritative biography of Lord Caitanya Mahāprabhu by Kṛṣṇadāsa Kavirāja Gosvāmī—before the International Society for Krishna Consciousness, New York City, April 10–14, 1967.)*

The word *caitanya* means "living force," *carita* means "character," and *amṛta* means "immortal." As living entities we can move, but a table cannot because it does not possess living force. Movement and activity may be considered signs of the living force. Indeed, it may be said that there can be no activity without the living force. Although the living force is present in the material condition, this condition is not *amṛta*, immortal. The words *caitanya-caritāmṛta*, then, may be translated as "the character of the living force in immortality."

But how is this living force displayed immortally? It is not displayed by man or any other creature in this material universe, for none of us are immortal in these bodies. We possess the living force, we perform activities, and we are immortal by our nature and constitution, but the material condition into which we have been put does not allow our immortality to be displayed. It is stated in the *Kaṭha Upaniṣad* that eternality and the living force are characteristics of both ourselves and God. Although this is true in that both God and ourselves are immortal living beings, there is a difference. As living entities, we perform many activities, but we have a tendency to fall down into material nature. God has no such tendency. Being all-powerful, He never comes under the control of material nature. Indeed, material nature is but one display of His inconceivable energies.

An analogy will help us understand the distinction between ourselves and God. From the ground we may see only clouds in the sky, but if we fly above the clouds we can see the sun shining. From the sky, skyscrapers and cities seem very tiny; similarly, from God's position this entire material creation is insignificant. The living entity is also insignificant, and his tendency is to come down from the heights, where everything can be seen in perspective. God, however, does not have this tendency. The Supreme Lord is not subject to falling down into illusion (*māyā*), any more than the sun is subject to falling beneath the clouds. Impersonalist philosophers (Māyāvādīs) maintain that because we fall under the control of *māyā* when we come into this material world God must also fall under *māyā's* control. This is the fallacy of their philosophy.

Lord Caitanya Mahāprabhu should therefore not be considered one of us. He is Kṛṣṇa Himself, the supreme living entity, and as such He never comes under the cloud of *māyā*. Kṛṣṇa, His expansions and even His higher devotees never fall into the clutches of illusion. Lord Caitanya came to earth simply to preach *kṛṣṇa-bhakti*, love of Kṛṣṇa. In other words, He is Lord Kṛṣṇa Himself teaching the living entities the proper way to approach Kṛṣṇa. He is like a teacher who, seeing a student doing poorly, takes up a pencil and writes, saying, "Do it like this: A, B, C." From this one should not foolishly think that the teacher is learning his ABC's. Similarly, although Lord Caitanya appears in the guise of a devotee, we should not foolishly think He is an ordinary human being; we should always remember that Lord Caitanya is Kṛṣṇa (God) Himself teaching us how to become Kṛṣṇa conscious, and we must study Him in that light.

In the *Bhagavad-gītā* (18.66) Lord Kṛṣṇa says, "Give up all your nonsense and surrender to Me. I will protect you."

We say, "Oh, surrender? But I have so many responsibilities."

And Māyā, illusion, says to us, "Don't do it, or you'll be out of my clutches. Just stay in my clutches, and I'll kick you."

It is a fact that we are constantly being kicked by Māyā, just as the male ass is kicked in the face by the she-ass when he comes for sex. Similarly, cats and dogs are always fighting and whining when they have sex. Even an elephant in the jungle is caught by the use of a trained she-elephant who leads him into a pit. We should learn by observing these tricks of nature.

Māyā has many ways to entrap us, and her strongest shackle is the female. Of course, in actuality we are neither male nor female, for these designations refer only to the outer dress, the body. We are all actually Kṛṣṇa's servants. But in conditioned life we are shackled by iron chains in the form of beautiful women. Thus every male is bound by sex, and therefore one who wishes to gain liberation from the material clutches must first learn to control the sex urge. Unrestricted sex puts one fully in the clutches of *māyā* (illusion). Lord Caitanya Mahāprabhu officially renounced this *māyā* at the age of twenty-four, although His wife was sixteen and His mother seventy and He was the only male in the family. Although He was a *brāhmaṇa* and was not rich, He took *sannyāsa,* the renounced order of life, and thus extricated Himself from family entanglement, not caring for the *māyā* of wife and mother.

If we wish to become fully Kṛṣṇa conscious, we have to give up the shackles of *māyā*. Or, if we remain with *māyā,* we should live in such a way that we will not be subject to illusion, as did the many householders among Lord Caitanya's closest devotees. With His followers in the renounced order, however, Lord Caitanya was very strict. He even banished Junior Haridāsa, an important *kīrtana* leader, for glancing lustfully at a young woman. The Lord told him, "You are living with Me in the renounced order, and yet you are looking at a woman with lust." Other devotees of the Lord appealed to Him to forgive Haridāsa, but He replied, "All of you can forgive him and live with him. I shall live alone." On the other hand, when the Lord learned that the wife of one of His householder devotees was pregnant, He asked that the baby be given a certain auspicious name. So while the Lord approved of householders having regulated sex, He was like a thunderbolt with those in the renounced order who tried to cheat by the method known as "drinking water under water while bathing on a fast day." In other words, He tolerated no hypocrisy among His followers.

From the *Caitanya-caritāmṛta* we learn how Lord Caitanya taught people to break the shackles of Māyā and become immortal. Thus, as mentioned above, the title may be properly translated as "the character of the living force in immortality." The supreme living force is the Supreme Personality of Godhead. He is also the supreme entity. There are innumerable living entities, and all of them are individuals. This is very easy to understand: We are all individual in our thoughts and desires, and the Supreme Lord is also an individual person. He is different, though, in that He is the leader, the one whom no one can excel. Among the minute living entities, one being can excel another in one capacity or another. Like each of these living entities, the Lord is an individual, but He is different in that He is the supreme individual. God is also infallible, and thus in the *Bhagavad-gītā* He is addressed as Acyuta, which means "He who never falls down." This name is appropriate because in the *Bhagavad-gītā* Arjuna falls into illusion but Kṛṣṇa does not. Kṛṣṇa Himself reveals His infallibility when he says to Arjuna, "When I appear in this world, I do so by My own internal potency." (Bg. 4.6)

Thus we should not think that Kṛṣṇa is overpowered by the material potency when He is in the material world. Neither Kṛṣṇa nor His incarnations ever come under the control of material nature. They are totally free. Indeed, in *Śrīmad-Bhāgavatam* one who has a godly nature is actually defined as one who is not affected by the modes of material nature although in material nature. If even a devotee can attain this freedom, then what to speak of the Supreme Lord?

The real question is, How can we remain unpolluted by material contamination while in the material world? Śrīla Rūpa Gosvāmī explains that we can remain uncontaminated while in the world if we simply make it our ambition to serve Kṛṣṇa. One may then justifiably ask, "How can I serve?" It is not simply a matter of meditation, which is just an activity of the mind, but of performing practical work for Kṛṣṇa. In such work, we should leave no resource unused. Whatever is there, whatever we have, should be used for Kṛṣṇa. We can use everything—typewriters, automobiles, airplanes, missiles. If we simply speak to people about Kṛṣṇa consciousness, we are also rendering service. If our mind, senses, speech, money and energies are thus engaged in the service of Kṛṣṇa, then we are no longer in material nature. By virtue of spiritual consciousness, or Kṛṣṇa consciousness, we transcend the platform of material nature. It is a fact that Kṛṣṇa, His expansions and His devotees—that is, those who work for Him—are not in material nature, although people with a poor fund of knowledge think that they are.

The *Caitanya-caritāmṛta* teaches that the spirit soul is immortal and that our activities in the spiritual world are also immortal. The Māyāvādīs, who hold the view that the Absolute is impersonal and formless, contend that a realized soul has no need to talk. But the Vaiṣṇavas, devotees of Kṛṣṇa, contend that when one reaches the stage of realization, he really begins to talk. "Previously we only talked of nonsense," the Vaiṣṇava says. "Now let us begin our real talks, talks of Kṛṣṇa." In support of their view that the self-realized remain silent, the Māyāvādīs are fond of using the example of the waterpot, maintaining that when a pot is not filled with water it makes a sound, but that when it is filled it makes no sound. But are we waterpots? How can we be compared to them? A good analogy utilizes as many similarities between two objects as possible. A waterpot is not an active living force, but we are. Ever-silent meditation may be adequate for a waterpot, but not for us. Indeed, when a devotee realizes how much he has to say about Kṛṣṇa, twenty-four hours in a day are not sufficient. It is the fool who is celebrated as long as he does not speak, for when he breaks his silence his lack of knowledge is exposed. The *Caitanya-caritāmṛta* shows that there are many wonderful things to discover by glorifying the Supreme.

In the beginning of the *Caitanya-caritāmṛta*, Kṛṣṇadāsa Kavirāja Gosvāmī writes, "I offer my respects to my spiritual masters." He uses the plural here to indicate the disciplic succession. He offers obeisances not to his spiritual master alone but to the whole *paramparā,* the chain of disciplic succession beginning with Lord Kṛṣṇa Himself. Thus the author addresses the *guru* in the plural to show the highest respect for all his predecessor spiritual masters.

After offering obeisances to the disciplic succession, the author pays obeisances to all other devotees, to the Lord Himself, to His incarnations, to the expansions of Godhead and to the manifestation of Kṛṣṇa's internal energy. Lord Caitanya Mahāprabhu (sometimes called Kṛṣṇa Caitanya) is the embodiment of all of these: He is God, *guru,* devotee, incarnation, internal energy and expansion of God. As His associate Nityānanda, He is the first expansion of God; as Advaita, He is an incarnation; as Gadādhara, He is the internal potency; and as Śrīvāsa, He is the marginal living entity in the role of a devotee. Thus Kṛṣṇa should not be thought of as being alone but should be considered as eternally existing with all His manifestations, as described by Rāmānujācārya. In the Viśiṣṭādvaita philosophy, God's energies, expansions and incarnations are considered to be oneness in diversity. In other words, God is not separate from all of these: everything together is God.

Actually, the *Caitanya-caritāmṛta* is not intended for the novice, for it is the postgraduate study of spiritual knowledge. Ideally, one begins with the *Bhagavad-gītā* and advances through *Śrīmad-Bhāgavatam* to the *Caitanya-caritāmṛta.* Although all these great scriptures are on the same absolute level, for the sake of comparative study the *Caitanya-caritāmṛta* is considered to be on the highest platform. Every verse in it is perfectly composed.

In the second verse of the *Caitanya-caritāmṛta,* the author offers his obeisances to Lord Caitanya and Lord Nityānanda. He compares Them to the sun and the moon because They dissipate the darkness of the material world. In this instance the sun and the moon have risen together.

In the Western world, where the glories of Lord Caitanya are relatively unknown, one may inquire, "Who is Kṛṣṇa Caitanya?" The author of the *Caitanya-caritāmṛta,* Śrīla Kṛṣṇadāsa Kavirāja, answers that question in the third verse of his book. Generally, in the *Upaniṣads* the Supreme Absolute Truth is described in an impersonal way, but the personal aspect of the Absolute Truth is mentioned in the *Īśopaniṣad,* where we find the following verse:

hiraṇmayena pātreṇa satyasyāpihitaṁ mukham
tat tvaṁ pūṣann apāvṛṇu satya-dharmāya dṛṣṭaye

"O my Lord, sustainer of all that lives, Your real face is covered by Your dazzling effulgence. Kindly remove that covering and exhibit Yourself to Your pure devotee." (*Śrī Īśopaniṣad* 15) The impersonalists do not have the power to go beyond the effulgence of God and arrive at the Personality of Godhead, from whom this effulgence is emanating. The *Īśopaniṣad* is a hymn to that Personality of Godhead. It is not that the impersonal Brahman is denied; it is also described, but that Brahman is revealed to be the glaring effulgence of the body of Lord Kṛṣṇa. And in the *Caitanya-caritāmṛta* we learn that Lord Caitanya is Kṛṣṇa Himself. In other words, Śrī Kṛṣṇa Caitanya is the basis of the impersonal Brahman. The Paramātmā, or Supersoul, who is present within the heart of every living entity and within every atom of the universe, is but the partial representation of Lord Caitanya. Therefore Śrī Kṛṣṇa Caitanya, being the basis of both Brahman and the all-pervading Paramātmā as well, is the Supreme Personality of Godhead. As such, He is full in six opulences: wealth, fame, strength, beauty, knowledge and renunciation. In short, we should know that He is Kṛṣṇa, God, and that nothing is equal to or greater than Him. There is nothing superior to be conceived. He is the Supreme Person.

Śrīla Rūpa Gosvāmī, a confidential devotee taught for more than ten days continually by Lord Caitanya, wrote:

namo mahā-vadānyāya kṛṣṇa-prema-pradāya te
kṛṣṇāya kṛṣṇa-caitanya- nāmne gaura-tviṣe namaḥ

"I offer my respectful obeisances unto the Supreme Lord Śrī Kṛṣṇa Caitanya, who is more munificent than any other *avatāra,* even Kṛṣṇa Himself, because He is bestowing freely what no one else has ever given—pure love of Kṛṣṇa."

Lord Caitanya's teachings begin from the point of surrender to Kṛṣṇa. He does not pursue the paths of *karma-yoga* or *jñāna-yoga* or *haṭha-yoga* but begins at the end of material existence, at the point where one gives up all material attachment. In the *Bhagavad-gītā* Kṛṣṇa begins His teachings by distinguishing the soul from matter, and in the Eighteenth Chapter He concludes at the point where the soul surrenders to Him in devotion. The Māyāvādīs would have all talk cease there, but at that point the real discussion only begins. As the *Vedānta-sūtra* says at the very beginning, *athāto brahma-jijñāsā:* "Now let us begin to inquire about the Supreme Absolute Truth." Rūpa Gosvāmī thus praises Lord Caitanya as the most munificent incarnation of all, for He gives the greatest gift by teaching the highest form of devotional service. In other words, He answers the most important inquiries that anyone can make.

There are different stages of devotional service and God realization. Strictly speaking, anyone who accepts the existence of God is situated in devotional service. To acknowledge that God is great is something, but not much. Lord Caitanya, preaching as an *ācārya*, a great teacher, taught that we can enter into a relationship with God and actually become God's friend, parent or lover. In the *Bhagavad-gītā* Kṛṣṇa showed Arjuna His universal form because Arjuna was His very dear friend. Upon seeing Kṛṣṇa as the Lord of the universes, however, Arjuna asked Kṛṣṇa to forgive the familiarity of his friendship. Lord Caitanya goes beyond this point. Through Lord Caitanya we can become friends with Kṛṣṇa, and there will be no limit to this friendship. We can become friends of Kṛṣṇa not in awe or adoration but in complete freedom. We can even relate to God as His father or mother. This is the philosophy not only of the *Caitanya-caritāmṛta* but of *Śrīmad-Bhāgavatam* as well. There are no other scriptures in the world in which God is treated as the son of a devotee. Usually God is seen as the almighty father who supplies the demands of His sons. The great devotees, however, sometimes treat God as a son in their execution of devotional service. The son demands, and the father and mother supply, and in supplying Kṛṣṇa the devotee becomes like a father or mother. Instead of taking from God, we give to God. It was in this relationship that Kṛṣṇa's mother, Yaśodā, told the Lord, "Here, eat this or You'll die. Eat nicely." In this way Kṛṣṇa, although the proprietor of everything, depends on the mercy of His devotee. This is a uniquely high level of friendship, in which the devotee actually believes himself to be the father or mother of Kṛṣṇa.

However, Lord Caitanya's greatest gift was His teaching that Kṛṣṇa can be treated as one's lover. In this relationship the Lord becomes so much attached to His devotee that He expresses His inability to reciprocate. Kṛṣṇa was so obliged to the *gopīs,* the cowherd girls of Vṛndāvana, that He felt unable to return their love. "I cannot repay your love," He told them. "I have no more assets to give." Devotional service on this highest, most excellent platform of lover and beloved, which had never been given by any previous incarnation or *ācārya,* was given by Caitanya Mahāprabhu. Therefore Kṛṣṇadāsa Kavirāja, quoting Śrīla Rūpa Gosvāmī, writes in the fourth verse of his book, "Lord Caitanya is Kṛṣṇa with a yellow complexion, and He is Śacīnandana, the son of Mother Śacī. He is the most charitable personality because He came to deliver *kṛṣṇa-prema,* unalloyed love for Kṛṣṇa, to everyone. May you always keep Him in your heart. It will be easy to understand Kṛṣṇa through Him."

We have often heard the phrase "love of Godhead." How far this love of Godhead can actually be developed can be learned from the Vaiṣṇava philosophy. Theoretical knowledge of love of God can be found in many places and in many scriptures, but what that love of Godhead actually is and how it is developed can be found in the Vaiṣṇava literatures. It is the unique and highest development of love of God that is given by Caitanya Mahāprabhu.

Even in this material world we can have a little sense of love. How is this possible? It is due to the presence of our original love of God. Whatever we find within our experience within this conditioned life is situated in the Supreme Lord, who is the ultimate source of everything. In our original relationship with the Supreme Lord there is real love, and that love is reflected pervertedly through material conditions. Our real love is continuous and unending, but because that love is reflected pervertedly in this material world, it lacks continuity and is inebriating. If we want real, transcendental love, we have to transfer our love to the supreme lovable object—Kṛṣṇa, the Supreme Personality of Godhead. This is the basic principle of Kṛṣṇa consciousness.

In material consciousness we are trying to love that which is not at all lovable. We give our love to cats and dogs, running the risk that at the time of death we may think of them and consequently take birth in a family of cats or dogs. Our consciousness at the time of death determines our next life. That is one reason why the Vedic scriptures stress the chastity of women: If a woman is very much attached to her husband, at the time of death she will think of him, and in the next life she will be promoted to a man's body. Generally a man's life is better than a woman's because a man usually has better facilities for understanding the spiritual science.

But Kṛṣṇa consciousness is so nice that it makes no distinction between man and woman. In the *Bhagavad-gītā* (9.32), Lord Kṛṣṇa says, "Anyone who takes shelter of Me—whether a woman, *śūdra, vaiśya* or someone of low birth—is sure to achieve My association." This is Kṛṣṇa's guarantee.

Caitanya Mahāprabhu informs us that in every country and in every scripture there is some hint of love of Godhead. But no one knows what love of Godhead actually is. The Vedic scriptures, however, are different in that they can direct the individual in the proper way to love God. Other scriptures do not give information on how one can love God, nor do they actually define or describe *what* or *who* the Godhead actually is. Although they officially promote love of Godhead, they have no idea how to execute it. But Caitanya Mahāprabhu gives a practical demonstration of how to love God in a conjugal relationship. Taking the part of Śrīmatī Rādhārāṇī, Caitanya Mahāprabhu tried to love Kṛṣṇa as Rādhārāṇī loved Him. Kṛṣṇa was always amazed by Rādhārāṇī's love. "How does Rādhārāṇī give Me such pleasure?" He would ask. In order to study Rādhārāṇī, Kṛṣṇa lived in Her role and tried to understand Himself. This is the secret of Lord Caitanya's incarnation. Caitanya Mahāprabhu is Kṛṣṇa, but He has taken the mood and role of Rādhārāṇī to show us how to love Kṛṣṇa. Thus the author writes in the fifth verse, "I offer my respectful obeisances unto the Supreme Lord, who is absorbed in Rādhārāṇī's thoughts."

This brings up the question of who Śrīmatī Rādhārāṇī is and what Rādhā-Kṛṣṇa is. Actually Rādhā-Kṛṣṇa is the exchange of love—but not ordinary love. Kṛṣṇa has immense potencies, of which three are principal: the internal, the external and the marginal potencies. In the internal potency there are three divisions: *samvit, hlādinī* and *sandhinī*. The *hlādinī* potency is Kṛṣṇa's pleasure potency. All living entities have this pleasure-seeking potency, for all beings are trying to have pleasure. This is the very nature of the living entity. At present we are trying to enjoy our pleasure potency by means of the body in the material condition. By bodily contact we are attempting to derive pleasure from material sense objects. But we should not entertain the nonsensical idea that Kṛṣṇa, who is always spiritual, also tries to seek pleasure on this material plane. In the *Bhagavad-gītā* Kṛṣṇa describes the material universe as a nonpermanent place full of miseries. Why, then, would He seek pleasure in matter? He is the Supersoul, the supreme spirit, and His pleasure is beyond the material conception.

To learn how Kṛṣṇa enjoys pleasure, we must study the first nine cantos of *Śrīmad-Bhāgavatam,* and then we should study the Tenth Canto, in which Kṛṣṇa's pleasure potency is displayed in His pastimes with Rādhārāṇī and the damsels of Vraja. Unfortunately, unintelligent people turn at once to the sports of Kṛṣṇa in the *Daśama-skandha,* the Tenth Canto. Kṛṣṇa's embracing Rādhārāṇī or His dancing with the cowherd girls in the *rāsa* dance are generally not understood by ordinary men, because they consider these pastimes in the light of mundane lust. They foolishly think that Kṛṣṇa is like themselves and that He embraces the *gopīs* just as an ordinary man embraces a young girl. Some people thus become interested in Kṛṣṇa because they think that His religion allows indulgence in sex. This is not *kṛṣṇa-bhakti,* love of Kṛṣṇa, but *prākṛta-sahajiyā*—materialistic lust.

To avoid such errors, we should understand what Rādhā-Kṛṣṇa actually is. Rādhā and Kṛṣṇa display Their pastimes through Kṛṣṇa's internal energy. The pleasure potency of Kṛṣṇa's internal energy is a most difficult subject matter, and unless one understands what Kṛṣṇa is, one cannot understand it. Kṛṣṇa does not take any pleasure in this material world, but He has a pleasure potency. Because we are part and parcel of Kṛṣṇa, the pleasure potency is within us also, but we are trying to exhibit that pleasure potency in matter. Kṛṣṇa, however, does not make such a vain attempt. The object of Kṛṣṇa's pleasure potency is Rādhārāṇī; Kṛṣṇa exhibits His potency as Rādhārāṇī and then engages in loving affairs with Her. In other words, Kṛṣṇa does not take pleasure in this external energy but exhibits His internal energy, His pleasure potency, as Rādhārāṇī and then enjoys with Her. Thus Kṛṣṇa manifests Himself as Rādhārāṇī in order to enjoy His internal pleasure potency. Of the many extensions, expansions and incarnations of the Lord, this pleasure potency is the foremost and chief.

It is not that Rādhārāṇī is separate from Kṛṣṇa. Rādhārāṇī is also Kṛṣṇa, for there is no difference between the energy and the energetic. Without energy, there is no meaning to the energetic, and without the energetic, there is no energy. Similarly, without Rādhā there is no meaning to Kṛṣṇa, and without Kṛṣṇa there is no meaning to Rādhā. Because of this, the Vaiṣṇava philosophy first of all pays obeisances to and worships the internal pleasure potency of the Supreme Lord. Thus the Lord and His potency are always referred to as Rādhā-Kṛṣṇa. Similarly, those who worship Nārāyaṇa first of all utter the name of Lakṣmī, as Lakṣmī-Nārāyaṇa. Similarly, those who worship Lord Rāma first of all utter the name of Sītā. In any case—Sītā-Rāma, Rādhā-Kṛṣṇa, Lakṣmī-Nārāyaṇa—the potency always comes first.

Rādhā and Kṛṣṇa are one, and when Kṛṣṇa desires to enjoy pleasure, He manifests Himself as Rādhārāṇī. The spiritual exchange of love between Rādhā and Kṛṣṇa is the actual display of Kṛṣṇa's internal pleasure potency. Although we speak of "when" Kṛṣṇa desires, just when He did desire we cannot say. We only speak in this way because in conditioned life we take it that everything has a beginning; however, in spiritual life everything is absolute, and so there is neither beginning nor end. Yet in order to understand that Rādhā and Kṛṣṇa are one and that They also become divided, the question "When?" automatically comes to mind. When Kṛṣṇa desired to enjoy His pleasure potency, He manifested Himself in the separate form of Rādhārāṇī, and when He wanted to understand Himself through the agency of Rādhā, He united with Rādhārāṇī, and that unification is called Lord Caitanya. This is all explained by Śrīla Kṛṣṇadāsa Kavirāja in the fifth verse of the *Caitanya-caritāmṛta*.

In the next verse the author further explains why Kṛṣṇa assumed the form of Caitanya Mahāprabhu. Kṛṣṇa desired to know the glory of Rādhā's love. "Why is She so much in love with Me?" Kṛṣṇa asked. "What is My special qualification that attracts Her so? And what is the actual way in which She loves Me?" It seems strange that Kṛṣṇa, as the Supreme, should be attracted by anyone's love. A man searches after the love of a woman because he is imperfect—he lacks something. The love of a woman, that potency and pleasure, is absent in man, and therefore a man wants a woman. But this is not the case with Kṛṣṇa, who is full in Himself. Thus Kṛṣṇa expressed surprise: "Why am I attracted by Rādhārāṇī? And when Rādhārāṇī feels My love, what is She actually feeling?" To taste the essence of that loving exchange, Kṛṣṇa made His appearance in the same way that the moon appears on the horizon of the sea. Just as the moon was produced by the churning of the sea, by the churning of spiritual loving affairs the moon of Caitanya Mahāprabhu appeared. Indeed, Lord Caitanya's complexion was golden, just like the luster of the moon. Although this is figurative language, it conveys something of the meaning behind the appearance of Caitanya Mahāprabhu.

After offering respects to Lord Caitanya, Kṛṣṇadāsa Kavirāja begins offering them to Lord Nityānanda in the seventh verse of the *Caitanya-caritāmṛta*. The author explains that Lord Nityānanda is Balarāma, who is the origin of Mahā-Viṣṇu. Kṛṣṇa's first expansion is Balarāma, a portion of whom is manifested as Saṅkarṣaṇa, who then expands as Pradyumna. In this way so many expansions take place. Although there are many expansions, Lord Śrī Kṛṣṇa is the origin, as confirmed in the *Brahma-saṁhitā*. He is like the original candle, from which many thousands and millions of candles are lit. Although any number of candles can be lit, the original candle still retains its identity as the origin. In this way Kṛṣṇa expands Himself into so many forms, and all these expansions are called *viṣṇu-tattva*. Viṣṇu is a large light, and we are small lights, but all are expansions of Kṛṣṇa.

When it is necessary to create the material universes, Viṣṇu expands Himself as Mahā-Viṣṇu. Mahā-Viṣṇu lies down in the Causal Ocean and breathes all the universes from His nostrils. Thus from Mahā-Viṣṇu and the Causal Ocean spring all the universes, and all these universes, including ours, float in the Causal Ocean. In this regard there is the story of Vāmana, who, when He took three steps, stuck His foot through the covering of this universe. Water from the Causal Ocean flowed through the hole that His foot made, and it is said that that water became the river Ganges. Therefore the Ganges is accepted as the most sacred water of Viṣṇu and is worshiped by all Hindus, from the Himalayas down to the Bay of Bengal.

Mahā-Viṣṇu is actually an expansion of Balarāma, who is Kṛṣṇa's first expansion and, in the Vṛndāvana pastimes, His brother. In the *mahā-mantra*—Hare Kṛṣṇa, Hare Kṛṣṇa, Kṛṣṇa Kṛṣṇa, Hare Hare/ Hare Rāma, Hare Rāma, Rāma Rāma, Hare Hare—the word "Rāma" refers to Balarāma. Since Lord Nityānanda is Balarāma, "Rāma" also refers to Lord Nityānanda. Thus Hare Kṛṣṇa, Hare Rāma addresses not only Kṛṣṇa and Balarāma but Lord Caitanya and Lord Nityānanda as well.

The subject matter of the *Caitanya-caritāmṛta* deals primarily with what is beyond this material creation. The cosmic material expansion is called *māyā,* illusion, because it has no eternal existence. Because it is sometimes manifested and sometimes not, it is regarded as illusory. But beyond this temporary manifestation is a higher nature, as indicated in the *Bhagavad-gītā* (8.20):

paras tasmāt tu bhāvo 'nyo 'vyakto 'vyaktāt sanātanaḥ
yaḥ sa sarveṣu bhūteṣu naśyatsu na vinaśyati

"Yet there is another unmanifested nature, which is eternal and is transcendental to this manifested and unmanifested matter. It is supreme and is never annihilated. When all in this world is annihilated, that part remains as it is." The material world has a manifested state (*vyakta*) and a potential, unmanifested state (*avyakta*). The supreme nature is beyond both the manifested and the unmanifested material nature. This superior nature can be understood as the living force, which is present in the bodies of all living creatures. The body itself is composed of inferior nature, matter, but it is the superior nature that is moving the body. The symptom of that superior nature is consciousness. Thus in the spiritual world, where everything is composed of the superior nature, everything is conscious. In the material world there are inanimate objects that are not conscious, but in the spiritual world nothing is inanimate. There a table is conscious, the land is conscious, the trees are conscious—everything is conscious.

It is not possible to imagine how far this material manifestation extends. In the material world everything is calculated by imagination or by some imperfect method, but the Vedic literatures give real information of what lies beyond the material universe. Since it is not possible to obtain information of anything beyond this material nature by experimental means, those who believe only in experimental knowledge may doubt the Vedic conclusions, for such people cannot even calculate how far this universe extends, nor can they reach far into the universe itself. That which is beyond our power of conception is called *acintya,* inconceivable. It is useless to argue or speculate about the inconceivable. If something is truly inconceivable, it is not subject to speculation or experimentation. Our energy is limited, and our sense perception is limited; therefore we must rely on the Vedic conclusions regarding that subject matter which is inconceivable. Knowledge of the superior nature must simply be accepted without argument. How is it possible to argue about something to which we have no access? The method for understanding transcendental subject matter is given by Lord Kṛṣṇa Himself in the *Bhagavad-gītā,* where Kṛṣṇa tells Arjuna at the beginning of the Fourth Chapter:

imaṁ vivasvate yogaṁ proktavān aham avyayam
vivasvān manave prāha manur ikṣvākave 'bravīt

"I instructed this imperishable science of *yoga* to the sun god, Vivasvān, and Vivasvān instructed it to Manu, the father of mankind, and Manu in turn instructed it to Ikṣvāku." (Bg. 4.1) This is the method of *paramparā,* or disciplic succession. Similarly, *Śrīmad-Bhāgavatam* explains that Kṛṣṇa imparted knowledge into the heart of Brahmā, the first created being within the universe. Brahmā imparted those lessons to his disciple Nārada, and Nārada imparted that knowledge to his disciple Vyāsadeva. Vyāsadeva imparted it to Madhvācārya, and from Madhvācārya the knowledge came down to Mādhavendra Purī and then to Īśvara Purī, and from him to Caitanya Mahāprabhu.

One may ask that if Caitanya Mahāprabhu is Kṛṣṇa Himself, then why did He need a spiritual master? Of course, He did not need a spiritual master, but because He was playing the role of *ācārya* (one who teaches by example), He accepted a spiritual master. Even Kṛṣṇa Himself accepted a spiritual master, for that is the system. In this way the Lord sets the example for men. We should not think, however, that the Lord takes a spiritual master because He is in want of knowledge. He is simply stressing the importance of accepting the disciplic succession. The knowledge taught in that disciplic succession actually comes from the Lord Himself, and if the knowledge descends unbroken, it is perfect. Although we may not be in touch with the original personality who first imparted the knowledge, we may receive the same knowledge through this process of transmission. In *Śrīmad-Bhāgavatam* it is stated that Kṛṣṇa, the Absolute Truth, the Personality of Godhead, transmitted transcendental knowledge into the heart of Brahmā. This, then, is one way knowledge is received—through the heart. Thus there are two processes by which one may receive knowledge: One depends directly upon the Supreme Personality of Godhead, who is situated as the Supersoul within the heart of all living entities, and the other depends upon the *guru,* or spiritual master, who is an expansion of Kṛṣṇa. Thus Kṛṣṇa transmits information both from within and from without. We simply have to receive it. If knowledge is received in this way, it doesn't matter whether it is inconceivable or not.

In *Śrīmad-Bhāgavatam* there is a great deal of information given about the Vaikuṇṭha planetary systems, which are beyond the material universe. Similarly, a great deal of inconceivable information is given in the *Caitanya-caritāmṛta.* Any attempt to arrive at this information through experimental knowledge will fail. The knowledge simply has to be accepted. According to the Vedic method, *śabda,* or transcendental sound, is regarded as evidence. Sound is very important in Vedic understanding, for if it is pure it is accepted as authoritative. Even in the material world we accept a great deal of information sent thousands of miles by telephone or radio. In this way we also accept sound as evidence in our daily lives. Although we cannot see the informant, we accept his information as valid on the basis of sound. Sound vibration, then, is very important in the transmission of Vedic knowledge.

The *Vedas* inform us that beyond this cosmic manifestation there are extensive planets in the spiritual sky. This material manifestation is regarded as only a small portion of the total creation. The material manifestation includes not only this universe but innumerable others as well, but all the material universes combined constitute only one fourth of the total creation. The remaining three fourths is situated in the spiritual sky. In that sky innumerable planets float, and these are called Vaikuṇṭhalokas. In every Vaikuṇṭhaloka, Nārāyaṇa presides with His four expansions: Saṅkarṣaṇa, Pradyumna, Aniruddha and Vāsudeva. This Saṅkarṣaṇa, states Kṛṣṇadāsa Kavirāja in the eighth verse of the *Caitanya-caritāmṛta*, is Lord Nityānanda.

As stated before, it is in His form as Mahā-Viṣṇu that the Lord manifests the material universes. Just as a husband and wife combine to beget offspring, Mahā-Viṣṇu combines with His wife Māyā, or material nature. This is confirmed in the *Bhagavad-gītā* (14.4), where Kṛṣṇa states:

sarva-yoniṣu kaunteya mūrtayaḥ sambhavanti yāḥ
tāsāṁ brahma mahad yonir ahaṁ bīja-pradaḥ pitā

"It should be understood that all species of life, O son of Kuntī, are made possible by birth in this material nature, and that I am the seed-giving father." Viṣṇu impregnates Māyā, the material nature, simply by glancing at her. This is the spiritual method. Materially we are limited to impregnating by only one particular part of our body, but the Supreme Lord, Kṛṣṇa or Mahā-Viṣṇu, can impregnate by any part. Simply by glancing, the Lord can conceive countless living entities in the womb of material nature. The *Brahma-saṁhitā* confirms that the spiritual body of the Supreme Lord is so powerful that any part of His body can perform the functions of any other part. We can touch only with our hands or skin, but Kṛṣṇa can touch just by glancing. We can see only with our eyes; we cannot touch or smell with them. Kṛṣṇa, however, can smell and also eat with His eyes. When food is offered to Kṛṣṇa, we do not see Him eating, but He eats simply by glancing at the food. We cannot imagine how things work in the spiritual world, where everything is spiritual. It is not that Kṛṣṇa does not eat or that we imagine that He eats; He actually eats, but His eating is different from ours. Our eating process will be similar to His when we are completely on the spiritual platform. On that platform every part of the body can act on behalf of any other part.

Viṣṇu does not require anything in order to create. He does not require the goddess Lakṣmī in order to give birth to Brahmā, for Brahmā is born from a lotus flower that grows from the navel of Viṣṇu. The goddess Lakṣmī sits at the feet of Viṣṇu and serves Him. In this material world sex is required to produce children, but in the spiritual world a man can produce as many children as he likes without having to take help from his wife. So there is no sex there. Because we have no experience with spiritual energy, we think that Brahmā's birth from the navel of Viṣṇu is simply a fictional story. We are not aware that spiritual energy is so powerful that it can do anything and everything. Material energy is dependent on certain laws, but spiritual energy is fully independent.

Countless universes reside like seeds within the skin pores of Mahā-Viṣṇu, and when He exhales, they are all manifested. In the material world we have no experience of such a thing, but we do experience a perverted reflection in the phenomenon of perspiration. We cannot imagine, however, the duration of one breath of Mahā-Viṣṇu, for within one breath all the universes are created and annihilated. This is stated in the *Brahma-saṁhitā*. Lord Brahmā lives only for the duration of one breath, and according to our time scale 4,320,000,000 years constitute only twelve hours for Brahmā, and Brahmā lives one hundred of his years. Yet the whole life of Brahmā is contained within one breath of Mahā-Viṣṇu. Thus it is not possible for us to imagine the breathing power of Mahā-Viṣṇu, who is but a partial manifestation of Lord Nityānanda. This the author of the *Caitanya-caritāmṛta* explains in the ninth verse.

In the tenth and eleventh verses Kṛṣṇadāsa Kavirāja describes Garbhodakaśāyī Viṣṇu and Kṣīrodakaśāyī Viṣṇu, successive plenary expansions of Mahā-Viṣṇu. Brahmā appears upon a lotus growing from the navel of Garbhodakaśāyī Viṣṇu, and within the stem of that lotus are so many planetary systems. Then Brahmā creates the whole of human society, animal society—everything. Kṣīrodakaśāyī Viṣṇu lies on the milk ocean within the universe, of which He is the controller and maintainer. Thus Brahmā is the creator, Viṣṇu is the maintainer, and when the time for annihilation arrives, Śiva will finish everything.

In the first eleven verses of the *Caitanya-caritāmṛta,* Kṛṣṇadāsa Kavirāja Gosvāmī thus discusses Lord Caitanya Mahāprabhu as Śrī Kṛṣṇa Himself, the Supreme Personality of Godhead, and Lord Nityānanda as Balarāma, the first expansion of Kṛṣṇa. Then in the twelfth and thirteenth verses he describes Advaita Ācārya, who is another principal associate of Lord Caitanya Mahāprabhu's and an incarnation of Mahā-Viṣṇu. Thus Advaita Ācārya is also the Lord, or, more precisely, an expansion of the Lord. The word *advaita* means "nondual," and His name is such because He is nondifferent from the Supreme Lord. He is also called *ācārya,* teacher, because He disseminated Kṛṣṇa consciousness. In this way He is just like Caitanya Mahāprabhu. Although Lord Caitanya is Śrī Kṛṣṇa Himself, He appeared as a devotee to teach people in general how to love Kṛṣṇa. Similarly, although Advaita Ācārya is the Lord, He appeared just to distribute the knowledge of Kṛṣṇa consciousness. Thus He is also the Lord incarnated as a devotee.

In the pastimes of Lord Caitanya, Kṛṣṇa is manifested in five different features, known as the Pañca-tattva, to whom Śrīla Kṛṣṇadāsa Kavirāja offers his obeisances in the fourteenth verse of the *Caitanya-caritāmṛta.* Kṛṣṇa and His associates appear as devotees of the Supreme Lord in the form of Śrī Kṛṣṇa Caitanya Mahāprabhu, Śrī Nityānanda Prabhu, Śrī Advaita Ācārya, Śrī Gadādhara Prabhu and Śrīvāsa Prabhu. In all cases, Caitanya Mahāprabhu is the source of energy for all His devotees. Since this is the case, if we take shelter of Caitanya Mahāprabhu for the successful execution of Kṛṣṇa consciousness, we are sure to make progress. In a devotional song, Narottama Dāsa Ṭhākura sings, "My dear Lord Caitanya, please have mercy upon me. There is no one who is as merciful as You. My plea is most urgent because Your mission is to deliver all fallen souls, and no one is more fallen than I. Therefore I beg priority."

With verse 15, Kṛṣṇadāsa Kavirāja Gosvāmī begins offering his obeisances directly to Kṛṣṇa Himself. Kṛṣṇadāsa Kavirāja was an inhabitant of Vṛndāvana and a great devotee. He had been living with his family in Katwa, a small town in the district of Burdwan, in Bengal. He worshiped Rādhā-Kṛṣṇa with his family, and once when there was some misunderstanding among his family members about devotional service, he was advised by Nityānanda Prabhu in a dream to leave home and go to Vṛndāvana. Although he was very old, he started out that very night and went to live in Vṛndāvana. While he was there, he met some of the Six Gosvāmīs, the principal disciples of Lord Caitanya Mahāprabhu. He was requested to write the *Caitanya-caritāmṛta* by the devotees of Vṛndāvana. Although he began this work at a very old age, by the grace of Lord Caitanya he finished it. Today it remains the most authoritative book on Caitanya Mahāprabhu's philosophy and life.

When Kṛṣṇadāsa Kavirāja Gosvāmī was living in Vṛndāvana, there were not very many temples. At that time the three principal temples were those of Madana-mohana, Govindajī and Gopīnātha. As a resident of Vṛndāvana, Kṛṣṇadāsa Kavirāja offers his respects to the Deities in these temples and requests God's favor: "My progress in spiritual life is very slow, so I'm asking Your help." In the fifteenth verse of the *Caitanya-caritāmṛta,* Kṛṣṇadāsa offers his obeisances to the Madana-mohana *vigraha,* the Deity who can help us progress in Kṛṣṇa consciousness. In the execution of Kṛṣṇa consciousness, our first business is to know Kṛṣṇa and our relationship with Him. To know Kṛṣṇa is to know one's self, and to know one's self is to know one's relationship with Kṛṣṇa. Since this relationship can be learned by worshiping the Madana-mohana *vigraha,* Kṛṣṇadāsa Kavirāja Gosvāmī first establishes his relationship with Him.

When this is established, in the sixteenth verse Kṛṣṇadāsa offers his obeisances to the functional Deity, Govinda. The Govinda Deity is called the functional Deity because He shows us how to serve Rādhā and Kṛṣṇa. The Madana-mohana Deity simply establishes that "I am Your eternal servant." With Govinda, however, there is actual acceptance of service. Govinda resides eternally in Vṛndāvana. In the spiritual world of Vṛndāvana the buildings are made of touchstone, the cows are known as *surabhi* cows, givers of abundant milk, and the trees are known as wish-fulfilling trees, for they yield whatever one desires. In Vṛndāvana Kṛṣṇa herds the *surabhi* cows, and He is worshiped by hundreds and thousands of *gopīs,* cowherd girls, who are all goddesses of fortune. When Kṛṣṇa descends to the material world, this same Vṛndāvana descends with Him, just as an entourage accompanies an important personage. Because when Kṛṣṇa comes His land also comes, Vṛndāvana is considered to exist beyond the material world. Therefore devotees take shelter of the Vṛndāvana in India, for it is considered to be a replica of the original Vṛndāvana. Although one may complain that no *kalpa-vṛkṣas,* wish-fulfilling trees, exist there, when the Six Gosvāmīs were there, *kalpa-vṛkṣas* were present. It is not that one can simply go to such a tree and make demands; one must first become a devotee. The Gosvāmīs would live under a tree for one night only, and the trees would satisfy all their desires. For the common man this may all seem very wonderful, but as one makes progress in devotional service, all this can be realized.

Vṛndāvana is actually experienced as it is by persons who have stopped trying to derive pleasure from material enjoyment. "When will my mind become cleansed of all hankering for material enjoyment so I will be able to see Vṛndāvana?" one great devotee asks. The more Kṛṣṇa conscious we become and the more we advance, the more everything is revealed as spiritual. Thus Kṛṣṇadāsa Kavirāja Gosvāmī considered the Vṛndāvana in India to be as good as the Vṛndāvana in the spiritual sky, and in the sixteenth verse of the *Caitanya-caritāmṛta* he describes Rādhārāṇī and Kṛṣṇa as seated beneath a wish-fulfilling tree in Vṛndāvana, on a throne decorated with valuable jewels. There Kṛṣṇa's dear *gopī* friends serve Rādhā and Kṛṣṇa by singing, dancing, offering betel nuts and refreshments, and decorating Their Lordships with flowers. Even today in India people decorate swinging thrones and re-create this scene during the month of July–August. Generally at that time people go to Vṛndāvana to offer their respects to the Deities there.

Finally Kṛṣṇadāsa Kavirāja Gosvāmī offers his blessings to his readers in the name of the Gopīnātha Deity, who is Kṛṣṇa as master and proprietor of the *gopīs.* When Kṛṣṇa played upon His flute, all the *gopīs,* or cowherd girls, were attracted by the sound and left their household duties, and when they came to Him, He danced with them. These activities are all described in the Tenth Canto of

Śrīmad-Bhāgavatam. These *gopīs* were childhood friends of Kṛṣṇa, and many were married, for in India the girls are generally married by the age of twelve. The boys, however, are not married before eighteen, so Kṛṣṇa, who was fifteen or sixteen at the time, was not married. Nonetheless, He called these girls from their homes and invited them to dance with Him. That dance is called the *rāsa-līlā* dance, and it is the most elevated of all the Vṛndāvana pastimes. Kṛṣṇa is therefore called Gopīnātha because He is the beloved master of the *gopīs*.

Kṛṣṇadāsa Kavirāja Gosvāmī petitions the blessings of Lord Gopīnātha: "May that Gopīnātha, the master of the *gopīs,* Kṛṣṇa, bless you. May you become blessed by Gopīnātha." The author of the *Caitanya-caritāmṛta* prays that just as Kṛṣṇa attracted the *gopīs* by the sweet sound of His flute, He will also attract the reader's mind by that transcendental vibration.

Part I

Rūpa Gosvāmī and his younger brother Anupama (Vallabha) meet Lord Caitanya at Prayāg (Allahabad).

CHAPTER 1

Teachings to Rūpa Gosvāmī

Śrīla Rūpa Gosvāmī, the younger brother of Sanātana Gosvāmī, went to Prayāga, the modern city of Allahabad, with his younger brother Vallabha. When the two brothers heard that Lord Śrī Caitanya Mahāprabhu was staying there, they both became very much pleased and went to see the Lord. At that time the Lord was on His way to visit the temple of Bindu Mādhava. On the way to the temple the Lord was chanting and dancing, and thousands of people were following Him. Some were crying and some were laughing, some were dancing and some were singing, and some were falling on the ground, offering obeisances to the Lord. And all of them were roaring the holy name: "Kṛṣṇa! Kṛṣṇa!" It is said that in spite of being at the confluence of the rivers Ganges and Yamunā, Prayāga was never flooded until the appearance of Caitanya Mahāprabhu, at which time the city was overflooded by love of Kṛṣṇa.

The two brothers, Rūpa Gosvāmī and Vallabha, stayed aloof in an uncrowded place and witnessed the great crowd and wonderful scene. When the Lord danced, He raised His arms and shouted, "Haribol! Haribol!" The people all about Him were astonished to see His activities. Indeed, the wonderful scene is difficult to describe.

After visiting the temple, the Lord accepted *prasādam* (food offered to the Deity) at the house of a Deccanist (southern) *brāhmaṇa* with whom He was acquainted. While sitting alone at the *brāhmaṇa's* home, the Lord was visited by Rūpa Gosvāmī and Vallabha. From a distance the two brothers fell down on the ground to offer obeisances, and they chanted many Sanskrit verses from the scriptures. When the Lord saw Rūpa Gosvāmī offering obeisances before Him, He became very much pleased and said, "My dear Rūpa, please get up." The Lord then informed Rūpa Gosvāmī of the causeless mercy of Kṛṣṇa upon him, for Kṛṣṇa had just delivered him from the materialistic way of life, which is based simply on pounds-shillings-pence.

The Lord accepted the two brothers as His devotees, and He cited a verse from the scriptures stating that the Lord will not accept a *brāhmaṇa* who has studied the four *Vedas* if he is not a devotee but He will accept someone from a very low family if he is a pure devotee. Then the Lord embraced the two brothers, and out of His causeless mercy He touched their heads with His lotus feet. Blessed in this way, the brothers offered prayers to the Lord in their own words. The prayers indicated that Lord Śrī Kṛṣṇa Caitanya Mahāprabhu was Kṛṣṇa Himself, that He had assumed a fair-complexioned form (*gaurāṅga*), and that He was the most munificent incarnation of Kṛṣṇa because He was distributing love of Kṛṣṇa. Śrīla Rūpa Gosvāmī also recited a verse later found in the book *Govinda-līlāmṛta* (1.2):

yo 'jñāna-mattaṁ bhuvanaṁ dayālur
ullāghayann apy akarot pramattam
sva-prema-sampat-sudhayādbhutehaṁ
śrī-kṛṣṇa-caitanyam amuṁ prapadye

"Let me surrender unto the lotus feet of Śrī Kṛṣṇa Caitanya Mahāprabhu, who is the greatest, most merciful Personality of Godhead. He delivers those who are merged in ignorance and offers them the highest gift, love of Kṛṣṇa, and thus makes them mad after Kṛṣṇa consciousness."

After this incident, Vallabha Bhaṭṭa invited the Lord to go to the other side of the Ganges, and the Lord went. On this trip Rūpa Gosvāmī accompanied the Lord, and, indeed, wherever the Lord went

Rūpa Gosvāmī would follow Him and stay with Him. Because the Lord felt inconvenienced in crowded places, He asked Rūpa Gosvāmī to accompany Him to a place on the banks of the Ganges known as Daśāśvamedha-ghāṭa. For ten days He instructed Rūpa Gosvāmī about the truth of Kṛṣṇa, the principles of devotional service, and the transcendental mellows (relationships with Kṛṣṇa). All of this was described in full detail so that in the future Rūpa Gosvāmī could distribute the science of Kṛṣṇa in his book *Bhakti-rasāmṛta-sindhu.* Śrīla Rūpa Gosvāmī described this incident in the first verse of the *Bhakti-rasāmṛta-sindhu,* in which he speaks of the causeless mercy of the Lord upon him.

The Supreme Lord is cognizant and all-powerful, and by His causeless mercy He empowers a living entity to receive His mercy. People in general, being under the spell of conditioned life, are averse to rendering devotional service and practicing Kṛṣṇa consciousness. They are unaware of the teachings of Kṛṣṇa consciousness, which reveal one's eternal relationship with the Supreme Personality of Godhead, the process by which one can return to the spiritual world, and the ultimate goal of life, which is to return home, back to Godhead. Because these things are unknown to the conditioned soul, Lord Caitanya, out of His causeless mercy, instructed Rūpa Gosvāmī in the principles of devotional service. Later, Rūpa Gosvāmī distributed this science to the people in general.

In the prologue to the *Bhakti-rasāmṛta-sindhu* (1.1.2), Rūpa Gosvāmī describes Lord Caitanya as follows:

hṛdi yasya preraṇayā pravartito 'haṁ varāka-rūpo 'pi
tasya hareḥ pada-kamalaṁ vande caitanya-devasya

"I offer my respectful obeisances unto the lotus feet of Lord Caitanyadeva, the Supreme Personality of Godhead, because He has inspired me with the desire in my heart to write something about devotional service. For this reason I am writing this book on the science of devotion, known as the *Bhakti-rasāmṛta-sindhu.*"

Beginning His ten days of continual instruction to Rūpa Gosvāmī, Lord Śrī Caitanya Mahāprabhu said, "My dear Rūpa, the science of devotional service is just like a great ocean, and so it is not possible to show you its entire length and breadth. But I shall try to explain the nature of that ocean by taking just one drop out of it. In this way you can taste it and understand what that ocean of devotional service actually is."

The Lord then explained that within this *brahmāṇḍa,* or universe, there are innumerable living entities who, according to their own fruitive activities, are transmigrating from one species of life to another and from one planet to another. In this way their encagement in material existence has continued since time immemorial. In actuality, these living entities are atomic parts and parcels of the Supreme Spirit. It is said in the *Śvetāśvatara Upaniṣad* that the length and breadth of the individual soul is 1/10,000th part of the tip of a hair. The atomic magnitude of the living entity is confirmed in the Eleventh Canto of *Śrīmad-Bhāgavatam* (11.16.11). And in the Tenth Canto (10.87.30) Sanandana-kumāra, while performing a great sacrifice, quotes the following statement by the personified *Vedas:* "O Supreme Truth! If the living entities were not infinitesimal sparks of the Supreme Spirit, each minute spark would be all-pervading and could not be controlled by a superior power. But if the living entity is accepted as a minute part and parcel of the Supreme Lord, one can automatically understand how he is controlled by the supreme power. The latter is his actual constitutional position, and if he remains in this position he can attain full freedom. If one mistakenly considers his constitutional position equal to that of the Supreme Personality of Godhead, he becomes contaminated by the doctrine of nonduality and his efforts in transcendental life are rendered ineffective."

Lord Caitanya continued His teachings by pointing out that there are two kinds of living entities, the eternally liberated and the eternally conditioned. The eternally conditioned living entities can be divided into two types, the moving and the nonmoving. Those that remain in one place—trees, for example—are classified as *sthāvara,* or nonmoving entities, and those that move—such as birds and beasts—are called *jaṅgama,* or moving entities. The moving entities are further divided into three categories: those that fly in the sky, those that swim in the water, and those that walk on land. Out of the many millions and trillions of living entities on land, human beings are very few. Out of that small number of human beings, most are totally ignorant of the spiritual science, are unclean in their habits, and have no faith in the existence of the Supreme Personality of Godhead. In short, most human beings live like animals. Therefore these can be deducted from the number of human beings that constitute civilized human society.

We can hardly find any human beings who believe in the Vedic scriptures and the existence of God, or even in proper behavior. Those who do believe in these things, and in advancing in spiritual life, are known as Āryans. Out of those who believe in the scriptures and the advancement of human civilization, there are two classes—the righteous and the unrighteous. Those who are righteous generally execute fruitive activities to derive some good result for sense gratification. Out of many such persons who engage in righteous activities for sense gratification, only a few come to know about the Absolute Truth. These are called *jñānīs,* empiric philosophers in search of the Absolute Truth. Out of many hundreds and thousands of such empiric philosophers, only a handful actually attain liberation. When one is liberated, he theoretically understands that the living entity is not composed of material elements but is spirit soul, distinct from matter. Simply by understanding this doctrine, even theoretically, one qualifies as a *mukta,* or liberated soul. But the actual *mukta* is he who understands his constitutional position as part and parcel of the Lord and as His eternal servant. Such liberated souls engage with faith and devotion in the service of the Lord, and they are called *kṛṣṇa-bhaktas,* or Kṛṣṇa conscious persons.

Kṛṣṇa-bhaktas are free from all material desires. Although those who are theoretically liberated by knowing that the living entity is not material may be classified among liberated souls, they still have desires. Their main desire is to become one with the Supreme Personality of Godhead. Such persons are very much attached to performing Vedic rituals and righteous activities in order to enjoy material prosperity. Even when some of them transcend material enjoyment, they still try to enjoy in the spiritual world by merging into the existence of the Supreme Lord. Some of them also desire to attain mystic powers through the execution of *yoga*. As long as any of these desires are within a person's heart, he cannot understand the nature of pure devotional service, and on account of constantly being agitated by such desires, he is not peaceful. Indeed, as long as there is any desire for material perfection at all, one cannot be at peace. Since the devotees of Lord Kṛṣṇa do not desire anything material, they are the only peaceful persons within this material world. This is confirmed in *Śrīmad-Bhāgavatam* (6.14.5):

muktānām api siddhānāṁ nārāyaṇa-parāyaṇaḥ
su-durlabhaḥ praśāntātmā koṭiṣv api mahāmune

"O great sage, out of many millions of liberated persons and persons who have achieved success in mystic *yoga*, it is very rare to find one who is completely devoted to the Supreme Personality of Godhead and is therefore filled with peace."

Lord Caitanya next explained that of the many thousands and millions of living entities wandering in the material world, one who by the grace of Lord Kṛṣṇa and the spiritual master gets the seed of devotional service is very rare and fortunate. A pious or religious man is generally inclined to worship deities in various temples, but if by chance, even without his knowledge, he offers his obeisances and worshipful respects to Lord Viṣṇu and receives the favor of a Vaiṣṇava, a devotee of the Lord, at that time he acquires the asset necessary to approach the Supreme Personality of Godhead. This is plainly understood from the history of the great sage Nārada, which is related in *Śrīmad-Bhāgavatam*. By serving Vaiṣṇavas in his previous life, Nārada was favored by those devotees of the Lord and became the great sage Nārada Muni.

Vaiṣṇavas are generally very compassionate toward the conditioned souls. Without even being invited, a devotee will go from door to door to enlighten people, to bring them out of the darkness of nescience by imparting knowledge of the living entity's constitutional position as a servant of Lord Kṛṣṇa. Such devotees are empowered by the Lord to distribute devotional consciousness, or Kṛṣṇa consciousness, to the people in general. They are known as authorized spiritual masters, and it is by the mercy of such a spiritual master that a conditioned soul gets the seed of devotional service. The causeless mercy of the Supreme Personality of Godhead is first appreciated when one comes in touch with a bona fide spiritual master, who can enlighten the conditioned soul and bring him to the highest position of devotional life. Therefore Lord Caitanya said that by the mercy of the spiritual master one can achieve the causeless mercy of the Lord and by the mercy of the Supreme Personality of Godhead one can attain the mercy of the bona fide spiritual master.

Thus by the mercy of the spiritual master and Kṛṣṇa one receives the seed of devotional service. Then one has to sow the seed in the field of his heart, just as a gardener sows the seed of a valuable tree. After sowing this seed, one has to water it by chanting and hearing the holy name of the Supreme Lord and by taking part in discussions about the science of devotional service in a society of pure devotees. When the plant of devotional service sprouts up from the seed of devotion, it begins to grow freely. When it is fully grown, it surpasses the length and breadth of this universe and enters the transcendental atmosphere of the spiritual world, where everything is bathed in the effulgence of the *brahmajyoti.* The plant penetrates even the *brahmajyoti* and gradually enters the planet known as Goloka Vṛndāvana. There the plant takes shelter at the lotus feet of Kṛṣṇa. That is the ultimate goal of devotional service. After attaining this position, the plant produces the fruit of love of Godhead. To taste this fruit, however, it is necessary for the devotee, or transcendental gardener, to water the plant daily by chanting and hearing. Unless one waters the plant by chanting and hearing, there is every chance that it will dry up.

Lord Caitanya pointed out to Rūpa Gosvāmī that there was another danger to be encountered while watering the root of the devotional plant. After a plant has grown somewhat, an animal may come and either eat it or destroy it. When the green leaves of a plant are eaten by some animal, the plant generally dies. Thus one has to take precautions so that the plant of devotional service is not disturbed by animals, which represent offenses. The most dangerous animal is a mad elephant, for if a mad elephant enters a garden, it causes tremendous damage to plants and trees. An offense to a pure devotee of the Lord is called *vaiṣṇava-aparādha,* the mad elephant offense. In the discharge of devotional service, an offense to the feet of a pure devotee creates havoc and stops one's advancement. Thus one has to defend the plant of *bhakti* by fencing it off properly and taking care not to offend pure devotees. Then the plant of devotional service will be properly protected.

An offense to a pure devotee is one of the ten offenses against the holy name. The first offense is to blaspheme the great devotees who have tried to spread the glories of the holy name all over the world. The greatest offender at the feet of the holy name is the rascal who is envious of such devotees. The holy name of Kṛṣṇa is nondifferent from Kṛṣṇa, and Lord Kṛṣṇa cannot tolerate offenses against a pure devotee who, following the order of his spiritual master, is spreading the holy name all over the world. The second offense is to deny that Lord Viṣṇu is the Absolute Truth. Since there is no difference between the Lord and His name, qualities, form and pastimes, or activities, one who sees a difference is considered an offender. The Lord being supreme, no one is equal to or greater than Him. Consequently, one who thinks that the name of some demigod is equal to the Lord's name is an offender. The Supreme Lord and the demigods should never be considered on the same level.

The third offense is to consider the bona fide spiritual master to be a common man. The fourth offense is to blaspheme the Vedic literature—the *Vedas* and such corollaries as the *Purāṇas.* The fifth offense is to consider the glories of the holy name to be exaggerations. The sixth offense is to imagine a perverted meaning of the holy name. The seventh offense is to commit sinful activities on the strength of chanting the holy name. It is understood that by chanting the holy name one is freed from sinful reactions, but this does not mean that one should perversely act sinfully on the strength of chanting. That is the greatest offense. The eighth offense is to equate chanting the holy name with religious rituals, austerity, renunciation or sacrificial performances. Chanting the holy name is as good as associating with the Supreme Personality of Godhead, whereas these pious activities are only means of approaching the Supreme Personality of Godhead, and they can also be performed for some material reason. It is an offense to equate them with chanting the holy name. The ninth offense is to preach the glories of the holy name of God to a faithless person. The tenth and last offense is to maintain material attachments even after hearing and chanting the holy name of God. The idea is that by chanting the holy name without offense one is elevated to the liberated platform, where one is freed from all material attachments. Thus if one chants the holy names and still has material attachments, he is committing an offense.

There are still other factors which can disturb the plant of devotional service. As this plant grows, the weeds of material desires may also grow. When a person advances in devotional service, it is natural that many persons will come to him requesting to become disciples and will offer him some material gains. If one is attracted by a large number of disciples offering material conveniences and forgets his duty as a bona fide spiritual master, the growth of the plant will be impeded. Simply by taking advantage of material conveniences one may become addicted to enjoying material comforts.

Other impediments are to desire liberation or material name and fame by discharging devotional service, or to neglect the prohibitions. These prohibitions are mentioned in the authorized scriptures: One should not indulge in illicit sex, intoxication, gambling or eating meat—indeed, one should not eat anything other than *kṛṣṇa-prasādam*, food offered to Kṛṣṇa. These are the restrictions for one who is attempting to advance in devotional service. If one does not follow these principles strictly, there will be a severe disturbance in the discharge of devotional service.

If one is not particularly careful, by watering the plant of devotional service one will instead nourish the weeds described above, which will then grow very luxuriantly and hamper one's progress. The idea is that when one waters a garden, not only does the desired plant grow rapidly but the unwanted plants grow also. If the gardener does not see these weeds and cut them down, they will overcome and choke the plant of devotion. It is thus the duty of the neophyte devotee to cut down all the weeds that may grow by the watering process of devotional service. If one is careful to guard against the growth of these weeds, the plant of devotion will grow luxuriantly and reach the ultimate goal, Goloka Vṛndāvana. When the living entity engaged in devotional service relishes the fruit of love of Godhead, he forgets all religious rituals aimed at improving his economic condition. He no longer desires to satisfy his senses, and he no longer desires to become one with the Supreme Lord by merging into His effulgence.

There are many practices leading to spiritual knowledge and transcendental bliss, including the ritualistic sacrifices recommended in the *Vedas,* the execution of austerities and pious duties, and the practice of mystic *yoga.* These all reward different results to their performers. But all these rewards appear to glitter only as long as one is not elevated to the transcendental loving service of the Lord. Love of God is dormant in everyone, and it can be awakened from its dormant position by the execution of pure devotional service, just as a person bitten by a serpent and fallen unconscious can be revived by smelling ammonia.

After speaking in this way about pure devotional service, Lord Caitanya began to describe that service and its symptoms to Rūpa Gosvāmī. He explained that in pure devotional service there can be no desire other than the desire to advance in Kṛṣṇa consciousness. In Kṛṣṇa consciousness there is no scope for worshiping any demigod or even any other form of Kṛṣṇa, nor is there room for indulgence in speculative empiric philosophy or fruitive activities. One should be free from all these contaminations. A devotee should accept only those things that are favorable for keeping his body and soul together and should reject those things that increase the demands of the body. Only the bare necessities for bodily maintenance should be accepted. By making one's bodily necessities secondary, one can primarily devote his time to the cultivation of Kṛṣṇa consciousness through the chanting of the holy names of God. Pure devotional service means engaging all one's senses in the service of the Lord. At the present moment our senses are all designated because the body is designated. So we think that our body belongs to a particular society or a particular country or a particular family. In this way the body is bound by so many designations. Similarly, the senses belong to the body, and when the body is subject to such designations, the senses are also. Thus one engages the senses on behalf of family, society, nation and so on. When the senses are so engaged, one cannot cultivate Kṛṣṇa consciousness. The senses must be purified, and this is possible when one purely understands that he belongs to Kṛṣṇa and that his life belongs to Kṛṣṇa—in other words, that his identity is to be an eternal servant of Kṛṣṇa. In this way one can engage his senses in the service of the Lord, and such engagement is called pure devotional service.

A pure devotee accepts the transcendental loving service of the Lord but rejects all kinds of liberation for his personal sense gratification. This is stated by Lord Kapila in *Śrīmad-Bhāgavatam* (3.29.11–14), in His explanation of the nature of pure devotional service. As soon as a pure devotee hears the glories and transcendental qualities of the Supreme Personality of Godhead, who is seated in everyone's heart, his mind at once flows toward the Lord, just as the waters of the Ganges flow down toward the sea. Such spontaneous attraction of the devotee's mind to the service of the Supreme Personality of Godhead signifies pure devotional service.

Devotional service is pure when one engages in the service of the Supreme Lord without any selfish motive and without being hampered by any material impediment. The pure devotee does not desire to live on the same planet as the Supreme Lord, nor does he desire the same opulence as the Lord, nor does he desire to have the same form as the Lord, nor to live with Him side by side, nor to merge into His existence. Even if the Lord offers the pure devotee such rewards, he rejects them. The point is that a pure devotee is so much absorbed in the transcendental loving service of the Lord that he has no time to think of any benefit beyond his immediate engagement. Just as an ordinary materialistic businessman thinks of nothing else when he is absorbed in his business, a pure devotee, when engaged in the service of the Lord, does not think of anything beyond that engagement.

One who possesses the symptoms described above has been elevated to the topmost position of devotional service. And it is by such transcendental loving service alone that one can surpass the influence of *māyā* and relish pure love of Godhead. As long as one desires material benefit or liberation, which are called the two witches of allurement, one cannot relish the taste of transcendental loving service to the Supreme Lord.

There are three stages of devotional service: The first is the beginning stage of cultivation, the second is the realization of service, and the third, the supreme stage, is the attainment of love of Godhead. There are nine different methods of cultivating devotional service—hearing, chanting, remembering, etc.—and all these processes are employed by the neophyte in the first stage. If one is engaged in chanting and hearing with devotion and faith, his material misgivings gradually become vanquished. As his faith in devotional service increases more and more, he becomes assured of a higher perfectional position. In this way one becomes firmly fixed in devotional service, increases his taste for it, becomes attached to it, and feels ecstasy, the preliminary stage of love of Godhead. Attainment of ecstasy is produced by executing this process of cultivating devotional service. When one continues the process of hearing and chanting, attachment to Kṛṣṇa gradually thickens and at last is called love of Godhead.

In the stage of transcendental love of God there are further developments, known as transcendental affection, emotion, ecstasy, and extreme and intense attachment. These are technically known by the terms *rāga, anurāga, bhāva* and *mahābhāva.* The progress from one stage to another is like the thickening of sugarcane juice. In the first stage sugarcane juice is a thin liquid. When, by evaporation, it becomes thicker and thicker, it turns into molasses. Then it turns into granules of sugar, then rock candy, and so on. Just as sugarcane juice progresses from one stage to another, similarly transcendental love for the Supreme Lord develops by stages.

When one actually becomes situated on the transcendental platform, he becomes steady. Unless one is so situated, his position is not steady and he may fall down. When one is actually situated transcendentally, there is no fear of falling down. This stage is technically called *sthāyi-bhāva.* There are further developments within this stage, known as *vibhāva, anubhāva, sāttvika* and *vyabhicārī.* When these four ingredients are added to the steadfast position of pure transcendental life, there is actually an exchange of *rasa,* or transcendental mellows, with the Supreme Lord. This exchange in loving reciprocation between the lover and the beloved is generally called *kṛṣṇa-bhakti-rasa,* the transcendental taste of exchanging loving sentiments between the devotee and the Supreme Personality of Godhead. It should be noted, however, that the transcendental loving exchanges stand on the steadfast position of *sthāyi-bhāva,* as explained above. The basic principle of *vibhāva* is *sthāyi-bhāva,* and all other activities are auxiliary for the development of transcendental love.

The ecstasy of transcendental love has two components—the context and the cause of the excitement. The context is also divided into two parts—the subject and the object. The exchange of devotional service is the subject, and Kṛṣṇa is the object. His transcendental qualities are the causes of excitement. This means that a devotee who becomes enamored with the transcendental qualities of Kṛṣṇa becomes excited to serve Him. The impersonal (Māyāvādī) philosophers say that the Absolute Truth is *nirguṇa,* "without qualities," but the Vaiṣṇava philosophers say that the Absolute Truth is described as *nirguṇa* because He has no *material* qualities. This is not to say that He has no *spiritual* qualities. Indeed, the Lord's spiritual qualities are so great and so enchanting that even liberated persons become attracted to Him. This is explained in the *ātmārāma* verse of *Śrīmad-Bhāgavatam* (1.7.10), where it is said that those who are already situated on the platform of self-realization are attracted by the transcendental qualities of Kṛṣṇa. This means that Kṛṣṇa's qualities are not material but are pure and transcendental.

The highest stage of ecstasy is characterized by the following thirteen transcendental activities: (1) dancing, (2) rolling on the floor, (3) singing, (4) clapping, (5) stretching the body, (6) thundering, (7) yawning, (8) breathing heavily, (9) forgetting social conventions, (10) drooling, (11) laughing, (12) shaking the head, and (13) hiccoughing. All these symptoms are not awakened simultaneously; they appear according to the exchange of transcendental mellows. Sometimes one symptom is prominent, and at another time another is prominent.

There are five transcendental *rasas,* or mellows. The initial stage is called *śānta-rati,* wherein one who is liberated from material contamination appreciates the greatness of the Supreme Personality of Godhead. One who attains this stage does not exactly engage in the transcendental loving service of the Lord, for this is the neutral stage.

In the second stage, which is called *dāsya-rati,* a person appreciates his position as being everlastingly subordinate to the Supreme Lord, and he understands that he is eternally dependent on the causeless mercy of the Supreme Person. At that time there is an awakening of natural affection, such as is felt by a son who grows up and begins to appreciate his father's benedictions. At this stage the living entity wants to serve the Supreme Lord instead of serving *māyā,* illusion.

The third stage in the development of transcendental love is called *sakhya-rati.* In this stage one associates with the Supreme as a friend on an equal level, with love and respect. As this stage is further developed, there is joking and such relaxed exchanges as laughing. On this level there are fraternal exchanges with the Personality of Godhead, and one is free from all bondage. One forgets his inferior position as a living entity, but at the same time he has the greatest respect for the Supreme Person.

In the fourth stage, called *vātsalya-rati,* the fraternal affection of the preceding stage develops into parental affection. At this time the living entity acts as the parent of God. Instead of worshiping the Lord, the living entity, as a parent of the Supreme Person, becomes an object of worship for Him. At this stage the Lord depends on the mercy of His pure devotee and puts Himself under the control of the devotee to be raised nicely. Such a devotee can embrace the Supreme Lord and even kiss His head.

In the fifth stage, called *madhura-rati,* there is a transcendental exchange of conjugal love between the lover and the beloved. It is at this stage that Kṛṣṇa and the damsels of Vraja glanced lovingly at one another, for on this platform there is an exchange of glances, movements of the eyebrows, pleasant words, attractive smiles, etc.

Besides these five primary *rasas* there are seven secondary *rasas,* which consist of laughing, wonder, chivalry, pity, anger, ghastliness and devastation. For example, Bhīṣma related to Kṛṣṇa as a warrior in the chivalrous *rasa.* Hiraṇyakaśipu, however, experienced an exchange of the ghastly and devastating *rasas.* The five primary *rasas* constantly remain within the heart of the pure devotee, and the seven secondary *rasas* sometimes appear and disappear to enrich the flavors and tastes of the primary ones. After enriching the primary *rasas,* they disappear.

Examples of *śānta-bhaktas,* or devotees in the neutral stage, are the Nine Yogendras, namely Kavi, Havi, Antarīkṣa, Prabuddha, Pippalāyana, Āvirhotra, Draviḍa (Drumila), Camasa and Karabhājana. The Four Kumāras (Sanaka, Sanandana, Sanat and Sanātana) are also examples of this stage. Examples of devotees in the second stage, servitorship, are Raktaka, Citraka and Patraka. These are all servants of Kṛṣṇa in Gokula. In Dvārakā there is Dāruka, and in the Vaikuṇṭha planets there are Hanumān and others. Devotees in the third stage, friendship, include Śrīdāmā in Vṛndāvana and Bhīma and Arjuna in Dvārakā or on the Battlefield of Kurukṣetra. As for those relating to Kṛṣṇa in parental love, they include His mother, father, uncle and similar relatives. In conjugal love there are the damsels of Vraja (Vṛndāvana), the queens in Dvārakā, and the goddesses of fortune in Vaikuṇṭha. No one can count the vast number of devotees in this *rasa.*

In general, attachment to Kṛṣṇa is of two kinds. The first kind is attachment with awe and veneration. Characterized by a lack of freedom, such attachment is exhibited in Mathurā and on the Vaikuṇṭha planets. In these abodes of the Lord, the flavor of transcendental loving service is restricted. But in Gokula (Vṛndāvana) love is freely exchanged, and although the cowherd boys and damsels of Vṛndāvana know that Kṛṣṇa is the Supreme Personality of Godhead, they do not show awe and veneration, because of the great intimacy of their relationship with Him through thick and thin. In the five principal transcendental relationships, awe and veneration are sometimes impediments to one's service to the Lord. When there is friendship, parental affection or conjugal love, such awe and veneration are impediments. For example, when Kṛṣṇa appeared as the son of Vasudeva and Devakī, they prayed to the Lord with awe and veneration because they understood that the Supreme Lord Kṛṣṇa or Viṣṇu had appeared before them as their little child. This is confirmed in *Śrīmad-Bhāgavatam* (10.44.51): "Devakī and Vasudeva, knowing their son to be the Supreme Personality of Godhead, began to pray to Him although He was present before them as their child." Similarly, when Arjuna saw the universal form of the Lord, he was so afraid that he begged pardon for his dealings with Kṛṣṇa as an intimate friend. As a friend, Arjuna often behaved unceremoniously with the Lord, and upon seeing the awesome universal form, Arjuna said:

sakheti matvā prasabhaṁ yad uktaṁ
he kṛṣṇa he yādava he sakheti
ajānatā mahimānaṁ tavedaṁ
mayā pramādāt praṇayena vāpi

"My dear Kṛṣṇa, sometimes I insulted You by calling You 'my dear friend Kṛṣṇa' without knowing the greatness of your inconceivable power. Please forgive me. I was mad to address You like a common friend or a common man." (*Bhagavad-gītā* 11.41)

Similarly, when Kṛṣṇa was playing jokes on Rukmiṇī, she feared that He might leave her and became so perturbed that she dropped the fan with which she was fanning Him and fainted, falling unconscious to the floor as her hair scattered. She resembled a plantain tree blown down by a blast of wind.

But as far as Yaśodā, Kṛṣṇa's mother in Vṛndāvana, is concerned, *Śrīmad-Bhāgavatam* 10.8.45 states:

trayyā copaniṣadbhiś ca sāṅkhya-yogaiś ca sātvataiḥ
upagīyamāna-māhātmyaṁ hariṁ sāmanyatātmajam

"Mother Yaśodā thought that the Personality of Godhead, who is worshiped by all the *Vedas* and *Upaniṣads,* as well as by the *sāṅkhya* system of philosophy and all authorized scriptures, had been born from her womb." It is also stated in *Śrīmad-Bhāgavatam* (10.9.14) that Mother Yaśodā bound child Kṛṣṇa with a rope as if He were an ordinary son born of her body. Another description of Kṛṣṇa's being treated as an ordinary person appears in *Śrīmad-Bhāgavatam* 10.18.24. There it is stated that when Kṛṣṇa was defeated in games with His friends, the cowherd boys, He had to carry Śrīdāmā on His shoulders.

Regarding the *gopīs'* dealings with Śrī Kṛṣṇa in Vṛndāvana, *Śrīmad-Bhāgavatam* 10.30.36–38 describes how when Śrī Kṛṣṇa took Śrīmatī Rādhikā alone from the *rāsa* dance, She proudly thought, "My dear Lord Kṛṣṇa has left the other *gopīs,* although they are as beautiful as I am, and He is satisfied with Me alone." In the forest She told Kṛṣṇa, "My dear Kṛṣṇa, I am unable to move anymore. Now if You like You can take Me wherever You desire." Kṛṣṇa replied, "You can climb on My shoulder," but as soon as He said this He disappeared, whereupon Śrīmatī Rādhikā repented very much.

When Kṛṣṇa disappeared from the scene of the *rāsa* dance, all the *gopīs* began to lament, saying, "Dear Kṛṣṇa! We have come here and left aside our husbands, sons, relatives, brothers and friends! Neglecting their advice, we have come to You, and You know very well the reason for our coming here. You know that we have come because we are captivated by the sweet sound of Your flute. But You are so cunning that in the dead of night You have left girls and women like us! This is not very good of You."

The word *śama* means controlling the mind and keeping it from being diverted in various ways while fixing it on the Supreme Personality of Godhead. In other words, one whose mind is fixed on the Supreme Lord is situated on the *śama* platform. On that platform the devotee understands that Kṛṣṇa is the basic principle of everything within our experience. This is explained in the *Bhagavad-gītā* (7.19): "After many, many births of cultivating knowledge, one who has attained real knowledge surrenders unto Vāsudeva [Kṛṣṇa] because he can understand that Kṛṣṇa is present in everything, that He is distributed all over the cosmic manifestation." Although everything is under the control of the Supreme Lord and is situated in His energy, everything is nonetheless different from Kṛṣṇa in His personal form. It is stated in the *Bhakti-rasāmṛta-sindhu* that the platform of *śama,* on which one understands that Kṛṣṇa is the basic principle of everything, is the same as *śānta-rati*. Unless one is elevated to the platform of *śānta-rati,* one cannot be fixed in knowledge of the greatness of Kṛṣṇa or of the diffusion of His different energies, which are the cause of all manifestations. This same point is explained in *Śrīmad-Bhāgavatam* (11.19.36):

śamo man-niṣṭhatā buddher dama indriya-saṁyamaḥ
titikṣā duḥkha-sammarṣo jihvopastha-jayo dhṛtiḥ

"*Śama,* equilibrium of mind, is achieved by one who has concluded that the Supreme Personality of Godhead is the original source of everything. And when one can control his senses, that is called *dama.* When one is ready to tolerate all kinds of sufferings to control the senses and keep the mind steady, that is called *titikṣā,* or tolerance. And when one can control the urges of the tongue and genitals, that is called *dhṛti.*" One who has attained *dhṛti* is a *dhīra,* a pacified person. A pacified person is never disturbed by the urges of the tongue and genitals.

One who can fix his mind on Kṛṣṇa without deviation attains *śānta-rasa,* the steadfast position in Kṛṣṇa consciousness. One in *śānta-rasa* exhibits two main qualities: unflinching faith in Kṛṣṇa, and the cessation of all material desires. These specific characteristics of *śānta-rasa*—unflinching faith in Kṛṣṇa and cessation of all desires not connected with Kṛṣṇa—are common to all other *rasas* as well, just as sound is present not only in sky, where it is produced, but also in all the other elements—air, fire, water and earth. So these two characteristics of *śānta-rasa* are also present in *dāsya-rasa* (servitorship), *sakhya-rasa* (fraternity), *vātsalya-rasa* (parental affection) and *madhura-rasa* (conjugal love).

When we speak of desires not connected with Kṛṣṇa, or "non-Kṛṣṇa," this does not mean that anything exists without Kṛṣṇa. Actually there cannot be anything non-Kṛṣṇa because everything is a product of the energy of Kṛṣṇa. Since Kṛṣṇa and His energies are identical, everything is Kṛṣṇa indirectly. For example, consciousness is common to every living entity, but when consciousness is centered solely on Kṛṣṇa (Kṛṣṇa consciousness) it is pure, and when consciousness is centered on something other than Kṛṣṇa, or when it is directed to sense gratification, it may be called non-Kṛṣṇa consciousness. Thus it is in the polluted state that the conception of non-Kṛṣṇa comes. In the pure state, however, there is nothing but Kṛṣṇa consciousness.

Active interest in Kṛṣṇa—the understanding that Kṛṣṇa is mine and that I am Kṛṣṇa's and that my business is therefore to satisfy the senses of Kṛṣṇa—is typical of a higher stage than the neutrality of *śānta-rasa.* Simply by understanding the greatness of Kṛṣṇa, one achieves the status of *śānta-rasa,* in which the worshipable object may be the impersonal Brahman or Paramātmā. Worship of the impersonal Brahman and the Paramātmā is conducted by those engaged in empiric philosophical speculation and mystic *yoga.* But when one develops even further in Kṛṣṇa consciousness, or spiritual understanding, he can appreciate that the Paramātmā, the Supersoul, is his eternal worshipable object and master, and he surrenders unto Him. *Bahūnāṁ janmanām ante jñānavān māṁ prapadyate* (Bg. 7.19): "After many, many births of worshiping Brahman and Paramātmā, when one surrenders unto Vāsudeva as the supreme master and accepts himself as the eternal servant of Vāsudeva, he becomes a great transcendentally realized soul." At that time, due to his intimate relationship with the Supreme Absolute Truth, the devotee begins to render some sort of transcendental loving service to the Supreme Personality of Godhead. Thus the neutral relationship known as *śānta-rasa* is transformed into *dāsya-rasa,* servitorship.

On the platform of *dāsya-rasa* one exhibits the greatest quantity of awe and veneration for the Supreme Lord. That is, in *dāsya-rasa* one appreciates the greatness of the Supreme Lord. It should be noted here that on the platform of *śānta-rasa* there is no spiritual activity but on the platform of *dāsya-rasa* service begins. Thus in *dāsya-rasa* the quality of *śānta-rasa* is exhibited, and, in addition, there is consciousness of the transcendental taste of service.

In *sakhya-rasa,* fraternity, the transcendental qualities of *śānta-rasa* and *dāsya-rasa* are certainly present, but beyond these there is another quality, confidential attachment, which is pure transcendental love. This confidential attachment for the Supreme Personality is technically known as *viśrambha.* On the platform of *viśrambha* there is no sense of awe or veneration toward the Supreme Personality of Godhead. Thus in the transcendental fraternal relationship, *sakhya-rasa,* there are three transcendental characteristics: the sense of greatness, the sense of service, and the sense of intimacy without awe or veneration. Thus *sakhya-rasa* adds one transcendental quality to the qualities of *śānta-* and *dāsya-rasa.*

Similarly, on the platform of parental affection (*vātsalya-rasa*) there are four qualities. In addition to the three qualities already mentioned, there is the sense that the Supreme Lord is dependent on the mercy of the devotee. As a parent of the Supreme Personality of Godhead, the devotee sometimes chastises the Lord and considers himself the Lord's maintainer. This transcendental sense of being the maintainer of the supreme maintainer is very pleasing to both the devotee and the Supreme Lord.

The Lord instructed Śrīla Rūpa Gosvāmī to write the transcendental literature named *Bhakti-rasāmṛta-sindhu,* the science of devotional service, and indicate therein the substance of the five transcendental relationships with the Lord—*śānta-, dāsya-, sakhya-, vātsalya-* and *madhura-rasa.* It is explained in that great literature how the transcendental relationship of *śānta-rasa,* taking the shape of unflinching faith in Kṛṣṇa, is further developed into *dāsya-rasa* with the spirit of service, and then to *sakhya-rasa,* or undeterred fraternity, and further to the transcendental platform of parental love, wherein one feels himself to be maintaining the Lord. All these transcendental relationships culminate on the highest platform, conjugal love (*madhura-rasa*), wherein they all exist simultaneously.

His Divine Grace A.C. Bhaktivedanta Swami Prabhupāda

The founder-*ācārya* of ISKCON and greatest exponent of Kṛṣṇa consciousness in the modern world.

Śrīla Bhaktisiddhānta Sarasvatī Gosvāmī Mahārāja
The spiritual master of His Divine Grace A. C. Bhaktivedanta Swami Prabhupāda and foremost scholar and devotee in the recent age.

Śrīla Gaura-Kiśora Dāsa Bābājī Mahārāja
The spiritual master of Śrīla Bhaktisiddhānta Sarasvatī Gosvāmī and intimate student of Śrīla Ṭhākura Bhaktivinoda.

Śrīla Ṭhākura Bhaktivinoda
The pioneer of the program to bless
the entire world with Kṛṣṇa consciousness.

Śrī Kṛṣṇa Caitanya Mahāprabhu (center), Lord Nityānanda (second from left), Śrī Advaita Ācārya (left), Śrī Gadādhara Paṇḍita (second from right), Śrīvāsa Ṭhākura (right). (p. 6)

The birthplace of Śrī Kṛṣṇa Caitanya Mahāprabhu in Śrīdhāma Māyāpur, West Bengal.

There He preached, there He sang, there He danced, and there He expressed all sorts of religious feelings. (p. *xiii*)

Lord Caitanya and Lord Nityānanda are compared to the sun and moon because They dissipate the darkness of the material world. (p. 6)

CHAPTER 2

Sanātana Gosvāmī

vande 'nantādbhutaiśvaryaṁ śrī-caitanya-mahāprabhum
nīco 'pi yat-prasādāt syād bhakti-śāstra-pravartakaḥ

I offer my respectful obeisances unto Lord Caitanya Mahāprabhu, by whose mercy even a person in the lowest status of life can find direction in transcendental devotional service to the Lord.

After Lord Caitanya Mahāprabhu accepted the renounced order of life (*sannyāsa*), He traveled all over India. During this period He went to Maldah, a district in Bengal. In that area there was a village named Rāmakeli, where two government ministers of the Nawab Hussain Shah's regime lived. These two ministers, who were brothers, were named Dabira Khāsa and Sākara Mallika; later they were renamed Rūpa Gosvāmī and Sanātana Gosvāmī, respectively. They had a chance to meet Lord Caitanya, and afterward they decided to retire from government service and join His *saṅkīrtana* movement.

Upon making this decision, the two brothers at once took steps to leave their material engagements, and they appointed two learned *brāhmaṇas* to perform certain Vedic religious rituals that would enable them to achieve complete freedom for the devotional service of Kṛṣṇa. These preliminary ritualistic functions are known as *puraścaryā*. They require that three times a day one worship and offer respects to one's forefathers, offer oblations to a fire, and respectfully offer food to a learned *brāhmaṇa*. Five items—the time, the worship, the offering of respect, the offering of oblations into the fire, and the offering of food to a *brāhmaṇa*—constitute *puraś-caryā*. These and other rituals are mentioned in the *Hari-bhakti-vilāsa,* an authoritative book of directions for Vaiṣṇavas.

After arranging for the performance of these religious rituals, the younger brother, Dabira Khāsa (Rūpa Gosvāmī), returned home with an immense amount of money, which he had acquired during his government service. The silver and gold coins he brought back filled a large boat. After arriving home, he first divided the accumulated wealth in half and distributed one part to the *brāhmaṇas* and Vaiṣṇavas. Thus for the satisfaction of the Supreme Personality of Godhead, he distributed fifty percent of his accumulated wealth to persons engaged in the Supreme Lord's transcendental loving service. *Brāhmaṇas* are meant to understand the Absolute Truth, and once they understand the Absolute Truth and actually engage in the loving service of the Lord, they are known as Vaiṣṇavas. Both *brāhmaṇas* and Vaiṣṇavas are supposed to fully engage in transcendental service, and Rūpa Gosvāmī, considering their important transcendental position, gave them fifty percent of his wealth. The balance he again divided in half: one part he distributed to his relatives and dependent family members, and the other he kept for personal emergencies.

Such distribution of personal wealth is very instructive for all who desire to be elevated in spiritual knowledge. Generally a person bequeaths all his accumulated wealth to his family members and then retires from family activities to make progress in spiritual knowledge. But here we find the behavior of Rūpa Gosvāmī to be exemplary: he gave fifty percent of his wealth for spiritual purposes. This should serve as an example for everyone. The twenty-five percent of his accumulated wealth he kept for personal emergencies was deposited with a Bengali grocer, since in those days there were no banks. Ten thousand coins were deposited for expenditures to be incurred by his elder brother, Sanātana Gosvāmī.

At this time Rūpa Gosvāmī received information that Lord Caitanya Mahāprabhu was preparing to go to Vṛndāvana from

Sanātana Gosvāmī resigns from the government service of Nawab Hussain Shah of Bengal (16th century).

Jagannātha Purī. Rūpa Gosvāmī sent two messengers to get actual information of the Lord's itinerary, and he made his own plans to go to Mathurā to meet the Lord. It appears that Rūpa Gosvāmī got permission to join Lord Caitanya, but Sanātana Gosvāmī did not. Therefore Sanātana Gosvāmī entrusted the responsibilities of his government service to his immediate assistants, and he remained at home to study *Śrīmad-Bhāgavatam*. He engaged ten or twenty learned *brāhmaṇas* and began an intensive study of *Śrīmad-Bhāgavatam* in their company. While he was thus engaged, he submitted sick-leave reports to his employer, the Nawab. But the ruler was so anxious for Sanātana Gosvāmī's advice in government matters that one day he suddenly appeared at his house. When the Nawab entered the room where Sanātana Gosvāmī and the *brāhmaṇas* were assembled, out of respect they all stood up to receive him, and they offered him a place to sit.

"You have submitted sick reports," the Nawab told Sanātana Gosvāmī, "but I sent my physician to see you, and he reported that you have no illness at all. Since I did not know why you were submitting sick reports and not attending to your service, I have personally come to see you. I am much perturbed by your behavior. As you know, I completely depend on you and your responsible work in government. I was free to act in other matters because I was depending on you, but if you do not join me, your past devotion will be spoiled. Now, what is your intention? Please tell me."

On hearing this, Sanātana Gosvāmī replied that he was unable to work anymore and that it would be very kind of the Nawab to appoint someone else to execute the work that had been entrusted to him. At this the Nawab became very angry and said, "Your elder brother lives like a hunter, and if you retire from the administration, everything will be finished." It was said that the Nawab used to treat Sanātana Gosvāmī like a younger brother. Since the Nawab was principally engaged in conquering different parts of the country and also in hunting, he depended largely on Sanātana Gosvāmī for government administration. Thus he pleaded with him: "If you retire from government service, how will the administration be run?"

"You are the governor of Gauḍa," Sanātana Gosvāmī replied very gravely, "and you punish different kinds of criminals in different ways. So you are at liberty to punish anyone according to his activity." By this reply Sanātana Gosvāmī indicated that since the governor was engaged in hunting animals and in killing men to expand his kingdom, let both of them suffer according to the acts they were performing. The Nawab, being intelligent, understood Sanātana Gosvāmī's purport. He left the house in an angry mood, and shortly afterward he went off to conquer Orissa. He ordered the arrest of Sanātana Gosvāmī and commanded that he be held until the Nawab returned.

When Rūpa Gosvāmī learned that the Nawab had arrested his elder brother Sanātana, Rūpa sent Sanātana a message that he could use the ten thousand coins in the care of the Bengali grocer to secure his release from the Nawab's detention. Having sent this message, Rūpa departed for Vṛndāvana with his younger brother Vallabha to meet Caitanya Mahāprabhu.

After receiving Rūpa Gosvāmī's message, Sanātana offered five thousand of the coins to the keeper of the jail in which he was being held in custody. He advised the jailkeeper to gladly accept the five thousand coins from him and let him go because by accepting the money he would not only be materially benefited but would also be acting very righteously by freeing Sanātana for spiritual purposes.

"Of course I would like to let you go," the jailkeeper replied, "for you have done many services for me and you are in government service. But I'm afraid of the Nawab. When he hears that you are free, I'll have to explain everything to him. How can I accept such a proposal?" Sanātana then invented a story the jailkeeper might submit to the Nawab to explain how he had escaped, and he raised his offer to ten thousand coins. Anxious to get the money, the jailkeeper agreed to the proposition and let him go.

Sanātana then departed to see the Lord. He did not travel on the open road but went through the jungles until he arrived at a place in Bihar called Pātaḍā. There he rested in a hotel, but the hotelkeeper was informed by an astrologer employed there that Sanātana Gosvāmī had some gold coins with him. The hotelkeeper, wanting to steal the money, spoke to Sanātana with superficial respect: "Just take your rest tonight, and in the morning I shall arrange for you to get out of this jungle trap."

However, Sanātana was suspicious of his behavior, and he inquired from his servant Īśāna whether he had some money. Īśāna told him that he had seven gold coins. Sanātana did not like the idea of the servant carrying such money. He became angry with him and said, "Why do you carry this death knell on the road?"

Sanātana at once took the gold coins and offered them to the hotelkeeper. He then requested the hotelkeeper to help him through the jungle. Sanātana informed him that he was on a special journey for the government and that since he could not travel on the open road, it would be very kind of the hotelkeeper to help him through the jungle and over the hills.

The hotelkeeper replied, "I learned that you had eight coins with you, and I was thinking of killing you to take them. But I can understand that you are a very good man, and so you don't have to offer me the money. I will get you over this hilly tract of land."

"If you don't accept these coins, then someone else will take them from me," Sanātana replied. "Someone will kill me for them, so it is better that you take them. I offer them to you." The hotelkeeper then gave him full assistance, and that very night he helped him get past the hills.

When Sanātana emerged from the hills, he requested his servant to go home with the one coin he still had with him, for Sanātana decided he would go on alone. After the departure of his servant, Sanātana felt completely free. With torn clothing and with a waterpot in his hand, he proceeded toward Lord Caitanya Mahāprabhu. On the way he met his rich brother-in-law, who was also in the government service and who offered him an excellent blanket, which Sanātana accepted at his special request. Then he departed from him and went on alone to see Caitanya Mahāprabhu at Benares.

When he reached Benares, Sanātana learned that the Lord was there, and he became overjoyed. He was informed by the people that the Lord was staying at the house of Candraśekhara, and Sanātana went there. Although Caitanya Mahāprabhu was inside the house, He could understand that Sanātana had arrived at the door, and He asked Candraśekhara to call in the man who was sitting there. "He is a Vaiṣṇava, a great devotee of the Lord," Caitanya Mahāprabhu said. Candraśekhara came out to see the man, but he saw no Vaiṣṇava at the door. He saw only a man who appeared to be a Muslim mendicant. The Lord then asked to see the mendicant, and when Sanātana entered the courtyard, Lord Caitanya hurriedly came out to receive him and embrace him. When the Lord embraced him, Sanātana became overwhelmed with spiritual ecstasy, and he said, "My dear Lord, please do not touch me." But they embraced each other and began to cry. Seeing Sanātana and Lord Caitanya acting thus, Candraśekhara was struck with wonder. Caitanya Mahāprabhu then asked Sanātana to sit down with Him on a bench. The Lord was touching the body of Sanātana with His hand, and again Sanātana asked Him, "My dear Lord, please do not touch me."

"I am touching you just for My purification," the Lord replied, "for you are a great devotee. By your devotional service you can deliver the whole universe and enable everyone to go back to Godhead."

The Lord then quoted a nice verse from the Vedic literature stating that a person who is a devotee of Lord Kṛṣṇa and is one hundred percent engaged in devotional service is far better than a *brāhmaṇa* who is versed in all the Vedic literatures but who does not engage in the devotional service of the Lord. Because the devotee carries the Supreme Lord within his heart, he can purify every place and everything.

The Vedic literature also states that the Supreme Personality of Godhead does not recognize a nondevotee who is very learned in all the divisions of the *Vedas* but He likes a devotee even if he was born in a low family. If one offers charity to a *brāhmaṇa* who is not a devotee, the Lord does not accept it; but if something is offered to a devotee, the Lord accepts. In other words, whatever a person wishes to offer the Lord may be given to His devotees. Caitanya Mahāprabhu also quoted *Śrīmad-Bhāgavatam* to the effect that even if a *brāhmaṇa* was born in a high family and is qualified with the twelve brahminical qualities, he is lower than the lowest of the low if he is not a devotee of the Supreme Lord. Although a devotee may have been born in a *caṇḍāla* (dog-eater) family, by devotional service he can purify his whole family for one hundred generations, past and future, whereas a proud *brāhmaṇa* cannot purify even himself. Lord Caitanya then said to Sanātana, quoting the *Hari-bhakti-sudhodaya* (13.2):

akṣṇoḥ phalaṁ tvādṛśa-darśanaṁ hi
tanoḥ phalaṁ tvādṛśa-gātra-saṅgaḥ
jihvā-phalaṁ tvādṛśa-kīrtanaṁ hi
su-durlabhā bhāgavatā hi loke

"O devotee of the Lord, to see you is the perfection of the eyes, to touch your body is the perfection of bodily activities, and to glorify your qualities is the perfection of the tongue, for it is very rare to find a pure devotee like you."

Next the Lord told Sanātana, "Kṛṣṇa is very merciful and is the deliverer of fallen souls. He has saved you from Mahāraurava." *Śrīmad-Bhāgavatam* describes Mahāraurava as a hell meant for persons engaged in killing animals, for it is stated there that butchers and animal eaters go to that hell.

"I do not know the mercy of Kṛṣṇa," Sanātana replied, "but I can understand that Your mercy upon me is causeless. You have delivered me from the entanglement of material life."

Then the Lord asked, "How did you get free from custody? I understand that you were arrested." Sanātana then narrated the whole story of his release. The Lord then informed him: "I saw your two brothers and advised them to proceed toward Vṛndāvana."

Lord Caitanya then introduced Candraśekhara and Tapana Miśra to Sanātana, and Tapana Miśra pleasantly invited Sanātana to dine with him. The Lord requested Candraśekhara to take Sanātana to a barber and make him "gentle," for Sanātana had grown a long beard, which Śrī Caitanya Mahāprabhu did not like. He asked Candraśekhara to provide Sanātana not only with a bath and clean shave but with a change of clothes as well.

After Sanātana had bathed, Candraśekhara offered him some good cloth. When Lord Caitanya was informed that Sanātana had not accepted the new garments but later accepted only some used garments from Tapana Miśra, He was very glad. The Lord went to Tapana Miśra's house for lunch and asked him to keep food for Sanātana. Tapana Miśra did not offer Sanātana food immediately, however, but after the Lord had finished eating there were some remnants of His food, and those remnants were offered to Sanātana while the Lord took His rest.

After resting, Lord Caitanya introduced a Maharashtriyan *brāhmaṇa,* a devotee of His, to Sanātana, and that *brāhmaṇa* invited Sanātana to accept lunch daily at his place as long as he remained in Benares.

"As long as I remain in Benares, I will beg from door to door," Sanātana said. "But the Lord will be so good as to accept this invitation for daily lunch at your house."

Lord Caitanya was very much pleased by this behavior of Sanātana's, but He noticed the valuable blanket that had been given to him by his brother-in-law while Sanātana was en route to Benares. Although Lord Caitanya did not say anything about the blanket, Sanātana understood that He did not approve of such a valuable garment on his body, and therefore Sanātana decided to get rid of it. He immediately went to the bank of the Ganges, and there he saw a mendicant washing an old quilt. When Sanātana asked him to trade the old quilt for the valuable blanket, the poor mendicant thought that Sanātana was joking with him. "How is this?" the mendicant replied. "You appear to be a very nice gentleman, but you are mocking me in this unmannerly way."

"I am not joking with you," Sanātana informed him. "I am very serious. Will you kindly exchange your torn quilt for this blanket?" Finally the mendicant exchanged his torn quilt for the blanket, and Sanātana returned to the Lord.

"Where is your valuable blanket?" the Lord immediately inquired. Sanātana informed Him about the exchange, and the Lord loved him for this and thanked him. "You are intelligent enough, and you have now exhausted all your attraction for material wealth." In other words, the Lord accepts a person for devotional service only when he is completely free from all material possessions. The Lord then told Sanātana: "It would not look good for you to be a mendicant and beg from door to door with such a valuable blanket on your body. It is contradictory, and people would look on it with abhorrence."

"Whatever I am doing to become free from material attachment is all Your mercy," Sanātana replied. The Lord was very much pleased with him, and they discussed spiritual advancement.

Previous to this meeting between Lord Caitanya and Sanātana Gosvāmī, the Lord had met a householder devotee named Rāmānanda Rāya. At that meeting, which is discussed in a later chapter, Lord Caitanya asked Rāmānanda Rāya questions, and Rāmānanda replied as if he were the Lord's teacher. However, in this case Sanātana put questions to the Lord, and the Lord answered them.

The instructions of Lord Caitanya to Sanātana Gosvāmī are very important for people in general. The Lord taught him the process of devotional service, which is the constitutional occupation of every living entity. Because this is so, it is every man's duty to advance in spiritual science. Many subjects were thoroughly discussed in the talks between Lord Caitanya and Sanātana Gosvāmī. Due to the mercy of Lord Caitanya, Sanātana was able to put important questions before Him, and these questions were replied to properly.

The meeting of Sanātana Gosvāmī and Lord Caitanya teaches us that to understand spiritual subject matters one must approach a spiritual master like Lord Caitanya Mahāprabhu and make submissive inquiries. This is confirmed in the instructions of the *Bhagavad-gītā* (4.34), where Lord Kṛṣṇa says that one should approach a man of authority and learn the spiritual science from him.

CHAPTER 3

Teachings to Sanātana Gosvāmī

From the instructions of Lord Caitanya to Sanātana Gosvāmī we can understand the science of God as it relates to God's transcendental form, His opulences, and His devotional service. Indeed, everything will be explained to Sanātana Gosvāmī by the Lord Himself.

First Sanātana fell at the feet of the Lord and with great humility asked about his own real identity. "I was born in a lower family," Sanātana said, "my associations are all abominable, and I am fallen, the most wretched of mankind. I was suffering in the dark well of material enjoyment, and I never learned the actual goal of my life. Indeed, I do not even know what is beneficial for me. Although in the mundane sphere I am what is known as a greatly learned man, I am in fact such a fool that I also think I am learned. You have accepted me as Your servant, and You have delivered me from the entanglement of material life. Now please tell me what my duty is in this liberated state."

From this plea we can understand that liberation is not the final word in perfection. There must be activities in liberation. Sanātana clearly says, "You have saved me from the entanglement of material existence. Now, after liberation, what is my duty? Kindly explain it to me." Sanātana further inquired, "Who am I? Why are the threefold miseries always giving me trouble? And finally, please tell me how I can be relieved from this material entanglement? I do not know how to question You about advancement in spiritual life, but I beg that You kindly, mercifully, let me know everything I should know."

This is the process of accepting a spiritual master. One should approach a spiritual master, humbly submit to him and then inquire from him about one's spiritual progress.

The Lord was pleased by Sanātana's submissive behavior, and He replied, "You have already been blessed by Lord Kṛṣṇa, and therefore you know everything and are free from all the miseries of material existence. Yet even though due to your Kṛṣṇa consciousness you have naturally achieved the grace of Kṛṣṇa and are thus already conversant with everything, because you are a humble devotee you are asking Me to confirm what you have already realized. This is very nice." These are the characteristics of a true devotee. In the *Nāradīya Purāṇa* it is said that by the grace of the Lord one who is very serious about developing Kṛṣṇa consciousness has his desire to understand Kṛṣṇa fulfilled very soon.

"You are a suitable person to protect the devotional service of the Lord," Caitanya Mahāprabhu continued. "Therefore it is My duty to instruct you in the science of God, and I will explain everything to you, step by step."

It is the duty of a disciple to inquire about his constitutional position when approaching a spiritual master. In conformity to that spiritual process, Sanātana has already asked, "What am I, and why am I suffering from the threefold miseries?" The threefold miseries are called *ādhyātmika*, *ādhibhautika* and *ādhidaivika*. The word *ādhyātmika* refers to those miseries caused by the body and mind. Sometimes the living entity suffers physically, and sometimes he is distressed mentally. Both are *ādhyātmika* miseries. We experience these miseries even in the womb of our mother. In general, there are many types of miseries that take advantage of the delicate human body and give us pain. Miseries inflicted by other living entities are called *ādhibhautika*. For example, bedbugs can make us miserable while we are sleeping. Cockroaches can also sometimes give us pain, and there are other living entities born on different planets who can cause us misery. As far as the *ādhidaivika* miseries are concerned, these originate with the demigods of the higher planets. For instance, we sometimes suffer from severe cold weather, from thunderbolts, or from earthquakes, tornadoes, droughts or other natural disasters. In any case, we are always suffering from one or more of these three kinds of miseries.

Sanātana's inquiry was therefore an intelligent one. "What is the position of the living entities?" he asked. "Why are they always undergoing these three kinds of miseries?" Sanātana had admitted his weakness: Although he was known by the masses of people as a greatly learned man (and he actually was a highly learned Sanskrit scholar), and although he accepted this designation, he did not know what his constitutional position was or why he was subjected to the threefold miseries.

Approaching a spiritual master is not just a fashion but is a necessity for one who is seriously conscious of the material miseries and who wants to be free of them. It is the duty of such a person to approach a spiritual master. In this regard, we should note Arjuna's similar circumstances in the *Bhagavad-gītā*. When he was perplexed by so many problems involving whether to fight or not, he accepted Lord Kṛṣṇa as his spiritual master. Like Lord Caitanya's instructing Sanātana Gosvāmī, the *Bhagavad-gītā* is also a case of the supreme spiritual master instructing His disciple about the constitutional position of the living entity.

In the *Bhagavad-gītā* we are informed that the constitutional nature of the individual entity is spirit soul. He is not matter. As spirit soul, he is part and parcel of the Supreme Soul, the Absolute Truth, the Personality of Godhead. We also learn that it is the duty of the spirit soul to surrender to the Supreme Soul, for only then can he be happy. The last instruction of the *Bhagavad-gītā* is that the spirit soul should surrender completely unto the Supreme Soul, Kṛṣṇa, and in that way realize happiness.

Here also, Lord Caitanya, answering the questions of Sanātana, repeats the same truth. There is a difference, however. Here Lord Caitanya does not give the information about the spirit soul that is already described in the *Bhagavad-gītā*. Rather, He begins from the point where Kṛṣṇa ended His instruction. It is accepted by great devotees that Lord Caitanya is Kṛṣṇa Himself, and, as such, He begins His instruction to Sanātana from the point where He ended His instructions to Arjuna in the *Gītā*.

"Your constitutional position is that you are pure living soul," the Lord told Sanātana. "Your material body is not your real self, nor is your mind your real identity, nor your intelligence, nor your false ego. Your identity is that of an eternal servitor of the Supreme Lord, Kṛṣṇa. Your position is that you are transcendental. The superior energy of Kṛṣṇa is spiritual in constitution, and the inferior, external energy is material. Since you are between the material energy and the spiritual energy, your position is marginal. Belonging to the marginal potency of Kṛṣṇa, you are simultaneously one with and different from Him. Because you are spirit, you are not different from Kṛṣṇa, but because you are only a minute particle of Kṛṣṇa, you are different from Him."

This simultaneous oneness and difference always exists in the relationship between the living entities and the Supreme Lord. From the fact that the living entities are always in the marginal position, this conception of "simultaneously one and different" can be understood. The living entity is just like a molecular particle of sunshine, whereas Kṛṣṇa is like the blazing sun itself. Lord Caitanya also compared the living entities to sparks in a fire, and the Supreme Lord to the blazing fire itself. In this connection the Lord cited a verse from the *Viṣṇu Purāṇa* (1.22.53):

eka-deśa-sthitasyāgner jyotsnā vistāriṇī yathā
parasya brahmaṇaḥ śaktis tathedam akhilaṁ jagat

"Everything manifested within this cosmic world is but the energy of the Supreme Lord. As fire situated in one place spreads its illumination and heat all around, so the Lord, although situated in one place in the spiritual world, manifests His different energies everywhere. Indeed, the whole cosmic creation is but a manifestation of His various energies."

Lord Caitanya continued citing the *Viṣṇu Purāṇa* (6.7.61): "The Supreme Lord's original energy is transcendental and spiritual, and the living entities are part and parcel of that energy. There is a third energy, however, called the material energy, which is covered by the cloud of ignorance." This energy, which is material nature, is divided into three modes, or *guṇas* (goodness, passion and ignorance). Lord Caitanya then quoted another verse from the *Viṣṇu Purāṇa* (1.3.2) to the effect that all inconceivable energies reside in the Supreme Personality of Godhead and that the whole cosmic manifestation acts due to those energies.

The Lord also said that the living entity is known as the *kṣetra-jña,* or "the knower of the field of activities." This is confirmed in the Thirteenth Chapter of the *Bhagavad-gītā,* where Kṛṣṇa describes the body as the field of activities and the living entity as the *kṣetra-jña,* the knower of that field. Although the living entity is constitutionally conversant with the spiritual energy, or has the potency to understand it, he is covered by the material energy and consequently believes himself to be the body. This false identification is called "false ego." Deluded by the false ego, the bewildered living entity in material existence passes through different bodies and suffers various kinds of miseries. Knowledge of the living entity's true position is possessed to different extents by different types of living entities.

In other words, it is to be understood that the living entity is part and parcel of the spiritual energy of the Supreme Lord. Because the material energy is inferior, man has the ability to get free from the covering of this material energy and utilize the spiritual energy. It is stated in the *Bhagavad-gītā* that in the conditioned state the superior energy (the living entity) is covered by the inferior energy. Due to this covering, the living entity is subjected to the miseries of the material world, and, in proportion to how much he is covered, he suffers material miseries. Those who are a little enlightened suffer less, but on the whole everyone is subjected to material miseries due to being covered by the material energy.

Caitanya Mahāprabhu also quoted from the Seventh Chapter of the *Bhagavad-gītā,* in which it is stated that earth, water, fire, air, ether, mind, intelligence and false ego all combine to form the inferior energy of the Supreme Lord. But the superior energy is the real identity of the living being, and it is because of that energy that the whole material world functions. The cosmic manifestation, which is made of the material elements, has no power to act unless it is moved by the superior energy, the living entity. The conditioned life of the living entity is due to forgetfulness of his relationship with the Supreme Lord in the superior energy. When that relationship is forgotten, conditioned life is the result. Only when a man revives his real identity as the eternal servitor to the Lord does he become liberated.

CHAPTER 4

The Wise Man

Since no one can trace the history of the living entity's entanglement in material energy, Lord Caitanya said that it is beginningless. By "beginningless" He meant that conditioned life exists prior to the creation; it simply becomes manifest during and after the creation. Due to forgetfulness of his real nature, the living entity, although spirit, suffers all kinds of miseries in material existence. It should be understood that there are also living entities who are not entangled in this material energy but are situated in the spiritual world. They are called liberated souls and are always engaged in Kṛṣṇa consciousness, devotional service.

The activities of those who are conditioned by material nature are taken into account, and in their next life, according to these activities, they are offered different grades of material bodies. Thus in the material world the conditioned spirit soul is subjected to various rewards and punishments. When he is rewarded for his righteous activities, he is elevated to the higher planets, where he becomes one of the many demigods, and when he is punished for his abominable activities, he is thrown into various hellish planets, where he suffers the miseries of material existence more acutely. Caitanya Mahāprabhu gives a very nice example of this punishment. Formerly a king used to punish a criminal by having him dunked in a river, raised up again for breath, and then again dunked in the water. Material nature punishes and rewards the individual living entity in just the same way. When he is punished, he is dunked in the water of material miseries, and when he is rewarded, he is taken out of it for some time. Elevation to the higher planets or to a higher status of life on this planet is never permanent. One must again come down to be submerged in the water. All this is constantly going on in this material existence: sometimes one is elevated to higher planetary systems, and sometimes one is thrown into the hellish condition of material life.

In this regard Caitanya Mahāprabhu recited a nice verse from *Śrīmad-Bhāgavatam* (11.2.37) that is part of the instructions of Nārada Muni to Vasudeva, the father of Kṛṣṇa:

bhayaṁ dvitīyābhiniveśataḥ syād
īśād apetasya viparyayo 'smṛtiḥ
tan-māyayāto budha ābhajet taṁ
bhaktyaikayeśaṁ guru-devatātmā

In this verse, which Nārada Muni quotes from the instructions that the Nine Yogendras imparted to Mahārāja Nimi, *māyā* is defined as "forgetfulness of one's relationship with Kṛṣṇa." Actually, *māyā* means "that which is not." Thus it is false to think that the living entity has no connection with the Supreme Lord. He may not believe in the existence of God, or he may think he has no relationship with God, but these ideas are all illusions, or *māyā*. Due to absorption in this false conception of life, a man is always fearful and full of anxieties. In other words, *māyā* is the godless concept of life. One who is actually learned in the Vedic literature surrenders unto the Supreme Lord with great devotion and accepts Him as the supreme goal. When a living entity forgets the constitutional nature of his relationship with God, he is at once overwhelmed by the external energy. This is the cause of his false ego, his false identification of the body with the self. Indeed, his whole conception of the material universe arises from this false identification with the body, for he becomes attached to the body and its by-products. To escape this entanglement, he has only to perform his duty, namely, to surrender unto the Supreme Lord with intelligence, with devotion, and with sincere Kṛṣṇa consciousness.

A conditioned soul falsely thinks himself happy in the material world, but if he is favored by an unalloyed devotee—if he hears the unalloyed devotee's instructions—he gives up his desire for material enjoyment and becomes enlightened in Kṛṣṇa consciousness. As soon as one enters into Kṛṣṇa consciousness, his desire for material enjoyment is at once vanquished, and he gradually becomes free from material entanglement. There is no question of darkness where there is light, and Kṛṣṇa consciousness is the light that dispels the darkness of material sense enjoyment.

A Kṛṣṇa conscious person is never under the false conception that he is one with God. Knowing that he would not be happy working for himself, he engages all his energies in the service of the Supreme Lord and thereby gains release from the clutches of the illusory material energy. In this connection, Caitanya Mahāprabhu quoted a verse from the *Bhagavad-gītā* (7.14), where Kṛṣṇa states:

daivī hy eṣā guṇa-mayī mama māyā duratyayā
mām eva ye prapadyante māyām etāṁ taranti te

"My material energy, composed of the three modes of material nature, is very strong. It is very difficult to escape the clutches of the material energy, but one who surrenders unto Me is easily freed from the clutches of *māyā*."

Caitanya Mahāprabhu went on to teach that each and every moment the conditioned soul is engaged in some fruitive activity, he forgets his real identity. Sometimes, when he is tired of material activities, he wants liberation and hankers to become one with the Supreme. But at other times he thinks that by working hard to gratify his senses he will be happy. In both cases he is covered by the material energy. For the enlightenment of such bewildered conditioned souls, who are working under a false identification, the Supreme Lord has presented us with voluminous Vedic literature, including the *Vedas,* the *Purāṇas* and the *Vedānta-sūtra*. These are all intended to guide the human being back to Godhead. Caitanya Mahāprabhu further explained that when a conditioned soul is accepted by a spiritual master out of his mercy and is guided by the

Supersoul, the soul can take advantage of the various Vedic scriptures, become enlightened and make progress in spiritual realization. It is because Lord Kṛṣṇa is always merciful to His devotees that He has presented all this Vedic literature, by which one can understand his relationship with Him and can act on the basis of that relationship. In this way one is gifted with the ultimate goal of life.

Actually, every living entity is destined to understand his relationship with the Supreme Lord and ultimately to reach Him. The execution of duties to attain this perfection is known as devotional service, and in maturity such devotional service becomes love of God, the true goal of life for every living being. The living entity should not desire success in religious rituals, economic development or sense enjoyment, or even liberation. One should desire only to achieve the stage of transcendental loving service to the Lord—pure Kṛṣṇa consciousness. The all-attractive features of Lord Kṛṣṇa help one attain this stage of pure devotional service, and one who engages in the preliminary practices of Kṛṣṇa consciousness can ultimately realize the relationship between himself and Kṛṣṇa.

In this connection Caitanya Mahāprabhu related a story from Śrīla Madhvācārya's commentary on the Fifth Canto of *Śrīmad-Bhāgavatam* (5.5.10–13). This story involves the instructions of an astrologer (*sarva-jña*) to a poor man who came to him to have his future told. When the astrologer saw the man's horoscope, he was astonished that the man was so poor, and he said to him, "Why are you so unhappy? From your horoscope I can see that you have a hidden treasure left to you by your father. However, the horoscope indicates that your father could not disclose this to you because he died in a foreign place. But now you can search out this treasure and be happy." This story is cited because the living entity is suffering due to his ignorance of the hidden treasure of his supreme father, Kṛṣṇa. That treasure is love of Godhead, and in every Vedic scripture the conditioned soul is advised to find it. As stated in the *Bhagavad-gītā,* although the conditioned soul is the son of the wealthiest personality—the Personality of Godhead—he does not realize it. Therefore the Vedic literature is given to him to help him search out his father and his paternal property.

The astrologer further advised the poor man: "Don't dig on the southern side of your house to find the treasure, for if you do so you will be attacked by a poisonous wasp and will be baffled in your efforts to find the treasure. Search on the eastern side, where there is actual light, which is devotional service, or Kṛṣṇa consciousness. On the southern side there are Vedic rituals, on the western side there is mental speculation, and on the northern side there is meditational *yoga*."

The astrologer's advice should be carefully noted by everyone. If one searches for the ultimate goal by the Vedic ritualistic process, he will surely be baffled. Such a process involves the performance of rituals under the guidance of a priest who takes money in exchange for service. A man may think he will be happy by performing such rituals, but this is not true. Even if he does gain some result from them, it is only temporary. His material distresses will continue. So he will never become truly happy by following the ritualistic process. Instead, his material pangs will increase more and more. The same may be said for digging on the northern side, or searching for the treasure of love of Godhead by means of the meditational *yoga* process. The perfection of this process is to think oneself one with the Supreme Lord. But this merging into the Supreme is like being swallowed by a large serpent. Sometimes a small serpent is swallowed by a large serpent, and merging into the spiritual existence of the Supreme is analogous. While the small serpent is searching after perfection, he is swallowed. This is spiritual suicide. On the western side there is also an impediment in the form of a *yakṣa,* an evil spirit who protects the treasure. This *yakṣa* is *jñāna-yoga,* the speculative process of self-realization. The idea is that a hidden treasure can never be found by one who asks the favor of a *yakṣa* to attain it. The result is that one will simply be killed. So while the *yogī's* practicing meditation is like a small serpent's being swallowed by a large serpent, practicing the speculative process to attain the treasure of love of Godhead is also suicidal.

The only possibility, then, is to search for the hidden treasure on the eastern side, which represents the process of devotional service in full Kṛṣṇa consciousness. Indeed, the process of devotional service is itself the perpetual hidden treasure, and one who attains to it becomes perpetually rich. One who is poor in devotional service to Kṛṣṇa is always in need of material gain. Sometimes he suffers the bites of poisonous creatures and is baffled, and sometimes he follows the philosophy of monism and thereby loses his identity and is swallowed by a large serpent. It is only by abandoning all this and becoming fixed in Kṛṣṇa consciousness, devotional service to the Lord, that one can actually achieve the perfection of life.

CHAPTER 5

How to Approach God

In truth, all Vedic literature directs the human being toward the perfect stage of devotion. The paths of fruitive activities, speculative knowledge, and meditation do not lead one to the perfectional stage, but the Lord is actually approachable by one who follows the process of devotional service. Therefore all Vedic literature recommends that one accept this process. In this regard, Caitanya Mahāprabhu quoted from the Lord's instructions to Uddhava in *Śrīmad-Bhāgavatam* (11.14.20–21):

na sādhayati māṁ yogo na sāṅkhyaṁ dharma uddhava
na svādhyāyas tapas tyāgo yathā bhaktir mamorjitā

bhaktyāham ekayā grāhyaḥ śraddhayātmā priyaḥ satām
bhaktiḥ punāti man-niṣṭhā śva-pākān api sambhavāt

"My dear Uddhava, neither philosophical speculation nor meditational *yoga* nor penances can give Me such pleasure as devotional service practiced by the living entities. I am dear only to My devotees, and I can be achieved only by devotional service. Even an extremely lowborn person will become free from all contamination if he takes to My devotional service." Devotional service is the only path by which one can achieve the Supreme Person.

Devotional service is the only perfection accepted by all Vedic literatures. Just as when a poor man receives some treasure he becomes happy, when one attains to devotional service his material pains are automatically vanquished. As one advances in devotional service, he attains love of Godhead, and as he advances in this love, he becomes free from all material bondage. One should not think, however, that the disappearance of poverty and the liberation from bondage are the goals of devotional service. Love of Kṛṣṇa, love of God, is itself the goal, and it consists in relishing the reciprocation of loving service with the Lord. In all Vedic literatures we find that the attainment of this loving relationship between the living entity and the Supreme Lord is the goal of devotional service. Our actual function is devotional service, and our ultimate goal is love of Godhead. Therefore in all Vedic literatures Kṛṣṇa is the ultimate center, and through knowledge of Kṛṣṇa all problems of life are solved.

Caitanya Mahāprabhu then quoted a verse from the *Padma Purāṇa:* "There are many different *Purāṇas* with instructions for worshiping different types of demigods, but such instructions only bewilder people into thinking that the demigods are supreme. Yet if one carefully studies the *Purāṇas,* he will find that Kṛṣṇa, the Supreme Personality of Godhead, is the only object of worship." For example, in the *Mārkaṇḍeya Purāṇa* there is mention of Devī worship, or worship of the goddess Durgā, or Kālī, but in this same *Purāṇa* it is also stated that all the demigods—even Durgā—are but different energies of Viṣṇu. Thus the study of the *Purāṇas* reveals Viṣṇu, the Supreme Personality of Godhead, to be the only object of worship.

The conclusion is that, directly or indirectly, all types of worship are more or less directed to the Supreme Personality of Godhead, Kṛṣṇa. The *Bhagavad-gītā* (9.23) confirms that one who worships the demigods is in fact worshiping only Kṛṣṇa because the demigods are but different parts of the body of Viṣṇu, or Kṛṣṇa, but that such worship is irregular. *Śrīmad-Bhāgavatam* (11.21.42–43) confirms this irregularity by answering the question "What is the purpose of the different types of worship described in the Vedic literature?" In the Vedic literature there are various divisions: one is called the *karma-kāṇḍa,* which describes purely ritualistic activities, and another is the *jñāna-kāṇḍa,* which describes speculation on the Supreme Absolute Truth. What then is the purpose of the ritualistic sections of the Vedic literature, and what is the purpose of the *upāsanā-kāṇḍa,* which contains different *mantras* or hymns for worshiping various demigods? And what is the purpose of philosophical speculation on the subject of the Absolute Truth? *Śrīmad-Bhāgavatam* replies that in actuality all of these methods described in the Vedic literature indicate the worship of the Supreme Lord, Viṣṇu. In other words, they are all indirect ways of worshiping the Supreme Personality of Godhead. Sacrifices contained in the ritualistic portions of this literature are meant for the satisfaction of the Supreme Lord, Viṣṇu. Indeed, because *yajña,* sacrifice, is specifically meant for satisfying Viṣṇu, another name for Viṣṇu is Yajñeśvara, or the Lord of sacrifices.

Since neophytes are not on the transcendental level, the Vedic literature advises them to worship different types of demigods according to their situation in the different modes of material nature. The idea is that gradually such neophytes may rise to the transcendental plane and engage in the service of Viṣṇu, the Supreme Personality of Godhead. For example, the *Purāṇas* advise the neophytes attached to eating flesh to eat it only after offering it to the goddess Kālī.

The philosophical sections of the Vedic hymns are intended to enable one to distinguish the Supreme Lord from *māyā.* After one understands the position of *māyā,* one can approach the Supreme Lord in pure devotional service. That is the actual purpose of philosophical speculation, and Kṛṣṇa confirms this in the *Bhagavad-gītā* (7.19): "After speculating for many, many births, the philosophical speculators and empiric philosophers ultimately surrender unto Me, Vāsudeva, and accept that I am everything." It can thus be seen that all Vedic rituals and different types of worship and philosophical speculation ultimately aim at Kṛṣṇa.

Śrī Caitanya Mahāprabhu then told Sanātana Gosvāmī about Kṛṣṇa's multiforms and His unlimited opulence. He also described the nature of the spiritual manifestation, the material manifestation and the manifestation of the living entity. In addition, He informed Sanātana Gosvāmī that the planets in the spiritual sky, known as

Vaikuṇṭhas, and the universes of the material sky are different types of manifestations, for they are created by different energies, namely the spiritual energy and the material energy, respectively. As far as Kṛṣṇa Himself is concerned, He is directly situated in His spiritual energy, or specifically in His internal potency.

To help us understand the difference between the spiritual energy and the material energy, the Second Canto of *Śrīmad-Bhāgavatam* gives a clear analysis of the two. Śrīdhara Svāmī also gives a clear analytical study in his commentary on the first verse of the Tenth Canto of *Śrīmad-Bhāgavatam*. Accepting Śrīdhara Svāmī as an authorized commentator on *Śrīmad-Bhāgavatam,* Caitanya Mahāprabhu quoted his commentary as follows: "The Tenth Canto of the *Bhāgavatam* describes the life and activities of Kṛṣṇa because He is the shelter of all manifestations. Knowing Kṛṣṇa to be the shelter of everything, I worship Him and offer Him my obeisances."

In this world there are two kinds of principles operating: One principle is the origin or shelter of everything, and all other principles are derived from this original principle. The Supreme Truth is the *āśraya,* the shelter of all manifestations. All other principles, which remain under the control of the *āśraya-tattva,* or the Absolute Truth, are called *āśrita,* or subordinate corollaries and reactions. The purpose of the material manifestation is to give the conditioned souls a chance to become liberated and return to the *āśraya-tattva,* or the Absolute Truth. Since everything in the cosmic creation, which is manifested by Kṛṣṇa's Viṣṇu expansions, is dependent on the *āśraya-tattva,* the various demigods and manifestations of energy, the living entities, and all material elements are dependent on Kṛṣṇa, for Kṛṣṇa is the Supreme Truth. Thus *Śrīmad-Bhāgavatam* indicates that everything is sheltered by Kṛṣṇa directly and indirectly. Consequently perfect knowledge can be had only by an analytical study of Kṛṣṇa, as confirmed in the *Bhagavad-gītā*.

Lord Caitanya then asked Sanātana Gosvāmī to listen attentively as He described the different features of Kṛṣṇa. First the Lord informed him that Kṛṣṇa, the son of Nanda Mahārāja, is the Absolute Supreme Truth—the cause of all causes and the origin of all emanations and incarnations. Yet in Vraja, or Goloka Vṛndāvana,

He is just like a young boy. His form is eternal, full of bliss, and full of knowledge absolute. He is both the shelter of everything and the proprietor as well.

In this connection Lord Caitanya gave evidence from the *Brahma-saṁhitā* (5.1):

īśvaraḥ paramaḥ kṛṣṇaḥ sac-cid-ānanda-vigrahaḥ
anādir ādir govindaḥ sarva-kāraṇa-kāraṇam

"Kṛṣṇa is the Supreme Personality of Godhead, with a body full of knowledge, eternality and bliss. He has no origin. He is the original person, known as Govinda, and is the cause of all causes." In this way, Caitanya Mahāprabhu gave evidence that Kṛṣṇa is the original Personality of Godhead, full in all six opulences. His abode, known as Goloka Vṛndāvana, is the highest planet in the spiritual sky.

In addition, Lord Caitanya quoted a verse from *Śrīmad-Bhāgavatam* (1.3.28):

ete cāṁśa-kalāḥ puṁsaḥ kṛṣṇas tu bhagavān svayam
indrāri-vyākulaṁ lokaṁ mṛḍayanti yuge yuge

"All the incarnations described previously are either direct expansions of Kṛṣṇa or, indirectly, expansions of the expansions of Kṛṣṇa. But Kṛṣṇa is the original Personality of Godhead. He appears on earth, in this universe or any other universe, when there is a disturbance created by the demons, who are always trying to disrupt the administration of the demigods."

There are three different processes by which Kṛṣṇa can be understood: the empiric process of philosophical speculation, the process of meditation according to the mystic *yoga* system, and the process of Kṛṣṇa consciousness, or devotional service. By philosophical speculation, the impersonal Brahman feature of Kṛṣṇa is understood; by meditation, or mystic *yoga,* the Supersoul, the all-pervading expansion of Kṛṣṇa, is understood; and by devotional service in full Kṛṣṇa consciousness, the original Personality of Godhead, Kṛṣṇa, is realized. In this connection, Lord Caitanya quoted a verse from *Śrīmad-Bhāgavatam* (1.2.11):

vadanti tat tattva-vidas tattvaṁ yaj jñānam advayam
brahmeti paramātmeti bhagavān iti śabdyate

"Those who are knowers of the Absolute Truth describe the Absolute Truth in three features: the impersonal Brahman, the localized, all-pervading Supersoul, and the Supreme Personality of Godhead, Kṛṣṇa." In other words, Brahman, the impersonal manifestation, Paramātmā, the localized manifestation, and Bhagavān, the Supreme Personality of Godhead, are one and the same. But according to the process adopted, He is realized as Brahman, Paramātmā or Bhagavān.

By realizing the impersonal Brahman, one simply realizes the effulgence emanating from the transcendental body of Kṛṣṇa. This effulgence is compared to the sunshine. There is the sun god, the sun itself, and the sunshine, which is the effulgence of that original sun god. Similarly, the spiritual effulgence (*brahmajyoti*), the impersonal Brahman, is nothing but the personal effulgence of Kṛṣṇa. To support this analysis, Lord Caitanya quoted an important verse from the *Brahma-saṁhitā* (5.40), in which Lord Brahmā says:

yasya prabhā prabhavato jagad-aṇḍa-koṭi-
koṭiṣv aśeṣa-vasudhādi vibhūti-bhinnam
tad brahma niṣkalam anantam aśeṣa-bhūtaṁ
govindam ādi-puruṣaṁ tam ahaṁ bhajāmi

"I worship the Supreme Personality of Godhead, Govinda, whose personal effulgence is the unlimited *brahmajyoti*. In that *brahmajyoti* there are innumerable universes, each filled with innumerable planets."

Caitanya Mahāprabhu further explained that the Paramātmā, the all-pervading feature situated in everyone's body, is but a partial manifestation or expansion of Kṛṣṇa. It is for this reason that Kṛṣṇa is sometimes called Paramātmā, the Supreme Self, the soul of all souls. In this regard Lord Caitanya quoted another verse from *Śrīmad-Bhāgavatam* (10.14.55), concerning the talks between Mahārāja Parīkṣit and Śukadeva Gosvāmī. While hearing the transcendental pastimes of Kṛṣṇa in Vṛndāvana, Mahārāja Parīkṣit inquired from his spiritual master, Śukadeva Gosvāmī, as to why the inhabitants of Vṛndāvana were so much attached to Kṛṣṇa. To this question Śukadeva Gosvāmī answered:

kṛṣṇam enam avehi tvam ātmānam akhilātmanām
jagad-dhitāya so 'py atra dehīvābhāti māyayā

"Kṛṣṇa should be known as the soul of all souls, for He is the soul of all individual souls and the soul of the localized Paramātmā as well. At Vṛndāvana He acted just like a human being to attract people to Him and show that He is not formless." The Supreme Lord is as much an individual as other living beings, but He is different in that He is the Supreme and all other living beings are subordinate to Him. All other living beings can enjoy spiritual bliss, eternal life and full knowledge in His association.

Next Lord Caitanya quoted a verse from the *Bhagavad-gītā* (10.42) in which Kṛṣṇa, while telling Arjuna of His different opulences, indicates that He Himself enters this universe by one of His plenary portions, Garbhodakaśāyī Viṣṇu, and also enters into each universe as Kṣīrodakaśāyī Viṣṇu, and then expands Himself as the Supersoul in everyone's heart. Lord Caitanya then said that if anyone wants to understand the Supreme Absolute Truth in perfection, he must take to the process of devotional service in full Kṛṣṇa consciousness. Then it will be possible for him to understand the last word of the Absolute Truth.

CHAPTER 6

His Forms Are One and the Same

By devotional service one can understand that Kṛṣṇa first of all manifests Himself as *svayaṁ-rūpa,* His personal form, then as *tad-ekātma-rūpa,* and then as *āveśa-rūpa.* It is in these three features that He manifests Himself in His transcendental form. The feature of *svayaṁ-rūpa* is the form by which Kṛṣṇa can be understood by one who may not understand His other features. In other words, the form by which Kṛṣṇa is directly understood is called *svayaṁ-rūpa,* or His personal form. The *tad-ekātma-rūpa* is that form which most resembles the *svayaṁ-rūpa,* but there are some differences in the bodily features. The *tad-ekātma-rūpa* is divided into two manifestations: the personal expansion (*svāṁśa*) and the pastime expansion (*vilāsa*). As far as the *āveśa-rūpa* is concerned, when Kṛṣṇa empowers some suitable living entity to represent Him, that living entity is called *āveśa-rūpa* or *śaktyāveśa-avatāra.*

The personal form of Kṛṣṇa can be divided into two: *svayaṁ-rūpa* and *svayaṁ-prakāśa.* As far as His *svayaṁ-rūpa* (or pastime form) is concerned, it is in that form that He remains always in Vṛndāvana with the inhabitants of Vṛndāvana. This personal form (*svayaṁ-rūpa*) can be further divided into the *prābhava* and *vaibhava* forms. For example, Kṛṣṇa expanded Himself in multiple forms during the *rāsa* dance in order to dance with each and every *gopī* who took part in that dance. Similarly, He expanded himself into 16,108 forms in Dvārakā when he married 16,108 wives. There are some instances of great mystics' expanding their bodily forms by the *yoga* process, but Kṛṣṇa did not expand Himself in that way. In Vedic history, Saubhari Ṛṣi expanded himself into eight forms by the *yoga* process, but those expansions were simply reflections, for Saubhari remained one. But when Kṛṣṇa manifested Himself in different forms, each and every one of them was a separate individual. When Nārada Muni visited Kṛṣṇa at His different palaces in Dvārakā, he was astonished at this, and yet Nārada is never astonished to see the expansions of a *yogī's* body, since he knows the trick himself.

Śrīmad-Bhāgavatam describes Nārada Muni's astonishment at seeing Kṛṣṇa's expansions in Dvārakā. Nārada wondered how the Lord was present with His queens in each and every one of His 16,108 palaces. With each queen, Kṛṣṇa Himself was in a different form, acting in different ways. In one form He was talking with His wife, in another form He was petting His children, and in another form He was performing some household duty. These different activities are conducted by the Lord when He is in His "emotional" forms, which are known as *vaibhava-prakāśa* expansions. Similarly, there are other unlimited expansions of Kṛṣṇa's forms, but even when they are divided or expanded without limit, they are still one and the same. There is no difference between one form and another. That is the absolute nature of the Supreme Personality of Godhead.

In *Śrīmad-Bhāgavatam* (10.39.44–57) it is stated that when Akrūra was accompanying Kṛṣṇa and Balarāma from Gokula to Mathurā, he entered the waters of the Yamunā River and could see all the planets of the spiritual sky. He also saw the Lord in His Viṣṇu form, as well as Nārada and the Four Kumāras, who were worshiping Him. As stated in the *Bhāgavata Purāṇa* (*Śrīmad-Bhāgavatam* 10.40.7):

anye ca saṁskṛtātmāno vidhinābhihitena te
yajanti tvan-mayās tvāṁ vai bahu-mūrty-eka-mūrtikam

"The Supreme Lord's many worshipers—the Vaiṣṇavas, or Āryans—are purified by the various processes of worship they perform according to their convictions and spiritual understanding. Each process of worship involves understanding different forms of the Lord, as mentioned in the scriptures, but the ultimate idea is to worship the Supreme Lord Himself."

In His *vaibhava-prakāśa* feature, the Lord manifests Himself as Balarāma. The Balarāma feature is as good as Kṛṣṇa Himself, the only difference being that Kṛṣṇa's bodily hue is blackish and Balarāma's is whitish. The *vaibhava-prakāśa* form was also displayed when Kṛṣṇa appeared before His mother Devakī in the four-handed form of Nārāyaṇa, just when He entered the world. Then at the request of His parents He transformed Himself into a two-handed form. Thus He sometimes manifests four hands and sometimes two. The two-handed form is *vaibhava-prakāśa,* and the four-handed form is *prābhava-prakāśa.* In His personal form, Kṛṣṇa is just like a cowherd boy, and He thinks of Himself in that way. But when He is in the Vāsudeva form, He thinks of Himself as the son of a *kṣatriya* and feels like a *kṣatriya,* a princely administrator.

In His two-handed form as the cowherd son of Nanda Mahārāja, Kṛṣṇa fully exhibits His opulence, beauty, wealth, attractiveness and pastimes. Indeed, in some Vaiṣṇava literature it is found that sometimes, in His form as Vāsudeva, He becomes attracted to His form of Govinda in Vṛndāvana. Thus as Vāsudeva He sometimes desires to enjoy as Govinda does, although the Govinda form and the Vāsudeva form are ultimately one and the same. In this regard, there is a passage in the *Lalita-mādhava* (4.19), in which Kṛṣṇa addresses Uddhava as follows: "My dear friend, the form of this cowherd boy Govinda attracts Me. Indeed, I wish to be like the damsels of Vraja, who are also attracted by this form of Govinda." Similarly, later in the *Lalita-mādhava* (8.34), Kṛṣṇa says: "Oh, how wonderful it is! Who is this person? After seeing Him, I am so much attracted that I now desire to embrace Him just like Rādhikā."

There are also forms of Kṛṣṇa that are a little different from His original form, and these are called *tad-ekātma-rūpa* forms. These may be further divided into the *vilāsa* and *svāṁśa* forms, which in turn have many different features and can be divided into *prābhava* and *vaibhava* forms. As far as the *vilāsa* forms are concerned, there are innumerable *prābhava-vilāsas,* headed by Kṛṣṇa's expansions as Vāsudeva, Saṅkarṣaṇa, Pradyumna and Aniruddha. Sometimes the Lord thinks of Himself as a cowherd boy, and sometimes He thinks of Himself as Vasudeva's son, a *kṣatriya* prince, and this "thinking" of Kṛṣṇa is called His "pastimes." Actually, He is in the same form in His *vaibhava-prakāśa* and *prābhava-vilāsa,* but He appears differently as Kṛṣṇa and Balarāma. His expansions as Vāsudeva, Saṅkarṣaṇa, Pradyumna and Aniruddha are the original *catur-vyūha,* or four-armed forms.

There are innumerable four-armed manifestations in different planets and different places. For instance, They are manifested in Dvārakā and Mathurā eternally. From the four original four-handed forms are manifested the twenty-four principal four-armed forms, which are called *vaibhava-vilāsa.* They are named differently according to the placement of the conch, club, lotus and disc in Their hands. The same four principal manifestations of Kṛṣṇa are found on each planet in the spiritual sky, known as Nārāyaṇa-loka or Vaikuṇṭhaloka. In Vaikuṇṭhaloka Kṛṣṇa is manifested in the four-handed form of Nārāyaṇa. From each Nārāyaṇa are manifested the forms of Vāsudeva, Saṅkarṣaṇa, Pradyumna and Aniruddha. Thus Nārāyaṇa is the center, and the four forms of Vāsudeva, Saṅkarṣaṇa, Pradyumna and Aniruddha surround the Nārāyaṇa form. Each of these four forms again expands into three, and these all have different names, beginning with Keśava. These forms are twelve in all, and, again, They are known by different names according to the placement of the symbols in Their hands.

As far as the Vāsudeva form is concerned, the three expansions manifested from Him are Keśava, Nārāyaṇa and Mādhava. The three forms expanded from Saṅkarṣaṇa are known as Govinda, Viṣṇu and Śrī Madhusūdana. (It should be noted that this Govinda is not the same Govinda manifested in Vṛndāvana as the son of Nanda Mahārāja.) Similarly, from Pradyumna expand the three forms known as Trivikrama, Vāmana and Śrīdhara, and the three forms expanded from Aniruddha are known as Hṛṣīkeśa, Padmanābha and Dāmodara.

CHAPTER 7

Unlimited Forms of Godhead

According to the Vaiṣṇava almanac, the twelve months of the year are named according to the twelve Vaikuṇṭha forms of Lord Kṛṣṇa, and these forms are known as the predominating Deities for the twelve months. This calendar begins with the month of Mārgaśīrṣa, which is equivalent to late November and early December. The Vaiṣṇavas call this month Keśava. December-January is called Nārāyaṇa, January-February Mādhava, February-March Govinda, March-April Viṣṇu, April-May Śrī Madhusūdana, and May-June Trivikrama. June-July is called Vāmana, July-August Śrīdhara, August-September Hṛṣīkeśa, September-October Padmanābha, and October-November Dāmodara. This Dāmodara is different from the Dāmodara in Vraja. The name Dāmodara was given to Kṛṣṇa when He was bound with ropes by His mother, but the Dāmodara form who is the predominating Deity of the month of October-November is a different manifestation.

Just as the months of the year are known according to the twelve different names of the Supreme Lord, members of the Vaiṣṇava community mark twelve parts of the body according to these names. For instance, the *tilaka* mark on the forehead is called Keśava, and on the stomach, chest and arms the other names are also given. These are the same names as those given the months.

Vāsudeva, Saṅkarṣaṇa, Pradyumna and Aniruddha also expand into eight additional *vilāsa-mūrtis*. Their names are Puruṣottama,

Acyuta, Nṛsiṁha, Janārdana, Hari, Kṛṣṇa, Adhokṣaja and Upendra. Adhokṣaja and Puruṣottama are the *vilāsa* forms of Vāsudeva. Similarly, Upendra and Acyuta are the *vilāsa* forms of Saṅkarṣaṇa; Nṛsiṁha and Janārdana the *vilāsa* forms of Pradyumna; and Hari and Kṛṣṇa the *vilāsa* forms of Aniruddha. (This Kṛṣṇa is different from the original Kṛṣṇa.)

These twenty-four forms—the four original Viṣṇu forms, the twelve Vaikuṇṭha forms, and the eight *vilāsa-mūrtis* mentioned above—are known as *vilāsa* manifestations of the *prābhava* (four-handed) form, and they are named differently according to the position of the symbolic representations (mace, disc, lotus flower and conch shell). Out of these twenty-four *vilāsa* forms, some are *vaibhava* forms, such as Pradyumna, Trivikrama, Vāmana, Hari and Kṛṣṇa, which have different features. Thus Vāsudeva, Saṅkarṣaṇa, Pradyumna and Aniruddha are *prābhava-vilāsa* forms of Kṛṣṇa, and there are a total of twenty further variations. All of these have Vaikuṇṭha planets in the spiritual sky and are situated in eight different directions. Although each of them resides eternally in the spiritual sky, some of them nonetheless appear in the material world also.

In the spiritual sky all the planets dominated by the Nārāyaṇa feature are eternal. The topmost planet in the spiritual sky is called Kṛṣṇaloka, which is divided into three portions: Gokula, Mathurā and Dvārakā. In the Mathurā portion, the form of Keśava is always situated. He is represented on this earthly planet in Mathurā, India, where the Keśava *mūrti* is worshiped. Similarly, there is a Puruṣottama form in Jagannātha Purī, in Orissa. In Ānandāraṇya there is the form of Viṣṇu, and in Māyāpur, the birthplace of Lord Caitanya, there is the form of Hari. Many other forms are also situated in various places on the earth.

Not only in this universe but in all other universes as well these forms of Kṛṣṇa are distributed everywhere. It is indicated that this earth is divided into seven islands, which are the seven continents, and it is understood that on every island there are similar forms. But at the present moment these are found only in India. Although from the Vedic literature we can understand that there are similar forms in other parts of the world, at present there is no information of their location.

These forms of Kṛṣṇa are distributed throughout the world and throughout the universes to give pleasure to the devotees. It is not that devotees are born only in India. There are devotees in all parts of the world, but they have simply forgotten their identity. These forms incarnate not only to give pleasure to the devotees but to reestablish devotional service and perform other activities which vitally concern the Supreme Personality of Godhead. Some of these forms are incarnations mentioned in the scriptures, such as the Viṣṇu incarnation, Trivikrama incarnation, Nṛsiṁha incarnation and Vāmana incarnation.

In the *Siddhārtha-saṁhitā* there is a description of the twenty-four forms of Viṣṇu, and these forms are named according to the position of the symbols in Their four hands. When describing the positions of objects in the hands of the Viṣṇu *mūrtis,* one should begin with the lower right hand and then move to the upper right hand, to the upper left hand and finally to the lower left hand. In this way, Vāsudeva is represented by club, conch shell, disc and lotus flower. Saṅkarṣaṇa is represented by club, conch shell, lotus flower and disc. Similarly, Pradyumna is represented by disc, conch shell, club and lotus flower. Aniruddha is represented by disc, club, conch shell and lotus flower. In the spiritual sky the representations of Nārāyaṇa are twenty in number and are described as follows: Śrī Keśava (lotus, conch shell, disc and club), Nārāyaṇa (conch, lotus, club and disc), Śrī Mādhava (club, disc, conch and lotus), Śrī Govinda (disc, club, lotus and conch), Viṣṇu-mūrti (club, lotus, conch and disc), Madhusūdana (disc, conch, lotus and club), Trivikrama (lotus, club, disc and conch), Śrī Vāmana (conch, disc, club and lotus), Śrīdhara (lotus, disc, club and conch), Hṛṣīkeśa (club, disc, lotus and conch), Padmanābha (conch, lotus, disc and club), Dāmodara (lotus, disc, club and conch), Puruṣottama (disc, lotus, conch and club), Acyuta (club, lotus, disc and conch), Nṛsiṁha (disc, lotus, club and conch), Janārdana (lotus, disc, conch and club), Śrī Hari (conch, disc, lotus and club), Śrī Kṛṣṇa (conch, club, lotus and disc), Adhokṣaja (lotus, club, conch and disc), and Upendra (conch, club, disc and lotus).

According to the *Hayaśīrṣa-pañcarātra,* there are sixteen forms, and these are also named according to the positions of the disc and so on. The conclusion is that the Supreme Original Personality of Godhead is Kṛṣṇa. He is called *līlā-puruṣottama,* and He resides principally in Vṛndāvana as the son of Nanda. It is also learned from the *Hayaśīrṣa-pañcarātra* that there are nine forms protecting the two Purīs known as Mathurā Purī and Dvārakā Purī. These nine forms are Vāsudeva, Saṅkarṣaṇa, Pradyumna, Aniruddha, Nārāyaṇa, Nṛsiṁha, Hayagrīva, Varāha and Brahmā. These are different manifestations of the *prakāśa* and *vilāsa* forms of Lord Kṛṣṇa.

Lord Caitanya next informed Sanātana Gosvāmī that there are different forms of *svāṁśa* as well, and these are divided into the Saṅkarṣaṇa division and the incarnation division. The Saṅkarṣaṇa division includes the three *puruṣa-avatāras*—Kāraṇodakaśāyī Viṣṇu, Garbhodakaśāyī Viṣṇu and Kṣīrodakaśāyī Viṣṇu—and the other division comprises the *līlā-avatāras,* such as the Lord's incarnations as a fish and a tortoise.

There are six kinds of incarnations: (1) the *puruṣa-avatāras,* (2) the *līlā-avatāras,* (3) the *guṇa-avatāras,* (4) the *manvantara-avatāras,* (5) the *yuga-avatāras* and (6) the *śaktyāveśa-avatāras.* Out of the six *vilāsa* manifestations of Kṛṣṇa, there are two divisions based on His age, and these are called *bālya* and *paugaṇḍa.* As the son of Nanda Mahārāja, Kṛṣṇa in His original form enjoys both of these childhood aspects—namely *bālya* and *paugaṇḍa.*

We can conclude that there is no end to the expansions and incarnations of Kṛṣṇa. Lord Caitanya described some of them to Sanātana just to give him an idea of how the Lord expands and how He enjoys. These conclusions are confirmed in *Śrīmad-Bhāgavatam* (1.3.26). There it is said that there is no limit to the incarnations of the Supreme Lord, just as there is no limit to the waves of the ocean.

Kṛṣṇa first incarnates as the three *puruṣa-avatāras,* namely the Mahā-Viṣṇu or Kāraṇodakaśāyī *avatāra,* the Garbhodakaśāyī *avatāra* and the Kṣīrodakaśāyī *avatāra.* This is confirmed in the *Sātvata-tantra.* Kṛṣṇa's energies can also be divided into three: His energy of thinking, His energy of feeling, and His energy of acting. When He exhibits His thinking energy He is the Supreme Lord, when He exhibits His feeling energy He is Lord Vāsudeva, and when He exhibits His acting energy He is Saṅkarṣaṇa Balarāma.

Without the Lord's thinking, feeling and acting, there would be no possibility of creation. Although there is no creation in the spiritual world as there is in the material world, both worlds are manifestations of Kṛṣṇa's energy of acting, which He carries out in the form of Saṅkarṣaṇa Balarāma.

The spiritual world—the Vaikuṇṭha planets and Kṛṣṇaloka—is situated in Kṛṣṇa's energy of thinking. Although there is no creation in the spiritual world, which is eternal, it is still to be understood that the spiritual planets depend on the thinking energy of the Supreme Lord. This thinking energy is described in the *Brahma-saṁhitā* (5.2), where it is said, "The supreme abode, known as Goloka, is manifested like a lotus flower with hundreds of petals. Everything there is manifested by Ananta, who is a form of Balarāma, or Saṅkarṣaṇa." The material cosmic manifestation and its different universes are manifested through *māyā,* or the material energy, but one should not think that the material energy, or material nature, is the cause of this cosmic manifestation. Rather, it is caused by the Supreme Lord, who uses His different expansions to act through material nature. In other words, there is no possibility of any creation without the superintendence of the Supreme Lord. The form of the Lord who causes the energy of material nature to bring about creation is Saṅkarṣaṇa, and it is understood that this cosmic manifestation is created when the material nature comes in contact with the superintendent energy of the Supreme Lord, Saṅkarṣaṇa. The example is given of iron becoming hot in contact with fire and, when red hot, acting just like fire.

In *Śrīmad-Bhāgavatam* (10.46.31) it is said that Balarāma and Kṛṣṇa are the origin of all living entities and that these two personalities enter into everything. A list of incarnations is given in *Śrīmad-Bhāgavatam* (1.3), and they are as follows: (1) the Kumāras, (2) Nārada, (3) Varāha, (4) Matsya, (5) Yajña, (6) Nara-Nārāyaṇa, (7) Kārdami Kapila, (8) Dattātreya, (9) Hayaśīrṣa, (10) Haṁsa, (11) Dhruvapriya, or Pṛśnigarbha, (12) Ṛṣabha, (13) Pṛthu, (14) Nṛsiṁha, (15) Kūrma, (16) Dhanvantari, (17) Mohinī, (18) Vāmana, (19) Bhārgava (Paraśurāma), (20) Rāghavendra, (21) Vyāsa, (22) Pralambāri Balarāma, (23) Kṛṣṇa, (24) Buddha and (25) Kalki. Because almost all of these twenty-five *līlā-avatāras* appear in one day of Brahmā, which is called a *kalpa,* they are sometimes called *kalpa-avatāras.* Out of these incarnations, Haṁsa and Mohinī are not permanent, but Kapila, Dattātreya, Ṛṣabha, Dhanvantari and Vyāsa are five eternal forms, and they are more celebrated. Kūrma (the tortoise incarnation), Matsya (the fish), Nara-Nārāyaṇa, Varāha (the boar), Hayaśīrṣa, Pṛśnigarbha and Balarāma are considered incarnations of *vaibhava.* Similarly, there are three *guṇa-avatāras,* or incarnations of the qualitative modes of nature, and these are Brahmā, Viṣṇu and Śiva.

There are fourteen *manvantara-avatāras:* (1) Yajña, (2) Vibhu, (3) Satyasena, (4) Hari, (5) Vaikuṇṭha, (6) Ajita, (7) Vāmana, (8) Sārvabhauma, (9) Ṛṣabha, (10) Viṣvaksena, (11) Dharmasetu, (12) Sudhāmā, (13) Yogeśvara and (14) Bṛhadbhānu. Out of these fourteen *manvantara-avatāras,* Yajña and Vāmana are also *līlā-avatāras.* The *manvantara-avatāras* are also known as *vaibhava-avatāras.*

The four *yuga-avatāras* are also described in *Śrīmad-Bhāgavatam.* In the Satya-yuga the incarnation of God is white; in the Tretā-yuga He is red; in the Dvāpara-yuga He is blackish; and in the Kali-yuga He is also blackish, but sometimes, in a special Kali-yuga, His color is yellowish (as in the case of Caitanya Mahāprabhu). As far as the *śaktyāveśa-avatāras* are concerned, they include Kapila, Ṛṣabha, Ananta, Brahmā (although sometimes the Lord Himself becomes Brahmā), Catuḥsana (the Kumāras, who are the incarnation of knowledge), Nārada (the incarnation of devotional service), King Pṛthu (the incarnation of administrative power) and Paraśurāma (the incarnation who subdues evil principles).

CHAPTER 8

The Avatāras

Lord Caitanya continued explaining to Sanātana Gosvāmī about Lord Kṛṣṇa's *avatāras,* or incarnations, which are His expansions who come to the material creation. The word *avatāra* means "one who descends from the spiritual sky." In the spiritual sky there are innumerable Vaikuṇṭha planets, and from these planets the expansions of the Supreme Personality of Godhead come into this universe.

The first descent of the Supreme Personality of Godhead, from the expansion of Saṅkarṣaṇa, is the first *puruṣa* incarnation. It is stated in *Śrīmad-Bhāgavatam* (1.3.1) that when the Supreme Personality of Godhead descends as the first *puruṣa* incarnation of the material creation, He immediately manifests sixteen elementary energies. Known as Mahā-Viṣṇu, He lies within the Causal Ocean, and it is He who is the original incarnation in the material world. *Śrīmad-Bhāgavatam* 2.6.42 states that He is the Lord of time, nature, cause and effect, mind, ego, the five physical elements, the three modes of nature, the senses and the universal form. He is the independent master of all moving and nonmoving living beings in the material world,

The influence of material nature cannot reach beyond the Virajā, or Causal Ocean, as confirmed in *Śrīmad-Bhāgavatam* (2.9.10). Neither the modes of material nature (goodness, passion and ignorance) nor material time have any influence on the Vaikuṇṭha planets. On those planets the liberated associates of Kṛṣṇa live eternally, and they are worshiped by both the demigods and the demons.

Material nature acts in two capacities, as *māyā* and *pradhāna*. *Māyā* is the direct cause, and *pradhāna* refers to the elements of the material manifestation. When the first *puruṣa-avatāra,* Mahā-Viṣṇu, glances over material nature, material nature becomes agitated, and the *puruṣa-avatāra* thus impregnates matter with the living entities. Simply by the glance of Mahā-Viṣṇu, consciousness is created, and this consciousness is known as the *mahat-tattva.* The predominating Deity of the *mahat-tattva* is Vāsudeva. This created consciousness is then divided into three departmental activities according to the three *guṇas,* or modes of material nature. Consciousness in the mode of goodness is described in the Eleventh Canto of *Śrīmad-Bhāgavatam.* The predominating Deity of this mode is Aniruddha. Consciousness in the mode of passion produces intelligence, and the predominating Deity in this case is Pradyumna. He is the master of the senses. Consciousness in the mode of ignorance causes the production of ether (the sky) and the ear. The cosmic manifestation is a combination of all these modes, and in this way innumerable universes are created. No one can count the number of universes.

These innumerable universes are produced from the pores of Mahā-Viṣṇu's body. As innumerable atoms pass through the tiny holes in a screen, innumerable universes similarly emanate from the pores of Mahā-Viṣṇu's body. As He breathes out, innumerable universes are produced, and as He inhales, they are annihilated. All of the energies of Mahā-Viṣṇu are spiritual: they have nothing to do with the material energy. In the *Brahma-saṁhitā* (5.48) it is stated that the predominating deity of each universe, Brahmā, lives only during one breath of Mahā-Viṣṇu. Thus Mahā-Viṣṇu is the original Supersoul of all the universes and the master of all universes as well.

The second Viṣṇu incarnation, Garbhodakaśāyī Viṣṇu, enters each and every universe, spreads perspiration from His body and lies down on that water. From His navel grows the stem of a lotus flower, and on that lotus flower the first creature, Brahmā, is born. Within the stem of that lotus flower are the fourteen divisions of planetary systems, which are created by Brahmā. In the form of Garbhodakaśāyī Viṣṇu, the Lord maintains each universe and tends to its needs. Although He is within each material universe, the influence of the material energy cannot touch Him. When it is required, this very same Viṣṇu takes the form of Lord Śiva and annihilates the cosmic creation. The three secondary incarnations—Brahmā, Viṣṇu and Śiva—are the predominating deities of the three modes of material nature. The master of the universe, however, is Garbhodakaśāyī Viṣṇu, who is worshiped as the Hiraṇyagarbha Supersoul. The Vedic hymns describe Him as having thousands of heads.

The third incarnation of Viṣṇu, Kṣīrodakaśāyī Viṣṇu, is the incarnation of the mode of goodness. He is also the Supersoul of all living entities, and He resides on the ocean of milk within the universe. Thus Caitanya Mahāprabhu described the *puruṣa-avatāras.*

Lord Caitanya next described the *līlā-avatāras,* or pastime incarnations, and of these the Lord pointed out that there is no limit. Still, He described some of them—for example, Matsya, Kūrma, Raghunātha, Nṛsiṁha, Vāmana and Varāha.

As far as the *guṇa-avatāras,* or qualitative incarnations of Viṣṇu, are concerned, they are three—Brahmā, Viṣṇu and Śiva. Brahmā is one of the living entities, but due to his devotional service he is very powerful. This primal living entity, master of the mode of material passion, is directly empowered by Garbhodakaśāyī Viṣṇu to create innumerable living organisms. In the *Brahma-saṁhitā* (5.49) Brahmā is likened to a valuable jewel influenced by the rays of the sun, and the Supreme Lord, Garbhodakaśāyī Viṣṇu, is likened to the sun. If in some *kalpa* there is no suitable living entity who can act in Brahmā's capacity, Garbhodakaśāyī Viṣṇu Himself becomes Brahmā and acts accordingly.

Similarly, by expanding Himself as Lord Śiva, the Supreme Lord is engaged when there is a need to annihilate the universe. Lord Śiva, in association with *māyā,* has many forms, which are generally numbered at eleven. Lord Śiva is not one of the living entities; he is more or less Kṛṣṇa Himself. The example of milk and yogurt is often given in this regard: Yogurt is a preparation of milk, but still yogurt cannot be used as milk. Similarly, Lord Śiva is an expansion of Kṛṣṇa, but he cannot act like Kṛṣṇa, nor can we derive the spiritual restoration from Lord Śiva that we derive from Kṛṣṇa. The essential difference is that Lord Śiva has a connection with material nature but Viṣṇu, or Lord Kṛṣṇa, has nothing to do with material nature. In *Śrīmad-Bhāgavatam* (10.88.3) it is stated that Lord Śiva is a combination of three kinds of transformed consciousness known as *vaikārika, taijasa* and *tāmasa.*

The Viṣṇu incarnation, although master of the modes of goodness within each universe, is in no way in touch with the influence of material nature. Although Viṣṇu is equal to Kṛṣṇa, Kṛṣṇa is the original source. Viṣṇu is a part, but Kṛṣṇa is the whole. This is the verdict of the Vedic literature. The *Brahma-saṁhitā* (5.46) gives the example of an original candle which lights a second candle. Although the candles are of equal power, one is still accepted as the original and the other is said to be kindled from the original. The Viṣṇu expansion is like the second candle. He is as powerful as Kṛṣṇa, but the original Viṣṇu is Kṛṣṇa. Brahmā and Lord Śiva are obedient servants of the Supreme Lord, and the Supreme Lord as Viṣṇu is an expansion of Kṛṣṇa.

After describing the *līlā-* and *guṇa-avatāras* to Sanātana Gosvāmī, Lord Caitanya explained the *manvantara-avatāras,* incarnations associated with the Manus. He first stated that there is no possibility of counting the *manvantara-avatāras.* Fourteen Manus appear in one *kalpa,* or day of Brahmā, and for each Manu there is a *manvantara-avatāra.* It is calculated that each day of Brahmā lasts 4,320,000,000 earth years, and Brahmā lives for one hundred years on this scale. Thus if fourteen Manus appear in one day of Brahmā, there are 420 Manus during one month of Brahmā, and during one year of Brahmā there are 5,040 Manus. Since Brahmā lives for one hundred of his years, it is calculated that there are 504,000 Manus manifested during the lifetime of one Brahmā. Since there are innumerable universes, no one can imagine the totality of the *manvantara* incarnations. Countless universes are produced by the exhalation of Mahā-Viṣṇu, and thus no one can begin to calculate how many Manus are existing at one time.

Each Manu is known by a different name. The first Manu is Svāyambhuva, and he is a direct son of Brahmā. The second Manu, Svārociṣa, is the son of the predominating deity of fire. The third

Manu is Uttama, and he is the son of King Priyavrata. The fourth Manu, Tāmasa, is the brother of Uttama, as is the fifth Manu, Raivata. The sixth Manu, Cākṣuṣa, is the son of Cakṣus. The seventh Manu is Vaivasvata, and he is the son of the sun god. The eighth Manu is Sāvarṇi, and he is also a son of the sun god, born of a wife named Chāyā. The ninth Manu, Dakṣa-sāvarṇi, is the son of Varṣa. The tenth Manu, Brahma-sāvarṇi, is the son of Upaśloka. The four other Manus are Rudra-sāvarṇi, Dharma-sāvarṇi, Deva-sāvarṇi and Indra-sāvarṇi.

After describing the Manu incarnations, Lord Caitanya described the *yuga-avatāras* to Sanātana Gosvāmī. There are four *yugas,* or millenniums—Satya, Tretā, Dvāpara and Kali—and in each millennium the Supreme Lord appears in an incarnation of a different color. In the Satya-yuga the color of the principal incarnation is white, in the Tretā-yuga the color is red, in the Dvāpara-yuga blackish (Kṛṣṇa), and in the Kali-yuga yellow (Caitanya Mahāprabhu). This is confirmed in *Śrīmad-Bhāgavatam* (10.8.13) by the astrologer Garga Muni, who calculated Kṛṣṇa's horoscope in the house of Nanda Mahārāja.

In the Satya-yuga the process of self-realization was meditation, and this process was taught by the white incarnation of God. This incarnation gave a benediction to the sage Kardama by which he obtained an incarnation of the Personality of Godhead as his son. In the Satya-yuga everyone meditated on Kṛṣṇa, and each and every living entity was in full knowledge. In the present age, the Kali-yuga, people who are not in full knowledge are still attempting various meditative processes not recommended for this age.

In the Tretā millennium the process for self-realization was the performance of various sacrifices, and this process was taught by the red incarnation of God.

In the Dvāpara millennium Kṛṣṇa was personally present, and the process of self-realization for everyone in that age was worshiping Him. He was blackish in color, He was the incarnation of the Supreme Personality of Godhead Himself, and He induced people to worship Him, as stated in the *Bhagavad-gītā*. *Śrīmad-Bhāgavatam* (11.5.29) states that in the Dvāpara millennium people generally worshiped the Supreme Lord Kṛṣṇa by chanting the following hymn:

namas te vāsudevāya namaḥ saṅkarṣaṇāya
pradyumnāyāniruddhāya tubhyaṁ bhagavate namaḥ

"Let me offer my obeisances unto the Supreme Personality of Godhead in the forms of Vāsudeva, Saṅkarṣaṇa, Pradyumna and Aniruddha."

In the next millennium—the present age, Kali-yuga—the Lord is yellow, and He teaches people the process of attaining love of God by chanting the names of Kṛṣṇa. This process is shown personally by Kṛṣṇa in the form of Caitanya Mahāprabhu, and He exhibits love of Godhead by chanting, singing and dancing with thousands of people following Him. This particular incarnation of the Supreme Personality of Godhead is foretold in *Śrīmad-Bhāgavatam* (11.5.32):

kṛṣṇa-varṇaṁ tviṣākṛṣṇaṁ sāṅgopāṅgāstra-pārṣadam
yajñaiḥ saṅkīrtana-prāyair yajanti hi su-medhasaḥ

"In the Age of Kali the Lord incarnates as a devotee and is always chanting Hare Kṛṣṇa, Hare Kṛṣṇa, Kṛṣṇa Kṛṣṇa, Hare Hare/ Hare Rāma, Hare Rāma, Rāma Rāma, Hare Hare. Although He is Kṛṣṇa, His complexion is not blackish like Kṛṣṇa's in Dvāpara-yuga but is golden. He always engages in preaching love of Godhead through the *saṅkīrtana* movement, and those who are intelligent adopt this process of self-realization." *Śrīmad-Bhāgavatam* (12.3.52) also states:

kṛte yad dhyāyato viṣṇuṁ tretāyāṁ yajato makhaiḥ
dvāpare paricaryāyāṁ kalau tad dhari-kīrtanāt

"The self-realization achieved in the Satya millennium by meditation, in the Tretā millennium by the performance of different sacrifices, and in the Dvāpara millennium by worship of Lord Kṛṣṇa can be achieved in the Age of Kali simply by chanting the holy names, Hare Kṛṣṇa." This is confirmed in the *Viṣṇu Purāṇa* (6.2.17):

dhyāyan kṛte yajan yajñais tretāyāṁ dvāpare 'rcayan
yad āpnoti tad āpnoti kalau saṅkīrtya keśavam

"In this age there is no use in meditation, performance of sacrifices, or temple worship. Simply by chanting the holy name of Kṛṣṇa—Hare Kṛṣṇa, Hare Kṛṣṇa, Kṛṣṇa Kṛṣṇa, Hare Hare/ Hare Rāma, Hare Rāma, Rāma Rāma, Hare Hare—one can achieve perfect self-realization."

When Lord Caitanya described the incarnation for this Age of Kali, Sanātana Gosvāmī, who had been a government minister and was perfectly capable of drawing conclusions, asked the Lord, "How can one understand the advent of an incarnation?" From the description of the incarnation for the Kali millennium, Sanātana Gosvāmī could understand that Lord Caitanya Himself was that incarnation of Kṛṣṇa, and he could also understand that in the future many people would try to imitate Lord Caitanya because the Lord had played as an ordinary *brāhmaṇa* though His devotees accepted Him as an incarnation. Since Sanātana knew that there would be many pretenders, he asked the Lord, "How can one understand the symptoms of an incarnation?"

"As one can understand the different incarnations for previous millenniums by referring to the Vedic literature," the Lord replied, "one can similarly understand who is actually the incarnation of Godhead in this Age of Kali." In this way the Lord especially stressed reference to authoritative scriptures. In other words, one should not whimsically accept a person as an incarnation but should try to understand the characteristics of an incarnation by referring to the scriptures. An incarnation of the Supreme Lord never declares Himself to be an incarnation, but His followers must ascertain who is an incarnation and who is a pretender by referring to authoritative scriptures.

Any intelligent person can understand the characteristics of a real incarnation by understanding two kinds of features—the principal features, called personal characteristics, and the marginal features, comprising His activities. The scriptures describe both kinds of features. For example, in the beginning of *Śrīmad-Bhāgavatam* (1.1.1), the features of an incarnation are nicely described. In that verse, the two terms *param* (supreme) and *satyam* (truth) are used, and Lord Caitanya indicated that these words reveal Kṛṣṇa's principal feature. The other, marginal features are that

He taught Vedic knowledge to Brahmā and incarnated as the *puruṣa-avatāra* to create the cosmic manifestation. These are occasional features manifested for some special purposes. One should be able to understand and distinguish the principal and marginal features of an *avatāra*. No one can declare himself an incarnation without referring to these two features. An intelligent man will not accept anyone as an *avatāra* without studying the principal and marginal features. When Sanātana Gosvāmī tried to confirm Lord Caitanya's personal characteristics as being those of the incarnation for this age, Lord Caitanya Himself indirectly confirmed Sanātana's conclusion by simply saying, "Let us leave aside all these discussions and continue with a description of the *śaktyāveśa-avatāras*."

The Lord then pointed out that there is no limit to the *śaktyāveśa-avatāras* but that some can be mentioned as examples. The *śaktyāveśa* incarnations are of two kinds—direct and indirect. When the Lord Himself comes, He is called a *sākṣāt,* or direct, *śaktyāveśa-avatāra,* and when He empowers a living entity to represent Him, that living entity is called an indirect, or *āveśa,* incarnation. Examples of indirect *avatāras* are the Four Kumāras, Nārada, Pṛthu and Paraśurāma. These are actually living entities who are given some specific power by the Supreme Personality of Godhead. When a specific opulence of the Supreme Lord is invested in specific entities, they are called *āveśa-avatāras.* The Four Kumāras represent the Supreme Lord's opulence of knowledge. Nārada represents devotional service to the Supreme Lord. Devotional service is also represented by Lord Caitanya, who is considered the full representation of devotional service. In Brahmā the opulence of creative power is invested, and King Pṛthu is invested with the power for maintaining the living entities. Similarly, in Paraśurāma the power for killing evil elements is invested. As for *vibhūti,* or the special favor of the Supreme Personality of Godhead, in the Tenth Chapter of the *Bhagavad-gītā* Lord Kṛṣṇa says that a living entity who is especially powerful or beautiful should be known to be especially favored by the Supreme Lord.

Examples of direct, or *sākṣāt*, *śaktyāveśa-avatāras* are the Śeṣa incarnation and the Ananta incarnation. In Ananta the power for sustaining all the planets is invested, and the Śeṣa incarnation is invested with the power for serving the Supreme Lord.

After describing the *śaktyāveśa* incarnations, Caitanya Mahāprabhu began to speak about the age of the Supreme Lord. He said that the Supreme Lord Kṛṣṇa is always like a sixteen-year-old boy, and when He desires to descend to this universe He first sends His father and mother, who are His devotees, and then He Himself appears. All His activities—beginning with the killing of the Pūtanā demon—are displayed in innumerable universes, and there is no limit to them. Indeed, at every moment, at every second, His manifestations and various pastimes are seen in different universes (*brahmāṇḍas*). Thus His activities are just like the waves of the Ganges River. Just as there is no limit to the flowing of the waves of the Ganges, there is no cessation of various features of Lord Kṛṣṇa's pastimes in different universes. From childhood He displays many pastimes, and ultimately He exhibits the *rāsa* dance.

It is said that all the pastimes of Kṛṣṇa are eternal, and this is confirmed in every scripture. Generally people cannot understand how Kṛṣṇa performs His pastimes, but Lord Caitanya clarified this by comparing the performance of His pastimes to the orbit of the sun. According to Vedic astrological calculations, the twenty-four hours of a day are divided into sixty *daṇḍas*. The days are again divided into 3,600 *palas*. The sun disc can be perceived crossing the sky in steps of sixty *palas* each, and that time constitutes a *daṇḍa*. Eight *daṇḍas* make one *prahara,* and the sun rises and sets within four *praharas*. Similarly, four *praharas* constitute one night, and after that the sun rises. And just as the sun can be seen in its movement through 3,600 *palas*, all the pastimes of Kṛṣṇa can be seen in any of the universes.

Lord Kṛṣṇa remains in this universe for only 125 years, but all the pastimes of that period are exhibited in each and every universe. These pastimes include His appearance, the activities of His boyhood and youth, and His later pastimes, including those at Dvārakā. Since all these pastimes are present in one or another of the myriad universes at any given time, they are called eternal. Just as the sun is eternally existing, although we see it rise and set, appear and disappear, according to our position on the earth, so

Kṛṣṇa's pastimes are eternally going on, although we can see them in this particular universe only at certain intervals. As stated earlier, Kṛṣṇa's abode is the supreme planet, known as Goloka Vṛndāvana, and by His will this Goloka Vṛndāvana is manifested in this universe and in other universes as well. Like Kṛṣṇa's name, fame and everything else directly connected to Him, Goloka Vṛndāvana is absolute and is therefore equal to Him.

Thus the Lord is always in His supreme abode, Goloka Vṛndāvana, and by His supreme will His activities there are also manifested at particular places in innumerable universes. And whenever and wherever Kṛṣṇa appears, He displays His six opulences.

CHAPTER 9

The Opulences of Kṛṣṇa

Since Lord Caitanya is especially merciful to innocent, unsophisticated persons, His name is also Patita-pāvana, the deliverer of the most fallen conditioned souls. Although a conditioned soul may be fallen to the lowest position, such a lowly state will not prevent him from advancing in the spiritual science, provided he is innocent. Sanātana Gosvāmī was considered fallen in society because he was in the service of the Muslim government and had thus been excommunicated from brahminical society. But because he was a sincere soul, Lord Caitanya showed him special favor by granting him a wealth of spiritual information.

The Lord next explained to Sanātana Gosvāmī how the different spiritual planets are situated in the spiritual sky. The spiritual planets are also known as Vaikuṇṭha planets. The planets of the material creation have a limited length and breadth, but as far as the Vaikuṇṭha planets are concerned, because they are spiritual there is no limit to their dimensions. Lord Caitanya informed Sanātana Gosvāmī that the length and breadth of every Vaikuṇṭha planet is thousands of billions of miles—in other words, no one can measure any Vaikuṇṭha planet's actual extent. Each of these planets is unlimitedly expanded, and in each of them the residents are full in all six opulences—wealth, strength, knowledge, beauty, fame and renunciation. The Supreme Personality of Godhead is present in every

Vaikuṇṭha planet. Indeed, in each Vaikuṇṭha planet an expansion of Kṛṣṇa has His eternal abode, and Kṛṣṇa Himself has His original eternal abode, called Kṛṣṇaloka or Goloka Vṛndāvana.

In this universe even the largest planet lies in one corner of outer space. For example, although the sun is a million times larger than the earth, it still lies in one corner of outer space. Similarly, each of the Vaikuṇṭha planets, although unlimited in length and breadth, lies in a corner of the spiritual sky, known as the *brahmajyoti*. In the *Brahma-saṁhitā* (5.40) the *brahmajyoti* is described as *niṣkalam anantam aśeṣa-bhūtam*, or undivided and unlimited and without a trace of the material modes of nature. All the Vaikuṇṭha planets are like petals of a lotus flower, and the principal part of that lotus, the center of all the Vaikuṇṭhas, is called Kṛṣṇaloka or Goloka Vṛndāvana.

Thus the expansions of Kṛṣṇa in various forms, as described herein, as well as His various abodes on the spiritual planets in the spiritual sky, are unlimited. Even demigods like Brahmā and Śiva cannot see the Vaikuṇṭha planets or even estimate their number or vast extent. This is confirmed in *Śrīmad-Bhāgavatam* (10.14.21): "No one can estimate the length and breadth of all the Vaikuṇṭha planets." Elsewhere in the *Bhāgavatam* (2.7.41) it is stated that not only are demigods like Brahmā and Śiva unable to make such an estimate, but even Ananta, the incarnation of the Lord's opulence of strength, cannot ascertain any limit to the Lord's potency or to the area of the different Vaikuṇṭha planets.

Again, *Śrīmad-Bhāgavatam* 10.14.21, one of the prayers of Brahmā, is very convincing in this connection: "O my dear Lord, O Supreme Personality of Godhead, O Supersoul, O master of all mystic powers, no one can know or explain the extent of Your Vaikuṇṭha planets or how You expand Your *yogamāyā* energy throughout the three worlds." And a few verses earlier (*Śrīmad-Bhāgavatam* 10.14.7) Brahmā prays:

guṇātmanas te 'pi guṇān vimātuṁ
hitāvatīrṇasya ka īśire 'sya
kālena yair vā vimitāḥ su-kalpair
bhū-pāṁśavaḥ khe mihikā dyu-bhāsaḥ

"Scientists and learned men cannot even measure the atomic constitution of a single planet. Even if they could count the molecules of snow in the sky or the number of stars in space, they could not understand how You descend to this earth or in this universe with Your innumerable transcendental potencies and qualities." In *Śrīmad-Bhāgavatam* (2.7.41) Lord Brahmā informs Nārada that none of the great sages born before Nārada, including Brahmā himself, can measure the extent of the Supreme Lord's potencies. Indeed, Brahmā declared that even Ananta, with His thousands of tongues, fails when He tries to fully describe the Lord's energies. Similarly, in *Śrīmad-Bhāgavatam* (10.87.41) the personified *Vedas* pray:

dyu-pataya eva te na yayur antam anantatayā
tvam api yad-antarāṇḍa-nicayā nanu sāvaraṇāḥ
kha iva rajāṁsi vānti vayasā saha yac chrutayas
tvayi hi phalanty atan-nirasanena bhavan-nidhanāḥ

"My Lord, You are unlimited, and therefore no one can measure the extent of Your potencies. I think that even You do not know the range of Your energies. An unlimited number of planets float in the sky just like atoms, and great Vedāntists, who are engaged in research to find You, discover that everything is different from You. At last they conclude that You are everything."

When Lord Kṛṣṇa was within this universe, Brahmā played a trick on Him in order to confirm that the special cowherd boy in Vṛndāvana was actually Kṛṣṇa Himself. By his mystic power Brahmā stole all the cows, calves and cowherd friends of Kṛṣṇa and hid them. But when Brahmā returned to see what Kṛṣṇa was doing alone, he saw that Kṛṣṇa was still playing with the same cows, calves and cowherd boys. By His Vaikuṇṭha potency Lord Kṛṣṇa had expanded all the stolen cows, calves and friends. Indeed, Brahmā saw millions and billions of them, and he also saw millions and billions of herding sticks and fruits, lotus flowers and horns. All the cowherd boys were wearing different clothes and ornaments, and no one could count their vast numbers. Then Brahmā saw each of the cowherd boys become a four-handed Nārāyaṇa, and he also saw innumerable Brahmās from different universes offering obeisances to the Lord. He saw that all these personalities were emanating from the body of Kṛṣṇa and, after a second, entering into His body. Lord Brahmā became struck with wonder by this extraordinary feat of Kṛṣṇa's, and in a prayer he stated that although anyone and everyone could say they knew all about Kṛṣṇa, as far as he was concerned, he did not know anything about Him. "My dear Lord," he said, "the potencies and opulences You have exhibited just now are beyond the ability of my mind to understand."

Lord Caitanya further explained that not only is the potency of Kṛṣṇaloka limitless, but so also is that of Vṛndāvana, Lord Kṛṣṇa's abode on this planet. From one point of view, Vṛndāvana is about thirty-two square miles in area, yet in one part of this Vṛndāvana all the Vaikuṇṭhas exist. The area of present-day Vṛndāvana contains twelve forests and covers about eighty-four *krośas,* or 168 miles in area, and Vṛndāvana City is estimated to be about sixteen *krośas,* or thirty-two square miles. How all the Vaikuṇṭhas can exist there is beyond material calculation. Thus Caitanya Mahāprabhu concluded that the potencies and opulences of Kṛṣṇa are unlimited. Whatever He told Sanātana Gosvāmī was only partial, but by such a partial presentation one can try to imagine the whole.

While Lord Caitanya was speaking to Sanātana Gosvāmī about the opulences of Kṛṣṇa, He became deeply immersed in ecstasy, and in that transcendental state He recited a verse from *Śrīmad-Bhāgavatam* (3.2.21) in which Uddhava, after the disappearance of Kṛṣṇa, told Vidura:

svayaṁ tv asāmyātiśayas try-adhīśaḥ
svārājya-lakṣmy-āpta-samasta-kāmaḥ
baliṁ haradbhiś cira-loka-pālaiḥ
kirīṭa-koṭīḍita-pāda-pīṭhaḥ

"Kṛṣṇa is the master of all demigods, including Lord Brahmā, Lord Śiva and the expansion of Viṣṇu within this universe. Therefore no one is equal to or greater than Him, and He is full in six opulences. All the demigods engaged in the administration of each universe offer their respectful obeisances unto Him. Indeed, the helmets on their heads are beautiful because they are decorated with the imprints of the lotus feet of the Supreme Lord." It is similarly stated in the *Brahma-saṁhitā* (5.1) that Kṛṣṇa is the Supreme Personality of Godhead and no one can be equal to or greater than Him. That is Brahmā's conclusion. Although the universal rulers—Brahmā, Śiva and Viṣṇu—are masters of each and every universe, they too are servants of the Supreme Lord Kṛṣṇa.

As the cause of all causes, Lord Kṛṣṇa is also the cause of Mahā-Viṣṇu, the first of the incarnations who control this material creation. From Mahā-Viṣṇu come Garbhodakaśāyī Viṣṇu and Kṣīrodakaśāyī Viṣṇu. Thus Kṛṣṇa is the master of Garbhodakaśāyī Viṣṇu and Kṣīrodakaśāyī Viṣṇu, and He is also the Supersoul within every living entity in the universe. The *Brahma-saṁhitā* (5.48) states: By Mahā-Viṣṇu's breathing innumerable universes are produced. In each universe there are innumerable Viṣṇu-tattvas, but it should be understood that Lord Kṛṣṇa is the master of them all and that they are but His partial plenary expansions.

From the revealed scriptures it is understood that Kṛṣṇa lives in three transcendental places. His most confidential residence is Goloka Vṛndāvana. It is there that He stays with His father, mother and friends, exhibits His transcendental relationships and bestows His mercy upon His eternal entourage. There Yogamāyā acts as His maidservant in the *rāsa-līlā* dance. The residents of Vrajabhūmi think, "The Lord is glorified by particles of His transcendental mercy and affection, and due to His merciful existence we, the residents of Vṛndāvana, have not the slightest anxiety." As stated in the *Brahma-saṁhitā* (5.43), in the spiritual sky all the Vaikuṇṭha planets (which make up Viṣṇuloka) are below the planet known as Kṛṣṇaloka, Goloka Vṛndāvana. On that supreme planet the Lord enjoys His transcendental bliss in multiple forms, and all the opulences of the Vaikuṇṭhas are fully displayed on that one planet. Like Kṛṣṇa, His associates are also full with six opulences. In the *Padma Purāṇa* (*Uttara-khaṇḍa* 255.57) it is stated that the material energy and the spiritual energy are separated by the Virajā River. That river flows from the perspiration of the first *puruṣa* incarnation. On the far bank of the Virajā is the eternal nature, unlimited and all-blissful, called the spiritual sky, the spiritual kingdom, or the kingdom of God.

The spiritual planets are called Vaikuṇṭhas because there is no lamentation or fear there and everything is eternal. The spiritual world has been calculated to comprise three fourths of the energies of the Supreme Lord, and the material world comprises one fourth. But no one can understand what that three fourths is, since even this material universe cannot be described. Trying to convey to Sanātana Gosvāmī something of the extent of this display of one fourth of Kṛṣṇa's energy, Caitanya Mahāprabhu next cited an incident from the scriptures in which Brahmā, the lord of this universe, came to see Kṛṣṇa at Dvārakā. When Brahmā, the first created being in the universe, approached Kṛṣṇa, the doorman informed Kṛṣṇa that Brahmā had arrived to see Him. Upon hearing this, Kṛṣṇa inquired as to which Brahmā had come, and the doorman returned to Brahmā and asked, "Which Brahmā are you? Kṛṣṇa has asked."

Brahmā was struck with wonder. Why did Kṛṣṇa ask such a question? Brahmā informed the doorman, "Please tell Him that the Brahmā who is the father of the Four Kumāras and who has four heads has come to see Him."

The doorman informed Kṛṣṇa and then asked Brahmā to come inside. Brahmā offered his obeisances unto the lotus feet of Kṛṣṇa, and after Kṛṣṇa had received him with all honor, the Lord asked him why he had come.

"I shall tell You of my purpose in coming here," Lord Brahmā replied, "but first I ask You to kindly remove a doubt I have. Your doorman told me that You asked which Brahmā had come to see You. May I inquire if there are other Brahmās besides me?"

Upon hearing this, Kṛṣṇa smiled and at once called for many Brahmās from many other universes. The four-headed Brahmā then saw many other Brahmās coming to see Kṛṣṇa and offer their respects. Some of them had ten heads, some had twenty, some had a hundred, and some even had a million heads. Indeed, the four-headed Brahmā could not even count the Brahmās who came to offer their obeisances to Kṛṣṇa. Kṛṣṇa then called many other demigods from various universes, and they all came to offer their respects to the Lord. Upon seeing this wonderful exhibition by Kṛṣṇa, the four-headed Brahmā became nervous and began to think he was just like a mosquito in the midst of many elephants.

Since so many demigods were offering obeisances unto the lotus feet of Kṛṣṇa, Brahmā concluded that no one can measure Kṛṣṇa's unlimited potency. All the helmets of the various demigods and Brahmās shone brightly in the assembly, and when the helmets struck one another as the demigods offered obeisances, the helmets seemed to make a great sound of prayer.

"Dear Lord," the demigods said, "it is Your great mercy upon us that You have called us to see You. Is there any particular order? If so, we will carry it out at once."

"There is nothing especially required of you," Lord Kṛṣṇa replied. "I only wanted to see you all together at one time. I offer My blessings to you. Don't be afraid of the demons."

"By Your mercy, everything is all right," they all replied. "There are no disturbances at present, for by appearing on the earth You have vanquished everything inauspicious."

As each Brahmā saw Kṛṣṇa, each thought that Kṛṣṇa was only within his universe. After this incident, Kṛṣṇa wished all the Brahmās farewell, and after offering respects to Him they returned to their respective universes. Upon seeing this, the four-headed Brahmā at once fell down at the feet of Kṛṣṇa and said, "What I thought about You before was all nonsense. People may say they know You perfectly, but as far as I am concerned, I cannot begin to conceive how great You are. You are beyond my understanding."

Kṛṣṇa then informed him, "This particular universe is only four thousand million miles across, but there are many millions and billions of universes which are far, far greater than this one. Some of these are many trillions of miles across, and all these universes require strong Brahmās with many more than four heads." Kṛṣṇa further informed Brahmā, "This material creation is only one quarter of My creative potency. Three quarters is in the spiritual kingdom."

The four-headed Brahmā then offered obeisances to Kṛṣṇa and departed, now understanding the meaning of the Lord's "three-quarters energy."

The Lord is known as Tryadhīśvara, a name indicating His principal abodes—Gokula, Mathurā and Dvārakā. These three abodes are full of opulences, and Lord Kṛṣṇa is the master of them all, situated as He is in His transcendental potency. Lord Kṛṣṇa, the master of all transcendental energies, is thus full with six opulences, and because He is the master of all opulences, all the Vedic literatures acclaim Him as the Supreme Personality of Godhead.

Lord Caitanya then sang a nice song to Sanātana Gosvāmī about the opulences of Kṛṣṇa: "All the pastimes of Kṛṣṇa are exactly like the activities of human beings. Therefore it is to be understood that His form is like that of a human being. Indeed, the human form is an imitation of His form. Kṛṣṇa is dressed just like a cowherd boy. He has a flute in His hand, and He seems to be just like a newly grown youth. He is always playful, and He plays just like an ordinary boy."

Thus Lord Caitanya began telling Sanātana Gosvāmī about the beautiful aspects of Kṛṣṇa. The Lord said that anyone who understands these beautiful qualities is dipped into an ocean of nectar. Kṛṣṇa's *yogamāyā* potency is transcendental, beyond the material energy, but the Lord exhibits His transcendental potency even within this material world just to satisfy His confidential devotees. In other words, Kṛṣṇa appears in the material world to satisfy His devotees. His qualities are so attractive that Kṛṣṇa Himself becomes eager to understand Himself. When He is fully decorated and stands with His body curved in three ways, with His eyebrows always moving and His eyes so attractive, the *gopīs* become enchanted. His special abode is at the top of the spiritual sky, and He resides there with His associates—the cowherd boys, the *gopīs* and all the goddesses of fortune. It is there that He is known as Madana-mohana.

There are many different pastimes of Kṛṣṇa, such as His pastimes in the forms of Vāsudeva and Saṅkarṣaṇa. In the material sky He performs pastimes as the first *puruṣa* incarnation, the creator of the material world. There are also pastimes in which He incarnates as a fish or a tortoise or takes the forms of Lord Brahmā and Lord Śiva, incarnations of the material qualities. In His pastimes as an empowered incarnation, He takes the form of King Pṛthu, and He also performs pastimes as the Supersoul in everyone's heart and as the impersonal Brahman as well.

Among Kṛṣṇa's innumerable pastimes, however, the most important are His humanlike activities—frolicking in Vṛndāvana, dancing with the *gopīs,* playing with the Pāṇḍavas on the Battlefield of Kurukṣetra and playing in Mathurā and Dvārakā. And His most important pastimes in the human form are those in which He appears as a cowherd boy, a newly grown youth who plays a flute. Just a partial manifestation of His pastimes in Goloka—in Gokula, Mathurā and Dvārāvatī, or Dvārakā—can overflood the whole universe with love of Godhead. Everyone can be attracted by the beautiful qualities of Kṛṣṇa.

The manifestation of Kṛṣṇa's internal potency (*yogamāyā*) is not exhibited in the part of the kingdom of God comprising the Vaikuṇṭha planets, but Kṛṣṇa does exhibit that internal potency within the universe when He descends from His personal abode out of His inconceivable mercy. Kṛṣṇa is so wonderful and attractive that He Himself becomes attracted by His own beauty, and this is proof that He is full of all inconceivable potencies. As far as the ornaments decorating Kṛṣṇa's body are concerned, it appears that they do not beautify Him but that they themselves become beautiful simply by being on His body. Always standing in a three-curved way, He attracts all living entities, including the demigods. Indeed, He even attracts the Nārāyaṇa form who presides in every Vaikuṇṭha planet.

CHAPTER 10

The Beauty of Kṛṣṇa

Kṛṣṇa is known as Madana-mohana because He conquers the mind of Cupid. He is also known as Madana-mohana due to His bestowing favors upon the damsels of Vraja and accepting their devotional service. After conquering Cupid's pride, the Lord engages in the *rāsa* dance as the new Cupid. He is also known as Madana-mohana because of His ability to conquer the minds of women with His five arrows of form, taste, smell, sound and touch. The pearls of the necklace hanging on Kṛṣṇa's neck are as white as ducks, and the peacock feather decorating His head is colored like a rainbow. His yellow garment is like lightning in the sky, and Kṛṣṇa Himself is like a newly arrived cloud. The *gopīs* are like food grains in the field, and when the cloud pours rain on those grains, it appears that Kṛṣṇa is nourishing the hearts of the *gopīs* by calling down His pastime rain of mercy. Indeed, ducks fly in the sky during the rainy season, and rainbows can also be seen at that time. Kṛṣṇa freely moves among His friends as a cowherd boy in Vṛndāvana, and when He plays His flute, all living creatures, mobile and immobile, are overwhelmed with ecstasy. They quiver, and tears flow from their eyes.

Kṛṣṇa's conjugal love is the summit of His various opulences. He is the master of all riches, all strength, all fame, all beauty, all knowledge and all renunciation, and out of these, His perfect beauty is His conjugal attraction. Such perfect conjugal beauty eternally exists only in the form of Kṛṣṇa, whereas His other opulences are present in His Nārāyaṇa form.

As Lord Caitanya described the superexcellence of Kṛṣṇa's conjugal attraction, He felt transcendental ecstasy, and, catching the hands of Sanātana Gosvāmī, He began to proclaim how fortunate the damsels of Vraja were, reciting a verse from *Śrīmad-Bhāgavatam* (10.44.14):

gopyas tapaḥ kim acaran yad amuṣya rūpaṁ
lāvaṇya-sāram asamordhvam ananya-siddham
dṛgbhiḥ pibanty anusavābhinavaṁ durāpam
ekānta-dhāma yaśasaḥ śriya aiśvarasya

"What great penance and austerities the damsels of Vṛndāvana must have undergone, for they are able to drink the nectar of Kṛṣṇa, who is all beauty, all strength, all riches and all fame, and who is the essence of all beautiful bodily luster."

The body of Kṛṣṇa, the ocean of the eternal beauty of youth, can be seen to move in waves of beauty, and there is a whirlwind at the sound of His flute. Those waves and that whirlwind make the hearts of the *gopīs* flutter like dry leaves on trees, and when those leaves fall down at Kṛṣṇa's lotus feet, they can never rise up again. There is no beauty to compare with that of Kṛṣṇa, who is the origin of Nārāyaṇa and all other incarnations, for no one possesses beauty equal to or greater than Kṛṣṇa's. Otherwise, why would the goddess of fortune, the constant companion of Nārāyaṇa, give up His association and engage herself in penance to gain the association of Kṛṣṇa? Such is the superexcellent beauty of Kṛṣṇa, the everlasting mine of all beauty. It is from that beauty that all other beautiful things emanate.

The attitude of the *gopīs* is like a mirror upon which the reflection of Kṛṣṇa's beauty develops at every moment. Both Kṛṣṇa and the *gopīs* increase their transcendental beauty at every moment, and there is always transcendental competition between them. No one can appreciate the beauty of Kṛṣṇa by properly discharging his occupational duty or by undergoing austerities, practicing mystic *yoga*, cultivating knowledge or offering various kinds of prayers.

Only those who are on the transcendental platform of love of God, who engage in devotional service only out of love, can appreciate the transcendental beauty of Kṛṣṇa. Such beauty is the essence of all opulences and is appreciated only in Goloka Vṛndāvana and nowhere else. In the form of Nārāyaṇa the beauties of mercy, fame, etc., are all established by Kṛṣṇa, but Kṛṣṇa's gentleness and magnanimity do not exist in Nārāyaṇa. They are found only in Kṛṣṇa.

Lord Caitanya, greatly relishing the verses of *Śrīmad-Bhāgavatam* He was explaining to Sanātana, quoted another verse (9.24.65):

yasyānanaṁ makara-kuṇḍala-cāru-karṇa-
bhrājat-kapola-subhagaṁ sa-vilāsa-hāsam
nityotsavaṁ na tatṛpur dṛśibhiḥ pibantyo
nāryo narāś ca muditāḥ kupitā nimeś ca

"The *gopīs* used to relish the beauty of Kṛṣṇa as a ceremony of perpetual enjoyment. They enjoyed the beautiful face of Kṛṣṇa—His beautiful ears with earrings, His broad forehead, His smile—and while enjoying this sight of Kṛṣṇa's beauty they used to criticize the creator, Brahmā, for causing their vision of Kṛṣṇa to be momentarily impeded by the blinking of their eyelids."

The Vedic hymn known as Kāma-gāyatrī describes the face of Kṛṣṇa as the king of all moons. In metaphorical language, there are many different full moons, but they are all one in Kṛṣṇa. There is the full moon of His face, the full moons of His cheeks, the full moon of the sandalwood-pulp spot on His forehead, which is a half-moon, and the beautiful full moons of His fingernails and toenails. In this way there are twenty-four and a half moons, and Kṛṣṇa is the central figure of all of them.

The dancing movement of Kṛṣṇa's earrings, eyes and eyebrows is very attractive to the damsels of Vraja. Activities in devotional service increase the sense of devotional service. What else is there for two eyes to see beyond the face of Kṛṣṇa? Since one cannot sufficiently see Kṛṣṇa with only two eyes, one feels incapable and thus becomes bereaved. Such bereavement is slightly reduced when one criticizes the creative power of the creator. The unsatiated seer of Kṛṣṇa's face thus laments: "I do not have thousands of eyes but only two, and even these two eyes are disturbed by the movements of my eyelids. So it is to be understood that the creator of this body is not very intelligent. He is not conversant with the art of ecstasy but is simply a prosaic creator. He does not know how to arrange things properly so one can see only Kṛṣṇa."

The *gopīs'* minds are always engaged in relishing the sweetness of Kṛṣṇa's body. He is the ocean of beauty, and the luster of His body and the beauty of His face and smile are all-attractive to the minds of the *gopīs*. In the *Kṛṣṇa-karṇāmṛta,* Kṛṣṇa's body, face and smile have been described as sweet, sweeter and sweetest. When there are three kinds of contamination in the bodily constitution, convulsions take place. Similarly, a perfect devotee of Kṛṣṇa experiences convulsions when he is overwhelmed by seeing the beauty of Kṛṣṇa's body, face and smile. Before Kṛṣṇa's beauty, the devotee sometimes stays immersed in this ocean of transcendental convulsions without receiving treatment, just as a patient suffering ordinary convulsions may be prevented by a physician from receiving a drink of water for relief.

The devotee increasingly feels the absence of Kṛṣṇa, for without Him one cannot drink the nectar of His beauty. When the transcendental sound of Kṛṣṇa's flute vibrates, the devotee's anxiety to hear that flute penetrates the covering of the material world and enters the spiritual sky, where the transcendental sound of the flute enters into the ears of the *gopīs* and their followers. The sound of Kṛṣṇa's flute always resides within the ears of the *gopīs* and increases their ecstasy. When they hear it, no other sound can enter their ears, and they are unable to reply properly to their family members' questions, for all these beautiful sounds are vibrating in their ears.

Thus Lord Caitanya explained the transcendental constitution of Kṛṣṇa—His expansions, His bodily luster and everything connected with Him. In short, Lord Caitanya explained Kṛṣṇa, the essence of everything, as He is.

CHAPTER 11

Service to the Lord

Next Lord Caitanya explained to Sanātana Gosvāmī the process by which one can approach Kṛṣṇa. The only process, said Caitanya Mahāprabhu, is devotional service to Kṛṣṇa. This is the verdict of all Vedic literature. As the sages declare, "If someone inquires into the *Vedas* to determine the process of transcendental realization, or if someone consults the *Purāṇas* (which are considered sister literatures), one will find that in all of them the conclusion is that the Supreme Personality of Godhead, Kṛṣṇa, is the only object of worship."

Kṛṣṇa is the Absolute Truth, the Supreme Personality of Godhead, and He is situated in His internal potency, which is known as *svarūpa-śakti* or *ātma-śakti*, as described in the *Bhagavad-gītā*. He expands Himself in multiple forms, some of which are known as His personal forms and some as His separated forms. Thus He enjoys Himself in all the spiritual planets, as well as in the material universes.

Kṛṣṇa's separated expanded forms are the living entities, who are classified according to which of the Lord's energies they are under. They are divided into two classes—eternally liberated and eternally conditioned. Eternally liberated living entities never come into contact with the material nature, and therefore they do not have any experience of material life. They are eternally engaged in Kṛṣṇa consciousness, or devotional service to the Lord, and they are counted among the associates of Kṛṣṇa. Their pleasure, the only enjoyment of their life, is derived from rendering transcendental loving service to Kṛṣṇa.

On the other hand, those who are eternally conditioned are always divorced from the transcendental loving service of Kṛṣṇa and are thus subjected to the threefold miseries of material existence. On account of the conditioned soul's eternal attitude of separation from Kṛṣṇa, the spell of the material energy awards him two kinds of bodies—the gross body, consisting of five elements, and the subtle body, consisting of mind, intelligence and ego. Being covered by these two bodies, the conditioned soul eternally suffers the pangs of material existence, known as the threefold miseries. He is also subjected to six enemies (lust, anger, etc.). Such is the everlasting disease of the conditioned soul.

Diseased and conditioned, the living entity transmigrates all over the universe. Sometimes he is situated in the upper planetary system, and sometimes he travels in the lower planetary system. In this way he leads his diseased, conditioned life. His disease can be cured only when he meets and follows the expert physician, the bona fide spiritual master. When the conditioned soul faithfully follows the instructions of a bona fide spiritual master, his material disease is cured, he is promoted to the liberated stage, and he again attains to the devotional service of Kṛṣṇa and goes back home, back to Kṛṣṇa.

A conditioned living entity should become aware of his real position and pray to the Lord, "How much longer will I be ruled by all these bodily functions, such as lust and anger?" As masters of the conditioned soul, lust and anger are never merciful. Indeed, such bad masters never cease demanding service from the conditioned soul. But when he comes to his real consciousness, Kṛṣṇa consciousness, he stops serving these bad masters and approaches Kṛṣṇa with a frank and open heart to achieve His shelter. At such a time he prays to Kṛṣṇa to be engaged in His transcendental loving service.

Sometimes the Vedic literature highly praises fruitive activities, mystic *yoga* and the speculative search for knowledge as different ways to self-realization. Yet despite such praise, in all Vedic literature the path of devotional service is accepted as foremost. In other words, devotional service to Lord Kṛṣṇa is the highest perfectional path to self-realization, and it is recommended that it be performed directly. Fruitive activity, mystic meditation and philosophical speculation are not direct methods of self-realization. They are indirect because without devotional service they cannot lead to the highest perfection of self-realization. Indeed, all paths to self-realization ultimately depend on the path of devotional service.

When Vyāsadeva was not satisfied even after compiling heaps of books of Vedic knowledge, Nārada Muni, his spiritual master, explained that no path of self-realization can be successful unless it is mixed with devotional service. When Nārada Muni arrived, Vyāsadeva was sitting by the banks of the river Sarasvatī in a state of depression. Upon seeing Vyāsa so dejected, Nārada explained the deficiency in his compilation of various books: "Even pure knowledge does not look well unless it is complemented by transcendental devotional service. And what to speak of fruitive activities when they are devoid of devotional service? How can they be of any benefit to their performer?"

Similarly, Śukadeva Gosvāmī prays in *Śrīmad-Bhāgavatam* (2.4.17): "There are many sages who are expert in performing austerities, there are many men who give much in charity, there are many famous men, scholars and thinkers, and there are those who are very expert in reciting Vedic hymns. Although all the activities of these men are auspicious, unless one performs them in order to attain devotional service to the Lord, they cannot award the desired results. Therefore I offer my respectful obeisances unto the Supreme Lord, the only one who can award such results."

Although many types of philosophers and transcendentalists believe that one who lacks knowledge cannot be liberated from material entanglement, there is no possibility that knowledge without devotional service can award liberation. In other words, when *jñāna*, or the cultivation of knowledge, leads one onto the path of devotional service, then only does it help one gain liberation, but not otherwise. This is confirmed by Brahmā in *Śrīmad-Bhāgavatam* (10.14.4):

śreyaḥ-sṛtiṁ bhaktim udasya te vibho
kliśyanti ye kevala-bodha-labdhaye

teṣām asau kleśala eva śiṣyate
nānyad yathā sthūla-tuṣāvaghātinām

"My dear Lord, devotional service unto You is the best path for self-realization. If someone gives up that path and engages in the cultivation of knowledge or in speculation, he will simply undergo a troublesome process and will not achieve his desired results. Just as a person who beats an empty husk of wheat cannot get grain, one who engages simply in speculative knowledge cannot achieve the desired result of self-realization. His only gain is trouble."

In the *Bhagavad-gītā* (7.14) it is stated that material nature is so strong that it can be surmounted only by those living entities who surrender unto the lotus feet of Kṛṣṇa. Only they can cross the ocean of material existence. When a living entity forgets that he is eternally the servitor of Kṛṣṇa, that forgetfulness causes his bondage in conditioned life and his attraction for the material energy. Indeed, that attraction is the shackle of the material energy. Since it is very difficult for a person to become free as long as he desires to lord it over the material nature, it is recommended that he approach a spiritual master who can train him in devotional service. In this way he can get out of the clutches of the material nature and achieve the lotus feet of Kṛṣṇa.

There are four social divisions of human society: the *brāhmaṇas,* or intellectuals; the *kṣatriyas,* or administrators; the *vaiśyas,* or businessmen and farmers; and the *śūdras,* or laborers. There are also four spiritual orders, or *āśramas:* the *brahmacārīs,* or students; the *gṛhasthas,* or householders; the *vānaprasthas,* or retired persons; and the *sannyāsīs,* or those in renounced life. Regardless of one's social or spiritual position, however, one who is lacking in devotional service, or Kṛṣṇa consciousness, cannot be released from material bondage, even if he executes his prescribed duty. On the contrary, he will glide down to hell due to material consciousness. Therefore, whoever is engaged in his occupational or spiritual duty must simultaneously cultivate Kṛṣṇa consciousness in devotional service if he wants liberation from the material clutches.

In this regard, Lord Caitanya recited two verses from *Śrīmad-Bhāgavatam* (11.5.2–3) that were spoken by Nārada Muni to indicate the path of *bhāgavata* cultivation. Nārada pointed out that the four social divisions of human society, as well as the four orders of life, are born from the gigantic universal form of the Lord, the *virāṭ-puruṣa*. The *brāhmaṇas* are born from the mouth of the universal form, the *kṣatriyas* are born from the arms, the *vaiśyas* from the waist, and the *śūdras* from the legs. As such, the members of all these social orders are qualified in the different modes of material nature within the form of the *virāṭ-puruṣa*. But if a person is not engaged in the devotional service of the Lord, he falls from his position, regardless of whether he executes his prescribed occupational duty or not.

Lord Caitanya further pointed out that although those who belong to the Māyāvāda, or impersonalist, school consider themselves to be one with God, or liberated, they are not actually liberated, as confirmed in *Śrīmad-Bhāgavatam* (10.2.32):

ye 'nye 'ravindākṣa vimukta-māninas
tvayy asta-bhāvād aviśuddha-buddhayaḥ
āruhya kṛcchreṇa paraṁ padaṁ tataḥ
patanty adho 'nādṛta-yuṣmad-aṅghrayaḥ

"Those who think that they are liberated according to Māyāvāda philosophy but who do not take to the devotional service of the Lord fall down for want of devotional service, even after they undergo the severest types of penances and austerities, and even after they sometimes approach the supreme position."

Caitanya Mahāprabhu explained that Kṛṣṇa is just like the sun and that Māyā, the illusory material energy, is just like darkness. Therefore one who is constantly in the sunshine of Kṛṣṇa cannot possibly be deluded by the darkness of the material energy. This is very clearly confirmed in the last of the four principal verses of *Śrīmad-Bhāgavatam* (2.9.34), as well as in *Śrīmad-Bhāgavatam* 2.5.13, which states: "The illusory energy, or Māyā, is ashamed to stand before the Lord." Nonetheless, the living entities are constantly being bewildered by this very same illusory energy. In his conditioned state, the living entity discovers many forms of word jugglery to get apparent liberation from the clutches of Māyā, but if he sincerely surrenders unto Kṛṣṇa by simply once saying "My dear Lord Kṛṣṇa, from this day I am Yours," he at once gets out of the clutches of the material energy. This is confirmed in the *Rāmāyaṇa* (*Yuddha-kāṇḍa* 12.20), wherein the Lord says:

sakṛd eva prapanno yas tavāsmīti ca yācate
abhayaṁ sarvadā tasmai dadāmy etad vrataṁ mama

"It is My duty and vow to give all protection to one who surrenders unto Me without reservation." One may develop the desire to enjoy fruitive activities, liberation, *jñāna* or the perfection of the *yoga* system, but if one becomes very intelligent he will give up all these paths and engage himself in sincere devotional service to the Lord. *Śrīmad-Bhāgavatam* 2.3.10 confirms that an intelligent person, whether free of desires or full of desires for material enjoyment or desirous of liberation, should engage in intense devotional service. Those who are ambitious to derive material benefit from devotional service are not pure devotees, but because they are engaged in devotional service they are considered fortunate. They do not know that the result of devotional service is not material benediction, but because they engage in devotional service of the Supreme Lord they ultimately come to understand that material enjoyment is not its goal. Kṛṣṇa says that persons who want some material benefit in exchange for devotional service are certainly foolish because they want something that is poisonous for them. Yet although a person may desire material benefits from Kṛṣṇa, the Lord, being all-powerful, considers the person's position and gradually liberates him from a materially ambitious life and engages him in more devotional service. When one is actually engaged in devotional service, he forgets his material ambitions and desires. This is confirmed in *Śrīmad-Bhāgavatam* (5.19.27):

satyaṁ diśaty arthitam arthito nṛṇāṁ
naivārtha-do yat punar arthitā yataḥ
svayaṁ vidhatte bhajatām anicchatām
icchā-pidhānaṁ nija-pāda-pallavam

"Lord Kṛṣṇa certainly fulfills the desires of His devotees who come to Him in devotional service, but He does not fulfill desires that would again cause miseries. In spite of being materially ambitious, such devotees, by rendering transcendental service to the Lord, are gradually purified of desires for material enjoyment and come to desire the pleasure of devotional service."

Generally people come into the association of devotees to mitigate some material wants, but the influence of a pure devotee frees a man from all material desires by enabling him to relish the taste of devotional service. Devotional service is so nice and pure that it purifies the devotee, and he forgets all material ambitions as soon as he engages fully in the transcendental loving service of Kṛṣṇa. A practical example is Dhruva Mahārāja, who wanted something material from Kṛṣṇa and therefore engaged in devotional service. When the Lord appeared before Dhruva as four-handed Viṣṇu, Dhruva told Him: "My dear Lord, because I engaged in Your devotional service with great austerity and penances, I am now seeing You, whom even great demigods and sages have difficulty seeing. Now I am pleased, and all my desires are satisfied. I do not want anything else. I was searching for some broken glass, but instead I have found a great and valuable gem." Thus Dhruva Mahārāja expressed his full satisfaction and refused to ask anything from the Lord.

The living entity transmigrating through 8,400,000 species of life is sometimes likened to a log gliding downstream on the waves of a river. Sometimes, by chance, a log washes up on shore and is thus saved from being forced to drift further downstream. In this regard there is a nice verse in *Śrīmad-Bhāgavatam* (10.38.5) that encourages every conditioned soul: "No one should be depressed by thinking he will never be out of the clutches of matter, for there is the possibility of being rescued, exactly as it is possible for a log floating down a river to come to rest on the bank." This fortunate opportunity was also discussed by Lord Caitanya. Such fortunate incidents are considered the beginning of the decline of one's conditioned life, and they occur if one associates with the pure devotees of the Lord. By associating with pure devotees, one develops attraction for Kṛṣṇa. There are various types of rituals and activities, some of which lead to material enjoyment and others to material liberation. But if a living entity takes to those ritualistic activities by which pure devotional service to the Lord is developed in the association of pure devotees, then his mind naturally becomes attracted to devotional service. In *Śrīmad-Bhāgavatam* (10.51.53) Mucukunda states:

bhavāpavargo bhramato yadā bhavej
janasya tarhy acyuta sat-samāgamaḥ
sat-saṅgamo yarhi tadaiva sad-gatau
parāvareśe tvayi jāyate ratiḥ

"My dear Lord, while traveling in this material world through different species of life, a living entity may progress toward liberation. But only when he gets the chance to come in contact with a pure devotee can he actually be liberated from the clutches of material energy and become a devotee of You, the Personality of Godhead."

When a conditioned soul becomes a devotee of Kṛṣṇa, the Lord, by His causeless mercy, trains him in two ways: He trains him from without as the spiritual master, and He trains him from within as the Supersoul. In this connection there is a very nice verse in *Śrīmad-Bhāgavatam* (11.29.6), in which Uddhava says to Lord Kṛṣṇa: "My dear Lord, even if someone lives as long as Brahmā, he would still be unable to express his gratitude to You for the benefits derived from remembering You. Out of Your causeless mercy You drive away all inauspicious conditions for Your devotee, expressing Yourself from outside as the spiritual master and from inside as the Supersoul."

If one somehow or other gets in touch with a pure devotee and thus develops a desire to render devotional service to Kṛṣṇa, he gradually rises to the platform of love of Godhead and is thus freed from the clutches of the material energy. This is confirmed in *Śrīmad-Bhāgavatam* (11.20.8), where the Lord says, "For one who, out of his own accord, becomes attracted to topics of My activities—being neither allured nor repelled by material activities—following the path of devotional service leading to the perfection of love of God becomes possible." However, it is not possible to achieve the stage of perfection without being favored by a pure devotee, or a *mahātmā*, a great soul. Without the mercy of a great soul, one cannot even be liberated from the material clutches, and what to speak of rising to the platform of love of Godhead. This also is confirmed in *Śrīmad-Bhāgavatam* (5.12.12), in a conversation between Jaḍa Bharata and King Rahūgaṇa, ruler of the Sindhu and Sauvīra provinces. When King Rahūgaṇa expressed surprise upon seeing Bharata's spiritual achievements, Bharata replied:

rahūgaṇaitat tapasā na yāti
na cejyayā nirvapaṇād gṛhād vā
na cchandasā naiva jalāgni-sūryair
vinā mahat-pāda-rajo 'bhiṣekam

"My dear Rahūgaṇa, no one can attain the perfected stage of devotional service without being favored by a great soul, a pure devotee. No one can attain the perfectional stage simply by following the regulative principles of scriptures, or by accepting the renounced order of life, or by prosecuting the prescribed duties of householder life, or by becoming a great student of spiritual science, or by accepting severe austerity and penances for realization." Similarly, when the atheist Hiraṇyakaśipu asked his son Prahlāda Mahārāja how he had attained such a devotional attitude, the boy replied, "As long as one is not favored by the dust of the feet of pure devotees, one cannot even touch the path of devotional service, which is the solution to all the problems of material life." (*Śrīmad-Bhāgavatam* 7.5.32)

Thus Lord Caitanya told Sanātana Gosvāmī that all scriptures stress association with pure devotees of the Lord. The opportunity to associate with a pure devotee of the Supreme Lord is the beginning of one's complete perfection. This is confirmed in *Śrīmad-Bhāgavatam* (1.18.13), where it is said that the facilities and benedictions one achieves by associating with a pure devotee are incomparable. They cannot be compared to anything—neither elevation to the heavenly kingdom nor liberation from the material energy. Lord Kṛṣṇa also confirms this in the most confidential instruction in the *Bhagavad-gītā* (18.64–65), wherein He tells Arjuna:

sarva-guhyatamaṁ bhūyaḥ śṛṇu me paramaṁ vacaḥ
iṣṭo 'si me dṛḍham iti tato vakṣyāmi te hitam

man-manā bhava mad-bhakto mad-yājī māṁ namaskuru
mām evaiṣyasi satyaṁ te pratijāne priyo 'si me

"My dear Arjuna, you are My affectionate friend and relative, and therefore I am imparting to you this most confidential knowledge for your benefit. Just become always mindful of Me, become My constant devotee, become My constant worshiper, and become a soul surrendered to Me. Only in this way will you be sure to achieve My abode. Because you are My very dear friend, I hereby disclose to you this most confidential knowledge."

Such a direct instruction from Kṛṣṇa is more important than any Vedic injunction or regulative service. There are certainly many Vedic injunctions, ritualistic and sacrificial performances, regulative duties, meditative techniques, and speculative processes for attaining knowledge, but Kṛṣṇa's direct order—"Just give up everything else and become My devotee, My worshiper"—should be taken as the final order of the Lord and should be followed. If one is simply convinced of this direct order of the Lord in the *Bhagavad-gītā,* becomes attached to His devotional service, and gives up all other engagements, one will undoubtedly attain success. To confirm this statement, in *Śrīmad-Bhāgavatam* (11.20.9) Kṛṣṇa says that one should follow other paths of self-realization only as long as one is not convinced of His direct order to become His devotee. It is the conclusion of the *Śrīmad-Bhāgavatam* and *Bhagavad-gītā* that the direct order of the Lord is to give up everything and engage in devotional service.

Firm conviction that one should execute the order of the Lord is known as faith. One who has faith is firmly convinced that simply by rendering devotional service to Lord Kṛṣṇa all other activities are automatically performed, including ritualistic duties, sacrifices, *yoga* and the speculative pursuit of knowledge. In fact, devotional service to the Lord includes everything. As stated in *Śrīmad-Bhāgavatam* (4.31.14):

yathā taror mūla-niṣecanena
tṛpyanti tat-skandha-bhujopaśākhāḥ
prāṇopahārāc ca yathendriyāṇāṁ
tathaiva sarvārhaṇam acyutejyā

"By watering the root of a tree, one automatically nourishes the branches, twigs, leaves and fruits, and by supplying food to the stomach, one satisfies all the senses. Similarly, by rendering devotional service to Kṛṣṇa, one automatically satisfies the requirements for all other forms of worship and all other spiritual processes." One who is faithful and firmly convinced of this is eligible to be elevated as a pure devotee.

There are three classes of devotees, according to the degree of conviction. The first-class devotee is conversant with all kinds of Vedic literature and at the same time has the firm conviction mentioned above. He can deliver all others from the pangs of material miseries. The second-class devotee is firmly convinced and has strong faith, but he has no power to cite evidence from the revealed scriptures. The third-class devotee is one whose faith is not very strong, but by the gradual cultivation of devotional service he can be promoted to the second- or first-class position. It is said in *Śrīmad-Bhāgavatam* (11.2.45) that the first-class devotee always sees the Supreme Lord as the soul of all living entities. Thus in seeing all living entities, he sees Kṛṣṇa and nothing but Kṛṣṇa. The second-class devotee places his full faith in the Supreme Personality of Godhead, makes friends with pure devotees, shows favor to innocent persons and avoids those who are atheistic or against devotional service. The third-class devotee engages in devotional service according to the directions of the spiritual master, or engages out of family tradition, and worships the Deity of the Lord, but he has not cultivated knowledge of devotional service, and he does not know a devotee from a nondevotee. Such a third-class devotee cannot actually be considered a pure devotee; he is almost in the devotional line, but his position is not very secure.

One can thus conclude that when a person shows love for God and friendship for devotees, displays mercy toward the innocent and is reluctant to associate with nondevotees, he may be considered a pure devotee. By developing devotional service, such a person can perceive that every living entity is part and parcel of the Supreme. In each and every living entity he can see the Supreme Person, and therefore he becomes highly developed in Kṛṣṇa consciousness. At this stage he does not distinguish between the devotee and the nondevotee, for he sees that everyone is engaged in the service of the Lord. Such a pure devotee continues to develop all great qualities while engaged in Kṛṣṇa consciousness and devotional service. As stated in *Śrīmad-Bhāgavatam* (5.18.12):

yasyāsti bhaktir bhagavaty akiñcanā
sarvair guṇais tatra samāsate surāḥ
harāv abhaktasya kuto mahad-guṇā
mano-rathenāsati dhāvato bahiḥ

"One who attains pure, unalloyed devotional service to the Supreme Lord develops all the good qualities of the demigods, whereas a person who doesn't attain such service is sure to go astray despite all his material qualifications, for he hovers on the mental platform. Thus his material qualifications are valueless."

CHAPTER 12

The Devotee

As mentioned above, a person in Kṛṣṇa consciousness, being fully devoted to the transcendental loving service of the Lord, develops all the godly qualities of the demigods. There are many such qualities, but Lord Caitanya described only some of them to Sanātana Gosvāmī.

A devotee of the Lord is always kind to everyone; he does not pick quarrels. His interest is in the essence of life, which is spiritual. He is equal to everyone, no one can find fault in him, his magnanimous mind is always fresh and clean, and he is without material possessions. He is a benefactor to all living entities and is peaceful and always surrendered to Kṛṣṇa. He has no material desires. He is very humble and is fixed in his purpose. He is victorious over the six material qualities, such as lust and anger, and he does not eat more than he needs. He is always sane and is respectful to others, but he does not require respect for himself. He is grave, merciful, friendly, poetic, expert and silent.

Śrīmad-Bhāgavatam 3.25.21 also describes the person in Kṛṣṇa consciousness, one who is devoted to the loving service of the Lord. There the devotee is said to be always tolerant and merciful, and a friend to all living entities. He has no enemies, he is peaceful, and he possesses all good qualities. These are a few of the characteristics of a person in Kṛṣṇa consciousness.

It is also said in *Śrīmad-Bhāgavatam* (5.5.2) that if one gets the opportunity to serve a great soul—a *mahātmā*—his path to liberation is open. However, those who are attached to materialistic persons are on the path of darkness. Those who are actually holy are transcendentalists; they are equipoised, very peaceful, free from anger, and friendly to all living entities. Simply by associating with such holy men one can become a Kṛṣṇa conscious devotee of the Lord. Indeed, to develop love of Godhead, the association of such great souls is needed. The path of advancement in spiritual life opens for anyone who comes in contact with such holy men, and by following their path, one is sure to develop Kṛṣṇa consciousness in full devotional service.

In the Eleventh Canto, Second Chapter, of *Śrīmad-Bhāgavatam,* Vasudeva, the father of Kṛṣṇa, asks Nārada Muni about the welfare of all living entities, and in reply Nārada Muni quotes a passage from Mahārāja Nimi's discussion with the Nine Sages. "O holy sages," King Nimi said, "I am just trying to find the path of well-being for all living entities. A moment of association with holy men is the most valuable thing in life, for that moment opens the path of advancement in spiritual life." (SB 11.2.30) This statement is confirmed elsewhere in *Śrīmad-Bhāgavatam* (3.25.25). By associating with holy persons and discussing transcendental subject matters with them, one becomes convinced of the value of spiritual life. Very soon, hearing of Kṛṣṇa becomes pleasing to the ear and begins to satisfy one's heart. After receiving such spiritual messages from holy persons, or pure devotees, if one tries to apply them in his own life, one naturally and successively develops faith, attachment and devotion while progressing on the path of Kṛṣṇa consciousness. The Lord then informed Sanātana Gosvāmī about the behavior of a devotee. The sum and substance of such behavior is that one should always stay aloof from unholy association. And what is unholy association? It is association with one who is too much attached to women or one who is not a devotee of Lord Kṛṣṇa. These are unholy persons. One is thus advised to associate with holy devotees of the Lord and carefully avoid the association of unholy nondevotees. Pure devotees of Kṛṣṇa are very careful to keep aloof from the two kinds of nondevotees. The result of unholy association is described in *Śrīmad-Bhāgavatam* (3.31.33–35). There it is said that one should give up all association with a person who is a plaything for women, for by associating with such an unholy person one becomes bereft of all good qualities, such as truthfulness, cleanliness, mercy, gravity, intelligence, shyness, beauty, fame, forgiveness, control of the mind, control of the senses, and all the opulences that are automatically obtained by a devotee. A man is never so degraded as when he associates with persons who are too much attached to women.

Regarding remaining aloof from unholy persons, Lord Caitanya quoted a verse from the *Kātyāyana-saṁhitā:* "One should rather tolerate the miseries of being locked in a cage filled with fire than associate with those who are not devotees of the Lord." Indeed, one is advised not to even look at the faces of persons who are irreligious, or without any devotion to the Supreme Lord. In other words, Lord Caitanya recommended that one should scrupulously renounce the association of unwanted persons and completely take shelter of the Supreme Lord, Kṛṣṇa. Kṛṣṇa gave Arjuna this same instruction near the end of the *Bhagavad-gītā* (18.66): "Just give up everything and surrender unto Me. I will take care of you and protect you from all the reactions to sinful activities." The Lord is very kind to His devotees, and He is very grateful, able and magnanimous. Therefore it is our duty to believe His words, and if we are intelligent enough and educated enough, we will follow His instructions without hesitation. In *Śrīmad-Bhāgavatam* (10.48.26) Akrūra tells Kṛṣṇa:

kaḥ paṇḍitas tvad aparaṁ śaraṇaṁ samīyād
bhakta-priyād ṛta-giraḥ suhṛdaḥ kṛta-jñāt
sarvān dadāti suhṛdo bhajato 'bhikāmān
ātmānam apy upacayāpacayau na yasya

"Who can surrender to anyone other than You? Who is so dear? Who is so truthful? Who is so friendly? And who is so grateful? You are so perfect and complete that even though You give Yourself to Your devotee, You are still full and perfect. You can therefore satisfy all the desires of Your devotee and even deliver Yourself unto him."

A person who is intelligent and able to understand the philosophy of Kṛṣṇa consciousness naturally gives up everything and takes shelter only of Kṛṣṇa. In this regard, Lord Caitanya recited a verse spoken by Uddhava in *Śrīmad-Bhāgavatam* (3.2.23): "How can one take shelter of anyone but Kṛṣṇa? Who else is so kind? Even though Bakāsura's sister Pūtanā tried to kill Kṛṣṇa when He was an infant by applying poison to her breast and offering it to Him to suck, still that heinous woman received salvation and was elevated to the same platform as His own mother." Kṛṣṇa accepted the poisonous breast of that demonic woman Pūtanā, and when He sucked the milk from her breast, He sucked out her life also. Nonetheless, Pūtanā was elevated to the same position as Kṛṣṇa's own mother.

There is no essential difference between a fully surrendered soul and a man in the renounced order of life. The only difference is that a fully surrendered soul is completely dependent upon Kṛṣṇa. There are six qualifications for surrender. The first is that one should accept everything favorable for the discharge of one's duties in devotional service, and one should be determined to accept the process. The second is that one should give up everything that is unfavorable for the discharge of devotional service, and one should be determined to give it all up. Thirdly, one should be convinced that only Kṛṣṇa can protect him and should have full faith that the Lord will give that protection. An impersonalist thinks that his actual identity is in being one with Kṛṣṇa, but a devotee does not destroy his identity in this way. He lives with full faith that Kṛṣṇa will kindly protect him in all respects. Fourthly, a devotee should always accept Kṛṣṇa as his maintainer. Those who are interested in the fruits of activities generally expect protection from the demigods, but a devotee of Kṛṣṇa does not look to any demigod for protection. He is fully convinced that Kṛṣṇa will protect him from all kinds of unfavorable conditions. Fifthly, a devotee is always conscious that he is not independent in fulfilling his desires; unless Kṛṣṇa fulfills them, they cannot be fulfilled. Lastly, one should always think of himself as most fallen so that Kṛṣṇa will take care of him.

Such a surrendered soul should take shelter of a holy place like Vṛndāvana, Mathurā, Dvārakā or Māyāpur and should surrender himself unto the Lord, saying, "My Lord, from today I am Yours.

You can protect me or kill me as You like." When a devotee takes shelter of Kṛṣṇa in such a way, Kṛṣṇa is so grateful that He accepts him and gives him all kinds of protection. This is confirmed in *Śrīmad-Bhāgavatam* (11.29.34), where it is said that if a person who is about to die takes full shelter of the Supreme Lord and places himself fully under His care, he actually attains immortality at that time and becomes eligible to associate with the Supreme Lord and enjoy transcendental bliss.

The Lord then explained to Sanātana Gosvāmī the various types and symptoms of practical devotional service. When devotional service is performed with our present senses, it is called practical devotional service. Actually, devotional service is the eternal life of the living entity and is lying dormant in everyone's heart. The practice which invokes that dormant devotional service is called practical devotional service. The purport is that the living entity is constitutionally part and parcel of the Supreme Lord; the Lord can be compared to the sun, and the living entities can be compared to molecules of sunshine. Under the spell of the illusory energy, the spiritual spark is almost extinguished, but by practical devotional service one can revive his natural constitutional position. When one practices such devotional service, it should be understood that he is returning to his original and normal liberated position. Practical devotional service can be performed with one's senses under the direction of a bona fide spiritual master.

One begins spiritual activities for advancement in devotional service, or Kṛṣṇa consciousness, by hearing. Indeed, hearing is the most important method for advancement in Kṛṣṇa consciousness, and one should be very eager to hear favorably about Kṛṣṇa. Giving up all speculation and fruitive activity, one should simply worship Kṛṣṇa and desire to attain love of God. That love of God is eternally existing within everyone; it simply has to be evoked by the process of hearing. Hearing and chanting are the principal methods of devotional service.

Devotional service may be regulative or affectionate. One who has not developed transcendental affection for Kṛṣṇa should conduct his life according to scriptural injunctions and under the guidance of the spiritual master. In *Śrīmad-Bhāgavatam* (2.1.5) Śukadeva

Gosvāmī advises Mahārāja Parīkṣit:

tasmād bhārata sarvātmā bhagavān īśvaro hariḥ
śrotavyaḥ kīrtitavyaś ca smartavyaś cecchatābhayam

"O best of the Bhāratas, it is the prime duty of persons who want to become fearless to hear about the Supreme Personality of Godhead, Hari, and to chant about Him and always remember Him." Lord Viṣṇu is always to be remembered and is not to be forgotten for even a moment. This is the sum and substance of all regulative principles. The conclusion is that when all the rules, regulations and recommended and prohibited activities in the revealed scriptures are taken together, remembrance of the Supreme Lord is always the essence of everything. To always remember the Supreme Personality of Godhead within one's heart is the main practice of devotional service, and in that practice there are no regulative principles—there are no do's and don't's.

However, one should generally accept the following principles to properly execute devotional service. The devotee should (1) take shelter of a bona fide spiritual master, (2) receive initiation from the spiritual master, (3) serve the spiritual master, (4) inquire and learn love from the spiritual master, (5) follow in the footsteps of holy persons devoted to the transcendental loving service of the Lord, (6) be prepared to give up all kinds of enjoyment and suffer all kinds of miseries for the satisfaction of Kṛṣṇa, (7) live in a place where Kṛṣṇa had His pastimes, (8) be satisfied with whatever is sent by Kṛṣṇa for the maintenance of the body and not hanker for more than that, (9) observe fasting on Ekādaśī day (This occurs on the eleventh day after the full moon and the eleventh day after the new moon. On such days no grains, cereals or beans are eaten; simply vegetables and milk are moderately taken, and the chanting of Hare Kṛṣṇa and reading of scriptures are increased.), and (10) show respect to devotees, cows and sacred trees like the banyan tree.

It is essential for a neophyte devotee who is beginning to follow the path of devotional service to observe these ten principles.

The eleventh principle is to try to avoid offenses in serving the Lord and in chanting His holy names. There are ten kinds of offenses in the matter of chanting the holy name: (1) to blaspheme a devotee of the Lord, (2) to consider the Lord and the demigods on the same level or to think there are many gods, (3) to neglect the orders of the spiritual master, (4) to minimize the authority of the scriptures (the *Vedas*), (5) to interpret the holy names of God, (6) to commit sins on the strength of chanting, (7) to instruct the glories of the Lord's names to the unfaithful, (8) to compare the chanting of the holy name to material piety, (9) to be inattentive while chanting the holy name, and (10) to remain attached to material things in spite of chanting the holy names. These ten offenses against the holy name should be avoided.

The twelfth principle in the execution of devotional service is that one should avoid the association of unholy nondevotees; (13) one should not attempt to have many disciples; (14) one should not take the trouble to understand many books or to understand partially any particular book, and one should avoid discussing different doctrines; (15) one should be equipoised both in gain and in loss; (16) one should not be subject to any kind of lamentation; (17) one should not disrespect the demigods or other scriptures; (18) one should not tolerate blasphemy against the Supreme Lord or His devotees; (19) one should avoid ordinary topics of novels and fiction, but there is no injunction that one should avoid hearing ordinary news; (20) one should not give any trouble to any living creature, even a small bug.

The first ten of the twenty items mentioned above are affirmative, and the second ten are prohibitive. In the *Bhakti-rasāmṛta-sindhu*, compiled by Śrīla Rūpa Gosvāmī, it is said that one should be very liberal in behavior and should avoid any undesirable activities. Of the twenty regulations, the most important are the first three: to accept the shelter of a bona fide spiritual master, be initiated by him, and serve him.

In addition to these twenty, there are thirty-five more items of devotional service, and they can be analyzed as follows: (1) hearing about the Lord, (2) chanting about Him, (3) remembering Him, (4) worshiping Him, (5) praying to Him, (6) serving Him, (7) engaging as His servitor, (8) being friendly toward Him, (9) offering everything to Him, (10) dancing before the Deity, (11) singing before the Deity, (12) informing the Deity of one's thoughts, (13) offering obeisances to the Deity, (14) standing up to show respect to the Deity and the devotees, (15) following a devotee when he gets up to go to the door, (16) entering the temple of the Lord, (17) circumambulating the temple of the Lord, (18) reciting prayers to the Lord, (19) vibrating hymns in His honor, (20) performing *saṅkīrtana,* or congregational chanting of the holy name, (21) smelling the incense and flowers offered to the Deity, (22) accepting *prasādam* (food offered to Kṛṣṇa), (23) attending the *ārati* ceremony, (24) seeing the Deity, (25) offering palatable foodstuffs to the Lord, (26) meditating on the Lord, (27) offering water to the *tulasī* tree, (28) offering respect to the Vaiṣṇavas or advanced devotees, (29) living in Mathurā or Vṛndāvana, (30) understanding *Śrīmad-Bhāgavatam,* (31) trying one's utmost to attain Kṛṣṇa, (32) expecting the mercy of Kṛṣṇa, (33) joining with devotees in performing Kṛṣṇa's ceremonial functions, (34) surrendering to the Lord in all respects, (35) observing different ceremonial functions and vows.

To these thirty-five items are added another four: (1) marking one's body with sandalwood pulp to show that one is a Vaiṣṇava, (2) painting one's body with the holy names of the Lord, (3) covering one's body with the remnants of the Deity's coverings, (4) sipping *caraṇāmṛta,* the water that has washed the Deity. These four additional items make thirty-nine items for devotional service in all, and out of all of these the following five are most important: (1) to associate with devotees, (2) to chant the holy name of the Lord, (3) to hear *Śrīmad-Bhāgavatam,* (4) to live in a holy place such as Mathurā or Vṛndāvana, and (5) to serve the Deity with great devotion. These items are especially mentioned by Rūpa Gosvāmī in his book *Bhakti-rasāmṛta-sindhu.* The thirty-nine items above, plus these five items, total forty-four items. Add to these the twenty preliminary items and there are a total of sixty-four items for conducting devotional service. The devotional service of one who adopts these sixty-four items with his body, mind and senses gradually becomes pure. Some of the items are completely distinct from others, some are identical, and others appear to be mixed.

Śrīla Rūpa Gosvāmī has recommended that one live in the association of those who are of the same mentality; therefore it is necessary to form some association for Kṛṣṇa consciousness and live together for the cultivation of knowledge of Kṛṣṇa and devotional service. The most important item for living in that association is the mutual understanding of the *Bhagavad-gītā* and *Śrīmad-Bhāgavatam*. When faith and devotion are developed, they become transformed into the worship of the Deity, chanting of the holy name and living in a holy place like Mathurā and Vṛndāvana.

The last five items—mentioned after the first thirty-nine—are very important and essential. If one can simply discharge these five items, he can be elevated to the highest perfectional stage, even if he does not execute them perfectly. One may be able to perform one item or many items, according to one's capacity, but it is the principal factor of complete attachment to devotional service that makes one advance on the path. Some devotees in history, like Mahārāja Ambarīṣa, attained perfection in devotional service by executing all the items of devotional service, while many others attained perfection by discharging the duties of only one item. Some of them are Mahārāja Parīkṣit, who was liberated and fully perfected simply by hearing; Śukadeva Gosvāmī, who became liberated and attained perfection in devotional service simply by chanting; Prahlāda Mahārāja, who attained perfection by remembering; Lakṣmī, who attained perfection by serving the lotus feet of the Lord; King Pṛthu, who attained perfection simply by worshiping; Akrūra, who attained perfection simply by praying; Hanumān, who attained perfection simply by becoming the servant of Lord Rāma; Arjuna, who attained perfection simply by being a friend of Kṛṣṇa's; and Bali Mahārāja, who attained perfection simply by offering whatever he had in his possession.

As mentioned above, Mahārāja Ambarīṣa performed all the items of devotional service. He first of all engaged his mind by fixing it on the lotus feet of Kṛṣṇa. He engaged his words, his power of speaking, in describing the transcendental qualities of the Supreme Personality of Godhead. He engaged his hands in washing the temple of the Deity, his ears in hearing the words of Kṛṣṇa, and his eyes in beholding the Deity. He engaged his sense of touch by rendering service to the devotees, and he engaged his sense of smell by relishing the fragrance of the flowers offered to Kṛṣṇa. He engaged his tongue in tasting the *tulasī* leaves offered to the lotus feet of Kṛṣṇa, his legs in going to the temple of Kṛṣṇa, and his head in offering obeisances to the Deity of Kṛṣṇa. Because all his desires and ambitions were thus engaged in the devotional service of the Lord, Mahārāja Ambarīṣa is considered the leader in discharging devotional service in all kinds of ways.

Whoever engages in the devotional service of the Lord in full Kṛṣṇa consciousness becomes freed of all debts to the sages, demigods and forefathers, to whom everyone is generally indebted. This is confirmed in *Śrīmad-Bhāgavatam* (11.5.41):

devarṣi-bhūtāpta-nṛṇāṁ pitṝṇāṁ
na kiṅkaro nāyam ṛṇī ca rājan
sarvātmanā yaḥ śaraṇaṁ śaraṇyaṁ
gato mukundaṁ parihṛtya kartam

"Whoever fully engages himself in the service of the Lord, O King, giving up all other duties, is no longer indebted to the demigods, the sages, other living entities, his relatives, the forefathers or any man." Every man, just after his birth, is at once indebted to all the above-mentioned personalities, and one is expected to discharge many kinds of ritualistic functions because of this indebtedness. But a person who is fully surrendered unto Kṛṣṇa has no obligation. He becomes free from all debts.

It should be carefully noted, however, that when a person gives up all other duties and simply takes to the transcendental service of Kṛṣṇa, he has no material desire and is not apt to perform sinful activities. If, however, he performs sinful activities (not willfully but by chance), Kṛṣṇa gives him all protection. It is not necessary for him to purify himself by any other method, and this is confirmed in *Śrīmad-Bhāgavatam* (11.5.42): "A devotee who is fully engaged in the transcendental loving service of the Lord is protected by the Supreme Person, but in case such a devotee unintentionally commits some sinful activity or is obliged to act sinfully under certain circumstances, God, situated within his heart, gives him all protection."

The processes of speculative knowledge and renunciation are not chief items for elevation in devotional service. One does not have to take to the principles of nonviolence and sense control, although there are rules and regulations for acquiring these qualities in the other processes. Without even practicing these processes, a devotee develops all good qualities simply by discharging devotional service to the Lord. In the Eleventh Canto of *Śrīmad-Bhāgavatam* (11.20.31), the Lord Himself says that there is no necessity of cultivating speculative knowledge and renunciation if one is actually engaged in the devotional service of the Lord.

Out of sheer misunderstanding, some transcendentalists think that knowledge and renunciation are necessary for rising to the platform of devotional service. This is not so. The cultivation of knowledge and the renunciation of fruitive activities may be necessary for understanding one's spiritual existence in relation to the material conception of life, but they are not part and parcel of devotional service. The results of knowledge and fruitive activities are liberation and material sense gratification, respectively. Therefore they cannot be part and parcel of devotional service; rather, they have no intrinsic value in the discharge of devotional service. One who is freed from bondage to the results of knowledge and fruitive activities can be situated in devotional service. Since a devotee of Lord Kṛṣṇa is by nature nonviolent, and since his mind and senses are controlled, he does not have to make a special effort to acquire the good qualities which result from cultivating knowledge and performing fruitive activities.

When Uddhava was questioning Kṛṣṇa about the rules and regulations according to Vedic injunctions, he asked, "Why is it that the Vedic hymns encourage one in material enjoyment, while at the same time the Vedic instructions also free one from all illusion and encourage one toward liberation?" The Vedic rules are said to be ordained by the Supreme Personality of Godhead, but apparently there are contradictions, and Uddhava was anxious to know how one could resolve these contradictions. In reply, Lord Kṛṣṇa cited the verse mentioned above (SB 11.20.31), informing him of the superexcellence of devotional service: "For one who is already engaged in devotional service to Me and whose mind is fixed on Me, it is neither practical nor necessary to cultivate knowledge and renunciation."

Thus the Lord's conclusion is that devotional service is independent of any other process. The cultivation of knowledge, renunciation or meditation may be a little helpful in the beginning, but they cannot be considered necessary for discharging devotional service. In other words, devotional service can be discharged independently of the cultivation of knowledge and renunciation. In this regard, there is also a verse from the *Skanda Purāṇa,* in which Nārada Muni tells a hunter tribesman: "O hunter, the qualifications you have just now acquired—such as nonviolence and others—are not astonishing, because one who is engaged in devotional service to the Supreme Lord cannot be a source of trouble for anyone, under any circumstance."

Beneath a wish-fulfilling tree in Vṛndāvana, Kṛṣṇa's dear friends serve Rādhā and Kṛṣṇa by singing, dancing and offering refreshments. (p. 21)

For seven days Śrī Caitanya Mahāprabhu continually listened to Sārvabhauma Bhaṭṭācārya expound on the Vedānta philosophy. (p. 269)

When the Lord embraced him, Sanātana became overwhelmed with spiritual ecstasy, and they both began to cry. (p. 54)

There are twenty-four forms of Viṣṇu, and these forms are named according to the position of the symbolic representations in Their four hands. (p. 84)

Kṛṣṇa is the ocean of beauty, and His beautiful face and smile and the luster of His body are all-attractive to the minds of the *gopīs*. (p. 112)

After proceeding a few steps, Nārada saw the hunter engaged in hunting with bow and arrows. (p. 179)

Prakāśānanda took the Lord's hand and requested Him to please come and sit with him. (p. 205)

Lord Caitanya smiled and showed Rāmānanda Rāya His real form as the combination of Śrī Śrī Rādhā and Kṛṣṇa. (p. 348)

CHAPTER 13

Devotional Service in Attachment

Next Lord Caitanya said to Sanātana Gosvāmī, "Thus far I have explained devotional service according to regulative principles. Now I shall explain devotional service to you in terms of transcendental attachment."

The inhabitants of Vṛndāvana, Vrajabhūmi, are living examples of devotional service. Theirs is ideal devotional service with attachment, and such devotion cannot be found anywhere except Vṛndāvana. Developing devotional service with attachment by following in the footsteps of the Vrajavāsīs is called *rāga-mārga-bhakti,* or devotional service in pursuance of attachment to the Lord. According to the *Bhakti-rasāmṛta-sindhu* (1.2.272), "The ecstatic attachment for the Lord experienced in the course of the devotional service that is natural for the devotee is called *rāga,* or transcendental attachment. The devotional service discharged with such deep attachment, and with consequent deep absorption in the object of love, is called *rāgātmikā.*" Examples of such devotional service can be seen in the activities of the residents of Vrajabhūmi. One who becomes attracted to Kṛṣṇa by hearing of such attachment is certainly very fortunate. When one becomes deeply affected by the devotion of the residents of Vrajabhūmi and tries to footsteps, he does not care for the restrictions or regulations of the revealed scriptures. This is characteristic of one discharging *rāga-bhakti*.

Devotional service with attachment is natural, and one who has been attracted by it does not care for any arguments against his conviction, even though such arguments may be presented according to scriptural injunctions. The natural inclination to devotional service with attachment is also based on scriptural injunction, and thus one who has attachment for such devotional service is not required to give it up simply on the strength of scriptural argument. In this connection, we should note that the class of so-called devotees known as *prākṛta-sahajiyās* follow their own concocted ideas and, representing themselves as Kṛṣṇa and Rādhā, indulge in debauchery. Such devotional service with attachment is false, and those so engaged are actually gliding down a hellish path. This is not the standard of *rāgātmikā-bhakti*, or devotional service with attachment. The *prākṛta-sahajiyā* community is actually cheated and very unfortunate.

Devotional service with attachment can be executed in two ways—externally and internally. Externally the devotee strictly follows the regulative principles, beginning with chanting and hearing, while internally he thinks of the attachment which attracts him to serve the Supreme Lord. Indeed, he always thinks of his special devotional service and attachment. Such a real devotee's attachment does not violate the regulative principles of devotional service, and he adheres to them strictly, yet within his mind he always thinks of his particular attachment.

All the inhabitants of Vrajabhūmi are very dear to Kṛṣṇa. A devotee selects one of them and follows in his footsteps in order to be successful in his own devotional service. A pure devotee discharging devotional service with attachment always follows in the footsteps of a personality of Vrajabhūmi. It is advised in the *Bhakti-rasāmṛta-sindhu* (1.2.294) that such a pure devotee should always remember the activities of a particular inhabitant of Vraja, even though he is not able to live in Vraja. In this way he can always think of Vraja.

Such confidential devotees are divided into several categories:

some of them are servants, some are friends, some are parents, and some are conjugal lovers. In devotional service with attachment, one has to follow a particular type of devotee of Vrajabhūmi. In *Śrīmad-Bhāgavatam* (3.25.38) the Lord says:

na karhicin mat-parāḥ śānta-rūpe
naṅkṣyanti no me 'nimiṣo leḍhi hetiḥ
yeṣām ahaṁ priya ātmā sutaś ca
sakhā guruḥ suhṛdo daivam iṣṭam

"The word *mat-parā* is used only to refer to persons who are satisfied with the idea of becoming My adherents alone. They consider that I am their soul, I am their friend, I am their son, I am their master, I am their well-wisher, I am their God, and I am their supreme goal. My dear mother, time does not act on such devotees." In the *Bhakti-rasāmṛta-sindhu* (1.2.308), Rūpa Gosvāmī offers his respectful obeisances to those who always think of Kṛṣṇa as son, well-wisher, brother, father, friend, and so on. Whoever adheres to the principles of devotional service with attachment, following in the footsteps of a particular devotee of Vrajabhūmi, certainly attains the highest perfection of love of Godhead in that spirit.

There are two characteristics by which the seeds of love of Godhead can develop, and these are known as *rati,* or attachment, and *bhāva,* the condition immediately preceding love of Godhead. It is by such attachment and *bhāva* that the Supreme Lord Śrī Kṛṣṇa is conquered by His devotees. These two characteristics are present before any symptoms of love of Godhead are manifest. This was all explained to Sanātana Gosvāmī by Lord Caitanya. Lord Caitanya told him that since there is really no end to describing the system of devotional service with attachment, He is simply trying to offer a sampling.

Lord Caitanya then described the ultimate goal of devotional service, which is meant for one who wants to attain perfection. When one's attachment to Kṛṣṇa becomes very deep, one has attained the condition called love of Godhead. The devotee who attains such a state of existence is said to be in his permanent situation. In this regard, Kavirāja Gosvāmī offers his respectful obeisances to Lord Caitanya for His sublime teachings of love of Godhead. As stated in the *Caitanya-caritāmṛta* (*Madhya* 23.1): "O Supreme Personality of Godhead, who but You has ever awarded such pure devotional service? O most magnanimous incarnation of the Personality of Godhead, I offer my respectful obeisances to this incarnation, known as Gaurakṛṣṇa."

In the *Bhakti-rasāmṛta-sindhu* (1.3.1), love of Godhead is compared to sunshine, and this shining makes the devotee's heart more and more lovely. The heart of such a devotee is situated in a transcendental position, beyond even the material mode of goodness. As the devotee's heart becomes increasingly sterilized by the sunshine of love, he attains a state called *bhāva*. This is the description of *bhāva* given by Rūpa Gosvāmī. *Bhāva* is the permanent characteristic of the living entity, and the crucial point of progress for *bhāva* is called the marginal state of love of Godhead. When the *bhāva* state becomes deeper and deeper, learned devotees call it love of Godhead. As stated in the *Nārada-pañcarātra:*

ananya-mamatā viṣṇau mamatā prema-saṅgatā
bhaktir ity ucyate bhīṣma- prahlādoddhava-nāradaiḥ

"When one is firmly convinced that Viṣṇu is the only object of love and worship and that there is no one else—not even a demigod—worthy of receiving devotional service, one is said to feel intimacy in his loving relationship with God. This is the conclusion of such personalities as Bhīṣma, Prahlāda, Uddhava and Nārada."

If due to some righteous activities which provoke devotional service one acquires some faith, one takes shelter of the good association of pure devotees and is influenced by their service attitude. Then he develops attachment for hearing and chanting. By developing hearing and chanting, one can advance further and further in regulative devotional service to the Supreme Lord. As one so advances, his misgivings about devotional service and his attraction to the material world proportionately diminish. By advancing in hearing and chanting, a devotee becomes more firmly fixed in his faith. Gradually he develops a taste for devotional service, and that taste gradually develops into attachment for Kṛṣṇa. When that attachment becomes pure, it exhibits the two characteristics of *bhāva* (emotion) and *rati* (affection). When *rati* increases, it is called love of Godhead. Love of Godhead is the ultimate goal of human life.

This process is summarized by Rūpa Gosvāmī in the *Bhakti-rasāmṛta-sindhu* (1.4.15–16): "The first thing required is faith. Due to faith a person associates with pure devotees, and by such association he develops devotional service. As devotional service develops, his misgivings diminish. Then he is situated in firm conviction, and from that conviction he develops a taste for devotional service and advances to the stage of attachment for Kṛṣṇa, whereby he follows the regulative principles of devotional service spontaneously. After that point he makes still further progress and attains the state called *bhāva,* which is permanent. Such love of God becomes deeper and deeper, until it reaches the highest stage of love of Godhead."

In Sanskrit this highest stage is called *prema. Prema* can be defined as love of God without any expectation of exchange or return. Actually the words *prema* and love are not synonymous, yet one can still say that *prema* is the highest stage of love. One who has attained *prema* is the most perfect human being. *Śrīmad-Bhāgavatam* 3.25.25 confirms this statement: Only by the association of pure devotees can a person develop a taste for Kṛṣṇa consciousness, and when he tries to apply Kṛṣṇa consciousness in his life, he can achieve everything up to the stage of *bhāva* and *prema.*

Lord Caitanya next described the symptoms of a person who has developed from faith to the stage of *bhāva.* Such a person is never agitated, even if there are causes for agitation. Nor does he waste his time, not even a moment: he is always anxious to do something for Kṛṣṇa. Even if he has no engagement, he will find some work to do for Kṛṣṇa's satisfaction. Nor does such a person like anything which is not connected with Kṛṣṇa. Although he is situated in the best position, he does not hanker after praise. He is confident in his work—he is never under the impression that he is not making progress toward the supreme goal of life, going back to Godhead. Since he is fully convinced of his progress, he is always very busy achieving the highest goal. He is very much attached to gratifying the Lord and in chanting or hearing about the Lord, and he is always attached to describing the transcendental qualities of the Lord. He also wants to live in holy places like Mathurā, Vṛndāvana or Dvārakā. All these characteristics are visible in one who has developed to the stage of *bhāva*.

King Parīkṣit affords a good example of *bhāva*. When sitting on the bank of the Ganges waiting to meet his death due to the curse of a *brāhmaṇa* boy, he said: "All the *brāhmaṇas* present here, as well as Mother Ganges, should know that I am a soul completely surrendered to Kṛṣṇa. I do not mind if I am immediately bitten by the snake sent by the *brāhmaṇa* boy. Let the snake bite me as it likes. I shall be pleased if all of you present here will go on chanting the message of Kṛṣṇa." Such a devotee is always anxious to see that his time is not wasted in anything which is not connected with Kṛṣṇa. Consequently he does not like the benefits derived from fruitive activity, yogic meditation or the cultivation of knowledge. He is simply attached to words favorably related to Kṛṣṇa. Such pure devotees of the Supreme Lord always pray to Him with tears in their eyes, their minds always recollect His activities, and their bodies always offer Him obeisances. Thus they are satisfied. Any devotee who renders such devotional service dedicates his life and body for the purpose of the Lord.

King Bharata (after whom India is called Bhārata-varṣa) was also a pure devotee, and at an early age he left his household life, his beautiful devoted wife, his sons, friends and kingdom just as if they were stool. This is typical of a person who has developed *bhāva* in the course of his devotional service. Such a devotee always thinks of himself as the most wretched, and his only satisfaction is in thinking that some day or other Kṛṣṇa will be kind enough to favor him by engaging him in devotional service. In the *Padma Purāṇa* another instance of pure devotion is found. There it is recorded that King Bhagīratha, although the most elevated of human beings, was begging from door to door and was even praying to the *caṇḍālas*, the lowest members of human society.

Śrī Sanātana Gosvāmī later composed this verse:

na premā śravaṇādi-bhaktir api vā yogo 'tha vā vaiṣṇavo
jñānaṁ vā śubha-karma vā kiyad aho saj-jātir apy asti vā
hīnārthādhika-sādhake tvayi tathāpy acchedya-mūlā satī
he gopī-jana-vallabha vyathayate hā hā mad-āśaiva mām

"I am poor in love of Godhead, and I have no qualification for hearing about devotional service. Nor do I have any understanding of the science of devotional service, nor any cultivation of knowledge, nor any righteous activities to my credit. Nor am I born in a high family. Nonetheless, O darling of the damsels of Vraja, I still maintain a hope of achieving You, and this hope is always disturbing me." A devotee who is touched deeply by such a strong desire always chants Hare Kṛṣṇa, Hare Kṛṣṇa, Kṛṣṇa Kṛṣṇa, Hare Hare/ Hare Rāma, Hare Rāma, Rāma Rāma, Hare Hare.

In this regard, the following verse by Bilvamaṅgala appears in the *Kṛṣṇa-karṇāmṛta* (32):

tvac chaiśavaṁ tri-bhuvanādbhutam ity avehi
mac-cāpalaṁ ca tava vā mama vādhigamyam
tat kiṁ karomi viralaṁ muralī-vilāsi
mugdhaṁ mukhāmbujam udīkṣitum īkṣaṇābhyām

"O Kṛṣṇa, O flute-player, the beauty of Your boyhood activities is very wonderful in this world. You know the agitation of my mind, and I know what You are. No one knows how confidential our relationship is. Although my eyes are anxious to see Your face, I cannot see You. Please let me know what to do." A similar passage appears in the *Bhakti-rasāmṛta-sindhu* (1.3.38) in which Rūpa Gosvāmī states:

rodana-bindu-maranda-syandi-dṛg-indīvarādya govinda
tava madhura-svara-kaṇṭhī gāyati nāmāvalīṁ bālā

"O Govinda! This young girl with tears in Her eyes is crying in a sweet voice, chanting Your glories." Such pure devotees are always anxious to describe the glories of Kṛṣṇa and to live in a place where He exhibited His pastimes. A similar verse appears, again, in the *Kṛṣṇa-karṇāmṛta* (92): "The body of Kṛṣṇa is so nice, and His face is so beautiful. Everything about Him is simply sweet and fragrant." And in the *Bhakti-rasāmṛta-sindhu* (1.2.156): "O lotus-eyed one, when will I be able to always chant Your holy name, and being inspired by that chanting, when will I be able to dance on the banks of the Yamunā?"

In this way Lord Caitanya described to Sanātana Gosvāmī the symptoms of the *bhāva* stage of devotional service.

Lord Caitanya next described the symptoms of actual love for Kṛṣṇa. He said that no one can understand the words, activities or symptoms of a person who has developed love of Kṛṣṇa. Even if one is very learned, it is very difficult to understand a pure devotee in the stage of love of God. This is confirmed in the *Bhakti-rasāmṛta-sindhu.*

When a person engaged in devotional service in love of God sings the glories of the Supreme Lord, his heart melts. Because the Lord is very dear to him, when he glorifies the Lord's name, fame and so on, he becomes almost like an insane man, and in that condition he sometimes laughs, sometimes cries and sometimes dances. He continues in this way without even considering his situation. By gradually developing his love of Godhead, he increases his affection, his emotion and his ecstasy. The culmination of such attachment is *mahābhāva,* the highest stage of devotional love. It may be likened to rock candy, which is the most concentrated form of sugar. As it is concentrated, sugar cane juice goes through different stages—molasses, sugar, sugar candy—but the final and most palatable state is rock candy. Similarly, love of Godhead can gradually develop in such a way that transcendental pleasure is increased to the highest stage for the real devotee.

CHAPTER 14

The Ecstasy of the Lord and His Devotees

The symptoms of highly developed devotional service for Kṛṣṇa, which are exhibited by the pure devotees, are sometimes imitated by those who are not actually pure devotees. This is described in the *Bhakti-rasāmṛta-sindhu*. Without devotional service to Kṛṣṇa, such symptoms are artificial, not actual. Sometimes those who are not conversant with the science of devotional service are captivated by the exhibition of such symptoms, but learned devotees know that they are simply imitation.

According to the various divisions and gradations of devotees, permanent devotional attitudes can be divided into five categories: (1) peacefulness, (2) service to Kṛṣṇa, (3) friendship with Kṛṣṇa, (4) parental affection toward Kṛṣṇa, and (5) conjugal love for Kṛṣṇa. Each division has its own taste and relish, and a devotee situated in a particular division is happy in that position. Characteristic symptoms exhibited by a pure devotee are generally laughing and crying; when emotions are favorable, a pure devotee laughs, and when emotions are not favorable, he cries.

Situated above these two emotions is permanent love, which is called *sthāyi-bhāva*. In other words, when one's attachment to Kṛṣṇa is permanent, one is situated in *sthāyi-bhāva*. That permanent loving attitude is sometimes mixed with different kinds of taste, called *vibhāva, anubhāva* and *vyabhicārī*. *Vibhāva* is a particular taste or attachment for Kṛṣṇa, and it can be divided into two further categories—*ālambana* and *uddīpana*. In the *Agni Purāṇa* and other authoritative scriptures, that which increases one's love for Kṛṣṇa is said to be *vibhāva,* and when Kṛṣṇa is the objective, *vibhāva* is described as *ālambana*. *Uddīpanas* include Kṛṣṇa's transcendental qualities, His activities, His beautiful smiling face and the aroma of His body, the sounds of His flute, ankle bells, and conch shell, the marks on the soles of His feet, His dwelling place and His paraphernalia of devotional service (such as *tulasī* leaves, devotees, ceremonial performances and Ekādaśī). *Anubhāva* occurs when feelings and emotions within oneself are exhibited. In the attitude of *anubhāva,* one dances and sometimes falls down, sometimes sings loudly, shows convulsions, yawns and sometimes breathes very heavily—all without concern for circumstances.

The external features exhibited on the bodies of devotees are called *udbhāsvara*. The *vyabhicārī* symptoms are thirty-three in number, and they primarily involve words uttered by the devotee and various bodily features. Different bodily features—such as dancing, trembling and laughing—sometimes mix with the *vyabhicārī* symptoms, which are also called *sañcārī*. When *bhāva, anubhāva* and *vyabhicārī* symptoms are combined, they make the devotee dive into the ocean of immortality. That ocean is called the *bhakti-rasāmṛta-sindhu,* the ocean of the pure nectar of devotional service, and one who is merged in that ocean is always rapt in transcendental pleasure on the waves and sounds of that ocean.

The particular *rasas* (flavors or tastes) of the devotees who merge into that ocean of *bhakti-rasāmṛta* are known as neutrality, servitorship, friendship, parenthood and conjugal love. Conjugal love is very prominent, and it is symptomized by the devotee's decorating his body to attract Kṛṣṇa. The flavor of servitorship increases to include affection, anger, fraternity and attachment. The flavor of friendship increases to include affection, anger, fraternity, attachment and devotion, and in parenthood the attachment also increases to include affection, anger, fraternity, attachment, and devotion. There are also special flavors experienced in friendship with the

Lord Caitanya faints in the temple of Lord Jagannātha.

Supreme Lord, and these are manifested by friends such as Subala, whose devotion increases up to the point of *bhāva*. The different *rasas* are also divided into two kinds of ecstasy, called *yoga* and *viyoga*, or meeting and separation. In the *rasas* of friendship and parenthood, the feelings of meeting and separation are various.

The situations known as *rūḍha* (advanced) and *adhirūḍha* (highly advanced) are possible only in the *rasa* of conjugal love. Conjugal love exhibited by the queens at Dvārakā is called *rūḍha*, and conjugal love exhibited at Vṛndāvana by the damsels of Vraja is called *adhirūḍha*. The highest perfections of *adhirūḍha* affection in conjugal love involve meeting (*mādana*) and separation (*mohana*). In the ecstasy of *mādana* there is kissing, and in the ecstasy of *mohana* there are *udghūrṇā* (unsteadiness) and *citra-jalpa* (varieties of mad emotional talks). There are ten varieties of *citra-jalpa*, examples of which are given in *Śrīmad-Bhāgavatam* (10.47.12–21), in a portion known as the *Bhramara-gītā*. *Udghūrṇā* is also a symptom of transcendental insanity, in which one thinks that he himself has become the Supreme Personality of Godhead. In such an ecstasy, he imitates the symptoms of Kṛṣṇa in different ways.

The two divisions of ecstasies experienced in the relationship of conjugal love are *sambhoga* (meeting) and *vipralambha* (separation). On the *sambhoga* platform the ecstasies are unlimited, and on the *vipralambha* platform they are four in number. The ecstasy exhibited before the lover and beloved meet, the ecstasy experienced between them after meeting, the state of mind experienced by not meeting, and the state of mind experienced after meeting but fearing separation are called *vipralambha*. That *vipralambha* serves as a nourishing element for future meetings. When the lover and beloved meet all of a sudden and embrace one another, they feel an ecstasy of happiness, and the state of mind they experience in that ecstasy is called *sambhoga*. According to the situation, *sambhoga* ecstasy is also known by four names: (1) *saṅkṣipta*, (2) *saṅkīrṇa*, (3) *sampanna* or (4) *samṛddhimān*. Such symptoms are also visible during dreams.

The mental state experienced before meeting is called *pūrva-rāga*. The obstacles that impede the meeting between the lover and beloved are called *māna*, or anger. When the lover and beloved are separated, the mental state experienced is called *pravāsa*. Feelings of separation which are present under certain conditions even when the lovers meet are called love anxieties (*prema-vaicittya*). Such love anxieties are exhibited in *Śrīmad-Bhāgavatam* (10.90.15) by Kṛṣṇa's queens, who kept awake nights and watched Him sleep. Afraid of being separated from Kṛṣṇa, they talked among themselves about how they had been affected by His beautiful eyes and smile.

The supreme lover is Kṛṣṇa in Vṛndāvana, and the supreme beloved is Rādhārāṇī. Kṛṣṇa has sixty-four main qualities, and His devotee takes transcendental pleasure in hearing of them. As explained in the *Bhakti-rasāmṛta-sindhu,* the characteristics are as follows: (1) His body is well constructed; (2) His body is full of auspicious symptoms; (3) His body is beautiful; (4) He is very glorious; (5) He is very strong; (6) He always looks like a boy of sixteen; (7) He is well versed in various languages; (8) He is truthful; (9) He is decorated with pleasing words; (10) He is expert in speaking; (11) He is very learned; (12) He is very intelligent; (13) He is influential; (14) He is joyful; (15) He is cunning; (16) He is expert; (17) He is grateful; (18) He is firmly convinced; (19) He knows how to deal with different circumstances; (20) He is always conversant with scriptural injunctions; (21) He is clean; (22) He is controlled by His devotees; (23) He is steady; (24) He is self-controlled; (25) He is forgiving; (26) He is grave; (27) He is self-satisfied; (28) He is fair in His dealings; (29) He is magnanimous; (30) He is religious; (31) He is a great hero; (32) He is merciful; (33) He is respectful; (34) He is competent; (35) He is gentle; (36) He is modest; (37) He is the protector of the souls surrendered unto Him; (38) He is the deliverer; (39) He is the friend of the devotees; (40) He is submissive to love; (41) He is all-auspicious; (42) He is most powerful; (43) He is famous; (44) He is devoted to all living entities; (45) He is worshipable by everyone; (46) He is very attractive to all women; (47) He is partial to His devotees; (48) He is full of all opulence; (49) He is the supreme controller; (50) He possesses all honor.

These fifty qualities are fragmentally present in every living entity. When a human being is completely spiritually free and situated in his original condition, all these qualities can be perceived in him in minute quantity. In Kṛṣṇa, however, they exist in totality. There are five other transcendental qualities (mentioned below), which can be seen in Viṣṇu, the Supreme Lord, and partially in Lord Śiva also, but they are not visible in ordinary living entities. These qualities are as follows: (1) He is always situated in His original condition; (2) He is omniscient; (3) He is evergreen or always fresh; (4) He is eternally blissful; (5) He is the master of all perfection. Besides these five transcendental characteristics, there are five others which can be seen in the spiritual sky, especially in the Vaikuṇṭha planets, where Nārāyaṇa is the predominating Deity. These are: (1) He has inconceivable potencies; (2) He is able to sustain innumerable universes; (3) He is the seed of all incarnations; (4) He grants the highest perfection to those enemies whom He kills; (5) He is attractive to self-realized persons.

The above-mentioned sixty qualities are visible in Nārāyaṇa. But Kṛṣṇa has four special qualities, which are: (1) He is able to manifest wonderful pastimes; (2) He is expert at transcendental flute-playing; (3) He is surrounded by loving devotees; (4) He possesses unparalleled personal beauty.

Thus Kṛṣṇa has sixty-four transcendental qualities. Śrīmatī Rādhārāṇī has twenty-five transcendental qualities, with which She can control even Kṛṣṇa. Her transcendental qualities are as follows: (1) She is sweetness personified; (2) She is a fresh young girl; (3) Her eyes are always moving; (4) She is always brightly smiling; (5) She possesses all auspicious marks on Her body; (6) She can agitate Kṛṣṇa by the aroma of Her person; (7) She is expert in the art of singing; (8) She speaks very nicely and sweetly; (9) She is expert in presenting feminine attractions; (10) She is modest and gentle; (11) She is always very merciful; (12) She is transcendentally cunning; (13) She knows how to dress nicely; (14) She is always shy; (15) She is always respectful; (16) She is always patient; (17) She is very grave; (18) She is enjoyed by Kṛṣṇa; (19) She is always situated on the highest devotional platform; (20) She is the abode of love of the residents of Gokula; (21) She can give shelter to all kinds of devotees; (22) She is always affectionate to superiors and inferiors; (23) She is always obliged by the dealings of Her associates, (24) She is the greatest among Kṛṣṇa's girlfriends; (25) She always keeps Kṛṣṇa under Her control.

Thus Kṛṣṇa and Rādhārāṇī are both transcendentally qualified, and They attract one another. But Rādhārāṇī's transcendental attractiveness is greater than Kṛṣṇa's, for Her attractiveness is the transcendental taste in conjugal love. Similarly, there are transcendental tastes in servitorship, friendship and other relationships with Kṛṣṇa. These can be described with reference to the context of the *Bhakti-rasāmṛta-sindhu*.

Persons who have been thoroughly cleansed by devotional service and are always joyful, being situated in elevated consciousness, who are very much attached to studying *Śrīmad-Bhāgavatam*, who are always cheerful in the association of devotees, who have accepted the lotus feet of Kṛṣṇa as the ultimate shelter of their lives, and who are pleased to perform all details of devotional service—such devotees have in their pure hearts the transcendental ecstasy of attachment, which has been developed through old and new reformatory practices. That ecstatic state of being, enriched with love of Kṛṣṇa and transcendental experience, gradually develops into the mature bliss of spiritual life. Tasting such spiritual bliss is not possible for those who are not situated in Kṛṣṇa consciousness and devotional service. This fact is further corroborated in the *Bhakti-rasāmṛta-sindhu* (2.5.131), where it is said: "It is very difficult for the nondevotee to understand the taste of devotional service. Only one who has completely taken shelter of the lotus feet of Kṛṣṇa and whose life is merged in the ocean of devotional service can understand this transcendental pleasure."

Lord Caitanya thus briefly explained the transcendental situation, the spiritual relish of life, which He called the fifth stage of perfection. The first stage of perfection is to become a religious man in the ordinary sense, as known in the material world, the second stage of perfection is to become materially rich, the third stage of perfection is the attainment of complete sense enjoyment, and the fourth stage of perfection is liberation. But above liberation are those in the fifth stage of perfection, those who are established in Kṛṣṇa consciousness, or devotional service to the Lord. Already liberated, devotees who reach the highest perfection of devotional service in Kṛṣṇa consciousness experience the taste of the ecstasy of spiritual relish.

The Lord then told Sanātana Gosvāmī that He had previously taught his younger brother, Rūpa Gosvāmī, at Prayāga (Allahabad). The Lord assured Sanātana Gosvāmī that He had empowered Rūpa Gosvāmī to spread the knowledge He had given him. The Lord then similarly ordered Sanātana Gosvāmī to write books on the transcendental loving service of Lord Kṛṣṇa, and He authorized him to excavate the different sites of Kṛṣṇa's pastimes in the district of Mathurā. Sanātana Gosvāmī was also advised to construct temples in Vṛndāvana and to write books on the principles of Vaiṣṇavism, as authorized by Lord Caitanya Himself. Sanātana Gosvāmī executed all these desires of the Lord—he constructed the temple of Madana-mohana at Vṛndāvana, and he wrote books on the principles of devotional service, such as the *Hari-bhakti-vilāsa.*

Lord Caitanya further taught Sanātana Gosvāmī how one can live in the material world while being in a complete relationship with Kṛṣṇa, and He also taught him that there is no necessity for dry renunciation. The purport of these instructions is that in the present age there are many persons who accept the renounced order of life (*sannyāsa*) but who are not spiritually advanced. Lord Caitanya did not approve of such *sannyāsa,* explaining that it is wrong to accept *sannyāsa* without having perfect knowledge of Kṛṣṇa consciousness. Actually, we find that there are many so-called *sannyāsīs* whose actions are below those of ordinary men but who pass themselves off as being in the renounced order of life. Lord Caitanya Mahāprabhu did not accept such hypocrisy, and He instructed Sanātana Gosvāmī to elaborate on this subject in his different books.

The perfectional stage of spiritual life, which one can experience even while being in the material world, is described by Lord Kṛṣṇa in the Twelfth Chapter of the *Bhagavad-gītā*. There it is said that one who is not envious of any living entity, who is friendly, merciful and detached from material possessions, who is situated in his pure identity, without any false conception of the body as the self, who is equipoised in both happiness and distress, who is forgiving, always satisfied, always engaged in devotional service, and always surrendered unto the Supreme Lord with his body and mind—such a devotee is very dear to Kṛṣṇa. A devotee who never gives trouble to any living entity, either by his body or his mind, who is never affected by material distress and happiness, and who is never angry or pleased with anything material is very dear to the Supreme Lord. He who is never dependent on anyone in this world, who is completely surrendered to the Supreme Lord, who is purified, expert, neutral, free of pain, and aloof from any material endeavor which requires too much attention—such a devotee is also very dear to Lord Kṛṣṇa. A person who is never subjected to material happiness or hatred, lamentation or ambition, who is aloof from all materially auspicious and inauspicious activities, and who is fully devoted in Kṛṣṇa consciousness—such a devotee is very dear to Lord Kṛṣṇa. A devotee who treats equally a so-called enemy and a so-called friend in the material world, who is not disturbed by heat or cold, who is without any attachment, who is equally situated when respected or insulted, who is always grave, satisfied in any condition of life, without any fixed residence, and fixed in Kṛṣṇa consciousness—such a devotee is very dear to Lord Kṛṣṇa. Even if one is not situated in the transcendental position, still, if he approves the transcendental life described here, he also becomes very dear to Kṛṣṇa.

In *Śrīmad-Bhāgavatam* (2.2.5) there is a very nice verse stating that a devotee should always remain dependent on the mercy of the Supreme Lord and that as far as his material necessities are concerned, he should be satisfied with whatever is obtained without endeavor. In this regard, Śukadeva Gosvāmī advised that a devotee should never approach a materialistic person for any kind of help. As far as one's bodily necessities are concerned, one can pick up torn clothing from the street, take fruits offered by trees, drink water from flowing rivers, and live in a mountain cave constructed by nature herself. Even if one is unable to do all these things, he should nonetheless completely depend on the Supreme Lord, understanding that since the Lord provides everyone with food and shelter, He will never fail to care for His devotees who are fully surrendered unto Him. In any case, the devotee is always protected, and therefore he should not be at all anxious for his maintenance.

Sanātana Gosvāmī thus inquired into all phases of devotional service, or Kṛṣṇa consciousness, and Lord Caitanya taught him most confidentially from authoritative scriptures like *Śrīmad-Bhāgavatam*. The Lord also referred to the Vedic literature known as *Hari-vaṁśa,* which gives information about the transcendental abode of Kṛṣṇa. This information was disclosed by Indra when he offered his prayers after being defeated upon challenging the potency of Kṛṣṇa. In the *Hari-vaṁśa* it is stated that although birds and airplanes can fly high in the sky above the earth, they cannot reach the higher planetary systems. The higher planetary systems extend upward from the sun planet, which is situated in the middle of the universe. Above the sun are planetary systems where persons who are elevated by great austerities and penances are situated. The whole material universe is called Devī-dhāma, and above it is Śiva-dhāma, where Lord Śiva and his wife Pārvatī eternally reside. Above that planetary system is the spiritual sky, where innumerable spiritual planets, known as Vaikuṇṭhas, are situated. And above these Vaikuṇṭha planets is Kṛṣṇa's planet, known as Goloka Vṛndāvana. The word *goloka* means "planet of the cows." Because Kṛṣṇa is very fond of cows, His abode is known as Goloka. Goloka Vṛndāvana is larger than all the material and spiritual planets put together.

In his prayers in the *Hari-vaṁśa,* Indra admitted that he could not understand the situation of Goloka, even by asking Brahmā. Devotees of the Nārāyaṇa expansion of Kṛṣṇa attain the Vaikuṇṭha planets, but it is very difficult to reach the Goloka planet. Indeed, that planet can be reached only by devotees of Lord Caitanya or Lord Śrī Kṛṣṇa. Indra then said to Lord Kṛṣṇa: "You have descended from that Goloka planet in the spiritual world, and the disturbance I created was all due to my foolishness." Therefore Indra begged Lord Kṛṣṇa to excuse him.

The last phase of the pastimes of Lord Kṛṣṇa is described in *Śrīmad-Bhāgavatam* as *mauṣala-līlā*. This series of pastimes includes Kṛṣṇa's mysterious disappearance from the material world. In that pastime the Lord played the part of being killed by a hunter. There are many improper explanations of scriptural passages describing the last portion of Lord Kṛṣṇa's pastimes (such as the explanation of descriptions of Kṛṣṇa as the incarnation of a hair), but Lord Caitanya properly explained these passages and gave them the right interpretation. As far as Kṛṣṇa being the incarnation of a hair is concerned, this is mentioned in *Śrīmad-Bhāgavatam,* the *Viṣṇu Purāṇa* and the *Mahābhārata.* In the *Mahābhārata* it is stated that Lord Viṣṇu snatched a gray hair and a black hair from His head and that these two hairs entered into the wombs of two queens of the Yadu dynasty, namely Rohiṇī and Devakī. It is also stated there that Lord Kṛṣṇa descends to the material world in order to vanquish all the demons. Some say that Kṛṣṇa is the incarnation of Viṣṇu who lies in the ocean of milk within this universe. Śrīla Rūpa Gosvāmī, in his *Laghu-bhāgavatāmṛta,* along with his commentator, Śrī Baladeva Vidyābhūṣaṇa, have discussed these points fully and have established the exact truth. Śrī Jīva Gosvāmī also discusses these points in the *Kṛṣṇa-sandarbha.*

When Lord Caitanya finished His instructions to Śrī Sanātana Gosvāmī, Sanātana, being empowered and enlightened, was so transcendentally pleased that he at once fell at the feet of Lord Caitanya and said, "I was born in a very low family, and I have always associated with lowly people; therefore I am the lowest of sinners. Yet You are so kind that You have taught me lessons which are not even understood by Lord Brahmā, the greatest being in this universe. By Your grace I have appreciated the conclusions which You have taught me, but I am so low that I cannot even touch a drop of the ocean of Your instructions. Thus if You want me, who am nothing but a lame man, to dance, then please give me Your benediction by placing Your feet on my head."

Thus Sanātana Gosvāmī prayed for the Lord's confirmation that His teachings would actually evolve in his heart by His grace. Otherwise Sanātana knew that there was no possibility of his being able to describe the Lord's teachings. The purport of this is that the *ācāryas* (spiritual masters) are authorized by higher authorities. Instruction alone cannot make one an expert. Unless one is blessed by the spiritual master, or *ācārya,* such teachings cannot become fully manifested. Therefore one should seek the mercy of the spiritual master so that his instructions can develop within oneself. After receiving the prayers of Sanātana Gosvāmī, Lord Caitanya placed His feet on Sanātana's head and gave him the benediction that all the Lord's instructions would fully develop within him.

Thus the Lord described the ultimate stage of love of Godhead. Lord Caitanya said that such a description cannot be given very elaborately but that He had informed Sanātana as far as possible. The author of *Śrī Caitanya-caritāmṛta* concludes this chapter by writing that anyone who attentively hears these instructions of Lord Caitanya to Sanātana Gosvāmī very soon becomes situated in Kṛṣṇa consciousness and engages in pure devotional service to the Lord.

CHAPTER 15

Explanation of the Ātmārāma Verse in Śrīmad-Bhāgavatam

Lord Caitanya next explained to Sanātana Gosvāmī a very famous verse known as the *ātmārāma* verse (*Śrīmad-Bhāgavatam* 1.7.10):

ātmārāmāś ca munayo nirgranthā apy urukrame
kurvanty ahaitukīṁ bhaktim ittham-bhūta-guṇo hariḥ

The general meaning of this verse is that those who are liberated souls and are fully satisfied within themselves will eventually become devotees of the Lord. This especially describes the impersonalists, who have no information of the Supreme Personality of Godhead. They try to remain satisfied with the impersonal Brahman, but Kṛṣṇa is so attractive and so strong that He attracts their minds. This is the purport of this verse.

Lord Caitanya had previously explained this verse to the great Vedāntist Sārvabhauma Bhaṭṭācārya. Sanātana Gosvāmī, after taking lessons from Lord Caitanya, referred to this incident and prayed to the Lord to again explain the *ātmārāma* verse. Śrīla Kṛṣṇadāsa Kavirāja, the author of the *Caitanya-caritāmṛta*, appreciating the Lord's explanation of the *ātmārāma* verse, has glorified Lord Caitanya in a prayer.

Sanātana Gosvāmī fell flat at the feet of Lord Caitanya and requested Him to explain the verse as He had formerly explained it to Sārvabhauma Bhaṭṭācārya. Sanātana expressed his eagerness to hear the same explanation in order that he might be enlightened. When the Lord was thus requested by Sanātana, He replied: "I do not understand why Sārvabhauma Bhaṭṭācārya so much appreciated My explanation. As far as I am concerned, I don't even remember what I said to him. But because you are asking this of Me, with the help of your association I shall try to explain whatever I can remember." Thus the speaker and the audience are very intimately connected: the speaker is enlightened by the presence of the audience. The speaker, or master, can speak very nicely on transcendental subject matters before an understanding audience; therefore Lord Caitanya said that He did not know how to explain the Sanskrit verse but that since He was in the association of Sanātana He would try to explain it.

The Lord then went on to point out that there are eleven words in the *ātmārāma* verse: (1) *ātmārāmāḥ,* (2) *ca,* (3) *munayaḥ,* (4) *nirgranthāḥ,* (5) *api,* (6) *urukrame,* (7) *kurvanti,* (8) *ahaitukīm,* (9) *bhaktim,* (10) *ittham-bhūta-guṇaḥ* and (11) *hariḥ.* The Lord then began to explain each and every one of these words. As far as the word *ātmārāma* is concerned, the Lord explained that the word *ātmā* means (1) the Supreme Absolute Truth, (2) the body, (3) the mind, (4) endeavor, (5) intelligence, (6) conviction and (7) nature. The word *ārāma* means enjoyer; therefore anyone who takes pleasure in the cultivation of the knowledge of these seven items is known as an *ātmārāma.* (Later the Lord would describe the different kinds of *ātmārāmas,* or transcendentalists.) As for the word *munayaḥ,* or *muni,* those who are great thinkers are called *munis.* Sometimes the word *muni* is also applied to a person who is very grave. Great sages, great austere persons, great mystics and learned scholars are also called *munis.*

The next word, *nirgrantha,* indicates freedom from the bondage of illusion. *Nirgrantha* also means "one who has no connection with scriptural injunctions." *Grantha* means revealed scriptures, and *nir* is an affix which is used to mean "no connection," "constructing," and also "prohibiting." There are many instructions for spiritual realization, and persons who have no connection with such scriptural injunctions are known as *nirgrantha*. There are many people who are foolish, low-born and misbehaved and who have no entrance into the revealed scriptures and injunctions, and therefore they are called *nirgrantha*. Because the word *grantha* can also mean "collected riches," the word *nirgrantha* also indicates a poor man, bereft of all riches, who is attempting to collect riches.

The word *urukrama* is used to indicate a highly powerful person. Since the word *krama* is used to indicate the act of stepping, the word *urukrama* also indicates one who can step forward very far. The greatest step forward was taken by Lord Vāmanadeva, who covered the whole universe in two steps. Thus the Supreme Lord Vāmanadeva is also known as Lord Urukrama. This extraordinary feature of Lord Vāmanadeva is explained in *Śrīmad-Bhāgavatam* (2.7.40):

viṣṇor nu vīrya-gaṇanāṁ katamo 'rhatīha
yaḥ pārthivāny api kavir vimame rajāṁsi
caskambha yaḥ sva-raṁhasāskhalatā tri-pṛṣṭhaṁ
yasmāt tri-sāmya-sadanād uru-kampayānam

"No one can estimate the inconceivable potencies of Lord Viṣṇu. Even if one could count the number of atomic combinations in this material world, he still could not count the different energies of the Supreme Lord. As Vāmanadeva, the Lord was so powerful that simply by stepping forward He covered the whole universe from Brahmaloka down to Pātālaloka."

The inconceivable energies of the Lord are spread throughout the creation. He is all-pervading, and by His energy He sustains all planetary systems, yet through His pleasure potency He remains situated in His personal abode, known as Goloka. By the expansion of His opulence, He is present in all the Vaikuṇṭha planets as Nārāyaṇa. By expanding His material energy, He creates innumerable universes with innumerable planets within them. Thus no one can estimate the wonderful activities of the Supreme Lord, and therefore the Supreme Lord is known as Urukrama, the wonderful actor. In the *Viśva-prakāśa* dictionary, the word *krama* is defined as "an expert display of energies," as well as "stepping forward very quickly."

The word *kurvanti* means "working for others." There is another word, similar to this, which is used when one's activities are done for one's personal sense gratification, but the word *kurvanti* is used when activities are performed for the satisfaction of the Supreme. Thus in this verse the word can only indicate the rendering of transcendental service to the Lord.

The word *hetu* means "reason" or "cause." Generally people are engaged in transcendental activities for three reasons: some want material happiness, some want mystic perfection, and some want liberation from material bondage. As far as material enjoyment is concerned, there are so many varieties that no one can enumerate them. As far as perfections in mystic power are concerned, there are eighteen, and as far as types of liberation from material bondage are concerned, there are five. The state of being where all these varieties of enjoyment are conspicuous by their absence is called *ahaitukī*. The *ahaitukī* qualification is especially mentioned because by the *ahaitukī* service of the Lord, one can achieve the favor of the Lord.

The word *bhakti* can be used in ten different ways. One of these is *sādhana-bhakti,* or occupational devotional service. The other nine are varieties of *prema-bhakti,* love of Godhead. Those who are situated in the neutral position attain perfection up to love of Godhead. Similarly, those who are situated in the relationship of master and servant attain love of Godhead to the stage of attachment. Those who are related in friendship attain love of God to the point of fraternity. Those who are in love with God as His parents are elevated to the point of transcendental emotion. But only those who are related with the Supreme in conjugal love can experience the highest of ecstasies. These are some of the different meanings for the word *bhakti.*

The Lord next explained the different meanings of *ittham-bhūta-guṇa. Ittham-bhūta* indicates full transcendental pleasure, before which even the transcendental pleasure known as *brahmānanda* becomes like straw. In the *Hari-bhakti-sudhodaya* (14.36), a devotee says:

tvat-sākṣāt-karaṇāhlāda- viśuddhābdhi-sthitasya me
sukhāni goṣpadāyante brāhmāṇy api jagad-guro

"My Lord, O Supreme, simply by understanding You or seeing You, we derive a pleasure so great that the pleasure of *brahmānanda* becomes insignificant." In other words, the pleasure derived by understanding Kṛṣṇa as He is—as the all-attractive reservoir of all pleasures and the reservoir of all pleasure-giving tastes with all transcendental qualifications—attracts one to become His devotee. By virtue of such attraction, one can give up fruitive activities and all endeavors for liberation and can even abandon the intense desire to achieve mystic power through success in *yoga*. The attractive power of Kṛṣṇa is so intense that one loses respect for all other means of self-realization and simply surrenders unto the Supreme Personality of Godhead.

Next the Lord explained the word *guṇa*. In the *ātmārāma* verse *guṇa* indicates the unlimited transcendental qualities of Kṛṣṇa, primarily those pertaining to His *sac-cid-ānanda* form. In His transcendental blissful knowledge and eternity, He is fully perfect, and His perfection is increased when He is controlled by the attention of His devotee. God is so kind and merciful that He gives Himself in exchange for the devotional service of the devotee. His transcendental qualities are such that His perfect beauty, His perfect reciprocation of love between Himself and His devotees, and the fragrance of His transcendental qualities attract different kinds of transcendentalists and liberated souls. For example, Kṛṣṇa attracted the mind of Sanaka and the other Kumāras simply by the aroma emanating from the flowers offered to Him, and He attracted the mind of Śukadeva Gosvāmī by His transcendental pastimes. The minds of the damsels of Vṛndāvana were attracted by His personal beauty, Rukmiṇī's attention was attracted by His bodily features and transcendental qualities, and the mind of the goddess of fortune was attracted by His flute-playing and other transcendental features. In this way Lord Kṛṣṇa attracts the minds of all young girls. He also attracts the minds of elderly ladies by His childlike activities, and the minds of His friends by His friendly activities. When He appeared in Vṛndāvana, He even attracted the birds, beasts, trees and plants. Indeed, everyone became attracted in love and affection for Kṛṣṇa.

The word *hari* has different meanings, of which two are principal. The name Hari indicates that Kṛṣṇa takes away all inauspicious things from the devotee's life and that He attracts the mind of the devotee by awarding him transcendental love of Godhead. Kṛṣṇa is so attractive that anyone who can somehow or other remember Him becomes freed from the four kinds of material miseries. The Lord gives special attention to His devotee and banishes the devotee's various sinful activities, which are stumbling blocks for the advancement of devotional service. This is called routing the influence of ignorance. Simply by hearing about Him, one develops love for Him. That is the gift of the Lord. On one side He takes away inauspicious things, and on the other side He awards the most auspicious things. That is the meaning of *hari*. When a person is developed in love of Godhead, his body, mind and everything else are attracted by the transcendental qualities of the Lord. Such is the power of Kṛṣṇa's merciful activities and transcendental qualities. He is so attractive that out of transcendental attachment to Him a devotee will give up all four principles of material success—religiosity, economic development, regulated sense gratification and salvation.

The words *api* and *ca* are adverbs and can be used for virtually any purpose. The word *ca,* or "and," can render seven different readings to the whole construction.

The Lord thus established the import of the eleven words in the *ātmārāma* verse, and then He began to further explain the verse as follows. The word "Brahman" means "the greatest in all respects." The Lord is the greatest in all opulences. No one can excel Him in wealth, no one can excel Him in strength, no one can excel Him in fame, no one can excel Him in beauty, no one can excel Him in knowledge, and no one can excel Him in renunciation. Thus the word "Brahman" actually indicates the Supreme Personality of Godhead, Kṛṣṇa. In the *Viṣṇu Purāṇa* (1.12.57) the word "Brahman" is said to indicate the greatest of all, the Supreme Lord, who as the greatest expands with no limit. One may conceive of Brahman's greatness, yet this greatness grows in such a way that no one can estimate how great He actually is.

The Supreme Personality of Godhead is realized in three aspects, but they are all one and the same. The Absolute Truth, the Supreme Personality, Kṛṣṇa, is everlasting. In *Śrīmad-Bhāgavatam* (2.9.33) it is said that He exists before the manifestation of this cosmic world, that He exists during its continuance, and that He continues to exist after its annihilation. Therefore He is the great soul of everything. He is all-pervading and all-witnessing, and He is the supreme form of everything.

There are three different kinds of transcendental processes mentioned in the Vedic literature by which one can understand and achieve that supreme perfection of the Absolute Truth. They are the process of knowledge, the process of mystic *yoga* and the process of devotional service. The followers of these three processes realize the Absolute Truth in three different aspects. Those who follow the process of knowledge realize Him as impersonal Brahman, those who follow the process of *yoga* realize Him as the localized Supersoul, and those who follow the process of devotional service realize Him as the Supreme Personality of Godhead, Śrī Kṛṣṇa. In other words, although the word Brahman indicates Kṛṣṇa and nothing else, still, according to the process that is followed, the Lord is realized in three different aspects.

As far as devotional service is concerned, there are two divisions. In the beginning there is *vidhi-bhakti,* or devotional service with regulative principles. In the higher stage there is *rāga-bhakti,* or devotional service in pure love.

The Supreme Personality of Godhead is the Absolute Truth, but He is manifested by the expansions of His different energies also. Those who follow the regulative principles of devotional service ultimately attain to the Vaikuṇṭha planets in the spiritual world, but one who follows the principles of love in devotional service attains to the supreme abode, the highest planet in the spiritual world, known as Kṛṣṇaloka or Goloka Vṛndāvana.

Transcendentalists can also be divided into three categories. The word *akāma* refers to one who does not have any material desires, *mokṣa-kāma* refers to one who seeks liberation from material miseries, and *sarva-kāma* refers to one who wants to enjoy by fulfilling material desires. The most intelligent transcendentalist gives up all other processes and engages in the devotional service of the Lord, even though he may have many desires. Through no kind of activity—whether fruitive action or the cultivation of knowledge or the cultivation of mystic *yoga*—can a person achieve the highest perfection without adding a tinge of devotional service. Except for devotional service, all transcendental processes are just like nipples on the neck of a goat. The nipples on a goat's neck may be squeezed, but they do not supply milk. Therefore if one is to derive actual perfection from his process, he must take to the devotional service of Kṛṣṇa.

In the *Bhagavad-gītā* (7.16) Lord Kṛṣṇa states:

catur-vidhā bhajante māṁ janāḥ sukṛtino 'rjuna
ārto jijñāsur arthārthī jñānī ca bharatarṣabha

"O best of the Bhāratas, four kinds of people with very righteous backgrounds take up devotional service to Me. They are the distressed, the inquisitive, the seekers of material profit, and the *jñānīs,* or wise men." Out of these four, those who are distressed and those who desire wealth are called *sakāma* devotees, devotees with material desires, whereas the other two, the inquisitive and the searcher for wisdom, are *mokṣa-kāma* devotees, seekers of liberation. Because they all worship Kṛṣṇa, they are all considered to be very fortunate. In due course of time, if they give up all desires and become pure devotees of the Supreme Lord, they can be considered most fortunate. Such fortunate beginners can develop only in the association of pure devotees of Lord Kṛṣṇa. When one associates with pure devotees, he becomes a pure devotee himself. This is confirmed in *Śrīmad-Bhāgavatam* (1.10.11):

sat-saṅgān mukta-duḥsaṅgo hātuṁ notsahate budhaḥ
kīrtyamānaṁ yaśo yasya sakṛd ākarṇya rocanam

"A person who is actually intelligent is able, by the association of pure devotees, to hear descriptions of Lord Kṛṣṇa and His activities. These activities are so attractive that one who hears of them does not wish to give up such association with the Lord."

Except for the association of pure devotees, all association is *kaitava,* or cheating. This is confirmed in *Śrīmad-Bhāgavatam* (1.1.2), which states, "All cheating processes, which obstruct transcendental realization, are to be thrown off. By *Śrīmad-Bhāgavatam* one can understand reality as it is, and such understanding helps one transcend the three kinds of material miseries. The *Śrīmad-Bhāgavatam* was compiled by the greatest sage, Vyāsadeva, and it is a work coming out of his mature experience. By understanding *Śrīmad-Bhāgavatam* and rendering devotional service, one can immediately capture the Supreme Lord within his heart."

Lord Caitanya then explained that the word *projjhita* in this *Bhāgavatam* verse refers to the desire for liberation. One great commentator explained that desire for liberation is the most obstructive stumbling block on the path of God realization. But if one somehow or other comes to Kṛṣṇa and begins to hear about Him, Kṛṣṇa is so kind that He awards him His lotus feet as a shelter. Then the devotee or transcendentalist forgets everything and engages in the devotional service of the Lord. When one comes to the Lord in devotional service, or in full Kṛṣṇa consciousness, the reward is the Supreme Himself. Once engaged for the Supreme, one no longer asks for anything, as do the distressed man and he who desires material possessions. The association of pure devotees, the causeless mercy of the Lord, and devotional service itself—these three act so wonderfully that one can give up all other activities and become absorbed in Kṛṣṇa, whether one is distressed, in want of material possessions, or inquisitive, or even if one is a wise man cultivating knowledge.

In summary, Kṛṣṇa is the meaning behind all the words in the *ātmārāma* verse. Up to this point Lord Caitanya spoke only of the introduction to the *ātmārāma* verse. Next He explained its real position.

There are two kinds of transcendentalists who cultivate knowledge. One of them worships the impersonal Brahman, and the other desires liberation. The Brahman worshipers, or monists, are further divided into three categories: the neophyte, one who is absorbed in Brahman realization, and one who has actually realized himself as Brahman. If devotional service is added, the knower of Brahman can then become liberated; otherwise there is no possibility of liberation.

Anyone who is fully engaged in devotional service in Kṛṣṇa consciousness is understood to be already realized in Brahman. Devotional service is so strong that one is attracted to Kṛṣṇa even from the platform of Brahman worship. The Lord awards the devotee the perfection of a spiritual body, and the devotee eternally engages in the transcendental service of Kṛṣṇa. It is when the devotee understands and becomes attracted by Kṛṣṇa's transcendental qualities that he wholeheartedly engages in devotional service. For instance, the Four Kumāras and Śukadeva Gosvāmī were liberated from the beginning of their lives, yet in their later life they became attracted to the pastimes of Kṛṣṇa and became devotees. Sanaka and the other Kumāras were attracted by the aroma of the flowers offered to Kṛṣṇa and by His transcendental qualities, and thus they engaged in His devotional service. Similarly, the nine mystics mentioned in the Eleventh Canto of *Śrīmad-Bhāgavatam* are understood to have been transcendentalists from birth, but they became devotees of the Lord by virtue of hearing the transcendental qualities of Kṛṣṇa from Brahmā, Lord Śiva and Nārada.

Sometimes one becomes attracted to Kṛṣṇa and His transcendental qualities simply by looking upon the beautiful features of His transcendental body. In this case also one abandons the desire for liberation and engages in His devotional service. The devotee repents his loss of time in the so-called cultivation of knowledge and becomes a pure devotee of the Lord.

There are two kinds of souls who are liberated even while in material bodies: the soul liberated by devotional service and the soul liberated by the cultivation of knowledge. The liberated soul in devotional service, attracted by the transcendental qualities of Kṛṣṇa, becomes more and more elevated, whereas those who engage in dry speculation and simply cultivate knowledge without devotion fall on account of their many offenses. This is confirmed in *Śrīmad-Bhāgavatam* (10.2.32), where it is stated:

ye 'nye 'ravindākṣa vimukta-māninas
tvayy asta-bhāvād aviśuddha-buddhayaḥ
āruhya kṛcchreṇa paraṁ padaṁ tataḥ
patanty adho 'nādṛta-yuṣmad-aṅghrayaḥ

"O Lord, the intelligence of those who think themselves liberated but who are without even a touch of devotional service is not pure.

Even though they rise to the highest point of liberation by dint of severe penances and austerity, they are sure to fall down again into this material existence, for they do not take shelter at Your lotus feet." Lord Kṛṣṇa confirms this is in the *Bhagavad-gītā* (18.54):

brahma-bhūtaḥ prasannātmā na śocati na kāṅkṣati
samaḥ sarveṣu bhūteṣu mad-bhaktiṁ labhate parām

"One who is actually situated in Brahman realization is fully joyful, has no reason to lament or desire anything, and is equal to everyone. Thus he is eligible for pure devotional service." This was illustrated by Bilvamaṅgala Ṭhākura, who in his later life wrote: "I was situated as a monist in order to become one with the Supreme, but somehow or other I contacted a naughty boy and became His eternal servitor." In other words, those who attain self-realization by the execution of devotional service attain a transcendental body, and, being attracted to the transcendental qualities of Kṛṣṇa, engage fully in pure devotional service.

Anyone who is not attracted to Kṛṣṇa is understood to be still under the spell of Māyā, but one who is attempting to be liberated by the process of devotional service is actually liberated from this spell. In the Eleventh Canto of *Śrīmad-Bhāgavatam* there are many instances recorded of devotees who became liberated in this life simply by engaging in devotional service.

CHAPTER 16

Conclusion of Teachings to Sanātana Gosvāmī

Persons who cultivate knowledge for liberation are of three kinds: those who simply desire liberation, those who are liberated already, even while in this material existence, and those who are actually self-realized. There are many persons in this world who desire liberation, and sometimes they engage in devotional service for this purpose. It is corroborated in *Śrīmad-Bhāgavatam* (1.2.26) that those who actually desire liberation give up all kinds of demigod worship and, without envy, concentrate their minds in the worship of Nārāyaṇa, the Supreme Personality of Godhead. When such persons come in contact with a pure devotee, they engage in the devotional service of Kṛṣṇa and give up the idea of liberation. A verse in the *Hari-bhakti-sudhodaya* states:

aho mahātman bahu-doṣa-duṣṭo
'py ekena bhāty eṣa bhavo guṇena
sat-saṅgamākhyena sukhāvahena
kṛtādya no yena kṛśā mumukṣā

"O great soul, although there are many flaws within this miserable life, there is yet one glory—the association of pure devotees.

Cultivate such association. By it our desire for liberation diminishes."

In *Śrīmad-Bhāgavatam* (11.2.37) it is stated that man's fear is due to his material conception of life and to his forgetting his eternal relationship with the Supreme Lord. Consequently he finds himself having only perverted memories. This occurs due to the spell of material energy. One who has sufficient intelligence will engage in full devotional service and regard the Supreme Lord as his spiritual master and worshipable God. The conclusion is that no one can attain a revolution in consciousness without engaging in devotional service to the Lord. When one is actually free from material contamination, he can fully engage himself in Kṛṣṇa consciousness.

In *Śrīmad-Bhāgavatam* (10.14.4) it is clearly said that one who engages in spiritual life to understand things as they are but who lacks all intention of engaging in Kṛṣṇa consciousness simply achieves trouble for his undertaking. There is no substance to his life. Every living entity is part and parcel of the Supreme Lord, and therefore it is the duty of every living entity to serve that supreme whole. Without such service, the living entity falls into material contamination.

Lord Caitanya concluded His teachings to Sanātana Gosvāmī by pointing out that the six kinds of *ātmārāmas,* or transcendentalists, engage in some kind of devotional service to Kṛṣṇa. In other words, at some time or another all the transcendentalists ultimately come to understand the necessity of rendering devotional service to Kṛṣṇa and become fully Kṛṣṇa conscious. Even if one is very learned or extravagant, he can still engage in the devotional service of the Lord.

The six kinds of transcendentalists are the neophyte transcendentalist, the absorbed transcendentalist, one who is situated in transcendence, one who desires liberation, one who is actually liberated, and one who is engaged in activities in his constitutional position. All of these are *ātmārāmas*. When a person becomes an *ātmārāma,* or a great thinker in Kṛṣṇa consciousness, he fully engages in devotional service. According to the grammatical rules, there are many kinds of *ātmārāmas*, but one sense of the word is sufficient to represent the others. In the collective sense, all the *ātmārāmas* are inclined to worship the Supreme Lord, Kṛṣṇa.

The mystic who worships the Supersoul within himself is also an *ātmārāma*. The *ātmārāma yogīs* are of two kinds: *sagarbha* and *nigarbha*. It is stated in *Śrīmad-Bhāgavatam* (2.2.8): "Some *yogīs* meditate within their heart on the localized Viṣṇu, who is four-handed and who holds four symbols: conch, disc, mace and lotus." The *yogī* who thinks of the four-handed Viṣṇu becomes absorbed in devotional ecstasy and shows the symptoms of that state. Sometimes he cries, and sometimes he feels separation from the Lord. In this way he merges in transcendental bliss, resulting in his becoming entrapped like a fish.

The *sagarbha* and *nigarbha yogīs* can be further divided into three categories: the beginner, the advanced *yogī,* and he who has attained perfection. These *yogīs* are described in the Sixth Chapter of the *Bhagavad-gītā*. Those who are trying to ascend the path of mystic *yoga* are called *ārurukṣu-yogīs,* beginners. In *ārurukṣu yoga,* one practices various sitting postures and concentrates the mind. One ascends the path of *yoga* by means of meditation and detachment, and when one is no longer attached to working for sense gratification, he gradually becomes free. At that time he attains a state of ecstasy called *yogārūḍha*. If such a mystic *yogī* somehow or other comes in contact with a saintly person, he becomes a devotee of Kṛṣṇa.

The word *urukrama* has already been explained: it indicates the Supreme Lord. All the *ātmārāmas* are engaged in devotional service to Urukrama. Before engaging in devotional service, such transcendentalists are called *śāntas,* or pacified devotees.

The word *ātmā,* or self, is sometimes translated as "mind." Sometimes mental speculators present philosophical theories in different ways, but when they come in contact with saintly persons engaged in devotional service, they also become devotees.

Śrīmad-Bhāgavatam (10.87.18) describes the two classes of *yogīs* (*sagarbha* and *nigarbha*) as follows: "The *yogīs* begin their practice of *yoga* by worshiping the abdomen, and they try to concentrate their attention on their intestines. Gradually their meditation rises to the heart and they concentrate the mind there. Then they gradually direct their attention to the top of the head. One who can raise his meditation to that position is understood to have become perfect and to be no longer subject to birth and death." Even such *yogīs* render causeless devotional service to the Lord when they come in contact with pure devotees.

The word *ātmā* also means "an endeavor." In every practice there is some endeavor, and the ultimate endeavor is the endeavor to reach the highest perfectional stage of devotional service. In *Śrīmad-Bhāgavatam* (1.5.18) it is stated that one should try to attain the highest goal, which cannot be attained either in the higher or lower planetary systems. The idea is that material happiness and misery are automatically available in all planetary systems in the course of time, but the highest achievement, devotional service, cannot be attained anywhere without endeavor. Therefore in the *Bṛhan-nāradīya Purāṇa* it is said that one who is serious about understanding the highest perfectional stage of devotional service can become successful simply by his endeavor. One cannot attain the highest perfectional stage of devotional service without personal endeavor. As Kṛṣṇa states in the *Bhagavad-gītā* (10.10):

teṣāṁ satata-yuktānāṁ bhajatāṁ prīti-pūrvakam
dadāmi buddhi-yogaṁ taṁ yena mām upayānti te

"To those who are constantly rendering devotional service to Me with love, I, who am situated in everyone's heart, give the intelligence by which they can make undeterred progress in devotional activities."

The word *ātmā* also means *dhṛti,* "patience and perseverance." By patience and perseverance one can achieve the highest stage of devotional service.

As far as the word *muni* is concerned, there are additional meanings. The word also refers to a bird and a large black bee. Another meaning of the word *nirgrantha* is "a foolish person." Thus even birds, bees and foolish people engage in the service of the Supreme Lord when they are favored by the pure devotee. Indeed, it is stated in *Śrīmad-Bhāgavatam* (10.21.14) that the birds in Vṛndāvana are devoted to the service of the Supreme Lord. It is also stated in the *Bhāgavatam* (10.15.6) that the black bees in Vṛndāvana always follow Kṛṣṇa and Balarāma. In that verse Śrī Kṛṣṇa describes to

Balarāma the devotional service the bees were rendering unto Him (Lord Balarāma):

ete 'linas tava yaśo 'khila-loka-tīrthaṁ
gāyanta ādi-puruṣānupathaṁ bhajante
prāyo amī muni-gaṇā bhavadīya-mukhyā
gūḍhaṁ vane 'pi na jahaty anaghātma-daivam

"O supremely virtuous one, O original Personality of Godhead, just see how these bees are following You, glorifying Your transcendental fame and thus worshiping You. Actually, these bees are not as they appear: they are great sages who are taking this opportunity to worship the Supreme Soul. Although You are not knowable by ordinary persons, they know You, and they are following and glorifying You."

In the next verse in *Śrīmad-Bhāgavatam* (10.15.7) Kṛṣṇa describes the similar reception given to Balarāma by the peacocks and cuckoos of Vṛndāvana: "O worshipable one, just see how the peacocks returning to their nests are receiving You with full pleasure. These peacocks are just like the damsels of Vraja. The cuckoos on the branches of the trees are also receiving You in their own way. The residents of Vṛndāvana are so glorious that everyone is prepared to render devotional service to the Lord." Another verse of *Śrīmad-Bhāgavatam* (10.35.11) describes a similar reception given to Kṛṣṇa by the birds of Vṛndāvana: "O just see how the cranes and swans on the water are singing the glories of the Lord! Indeed, they are standing in the water meditating on Him and worshiping Him." It is stated elsewhere in *Śrīmad-Bhāgavatam* (2.4.18): "Even the aborigines and uncivilized human beings like Kirātas, Hūṇas, Āndhras, Pulindas, Pulkaśas, Ābhīras, Śumbhas, Yavanas and Khasas, as well as many other such human beings, can all be purified simply by taking shelter of the pure devotees." Therefore Śukadeva Gosvāmī offered his respectful obeisances unto Lord Viṣṇu, whose devotees can work so wonderfully.

Another meaning of the word *dhṛti* is "to realize oneself as elevated." In this state one feels that he is free from all miseries and is elevated to the highest platform of life. All devotees of Kṛṣṇa in full Kṛṣṇa consciousness are free from all kinds of material pleasures and miseries. They are fully absorbed in the service of the Lord, and they are always jolly by virtue of their engagement in His transcendental service. They are experienced men of happiness. Indeed, they are so happy that they do not even wish to be promoted to the spiritual planets, for they are happy in every sphere of life. Being fulfilled in the transcendental service of the Lord, they desire neither material objects nor material sense pleasures. As stated by the Six Gosvāmīs: "Persons whose senses are fixed in the service of the Supreme Lord can be called peaceful."

Thus the word *ātmārāma* indicates that even birds, beasts and fools—in short, everyone—can become attracted by the transcendental qualities of Kṛṣṇa, engage in His service and become liberated.

Still another meaning of *ātmā* is "intelligence." One who has special intelligence is also called *ātmārāma*. The *ātmārāmas* with special intelligence are of two kinds. One is the learned sage, and the other is the fool without book knowledge. Both of these can have an opportunity to associate with a pure devotee. Even the foolish *ātmārāmas* can give up everything and engage in Kṛṣṇa consciousness in pure devotional service. In the *Bhagavad-gītā* (10.8) it is said that the Supreme Lord Kṛṣṇa is the origin of everything—that everything emanates from Him—and that anyone who is actually intelligent understands this and engages in His service. A verse in *Śrīmad-Bhāgavatam* (2.7.46) states: "To say nothing of persons who are intelligent enough to study the *Vedas*, even less intelligent persons like women, laborers, Hūṇas and Śabaras, as well as the birds and beasts, can achieve the highest perfectional stage of life by engaging in the devotional service of the Lord." As previously quoted, *Bhagavad-gītā* (10.10) also indicates that when a person becomes highly intelligent and engages in Kṛṣṇa consciousness, Kṛṣṇa reciprocates by giving him the intelligence by which he can be promoted to the abode of the Supreme Lord.

The Lord then told Sanātana Gosvāmī that the association of good devotees, engagement in the transcendental service of the Lord, the understanding of *Śrīmad-Bhāgavatam*, the chanting of the holy name of the Lord, and residence in a holy place like Vṛndāvana or Mathurā are all very important for elevation to the transcendental plane. One need not practice all five of these items; if one is expert in just one of them, he will, without fail, be elevated to the stage of love of Godhead. One who is actually intelligent gives up all material desires and engages in the transcendental service of Kṛṣṇa. The influence of devotional service is such that a person who engages in it gives up all material desires and becomes fully attached to Kṛṣṇa, being inspired by the transcendental qualities of the Lord. Such is the beauty of the Lord in the eyes of His devotee.

Another meaning of the word *ātmā* is "nature." In this case the word *ātmārāma* indicates that everyone is enjoying the particular nature he has acquired. But the ultimate nature, the eternal nature of the living entity, is to serve the Supreme Lord. One who attains to the perfection of understanding his real nature—as eternal servant of the Lord—gives up his designative (material, or bodily) conception of life. That is real knowledge. Those who are in pursuit of knowledge and who get the opportunity to associate with a pure devotee also engage in the devotional service of the Lord. Sages like the Four Kumāras, as well as fools and birds, can engage in the Lord's transcendental service. By being favored with Kṛṣṇa's causeless mercy, anyone can be elevated to the platform of Kṛṣṇa consciousness.

One who becomes attracted by the transcendental qualities of Kṛṣṇa begins devotional service. In *Śrīmad-Bhāgavatam* (10.15.8) Kṛṣṇa glorifies the land of Vṛndāvana as He addresses Balarāma in this way:

dhanyeyam adya dharaṇī tṛṇa-vīrudhas tvat-
pāda-spṛśo druma-latāḥ karajābhimṛṣṭāḥ
nadyo 'drayaḥ khaga-mṛgāḥ sadayāvalokair
gopyo 'ntareṇa bhujayor api yat-spṛhā śrīḥ

"This land of Vrajabhūmi is made glorious by the touch of Your feet. Being touched by Your fingers, the creepers have also become glorious. When You look on the hills, rivers and lower animals, they too are all made glorious, and the *gopīs,* being embraced by Your transcendental arms, are also made glorious." The *gopīs* glorified Vṛndāvana in the following words: "Dear friends, all these inhabitants of Vrajabhūmi—everyone, including the birds, beasts and trees—are glorified when they see Lord Kṛṣṇa and Lord Balarāma singing on Their flutes as They go to the pasturing ground with Their friends."

The word *ātmā* also means "this body." The *yogīs* who practice bodily exercises, considering the body to be the self, are also elevated to the transcendental service of the Lord if they associate with pure devotees. There are many people who believe the body to be the self, and they are engaged in many fruitive activities, including bathing rituals and ordinary worldly activities. But when they come in contact with a pure devotee, they also engage in the transcendental service of the Lord.

In *Śrīmad-Bhāgavatam* (1.18.12) it is stated: "O my dear Sūta Gosvāmī, we have become darkened by the sacrificial smoke of fruitive activities, but you have given us the nectar of Kṛṣṇa's lotus feet." It is also stated in *Śrīmad-Bhāgavatam* (4.21.31): "The waters of the Ganges flow from the tip of the lotus feet of Kṛṣṇa, and by bathing in that water, everyone—including fruitive actors and all sages—can wash dirty things from the mind."

Even those who believe that the body is the self, or those who are full of material desires, are also, in a sense, *ātmārāma*. When they associate with the pure devotees of the Lord, they give up their material desires and become perfect in the service of the Lord. The best example of this is found in the *Hari-bhakti-sudhodaya* (7.28), wherein Dhruva Mahārāja said:

sthānābhilāṣī tapasi sthito 'haṁ
tvāṁ prāptavān deva-munīndra-guhyam
kācaṁ vicinvann api divya-ratnaṁ
svāmin kṛtārtho 'smi varaṁ na yāce

"My dear Lord, I came to worship You because I desired some land on this earth, but fortunately I have attained You, who are beyond even the perception of great sages and saintly persons. I came to search out some particles of colored glass, but instead I found a very valuable gem like You. I am satisfied, and I do not desire to ask anything of You."

There is also another meaning to the word *nirgrantha*. The word can also mean "foolish hunter," or "wretched poor man." There is an instance of such a hunter who attained salvation and engaged himself in the devotional service of the Lord simply by associating with the pure devotee Nārada. Indeed, Lord Caitanya told Sanātana Gosvāmī the following story of the hunter's meeting with Nārada.

Once there was a hunter in the forest of Prayāga who was fortunate enough to meet Nārada Muni when the great sage was returning from Vaikuṇṭha after visiting Lord Nārāyaṇa. Nārada came to Prayāga to bathe in the confluence of the Ganges and Yamunā. While passing through the forest, Nārada saw a bird lying on the ground. The bird was half-killed, having been pierced by an arrow, and it was chirping piteously. Further on, Nārada saw a deer flopping about in agony. Further, he saw that a boar was also suffering, and in another place he saw a rabbit twitching in pain. All this made him feel very compassionate, and he began to think, "Who is the foolish man who has committed such sins?" In general, devotees of the Lord are compassionate toward the suffering living entities, and so what to speak of the great sage Nārada? He became very much aggrieved by this scene, and after proceeding a few steps he saw the hunter engaged in hunting with bow and arrows. The hunter's complexion was very black, and his eyes were red. It appeared to be dangerous just to see him standing there with his bow and arrows, looking just like an associate of Yamarāja, death. Seeing him, Nārada Muni entered deeper into the forest to approach him. As Nārada Muni passed through the forest, all the animals who were caught in the hunter's traps fled away. The hunter became very angry at this, and he was just about to call Nārada vile names, but, due to the influence of saintly Nārada, the hunter could not utter such blasphemies. Rather, with gentle behavior he asked Nārada: "My dear sir, why have you come here while I am hunting? Have you strayed from the general path? Because you have come here, all the animals in my traps have fled."

"Yes, I am sorry," Nārada replied. "I have come to you to find my own path and to inquire from you. While on the path I have seen that there are many boars, deer and rabbits lying on the forest floor half-dead and flopping about. Who has committed these sinful acts?"

"What you have seen is all right," the hunter replied. "It was done by me."

"If you are hunting all these poor animals, why don't you kill them at once?" Nārada asked. "You half-kill them, and they are writhing in their death pangs. This is a great sin. If you want to kill an animal, why don't you kill it completely? Why do you leave it half-killed and allow it to die flopping around?"

"My dear Lord," the hunter replied, "my name is Mṛgāri, enemy of the animals. I am simply following the teachings of my father, who taught me to half-kill animals and leave them flopping about. When a half-dead animal suffers, I take great pleasure in it."

"I beg only one thing from you," Nārada implored. "Please accept it."

"Oh, yes sir, I shall give you whatever you like," the hunter said. "If you want some animal skins, come to my house. I have many skins of animals, including tigers and deer. I shall give you whatever you like."

"I do not want such things," Nārada replied. "But I do want something else. Since you kindly agreed to grant it to me, I shall tell you. Please, henceforth from tomorrow, whenever you kill an animal, please kill it completely. Don't leave it half dead."

"My dear sir, what are you asking of me? What is the difference between half-killing an animal and killing it completely?"

"If you half-kill the animals, they suffer great pain," Nārada explained. "And if you give too much pain to other living entities, you commit great sin. There is a great offense committed when you kill an animal completely, but the offense is much greater when you half-kill it. Indeed, the pain which you give half-dead animals will have to be accepted by you in a future birth."

Although the hunter was very sinful, his heart became softened, and he became afraid of his sins by virtue of his association with a great devotee like Nārada. Those who are grossly sinful are not at all afraid of committing sins, but here we can see that because his purification began in the association of a great devotee like Nārada, the hunter became afraid of his sinful activities. The hunter therefore replied: "My dear sir, from my very childhood I have been taught to kill animals in this way. Please tell me how I can counteract all the offenses and sinful activities I have committed. I am surrendering unto your feet. Please save me from all the reactions to the sinful activities I have committed in the past, and please direct me to the proper path so that I can be free."

"If you actually want to follow my directions, I can tell you the real path by which you can be freed from these sinful reactions."

"I shall follow whatever you say without hesitation," the hunter agreed.

Nārada then told him to first break his bow; only then would Nārada disclose the path of liberation.

"You are asking me to break my bow," the hunter protested, "but if I break it, what will be the means of my livelihood?"

"Don't worry about your livelihood," Nārada said. "I shall send you sufficient grain so you can live."

The hunter then broke his bow and fell down at the feet of Nārada. Nārada got him to stand up, and he instructed him: "Just go to your home and distribute whatever money and valuables you have to the devotees and the *brāhmaṇas*. Then come out and follow me wearing only one cloth. Construct a small thatched house on the riverbank and sow a *tulasī* plant by that house. Just circumambulate the *tulasī* tree, and every day taste one fallen leaf. Above all, always chant Hare Kṛṣṇa, Hare Kṛṣṇa, Kṛṣṇa Kṛṣṇa, Hare Hare/ Hare Rāma, Hare Rāma, Rāma Rāma, Hare Hare. As far as your livelihood is concerned, I shall send you the grain you need, but you must accept only as much grain as you require for yourself and your wife."

Nārada then revived the half-dead animals, and, getting freed from their dreadful condition, they fled away. Upon seeing Nārada execute this miracle, the black hunter was struck with wonder. After taking Nārada to his home, he bowed down again at his feet.

Nārada returned to his place, and the hunter, after returning home, began to execute the instructions Nārada had given him. In the meantime, news spread among all the villages that the hunter had become a devotee. Consequently the residents of the villages came to see the new Vaiṣṇava. It is the Vedic custom to bring grain or fruits whenever one goes to see a saintly person, and since all the villagers saw that the hunter had turned into a great devotee, they brought eatables with them. Thus every day he was offered grain and fruits, so much so that no less than ten to twenty people could have eaten there. But following Nārada's instructions, he did not accept more than what he and his wife required to live on.

After some days had passed, Nārada told his friend Parvata Muni: "I have a disciple. Let us go visit him and see if he is doing well."

When the two great sages, Nārada and Parvata, went to the hunter's home, the hunter saw his spiritual master coming from a distance and began to approach him with great respect. On his way to greet the great sages, the hunter saw that there were ants on the ground before him, and they were hindering his passage. When he reached the sages, he wanted to bow down before them, but before he did so he carefully cleared away the ants with his cloth. When Nārada saw that the hunter was trying to save the lives of the ants in this way, he was reminded of a verse from the *Skanda Purāṇa:* "Is it not wonderful that a devotee of the Lord is not inclined to give any sort of pain to anyone, not even an ant?" Although formerly the hunter had taken great pleasure in half-killing animals, since he had become a great devotee of the Lord he was not prepared to give pain even to an ant.

The hunter received the two great sages at his home and offered them a sitting place, brought water, and washed their feet. Then the hunter and his wife took some of the water and drank it, and finally they both sprinkled the water on their heads. After this they felt ecstasy and began to dance while singing Hare Kṛṣṇa, Hare Kṛṣṇa, Kṛṣṇa Kṛṣṇa, Hare Hare/ Hare Rāma, Hare Rāma, Rāma Rāma, Hare Hare. They raised their hands and danced with their clothes flying. When the two great sages saw this ecstasy of love of Godhead manifest in the body of the hunter, Parvata Muni told Nārada: "You are a touchstone, for by your association even a great hunter has turned into a great devotee."

There is a verse in the *Skanda Purāṇa* which states: "My dear Devarṣi [Nārada], you are glorious, and by your mercy even the lowest creature, a hunter of animals, also became elevated to the path of devotion and attained transcendental attachment for Kṛṣṇa."

At length, Nārada inquired of the hunter-devotee: "Are you getting your foodstuffs regularly?"

"You send so many people," the hunter replied, "and they bring so much food that we cannot eat it all."

"That's all right," Nārada replied. "Whatever you are getting is all right. Now just continue your devotional service in that way."

After Nārada had spoken this, both he and Parvata Muni disappeared from the hunter's home. Lord Caitanya recited this story to show that even a hunter can be engaged in the devotional service of Kṛṣṇa by the influence of pure devotees.

Continuing to explain the *ātmārāma* verse, Lord Caitanya pointed out that the word *ātmā* also indicates all varieties of the Personality of Godhead. Generally the Personality of Godhead Himself, Kṛṣṇa, and His different expansions are all known as the Personality of Godhead.

Anyone who is engaged in the devotional service of any form or expansion of the Supreme Personality of Godhead is also called *ātmārāma*. All such devotees engage either in the regulative principles of devotional service or in devotional service in transcendental love. These two groups of devotees are each divided into three categories: eternal associates, those perfected in devotional service, and those newly engaged in devotional service. Newly engaged devotees can be divided into two groups: those who have already attained attachment for the Lord and those who have not attained such attachment. When considered according to the two divisions of devotional service (namely due to attachment in transcendental love, and under regulation) these classes of devotees become eight in number. By following the regulative principles of devotion, the perfect associates of the Lord are further divided into four classes: the servants, the friends, the parental superiors and the fiancées.

Just as some devotees are perfected by the execution of devotional service, so some are eternally perfect. Of those following the regulative principles of devotional service, there are the advanced and the beginners, totaling sixteen categories; and in the transcendental loving service of the Lord, there are also sixteen types of devotees. Thus the *ātmārāmas* can be considered to exist in thirty-two divisions. If the words *muni, nirgrantha, ca* and *api* are applied to the thirty-two classes, then there are fifty-eight different types of devotees. All these devotees can be described by one word: *ātmārāma*. There may be many different kinds of trees standing in the forest, but the word "tree" describes them all.

Thus the Lord gave sixty different meanings to the *ātmārāma* verse. In addition, He said that *ātmā* means "any embodied living entity, from the first living creature, Brahmā, down to the ant." He cited a verse from the Sixth Chapter of the *Viṣṇu Purāṇa* in which it is stated that all the energies of the Lord are spiritual. Although this is the case, the energy which is known as the source of the living entity is called spiritual, but the other energy, which is full of ignorance and is manifested in material activities, is called material nature. Even in the material creation, the living entities are innumerable. If by chance a living entity in the material world can associate with a pure devotee, he can engage in the pure devotional service of Kṛṣṇa. "Formerly I thought of sixty different meanings for the *ātmārāma* verse," the Lord told Sanātana Gosvāmī, "but here another meaning has come to My mind by your association."

After hearing the different explanations of the *ātmārāma* verse, Sanātana Gosvāmī was struck with wonder, and he fell down in devotion at the feet of Lord Caitanya. "I understand that You are personally the Supreme Personality of Godhead, Kṛṣṇa," Sanātana said, "and by Your breathing have come many manifestations of Vedic literature. You are the teacher of *Śrīmad-Bhāgavatam,* and You best know the meanings of the verses of *Śrīmad-Bhāgavatam.* It is not possible for others to understand the confidential meanings of *Śrīmad-Bhāgavatam* without Your mercy."

"Do not try to eulogize Me in that way," the Lord told Sanātana. "Just try to understand the real nature of *Śrīmad-Bhāgavatam. Śrīmad-Bhāgavatam* is the sound representation of the Supreme Lord Kṛṣṇa; therefore *Śrīmad-Bhāgavatam* is not different from Kṛṣṇa. As Kṛṣṇa is unlimited, so each word and each syllable of *Śrīmad-Bhāgavatam* has unlimited meanings. One can understand these meanings through the association of devotees. Don't, then, say that the *Bhāgavatam* is simply a collection of answers to questions."

There were six questions put by the sages of Naimiṣāraṇya to Sūta Gosvāmī, and Sūta Gosvāmī answered the six questions in *Śrīmad-Bhāgavatam.* There is a verse in the Vedic literature in which Lord Śiva says, "As far as the *Bhāgavatam* is concerned, I may know it, or

Śukadeva or Vyāsadeva may know it, or we may not know it—but actually *Bhāgavatam* is to be understood by devotional service and from a devotee, and not by one's own intelligence or by academic commentaries." At the beginning of *Śrīmad-Bhāgavatam* (1.1.23) the sages of Naimiṣāraṇya asked Sūta Gosvāmī:

brūhi yogeśvare kṛṣṇe brahmaṇye dharma-varmaṇi
svāṁ kāṣṭhām adhunopete dharmaḥ kaṁ śaraṇaṁ gataḥ

"My dear sir, now that the Lord has departed for His own abode, kindly tell us whether the principles of religion have gone with Him. How can we find such principles after His departure?"

The reply was given in *Śrīmad-Bhāgavatam* (1.3.43):

kṛṣṇe sva-dhāmopagate dharma-jñānādibhiḥ saha
kalau naṣṭa-dṛśām eṣa purāṇārko 'dhunoditaḥ

"After Kṛṣṇa departed to His abode with all religious principles, His representation, *Śrīmad-Bhāgavatam,* the *Mahā-Purāṇa,* remains as the blazing, illuminating sun."

Lord Caitanya then told Sanātana Gosvāmī: "I was just like a madman in describing this *ātmārāma* verse in so many ways. Do not mind if I have said something mad. But if someone becomes a madman like Me, he can understand the real meaning of *Śrīmad-Bhāgavatam* as I have explained it."

Then Sanātana Gosvāmī, with folded hands, fell at the feet of Lord Caitanya and prayed as follows: "My dear Lord, You have asked me to prepare a book on the regulative principles of devotional service, but I belong to the lowest caste. I have no knowledge. I do not know how such an important task can be finished by me. If You will kindly give me some hints about the preparation of such a book on devotional service, it may be that I shall be qualified to write it."

The Lord then blessed him, saying, "By the grace of Kṛṣṇa, whatever you write will come out of your heart and be accepted. As you have requested, I will now give you some notes that you can take down. The first and foremost point is that one should accept a bona fide spiritual master. That is the beginning of spiritual life." Lord Caitanya then requested Sanātana Gosvāmī to write down the symptoms of a true guru and the symptoms of a true disciple. The symptoms of a guru are described in the *Padma Purāṇa:* "A person who is a qualified *brāhmaṇa* and at the same time has all the symptoms of a devotee can become a spiritual master for all classes of men. Such a devotee and spiritual master must be respected as God Himself. Even though a person may be born in a very respectable *brāhmaṇa* family, he cannot become a bona fide spiritual master if he is not a devotee of the Lord." One should not mistakenly think that a bona fide spiritual master has to be born in a so-called *brāhmaṇa* family. The idea is that a spiritual master must be a qualified *brāhmaṇa;* that is, he must be qualified by his activities.

This is confirmed in *Śrīmad-Bhāgavatam,* when Nārada speaks of the different symptoms characterizing the four divisions of social life. Nārada therein states that *brāhmaṇas, kṣatriyas, vaiśyas* and *śūdras* should be selected by their individual qualifications. In his commentary, Śrīdhara Svāmī has noted that birth in a family of *brāhmaṇas* does not necessarily mean that one is a *brāhmaṇa.* One must be qualified with a *brāhmaṇa's* symptoms, which are described in the *śāstras.* In the disciplic succession of the Gauḍīya Vaiṣṇava *sampradāya,* there are two great *ācāryas* (Ṭhākura Narottama and Śyāmānanda Gosvāmī) who were not born in *brāhmaṇa* families but were accepted as spiritual masters by many famous *brāhmaṇas,* including Gaṅgānārāyaṇa and Rāmakṛṣṇa.

In this way there are symptoms which both the prospective spiritual master and the prospective disciple must have, and both the disciple and the spiritual master must see whether the other is eligible to become either a bona fide spiritual master or a bona fide student. One should then know that the only worshipable object is the Supreme Personality of Godhead, and one should learn the various *mantras* and sacred songs.

The Lord then instructed Sanātana to describe the symptoms of those persons who are eligible to accept the *mantras* and to describe how the *mantras* should be understood and perfected by ritualistic performances. Then the Lord instructed Sanātana to describe initiation, morning duties and duties of cleanliness—washing the face, brushing the teeth, and so on—the process of work and the prayers to be recited both in the morning and the evening. The Lord also told him to describe how one should worship the spiritual master, how to mark one's body with *gopī-candana,* how to collect *tulasī* leaves, how to wash the room and temple of the Lord, and how to awaken Kṛṣṇa from sleep. Then Lord Caitanya instructed Sanātana to describe different methods for worshiping the Lord, with fivefold, sixteenfold or fiftyfold paraphernalia, how to worship the Lord by offering Him *ārati* five times a day, and how to offer food to Kṛṣṇa and lay Him down on His bed. Next Lord Caitanya instructed Sanātana to write about the characteristics of both the form of the Lord in the temple and the *śālagrāma-śilā,* and also to write about the effect of going to holy places where there are different temples of the Lord and seeing the form of God in the temple. Sanātana was also instructed to glorify the transcendental name of the Lord and to describe the different offenses one can commit while chanting the Lord's name or worshiping the Deity. In the worship of the Lord certain paraphernalia are used, such as a conchshell, water, incense and fragrant flowers. The Lord instructed Sanātana to describe these, along with the chanting of prayers and hymns, circumambulation, and the offering of obeisances. Other topics for Sanātana to explain included following the regulative principles of *puraścaraṇa,* accepting *kṛṣṇa-prasādam,* rejecting foodstuff not offered to Kṛṣṇa, and not indulging in defaming a devotee who has the actual symptoms of a devotee.

Lord Caitanya also instructed Sanātana to describe the symptoms of a holy man, the process of satisfying the sages, and the value of rejecting the society of undesirable persons and hearing *Śrīmad-Bhāgavatam* constantly. Also to be described were how to follow the daily, fortnightly and monthly duties, how to observe fasting on the Ekādaśī day, how to observe ceremonies like the birthday of the Lord, and how to observe fasting not only on Ekādaśī but also on Janmāṣṭamī, Vāmana-dvādaśī, Rāma-navamī and Nṛsiṁha-caturdaśī. Lord Caitanya also instructed Sanātana to explain that it is helpful in the advancement of devotional service to avoid fast days that overlap with other days (*viddhā*). Also to be explained were how to establish temples of the Lord, along with the general behavior, symptoms, duties and occupation of a Vaiṣṇava. And at every step, Lord Caitanya said, Sanātana Gosvāmī should give documentary evidence from the *purāṇas*. Thus the Lord gave a summary of all the topics Sanātana should include in his book on Vaiṣṇava regulative principles.

Sanātana Gosvāmī was a great devotee of the Lord, and he was directly instructed to spread the cult of *bhakti* by writing many books. There is a description of Sanātana in the *Caitanya-candrodaya,* where it is said that Sanātana Gosvāmī was one of the most important personalities in the government of Nawab Hussain Shah. Sanātana's brother, Rūpa Gosvāmī, was also a minister in the government, but both of them gave up their lucrative government posts to become mendicants and serve the Supreme Lord. Externally the brothers became just like ordinary mendicants, but their hearts were filled with transcendental loving service and a great love for the cowherd boy of Vṛndāvana. Indeed, Sanātana Gosvāmī was dear to all pure devotees of his time.

Part II

CHAPTER 17

Lord Caitanya, the Original Personality of Godhead

Following in the footsteps of Kavirāja Kṛṣṇadāsa Gosvāmī, we offer our respectful obeisances unto the lotus feet of Lord Caitanya.

Lord Caitanya is described as follows: He is the only shelter for the forlorn, the most fallen, and He is the only hope for those who are completely devoid of spiritual knowledge. Let us try to discuss His great contribution of devotional service.

The supremely powerful Lord Kṛṣṇa becomes manifest in five different features. Although He is one without a second, in order to serve five specific spiritual purposes He becomes manifest in five ways. Such diversity is eternal and blissful, in contrast to the conception of monotonous oneness. From the Vedic literature we can understand that the Absolute Truth, the Supreme Personality of Godhead, eternally exists with His diverse energies. Lord Caitanya appeared with full diverse energies, and they are five in number; therefore Lord Caitanya is said to be Kṛṣṇa with diverse energies.

There is no difference between the energy and the energetic in regard to the Lord's appearance as Śrī Caitanya Mahāprabhu and His four associates Nityānanda Prabhu, Advaita Prabhu, Gadādhara Paṇḍita and Śrīvāsa Ṭhākura. Among these five diverse manifestations of the Supreme Lord (as the Lord Himself and His expansion, incarnation, devotional energy and devotee) there is no spiritual difference. They are five in one Absolute Truth. For the sake of relishing transcendental flavors in the Absolute Truth, there are five diverse manifestations. These are called the form of a devotee, the identity of a devotee, the incarnation of a devotee, the devotional energy and the pure devotee.

Out of the five diversities in the Absolute Truth, the form of Lord Caitanya is that of the original Personality of Godhead, Kṛṣṇa. Lord Nityānanda is the manifestation of the first expansion of the Supreme Lord. Similarly, Advaita Prabhu is an incarnation of the Supreme Lord. These three—Caitanya, Nityānanda and Advaita—belong to the category of *viṣṇu-tattva,* or the Supreme Absolute Truth. Śrīvāsa represents the pure devotee, and Gadādhara represents the internal energy of the Lord for the advancement of pure devotion. Therefore Gadādhara and Śrīvāsa, although on the Viṣṇu platform, are dependent, diverse energies of the Supreme Lord. In other words, they are not different from the energetic, but they are manifested diversely for the sake of relishing transcendental relationships. The whole process of devotional service involves a transcendental reciprocation of the flavors of relationship between the worshiper and the worshiped. Without such a diverse exchange of transcendental flavors, devotional service has no meaning.

In the Vedic literature (*Kaṭha Upaniṣad*) it is stated that the Supreme Lord is the supreme living entity among all living entities. There are innumerable living entities, but there is one living entity who is the Supreme Absolute Godhead. The difference between the singular living entity and the plural living entities is that the singular living entity is the Lord of all. Lord Caitanya is that supreme living entity, and He descended to reclaim the innumerable fallen living entities. In other words, the specific purpose of Lord Caitanya's advent was to establish in the present age the Vedic fact that there is one Supreme Personality of Godhead predominating and maintaining all the other innumerable living entities. Because the impersonalist (Māyāvādī) philosophers cannot understand this, Lord Caitanya advented Himself to enlighten the people in general about the real nature of the relationship between the Supreme and the many dependent living entities.

In the *Bhagavad-gītā* Kṛṣṇa's last instruction is that everyone should give up all other engagements and render devotional service unto Him. But after Kṛṣṇa's disappearance, less intelligent people misunderstood Him. They became contaminated with the Māyāvāda philosophy, which produced so many mental speculators that people forgot the actual position of the Absolute Truth and the living entity. Therefore Lord Śrī Kṛṣṇa Himself, as Lord Caitanya, again appeared in order to teach the fallen souls of this material world the way to approach Lord Kṛṣṇa. The *Bhagavad-gītā* teaches that one should give up everything and be done with this world of material attachment. A pure devotee of Lord Kṛṣṇa and one who follows the philosophy of Lord Caitanya are one and the same. Caitanya's philosophy is that one should give up everything and worship God, Kṛṣṇa. Kṛṣṇa, as the Supreme Lord, the Personality of Godhead, spoke the same words, indicating Himself as the Supreme Lord. But the Māyāvādī philosophers misunderstood Him. Therefore Lord Caitanya, to clarify the situation, reiterated Lord Kṛṣṇa's message: One should not declare himself to be as good as Kṛṣṇa but should worship Kṛṣṇa as the Supreme Lord.

We make a great mistake if we think Lord Caitanya is a conditioned soul. He is to be understood as the Supreme Absolute Truth, the Personality of Godhead, Śrī Kṛṣṇa Himself. In the *Caitanya-caritāmṛta* it is therefore said of Lord Caitanya: "Kṛṣṇa is now present in His five diverse manifestations." Unless one is situated in uncontaminated goodness, it is very difficult to understand Lord Caitanya as the Supreme Personality of Godhead Himself. Thus in order to understand Lord Caitanya, one has to follow the direct disciples of Lord Caitanya—the Six Gosvāmīs—and especially the path chalked out by Śrīla Jīva Gosvāmī.

The most astonishing fact is that Lord Caitanya, although the Supreme Personality of Godhead, Kṛṣṇa, never displayed Himself as Kṛṣṇa. Rather, whenever intelligent devotees detected that He was Lord Kṛṣṇa and addressed Him as Lord Kṛṣṇa, He denied it. Indeed, He sometimes placed His hands over His ears, protesting that a human being should not be addressed as the Supreme Lord. Indirectly, He was teaching the Māyāvādī philosophers that one should never falsely pose himself as the Supreme Lord and thereby misguide his followers. Nor should the followers be foolish enough to accept anyone and everyone as the Supreme Personality of Godhead. One should test by consulting scriptures and by seeing the activities of the person in question. One should not, however, mistake Lord Caitanya and His five diverse manifestations for ordinary human beings. Lord Caitanya is the Supreme Personality of Godhead, Kṛṣṇa Himself. The beauty of Lord Caitanya is that although He is the Supreme Lord, He came as a great devotee to teach all conditioned souls how devotional service should be rendered. Conditioned souls who are interested in devotional service should follow in the exemplary footsteps of Lord Caitanya to learn how Kṛṣṇa can be attained by devotional service. Thus the Supreme Lord Himself teaches the conditioned soul how He should be approached by devotional service.

By analytically studying the five diverse manifestations of the Supreme Lord, we can come to know that Lord Śrī Caitanya Mahāprabhu is the Supreme Absolute Truth and that Lord Nityānanda is His immediate expansion. We can also come to understand that Advaita Prabhu is also in the category of the Supreme Personality of Godhead but is subordinate to Lord Caitanya and Nityānanda Prabhu. The Supreme Personality of Godhead and His immediate and subordinate expansion are worshipable by the other two—namely the representation of the internal potency and the representation of the marginal potency. The representation of the internal potency, Gadādhara, represents the confidential devotee, and the representation of the marginal potency, Śrīvāsa, represents the pure devotee. Both of these are worshipers of the other three. But all four of the Lord's expansions—whether in the worshipable category (Nityānanda and Advaita) or the worshiper category (Gadādhara and Śrīvāsa)—are engaged in the transcendental loving service of the Supreme Personality of Godhead, Śrī Caitanya Mahāprabhu.

There is a specific difference between the pure devotee and the confidential devotee. The different potencies of the Lord are engaged in serving the Supreme Lord in different transcendental relationships. They are situated in conjugal love, in parental affection, in friendship or in servitude. By judging impartially, one can find that the internal potencies of the Supreme Lord who are engaged in conjugal love with the Lord are the best of all devotees. Thus both internal devotees and confidential devotees are attracted by the conjugal love of the Supreme Absolute Truth. These are the most confidential devotees of Lord Caitanya. Other pure devotees, who are more or less attached to Śrī Nityānanda Prabhu and Advaita Prabhu, are attracted by other transcendental relationships, such as parental affection, friendship and servitorship. When such devotees are very much attached to the activities of Lord Caitanya, they at once become confidential devotees in conjugal love with the Supreme Lord.

There is a very nice song sung by Śrī Narottama Dāsa Ṭhākura, a great devotee and *ācārya* in the disciplic succession from Lord Caitanya. Narottama Dāsa sings: "When will there be transcendental eruptions all over my body simply by my hearing the name of Gaurāṅga? When will tears incessantly flow from my eyes simply by my uttering the names of the Lord? When will Lord Nityānanda have mercy upon me and make all my desires for material enjoyment insignificant? When shall I be purified by giving up all contaminations of material enjoyment? And when shall I be able to see the transcendental abode, Vṛndāvana? When shall I be eager to accept the Six Gosvāmīs as my prime guides? And when will I be able to understand the conjugal love of Kṛṣṇa?" No one should be eager to understand the conjugal love of Kṛṣṇa without undergoing disciplinary training under the Six Gosvāmīs of Vṛndāvana.

The *saṅkīrtana* movement inaugurated by Lord Caitanya is a transcendental pastime of the Lord. "By it I live simultaneously to preach and popularize this movement in the material world." In that *saṅkīrtana* movement of Lord Caitanya, Nityānanda and Advaita are His expansions and Gadādhara and Śrīvāsa are His internal and marginal potencies, respectively. The living entities are also called marginal potency because they have either of two attitudes—namely, the tendency to surrender unto Kṛṣṇa and the tendency to become independent of Him and try for material enjoyment. Due to this propensity for material enjoyment, the living entity becomes contaminated by the material world. When a living entity is dominated by a desire for material enjoyment and becomes entangled in material life, he is subjected to the threefold miseries of material existence.

There is a nice example showing how Lord Caitanya's *saṅkīrtana* movement can save one from the miseries of material existence. The desire for material enjoyment is just like a seed sown in the earth. If a seed is inundated by too much water, there is no possibility of its fructifying. Similarly, if a conditioned soul is captivated by material enjoyment because the seed of such enjoyment is within his heart, he can be overwhelmed and overpowered by a flood of transcendental activities performed in love of God. In this way his seed of material enjoyment cannot fructify into a conditioned life of material existence. The conditioned living entities in the present Age of Kali are being overpowered by the flood of love of God inaugurated by Lord Caitanya and His associates.

In this connection there is a verse written by His Holiness Prabodhānanda Sarasvatī in his book *Śrī Caitanya-candrāmṛta.* This verse states that materialistic persons are very enthusiastic to maintain their family members, wife and children, and that there are also many mystic speculators who are engaged in speculating about liberation from the miseries of material life and who therefore undergo various austerities and penances. But those who have discovered the greatest transcendental flavor in the movement of Lord Caitanya Mahāprabhu no longer have a taste for such activities.

Those who are under the impression that there is material contamination in the form of the Supreme Personality of Godhead and in His devotional service are called Māyāvādīs. According to their imperfect speculation, the impersonal Brahman is the only existence in the cosmic manifestation. As soon as the Supreme Personality of Godhead is introduced, they consider that His personality arises from *māyā,* or the external material energy. Such persons consider all incarnations of the Supreme Lord to be contaminated by this material nature. According to them, the material body and the activities of matter are all that give a living being an individual identity. According to them, liberation means the end of an individual identity for the pure living being. In other words, the Māyāvādīs maintain that when a living entity is liberated he becomes one with the supreme, impersonal Brahman. According to such Māyāvāda philosophy, the Personality of Godhead, His abode, His devotional service and His emotional devotees are all under the spell of *māyā* and are consequently subjected to the material condition. Those who forget the transcendental nature of the Supreme Lord, His abode, His devotional service and His devotees consider all these to be but manifestations of material activity. One who thinks that there is a possibility of arguing about transcendence is called an agnostic, and one who thinks that there is a possibility of criticizing transcendence is called an atheist. Lord Caitanya wanted to accept all kinds of agnostics, atheists, skeptics and unfaithfuls and swallow them in the flood of love of God. Therefore He accepted the renounced order of life to attract all these forces.

Lord Caitanya remained a householder until His twenty-fourth year, and in the twenty-fifth year of His life He accepted the renounced order. After accepting the renounced order (*sannyāsa*), He attracted many other *sannyāsīs*. When He had been spreading the *saṅkīrtana* movement as a family man, many Māyāvādī *sannyāsīs* did not take His movement very seriously, but after the Lord accepted the *sannyāsa* order of life, He delivered not only Māyāvādī *sannyāsīs* but speculative students, atheists and those who were attached to fruitive activities and unnecessary criticism. The Lord was so kind that He accepted all these people and delivered to them the most important factor in life: love of God.

To fulfill His mission of bestowing love of God upon the conditioned souls, Lord Caitanya devised many methods to attract those who were uninterested in love of God. After He accepted the renounced order, all the agnostics, critics, atheists and mental speculators became His students and followers. Even many who were not Hindus and who did not follow the Vedic principles accepted Lord Caitanya as the supreme teacher. The only persons who avoided the mercy of Śrī Caitanya Mahāprabhu were those *sannyāsīs* who were known as the Māyāvādī philosophers of Benares. Their plight is described by Śrīla Bhaktisiddhānta Sarasvatī Gosvāmī: "The Māyāvādī philosophers of Benares were less intelligent because they wanted to measure everything by direct perception. On this basis they calculated that whatever is perceived by material means is *māyā,* or illusion. Since *māyā* is full of variegatedness and the Absolute Truth is transcendental to *māyā,* they concluded that there is no variegatedness in the Absolute Truth."

During Caitanya Mahāprabhu's time there were also other impersonalist philosophers known as the Māyāvādī philosophers of Saranātha. Saranātha is a place near Benares where Buddhist philosophers used to reside, and even today many *stūpas* of the Buddhist Māyāvādīs can be seen. The Māyāvādī philosophers of Saranātha are different from the impersonalists who believe in the impersonal manifestation of Brahman. According to the Saranātha philosophers, there is no spiritual existence at all. The fact is that both the Māyāvādī philosophers of Benares and the philosophers of Saranātha are entrapped by material nature. None of them actually know the nature of the absolute transcendence. Although superficially accepting the Vedic principles and considering themselves transcendentalists, the philosophers of Benares do not accept spiritual variegatedness. Because they have no information about devotional service, they are called nondevotees, or those who are against the devotional service of Lord Kṛṣṇa.

The impersonalists speculate on the Supreme Personality of Godhead and His devotees and subject them to the tests of direct perception. But the Lord, His devotees and His devotional service are not subject to direct perception. In other words, spiritual variegatedness is unknown to the Māyāvādī philosophy; therefore all the Māyāvādī philosophers and *sannyāsīs* criticized Lord Caitanya when He was conducting His *saṅkīrtana* movement. They were surprised to see Lord Caitanya chanting and dancing after He accepted His *sannyāsa* order from Keśava Bhāratī, for Keśava Bhāratī belonged to the Māyāvādī school. Since Lord Caitanya therefore also belonged to the Māyāvādī sect of *sannyāsīs,* the Māyāvādīs were surprised to see Him engaged in chanting and dancing instead of hearing or reading the *Vedānta-sūtras,* as is the custom. The Māyāvādī philosophers are very fond of the *Vedānta,* and they misinterpret it in their own way. Misunderstanding their own position, they criticized Lord Caitanya as an unauthorized *sannyāsī,* arguing that because He was a sentimentalist He was not actually a bona fide *sannyāsī.*

All these criticisms were carried to Lord Caitanya when He was at Benares, and He was not at all surprised at them. He even smiled when the news was carried to Him. He did not associate with the Māyāvādī *sannyāsīs* but remained alone and executed His own mission. After staying for some days in Benares, He started for Mathurā.

CHAPTER 18

Conversations with Prakāśānanda

According to the principles of the Māyāvādī *sannyāsīs,* singing, dancing and playing musical instruments are strictly prohibited, for they are considered to be sinful activities. The Māyāvādī *sannyāsī* is simply supposed to engage in the study of the *Vedānta*. Therefore when the Māyāvādī *sannyāsīs* in Benares saw that Lord Caitanya was indulging in singing, dancing, playing musical instruments and always chanting Hare Kṛṣṇa, Hare Kṛṣṇa, Kṛṣṇa Kṛṣṇa, Hare Hare/ Hare Rāma, Hare Rāma, Rāma Rāma, Hare Hare, they concluded that He was not educated and that, out of sentiment, He was misleading His followers. Śaṅkarācārya's injunction was that a *sannyāsī* should always study the *Vedānta* and that he should be satisfied by simply having one cloth and nothing more. Because Lord Caitanya neither studied the *Vedānta* formally nor ceased from singing and dancing, He was criticized by all the *sannyāsīs* at Benares, as well as by their householder followers.

When Lord Caitanya received news of this criticism from His students and disciples, He simply smiled and started for Mathurā and Vṛndāvana. When He returned to Benares on His way from Mathurā to Jagannātha Purī, He stayed at the house of Candraśekhara, who was considered a *śūdra* because he was a clerk. In spite of this, Lord Caitanya Mahāprabhu made His residence at his home. Lord Caitanya made no distinctions between *brāhmaṇas* and *śūdras;* He accepted anyone who was devoted. Customarily, a *sannyāsī* is supposed to take shelter and eat in the home of a *brāhmaṇa,* but Caitanya Mahāprabhu, as the independent Supreme Personality of Godhead, used His own discretion and decided to stay at Candraśekhara's house.

In those days, by misusing their brahminical heritage, the *brāhmaṇas* had created a law to the effect that anyone not born in a *brāhmaṇa* family was to be considered a *śūdra*. Thus even the *kṣatriyas* and *vaidyas* were also considered *śūdras*. Because the *vaidyas* were said to be descendants of *brāhmaṇa* fathers and *śūdra* mothers, they were sometimes called *śūdras*. Thus Candraśekhara, although born in a *vaidya* family, was called a *śūdra* in Benares. As long as Lord Caitanya stayed in Benares, He remained at Candraśekhara's home, and He took His food at the home of Tapana Miśra.

When Sanātana Gosvāmī met Lord Caitanya at Benares, he learned the process and principles of devotional service during two months of continual teaching. Lord Caitanya's instructions to Sanātana Gosvāmī have been described in the first part of this book. After receiving these teachings, Sanātana Gosvāmī was authorized to propagate the principles of devotional service and *Śrīmad-Bhāgavatam*. It was during this time that both Tapana Miśra and Candraśekhara were feeling very sorry about the strong criticism against Lord Caitanya Mahāprabhu, and they came together and prayed for the Lord to meet the Māyāvādī *sannyāsīs*.

"We have been mortified by hearing unfavorable criticisms from the Māyāvādī *sannyāsīs* against You," they informed Lord Caitanya. "Indeed, it has become intolerable for us." They requested the Lord to do something so that these criticisms would be stopped. While they were discussing this subject, a *brāhmaṇa* came to Lord Caitanya and invited Him to his home. All the *sannyāsīs* but Caitanya Mahāprabhu had been invited, and now the *brāhmaṇa* came to invite Him. Knowing that the Lord did not mix with Māyāvādī *sannyāsīs,* the *brāhmaṇa* fell down at Caitanya Mahāprabhu's feet and implored Him: "Although I know that You do not accept invitations, I still implore You to come and take

Lord Caitanya meets Prakāśānanda Sarasvatī at Benares.

prasādam at my home with the other *sannyāsīs*. If You accept this invitation, I will consider it a special favor."

The Lord took this opportunity and accepted the *brāhmaṇa's* invitation in order to meet the Māyāvādī *sannyāsīs*. Actually this was an arrangement made by the Lord Himself. Although the *brāhmaṇa* who invited Him knew that the Lord did not accept any invitations, he was still very eager to invite Him.

The next day Lord Caitanya went to the house of the *brāhmaṇa* and saw that all the Māyāvādī *sannyāsīs* were sitting there. He offered His respects to all the *sannyāsīs,* as was customary, and then went to wash His feet. After washing, He sat down at that spot, a little distance from the other *sannyāsīs*. While He was sitting there, the *sannyāsīs* saw a glaring effulgence emanating from His body. Attracted by this glaring effulgence, all the Māyāvādī *sannyāsīs* stood up and showed Him their respects. Among them was a *sannyāsī* named Prakāśānanda Sarasvatī. He was the chief among the impersonalist *sannyāsīs,* and he addressed Lord Caitanya with great humility, asking Him to come and sit among them.

"My dear Sir, why are You sitting in that filthy place?" he asked. "Please come and sit with us."

"Oh, I belong to an inferior sect of *sannyāsīs,*" Lord Caitanya replied. "Therefore I think that I should not sit with you. Let Me remain down here."

Prakāśānanda was surprised to hear such a thing from such a learned man, and he took the Lord's hand and requested Him to please come and sit with him and the other *sannyāsīs*. When Lord Caitanya was finally seated among them, Prakāśānanda Sarasvatī said, "I think Your name is Śrī Kṛṣṇa Caitanya, and because You have taken *sannyāsa* from Keśava Bhāratī, who belongs to the Śaṅkarācārya *sampradāya,* I understand that You belong to our Māyāvādī sect."

According to the Śaṅkara sect, there are ten different names for *sannyāsīs*. Out of them, three names—Tīrtha, Āśrama and Sarasvatī—are given to the *sannyāsīs* considered to be the most enlightened and cultured. Since Lord Caitanya was a Vaiṣṇava, He was naturally humble and meek, and He wanted to give the better sitting place to Prakāśānanda, who belonged to the Sarasvatī *sampradāya*. According to Śaṅkara's principles, a *brahmacārī* of the Bhāratī school is called Caitanya. However, although Śrī Kṛṣṇa Caitanya Mahāprabhu took *sannyāsa,* He kept His *brahmacārī* name and did not take up the title of Bhāratī.

"Well, Sir," Prakāśānanda Sarasvatī continued, "You belong to our Śaṅkara sect, and You are living in Benares—so why don't You mix with us? What is the reason? Another thing: You are a *sannyāsī* and are supposed to engage simply in the study of the *Vedānta,* but we see that instead You are always engaged in chanting and dancing and playing musical instruments. What is the reason? These are the activities of emotional and sentimental people. But You are a qualified *sannyāsī*. Why not engage in the study of the *Vedānta*? By Your effulgence it appears to us that You are just like the Supreme Nārāyaṇa, the Personality of Godhead, but by Your behavior You appear to be otherwise. So we are inquisitive to know why You act in this way."

"My dear sir," Lord Caitanya replied, "My spiritual master considered Me a great fool. Therefore he has more or less punished Me by saying that because I am such a fool I have no capacity to study the *Vedānta*. So he kindly gave Me the chanting of Hare Kṛṣṇa, Hare Kṛṣṇa, Kṛṣṇa Kṛṣṇa, Hare Hare/ Hare Rāma, Hare Rāma, Rāma Rāma, Hare Hare. My spiritual master told Me, 'Just go on chanting this Hare Kṛṣṇa *mantra;* it will make You all-perfect.'"

Actually, Lord Caitanya was neither foolish nor ignorant of the principles of the *Vedānta*. His purpose was to demonstrate to modern society that fools who have no history of penance and austerity should not try to study the *Vedānta* just for some recreational purpose. In His *Śikṣāṣṭaka,* Lord Caitanya said that one should be in a humble state of mind, should think himself lower than the grass on the street, should be more tolerant than a tree, and should be devoid of all sense of prestige and ready to offer all kinds of respects to others. In such a state of mind, one can chant the Vedānta philosophy or the holy name of God constantly. The Lord also wanted to teach that a serious student of transcendental science should exactly follow the words of his spiritual master. According to the calculations of His spiritual master, Lord Caitanya appeared to be a fool; therefore he said that He should not indulge in the study of the *Vedānta* but should continue chanting the Hare Kṛṣṇa *mantra*. Lord Caitanya strictly obeyed this order. In other words, Lord Caitanya impressed on the Māyāvādīs that the words of a bona fide spiritual master must be strictly followed. One who does so becomes perfect in all respects.

The word *vedānta* means "the last word of Vedic knowledge," which is to understand Kṛṣṇa. As Kṛṣṇa states in the *Bhagavad-gītā* (15.15), *vedaiś ca sarvair aham eva vedyaḥ:* "By all the *Vedas,* I am to be known." When one actually comes to understand the *Vedānta,* he comes to know Kṛṣṇa and his relationship with Kṛṣṇa. And one who understands Kṛṣṇa understands everything. Moreover, the knower of Kṛṣṇa is always engaged in His transcendental loving service. As the Lord states in the *Bhagavad-gītā* (10.8):

ahaṁ sarvasya prabhavo mattaḥ sarvaṁ pravartate
iti matvā bhajante māṁ budhā bhāva-samanvitāḥ

"I am the source of everything, and everything emanates from Me. One who perfectly knows this fully engages in My transcendental loving service."

A living entity is eternally related with Kṛṣṇa in the relationship of servant and master. Once that service is wanting—or, in other words, when one is not situated in Kṛṣṇa consciousness—it is to be understood that his study of the *Vedānta* is insufficient. When one does not understand Kṛṣṇa or does not engage in His transcendental loving service, it is to be understood that he is averse to studying the *Vedānta* and understanding the Supreme Personality of Godhead. The path of *Vedānta* study shown by Lord Caitanya should be followed by all. A person who is puffed up by so-called education has no humility and therefore does not seek the protection of a bona fide spiritual master. He thinks that he does not require a spiritual master and that he can achieve the highest perfection by his own efforts. Such persons are not eligible for studying the *Vedānta-sūtra*. Those who are under the spell of the material energy do not follow the instructions of the disciplic succession but try to manufacture something on their own. In this way they step outside the sphere of *Vedānta* study. A bona fide spiritual master must always condemn such independent mental speculators. If the bona fide spiritual master directly points out the foolishness of a disciple, it should not be taken wrongly.

A person who is completely ignorant of the science of God cannot be considered learned. More or less, everyone who is not in Kṛṣṇa consciousness is subject to foolishness. Sometimes we display our foolishness by accepting someone who is barely educated as a spiritual master. It is our duty to understand the Supreme Personality of Godhead, whose lotus feet are worshiped by all the *Vedas*. One who does not understand Him and is proud of a false understanding of the *Vedānta* is actually a fool. Mundane attempts at academic knowledge are simply another type of foolishness. As long as one cannot understand the cosmic manifestation as a representation of the three modes of material nature, he must be considered to be in the darkness of inebriety and caught in the duality of this material world. A person who is in perfect knowledge of the *Vedānta* becomes a servitor of the Supreme Lord, who is the maintainer and sustainer of the whole cosmic manifestation. As long as one is not transcendental to the service of the limited, he cannot have knowledge of the *Vedānta*.

As long as one is within the limited jurisdiction of fruitive activities or is involved in mental speculation, he may perhaps be eligible to study or teach the theoretical knowledge of the *Vedānta-sūtra,* but he cannot understand the supreme, eternal, transcendental (completely liberated) vibration of Hare Kṛṣṇa, Hare Kṛṣṇa, Kṛṣṇa Kṛṣṇa, Hare Hare/ Hare Rāma, Hare Rāma, Rāma Rāma, Hare Hare. One who has achieved perfection in chanting this transcendental vibration does not have to separately learn the philosophy of the *Vedānta-sūtra*. According to the teachings of Caitanya Mahāprabhu, the bona fide spiritual master, those who do not understand that this transcendental vibration is nondifferent from the Supreme, yet who try to become Māyāvādī philosophers expert in the *Vedānta-sūtra,* are all fools. Studying the *Vedānta-sūtra* by one's own efforts (the ascending process of knowledge) is a sign of foolishness. On the other hand, he who has attained a taste for chanting this transcendental vibration has actually reached the conclusion of the

Vedānta. In this connection, there are two verses in *Śrīmad-Bhāgavatam* which are very instructive. The purport of the first is that if a person is chanting the transcendental vibration Hare Kṛṣṇa, Hare Kṛṣṇa, Kṛṣṇa Kṛṣṇa, Hare Hare/ Hare Rāma, Hare Rāma, Rāma Rāma, Hare Hare, then even if he was born in the family of the lowest of human beings it is to be understood that in his previous lives he performed all types of renunciation, austerities and sacrifice and studied all the *Brahma-sūtras.* The purport of the second verse is that one who chants the two syllables *ha-ri* must be considered to have studied all the *Vedas*—the *Ṛg Veda, Atharva Veda, Yajur Veda* and *Sāma Veda.*

On the other hand, there are many so-called devotees who think the *Vedānta* is not meant for devotees. Such people are ignorant of the fact that the *Vedānta* is the only platform of pure devotees. The great *ācāryas* of all four Vaiṣṇava *sampradāyas* have made commentaries on the *Vedānta-sūtra,* but the so-called devotees known as *prākṛta-sahajiyās* carefully avoid the study of the *Vedānta-sūtra.* The *prākṛta-sahajiyās* mistakenly take the pure devotees and Vaiṣṇava *ācāryas* to be mental speculators or fruitive actors. Consequently they themselves become Māyāvādīs and leave the service of the Supreme Lord.

Understanding the *Vedānta-sūtra* by academic knowledge never enables one to understand the value of the transcendental vibration. People who are entangled in academic knowledge are conditioned souls who are confused about the facts of "I"-and-"mine" understanding. Consequently they are unable to detach their minds from the external energy. When a person actually attains transcendental knowledge, he becomes free from this duality and engages in the transcendental loving service of the Supreme Lord. The Lord's service is the only means by which one can become detached from material activities. A person properly initiated by a bona fide spiritual master and engaged in chanting Hare Kṛṣṇa, Hare Kṛṣṇa, Kṛṣṇa Kṛṣṇa, Hare Hare/ Hare Rāma, Hare Rāma, Rāma Rāma, Hare Hare gradually becomes freed from the conception of "I" and "mine" and becomes attached to the Lord's transcendental loving service in one of the five transcendental relationships. Such transcendental service is not a subject matter for gross and subtle bodies.

Only when one can understand that there is no difference between the Supreme and His name can one be situated in Kṛṣṇa consciousness. At such a time one no longer needs to make grammatical adjustments. Rather, one becomes more interested in petitioning the Lord: "Hare Kṛṣṇa—O my Lord, O energy of the Lord, please engage me in Your service!"

Lord Caitanya explained all this to Prakāśānanda Sarasvatī and told him that He had heard all this from His spiritual master. He further informed Prakāśānanda Sarasvatī that His spiritual master had taught Him that *Śrīmad-Bhāgavatam* is the actual commentary on the *Vedānta-sūtra,* as stated in *Śrīmad-Bhāgavatam* by Vyāsadeva, the author of the *Vedānta-sūtra.*

A student's perfection is to understand the identity of the holy name and the Supreme Lord. Unless one is under the shelter of a realized spiritual master, his understanding of the Supreme is simply foolishness. However, one can fully understand the transcendental Lord by service and devotion. When Lord Caitanya offenselessly chanted the Hare Kṛṣṇa *mantra,* He declared that the *mantra* could at once deliver a conditioned soul from material contamination. In this Age of Kali there is no alternative to chanting this *mahā-mantra*. It is stated that the essence of all Vedic literature is the chanting of this holy name of Kṛṣṇa: Hare Kṛṣṇa, Hare Kṛṣṇa, Kṛṣṇa Kṛṣṇa, Hare Hare/ Hare Rāma, Hare Rāma, Rāma Rāma, Hare Hare. Lord Caitanya also told Prakāśānanda Sarasvatī, "In order to convince Me about this essential fact of Vedic knowledge, My spiritual master has taught Me a verse from the *Bṛhan-nāradīya Purāṇa* (38.126). *Harer nāma harer nāma harer nāmaiva kevalam/ kalau nāsty eva nāsty eva nāsty eva gatir anyathā:* "'In this age of quarrel and hypocrisy, the only means of deliverance is the chanting of the holy name of the Lord. There is no other way. There is no other way. There is no other way.'"

In three out of the four millenniums (namely Satya-yuga, Tretā-yuga and Dvāpara-yuga) people had the honor to strive to understand transcendence through the path of disciplic succession. But in the present age, due to the influence of Kali, people have no interest in the disciplic succession. Instead, they have invented many paths of logic and argument. This individual attempt to understand the supreme transcendence (called the ascending process) is not the Vedic way. The Absolute Truth must descend from the absolute platform. He is not to be understood by the ascending process. The holy name of the Lord—Hare Kṛṣṇa, Hare Kṛṣṇa, Kṛṣṇa Kṛṣṇa, Hare Hare/ Hare Rāma, Hare Rāma, Rāma Rāma, Hare Hare—is a transcendental vibration because it comes from the transcendental platform, the supreme abode of Kṛṣṇa. And because there is no difference between Kṛṣṇa and His name, the holy name of Kṛṣṇa is as pure, perfect and liberated as Kṛṣṇa Himself. Academic scholars, relying on logic and argument, have no entrance into the understanding of the transcendental nature of the holy name of God. The single path for understanding the transcendental nature of Hare Kṛṣṇa, Hare Kṛṣṇa, Kṛṣṇa Kṛṣṇa, Hare Hare/ Hare Rāma, Hare Rāma, Rāma Rāma, Hare Hare is the chanting of these names with faith and adherence. Such chanting will release one from designated conditions arising from the gross and subtle bodies.

In this age of logical argument and disagreement, the chanting of Hare Kṛṣṇa is the only means for self-realization. And because this transcendental vibration alone can deliver the conditioned soul, it is the essence of the *Vedānta-sūtra*. According to the material conception, there is a difference between a person himself and his name, form, qualities, emotions and activities, but as far as this transcendental vibration is concerned, there is no such limitation, for it descends from the spiritual world. In the spiritual world, unlike the material world, there is no difference between a person and his name and qualities. Because the Māyāvādī philosophers cannot understand this, they cannot utter the transcendental vibration.

Lord Caitanya then told Prakāśānanda Sarasvatī that because He received the order from His spiritual master He was constantly chanting Hare Kṛṣṇa, Hare Kṛṣṇa, Kṛṣṇa Kṛṣṇa, Hare Hare/ Hare Rāma, Hare Rāma, Rāma Rāma, Hare Hare. "As a result of this chanting," the Lord said, "I sometimes become very impatient and cannot restrain Myself from dancing and laughing or crying and singing. Indeed, I become just like a madman. When I first wondered whether I had become mad by chanting this Hare Kṛṣṇa, Hare Kṛṣṇa, Kṛṣṇa Kṛṣṇa, Hare Hare/ Hare Rāma, Hare Rāma, Rāma Rāma, Hare Hare, I approached My spiritual master and informed him that I had gone mad by chanting Hare Kṛṣṇa, Hare Kṛṣṇa, Kṛṣṇa Kṛṣṇa, Hare Hare/ Hare Rāma, Hare Rāma, Rāma Rāma, Hare Hare. Thus I asked him what was My actual position."

In the *Nārada-pañcarātra* it is stated:

eṣo vedāḥ ṣaḍ-aṅgāni chandāṁsi vividhāḥ surāḥ
sarvam aṣṭākṣarāntaḥsthaṁ yac cānyad api vāṅ-mayam
sarva-vedānta-sārārthaḥ saṁsārārṇava-tāraṇaḥ

"All Vedic rituals, *mantras* and understanding are compressed into the eight words Hare Kṛṣṇa, Hare Kṛṣṇa, Kṛṣṇa Kṛṣṇa, Hare Hare." Similarly, in the *Kali-santaraṇa Upaniṣad* it is stated:

hare kṛṣṇa hare kṛṣṇa kṛṣṇa kṛṣṇa hare hare
hare rāma hare rāma rāma rāma hare hare

iti ṣoḍaśakaṁ nāmnāṁ kali-kalmaṣa-nāśanam
nātaḥ paratаropāyaḥ sarva-vedeṣu dṛśyate

"The sixteen words Hare Kṛṣṇa, Hare Kṛṣṇa, Kṛṣṇa Kṛṣṇa, Hare Hare/ Hare Rāma, Hare Rāma, Rāma Rāma, Hare Hare are especially meant for counteracting the contaminations of Kali. To save oneself from the contamination of Kali, there is no alternative to the chanting of these sixteen words."

Lord Caitanya informed Prakāśānanda Sarasvatī that when His spiritual master understood Him he said, "It is the transcendental nature of the holy names Hare Kṛṣṇa, Hare Kṛṣṇa, Kṛṣṇa Kṛṣṇa, Hare Hare/ Hare Rāma, Hare Rāma, Rāma Rāma, Hare Hare to transport a man into spiritual madness. Anyone who sincerely chants this holy name is quickly elevated to the platform of love of God and becomes mad after God. This madness arising from love of God is the highest perfectional stage for a human being."

Generally a human being is interested in religion, economic development, sense gratification and liberation. But love of God is above all these. A bona fide spiritual master chants the holy names Hare Kṛṣṇa, Hare Kṛṣṇa, Kṛṣṇa Kṛṣṇa, Hare Hare/ Hare Rāma, Hare Rāma, Rāma Rāma, Hare Hare, and the transcendental sound vibration enters the ear of the disciple, and if the disciple follows in the footsteps of his spiritual master and chants the holy name with equal respect, this chanting constitutes worship of the transcendental name. When the transcendental name is worshiped by the devotee, the name Himself spreads His glories within the heart of the devotee. When the devotee is perfectly qualified in chanting the transcendental vibration of the holy name, he is quite fit to become a spiritual master and to deliver all the people of the world. The chanting of the holy name is so powerful that it gradually establishes its supremacy above everything in the world. The devotee who chants it becomes transcendentally situated in ecstasy and sometimes laughs, cries and dances in his ecstasy. Sometimes the unintelligent put hindrances in the path of the chanting of the Hare Kṛṣṇa *mahā-mantra,* but one who is situated on the platform of love of Godhead continues to chant the holy name loudly for the benefit of all concerned. As a result, everyone becomes initiated into the chanting of the holy names—Hare Kṛṣṇa, Hare Kṛṣṇa, Kṛṣṇa Kṛṣṇa, Hare Hare/ Hare Rāma, Hare Rāma, Rāma Rāma, Hare Hare. By chanting and hearing the holy names of Kṛṣṇa, a person can remember the forms and qualities of Kṛṣṇa.

CHAPTER 19

Further Talks with Prakāśānanda

Bhāva is the transcendental ecstatic attachment for Kṛṣṇa which results from perfectly understanding that the person Kṛṣṇa and the name Kṛṣṇa are identical. One who has attained *bhāva* is certainly not contaminated by material nature. He enjoys transcendental pleasure from *bhāva,* and when *bhāva* is intensified it is called love of Godhead. Lord Caitanya told Prakāśānanda Sarasvatī that the holy name of Kṛṣṇa—the *mahā-mantra,* or "great chant"—enables anyone who chants it to attain the stage of love of Godhead, or intensified *bhāva*. Love of Godhead is the ultimate human necessity, for when one compares it with other necessities (namely religion, economic development, sense gratification and liberation), one can see that these others are most insignificant. When one is absorbed in temporary, conditioned existence, he hankers after sense gratification and liberation. But love of Godhead is the eternal nature of the soul; it is unchangeable, without beginning or end. Therefore neither temporary sense gratification nor liberation can compare with the transcendental nature of love of God. Love of God is the fifth and ultimate goal of human life. Compared with the ocean of transcendental pleasure that is love of God, the conception of impersonal Brahman is no more significant than a drop of water.

Lord Caitanya next explained that His spiritual master had confirmed the validity of the ecstasy He had felt from chanting the holy name of God, and he had also confirmed that the essence of all Vedic literature is the attainment of love of Godhead. Lord Caitanya's spiritual master had said that the Lord was fortunate to have attained love of Godhead. The heart of one who attains such transcendental love becomes very anxious to attain direct contact with the Lord. Feeling such transcendental sentiment, one sometimes laughs, sometimes cries, sometimes sings, sometimes dances like a madman, and sometimes runs hither and thither. In this way there are various ecstatic symptoms manifest: crying, changing bodily color, madness, bereavement, silence, pride, ecstasy and gentleness. Often the person who has attained love of God dances, and such dancing places him in the ocean of the nectar of love of Kṛṣṇa.

Lord Caitanya said that His spiritual master told Him: "It is very good that You have attained such a perfectional stage of love of Godhead. Because of Your attainment, I am very much obliged to You." The father becomes enlivened when he sees his son advance beyond himself. Similarly, the spiritual master takes more pleasure in seeing his disciple advance than in advancing himself. Thus Lord Caitanya's spiritual master blessed Him, telling Him: "Dance, sing, propagate this *saṅkīrtana* movement and, by instructing people about Kṛṣṇa, try to deliver them from nescience." Lord Caitanya's spiritual master also taught Him the following very nice verse from *Śrīmad-Bhāgavatam* (11.2.40):

evaṁ-vrataḥ sva-priya-nāma-kīrtyā
jātānurāgo druta-citta uccaiḥ
hasaty atho roditi rauti gāyaty
unmāda-van nṛtyati loka-bāhyaḥ

"A person who constantly engages in devotional service to Kṛṣṇa by chanting His holy name becomes so transcendentally attached to the chanting that his heart becomes softened without extraneous endeavor. When this happens, he exhibits transcendental ecstasies by sometimes laughing, sometimes crying, sometimes singing and sometimes dancing—not exactly in an artistic way, but just like a madman."

Lord Caitanya further informed Prakāśānanda Sarasvatī: "Because I have full faith in My spiritual master's words, I always engage in chanting Hare Kṛṣṇa, Hare Kṛṣṇa, Kṛṣṇa Kṛṣṇa, Hare Hare/ Hare Rāma, Hare Rāma, Rāma Rāma, Hare Hare. I do not know how I have become just like a madman, but I believe the name of Kṛṣṇa has induced Me. I have realized that the transcendental pleasure derived from chanting Hare Kṛṣṇa, Hare Kṛṣṇa, Kṛṣṇa Kṛṣṇa, Hare Hare/ Hare Rāma, Hare Rāma, Rāma Rāma, Hare Hare is just like an ocean, in comparison to which all other pleasures, including the pleasure of impersonal realization, are like the shallow water in canals."

It appears from the talks of Lord Caitanya that a person who cannot keep his faith in the words of the spiritual master and who acts independently cannot attain the desired success in chanting Hare Kṛṣṇa. In the Vedic literature it is stated that the import of all transcendental literature is revealed to one who has unflinching faith in the Supreme Lord and his spiritual master. Lord Caitanya firmly believed in the statements of His spiritual master, and He never neglected the instructions of His spiritual master by stopping His *saṅkīrtana* movement. Thus the transcendental potency of the holy name encouraged Him more and more in chanting Hare Kṛṣṇa, the *mahā-mantra*.

Lord Caitanya next informed Prakāśānanda that in the modern age people in general are more or less bereft of spiritual intellect. When such people come under the influence of Śaṅkarācārya's Māyāvāda (impersonalist) philosophy before beginning the most confidential *Vedānta-sūtra,* their natural tendency toward obedience to the Supreme is checked. The supreme source of everything is naturally respected by everyone, but this natural tendency is hampered when one takes to the impersonalist conceptions of Śaṅkara. Thus the spiritual master of Lord Caitanya suggested that it is better not to study the *Śārīraka-bhāṣya* of Śaṅkarācārya, for it is very harmful to people in general. Indeed, the common man does not even have the intelligence to penetrate into the jugglery of words.

He is better advised to chant the *mahā-mantra:* Hare Kṛṣṇa, Hare Kṛṣṇa, Kṛṣṇa Kṛṣṇa, Hare Hare/ Hare Rāma, Hare Rāma, Rāma Rāma, Hare Hare. In this quarrelsome Age of Kali there is no alternative for self-realization.

After hearing the arguments and talks of Caitanya Mahāprabhu, all the Māyāvādī *sannyāsīs* who were present became pacified and replied with sweet words: "Dear sir, what You have spoken is all true. A person who attains love of Godhead is certainly very fortunate, and undoubtedly You are very fortunate to have attained this stage. But what is the fault in the *Vedānta*? It is the duty of a *sannyāsī* to read and understand the *Vedānta*. Why do You not study it?"

According to Māyāvādī philosophers, the *Vedānta* refers to the *Śārīraka* commentary of Śaṅkarācārya. When impersonalist philosophers refer to the *Vedānta* and the *Upaniṣads,* they are actually referring to these works as understood through the commentaries of Śaṅkarācārya, the greatest teacher of Māyāvāda philosophy. After Śaṅkarācārya came Sadānanda Yogīndra, who claimed that the *Vedānta* and *Upaniṣads* should be understood through the commentaries of Śaṅkarācārya. Factually, this is not so. There are many commentaries on the *Vedānta* and the *Upaniṣads* made by Vaiṣṇava *ācāryas,* and these are preferred to those of Śaṅkarācārya. But the Māyāvādī philosophers, influenced by Śaṅkarācārya, do not attribute any importance to the Vaiṣṇava understandings.

There are four different sects of Vaiṣṇava *ācāryas*, and each follows a different variation of personalism—*śuddhādvaita, viśiṣṭādvaita, dvaitādvaita* and *acintya-bhedābheda*. All the Vaiṣṇava *ācāryas* in these schools have written commentaries on the *Vedānta-sūtra,* but the Māyāvādī philosophers do not recognize them. The Māyāvādīs distinguish between Kṛṣṇa and Kṛṣṇa's body, and therefore they do not recognize the worship of Kṛṣṇa by the Vaiṣṇava philosophers. Thus when the Māyāvādī *sannyāsīs* asked Lord Caitanya why He did not study the *Vedānta-sūtra,* the Lord replied, "Dear sirs, you have asked why I do not study the *Vedānta,* and in answer to this I could speak something, but I am afraid you would be sorry to hear it."

All the Māyāvādī *sannyāsīs* replied, "We shall be very much pleased to hear You because we see that You are just like Nārāyaṇa and Your speeches are so nice that we are taking great pleasure in them. We are very much obliged to see and hear You. Therefore we shall be very glad to hear patiently and accept whatever You say."

The Lord then began to speak on Vedānta philosophy as follows: The *Vedānta-sūtra* is spoken by the Supreme Lord Himself. The Supreme Lord, in His incarnation as Vyāsadeva, has compiled this great philosophical treatise. Since Vyāsadeva is an incarnation of the Supreme Lord, he cannot be likened to an ordinary person, who has the four defects which arise due to contact with material existence. The defects of a conditioned soul are (1) he must commit mistakes, (2) he must be illusioned, (3) he must possess the tendency to cheat others, and (4) all his senses must be imperfect. We must understand that the incarnation of God is transcendental to all these defects. Thus whatever has been spoken and written by Vyāsadeva is considered to be perfect. The *Upaniṣads* and *Vedānta-sūtra* aim at the same goal: the Supreme Absolute Truth. When we accept the direct import of the *Vedānta-sūtra* and *Upaniṣads,* that is glorious. But the commentaries made by Śaṅkarācārya are indirect and are thus very dangerous for the common man to read, for by understanding the import of the *Upaniṣads* in such an indirect, disruptive way, one practically bars himself from spiritual realization.

According to the *Skanda* and *Vāyu Purāṇas,* the word *sūtra* refers to a condensed work which carries meaning and import of immeasurable strength without any mistake or fault. The word *vedānta* means "the end of Vedic knowledge." In other words, any book which deals with the subject matter indicated by all the *Vedas* is called *vedānta.* For example, the *Bhagavad-gītā* is *vedānta* because in the *Bhagavad-gītā* the Lord says that the ultimate goal of all Vedic research is Kṛṣṇa. Thus one should understand that the *Bhagavad-gītā* and *Śrīmad-Bhāgavatam,* which aim only at Kṛṣṇa, are *vedānta.*

In transcendental realization there are three divisions of knowledge, called *prasthāna-traya.* That department of knowledge which is proved by Vedic instruction (like the *Upaniṣads*) is called *śruti-prasthāna.* Authoritative books indicating the ultimate goal and written by liberated souls like Vyāsadeva (for example, the *Bhagavad-gītā, Mahābhārata* and *Purāṇas,* especially *Śrīmad-Bhāgavatam,* the

Mahā-Purāṇa) are called *smṛti-prasthāna*. From the Vedic literature we understand that the *Vedas* originated from the breathing of Nārāyaṇa. Vyāsadeva, who is an incarnation of the power of Nārāyaṇa, compiled the *Vedānta-sūtra* (*nyāya-prasthāna*), but according to Śaṅkara's commentaries, Apāntaratamā Ṛṣi is also sometimes credited with having compiled the aphorisms of the *Vedānta-sūtra*. According to Lord Caitanya, the conclusions of the verses of the *Pañcarātra* and the aphorisms of the *Vedānta* are one and the same. Since the *Vedānta-sūtra* is compiled by Vyāsadeva, it should be understood to be spoken by Nārāyaṇa Himself. From all the descriptive literature dealing with the *Vedānta-sūtra*, it appears that there were many other *ṛṣis* contemporary with Vyāsadeva who also discussed the *Vedānta-sūtra*. These sages were Ātreya, Āśmarathya, Auḍulomi, Kārṣṇājini, Kāśakṛtsna, Jaimini and Bādarī, while other sages such as Pārāśarī and Karmandī discussed the *Vedānta* before Vyāsadeva.

In the first two chapters of the *Vedānta-sūtra* the relationship between the living entities and the Supreme Lord is explained, and in the Third Chapter the discharge of devotional service is explained. The Fourth Chapter deals with the result of discharging devotional service. The natural commentary on the *Vedānta-sūtra* is *Śrīmad-Bhāgavatam*. The great *ācāryas* of the four Vaiṣṇava communities (*sampradāyas*)—namely, Rāmānujācārya, Madhvācārya, Viṣṇu Svāmī and Nimbārka—have also written commentaries on the *Vedānta-sūtra* by following the principles of *Śrīmad-Bhāgavatam*. The followers of these *ācāryas*, down to the present day, have written many books following the principles of *Śrīmad-Bhāgavatam* and accepting it as the natural commentary on the *Vedānta*. Śaṅkara's commentary on the *Vedānta-sūtra*, known as the *Śārīraka-bhāṣya*, is very much adored by the impersonalist scholars, but such materialistic commentaries are completely adverse to the transcendental service of the Lord. Consequently Lord Caitanya said that direct commentaries on the *Upaniṣads* and *Vedānta-sūtra* are glorious, but that anyone who follows the indirect path of Śaṅkarācārya's *Śārīraka-bhāṣya* is certainly doomed.

Lord Caitanya admitted that Śaṅkarācārya was an incarnation of Lord Śiva, and it is known that Lord Śiva is one of the greatest devotees, a *mahājana* of the Bhāgavata school. There are twelve *mahājanas,* great authorities on devotional service, and Lord Śiva is one of them. Why, then, did he adopt the process of Māyāvāda philosophy? The answer is given in the *Śiva Purāṇa,* where the Supreme Lord tells Śiva:

dvāparādau yuge bhūtvā kalayā mānuṣādiṣu
svāgamaiḥ kalpitais tvaṁ ca janān mad-vimukhān kuru

"In the beginning of the Kali-yuga, by My order, bewilder the people in general with Māyāvāda philosophy." In the *Padma Purāṇa,* Lord Śiva tells his wife Bhāgavatī Devī:

māyāvādam asac-chāstraṁ pracchannaṁ bauddham ucyate
mayaiva kalpitaṁ devi kalau brāhmaṇa-rūpiṇā

brahmaṇaś cāparaṁ rūpaṁ nirguṇaṁ vakṣyate mayā
sarva-svaṁ jagato 'py asya mohanārthaṁ kalau yuge

vedānte tu mahā-śāstre māyāvādam avaidikam
mayaiva vakṣyate devi jagatāṁ nāśa-kāraṇāt

"The Māyāvāda philosophy is veiled Buddhism. [In other words, the voidist philosophy of Buddha is more or less repeated in the Māyāvāda philosophy of impersonalism, although the Māyāvādī philosophers claim to be directed by the Vedic conclusions.] As a *brāhmaṇa* boy, I manufacture this philosophy in the Age of Kali to mislead the atheists. Actually, the Supreme Personality of Godhead has His transcendental body, but I describe the Supreme as impersonal. I also explain the *Vedānta-sūtra* according to the same principles of Māyāvāda philosophy."

Lord Śiva continues speaking to Bhāgavatī Devī as follows:

śṛṇu devi pravakṣyāmi tāmasāni yathā-kramam
yeṣāṁ śravaṇa-mātreṇa pātityaṁ jñāninām api

apārthaṁ śruti-vākyānāṁ darśayal loka-garhitam
karma-svarūpa-tyājyatvam atra ca pratipadyate

sarva-karma-paribhraṁśān naiṣkarmyaṁ tatra cocyate
parātma-jīvayor aikyaṁ mayātra pratipadyate

"My dear Devī, sometimes I teach Māyāvāda philosophy for those who are engrossed in the mode of ignorance. But anyone in the mode of goodness who happens to hear this Māyāvāda philosophy falls down, for when I teach Māyāvāda philosophy I say that the living entity and the Supreme Lord are one and the same."

Sadānanda Yogīndra, one of the greatest Māyāvādī *ācāryas,* has written in his book *Vedānta-sāra:* "The Absolute Truth of eternity, knowledge and bliss is Brahman. Ignorance and all products of ignorance are non-Brahman. All products of the three modes of material nature are covered by ignorance, and all are different from the supreme cause and effect. This ignorance is manifested in a collective and individual sense. Collective ignorance is called *viśuddha-sattva-pradhāna*. When that *viśuddha-sattva-pradhāna* is manifested within the ignorance of material nature, it is called the Lord, and the Lord manifests all kinds of ignorance. Therefore He is known as *sarvajña*." Thus according to Māyāvāda philosophy, the Lord is a product of this material nature and the living entity is in the lowest stage of ignorance. That is the sum and substance of Māyāvāda philosophy.

If, however, we accept the import of the *Upaniṣads* directly, it is clear that the Supreme Personality of Godhead is a person with unlimited potency. For example, in the *Śvetāśvatara Upaniṣad* it is stated, "The Supreme Personality of Godhead is the origin of everything, and He has multiple potencies. The Supreme Personality of Godhead is transcendental to the cosmic manifestation. He is the origin of all religion, the supreme deliverer, and the possessor of all opulences. I understand the Supreme Personality of Godhead to be just like the sun, profusely distributing His energies while situated beyond the cloud of this material cosmic manifestation. He is the master of masters, and He is the supreme of supremes. He is known as the greatest Lord, the Personality of Godhead. His multiple potencies are variously distributed." Also, the *Ṛg Veda* (1.22.20) states that Viṣṇu is the Supreme and that saintly persons are always anxious to see His lotus feet. And in the *Aitareya Upa-*

niṣad it is stated that the cosmic manifestation came about when the Lord glanced over material nature (1.1.1–2). This is confirmed by the *Praśna Upaniṣad* (6.3).

The negative descriptions of the Lord which occur in the Vedic literature (such as *apāṇi-pādaḥ:* "the Lord has no hands or feet") indicate that the Lord has no material body and no material form. But He does have His spiritual, transcendental body and His transcendental form. Because the Māyāvādī philosophers misunderstand His transcendental nature, they explain Him as impersonal. The Lord's name, form, qualities, entourage and abode are all in the transcendental world. How can He be a transformation of this material nature? Everything connected with the Supreme Lord is eternal, blissful and full of knowledge.

In effect, Śaṅkarācārya preached Māyāvāda philosophy to bewilder a certain type of atheist. Actually he never considered the Supreme Lord, the Personality of Godhead, to be impersonal, without body or form. It is best for intelligent persons to avoid lectures on Māyāvāda philosophy. We should understand that the Supreme Personality of Godhead Viṣṇu is not impersonal. He is a transcendental person, and the basic principle of the cosmic manifestation is His energy. Māyāvāda philosophy cannot trace the energy of the Supreme Lord back to its source, but all Vedic literatures give evidence of the Supreme Lord's various energetic manifestations. Viṣṇu is not a product of material nature, but material nature is a product of Viṣṇu's potency. The Māyāvādī philosophers understand Viṣṇu to be a product of material nature, but if Viṣṇu is a product of material nature, He can only be counted among the demigods. One who considers Viṣṇu to be a demigod is certainly mistaken and misled. How this is so is explained in the *Bhagavad-gītā* (7.13–14): "Deluded by the three modes of material nature, the whole world does not know Me, who am above the material nature and inexhaustible. My material nature is so powerful that it is very difficult to surpass its spell, even for the greatest scholar, but those who have surrendered unto Me can easily cross beyond it."

CHAPTER 20

The Goal of Vedānta Study

It is concluded that Lord Kṛṣṇa, or Viṣṇu, is not of this material world. He belongs to the spiritual world. One who considers Him to be a demigod of the material world is a great offender and blasphemer. Lord Viṣṇu is not subject to perception by material senses, nor can He be realized by mental speculation. Unlike in the material world, where there is always a difference between the body and the soul, there is no difference between the body and soul of the Supreme Lord Viṣṇu.

Material things are enjoyed by the living entities because the living entities are superior in quality whereas material nature is inferior. Thus the superior nature, the living entities, can enjoy the inferior nature, matter. Because Lord Viṣṇu is in no way touched by matter, He has no tendency to enjoy material nature the way the living entities do. The living entities cannot attain knowledge of Viṣṇu by enjoying their habits of mental speculation. The infinitesimal living entities are not the enjoyers of Viṣṇu, but they are enjoyed by Viṣṇu. Only the greatest offender thinks that Viṣṇu is enjoyed. The greatest blasphemy is to consider Viṣṇu and the living entity on the same level.

The Supreme Absolute Truth, the Personality of Godhead, is compared to a blazing fire, and the innumerable living entities are compared to sparks emanating from that fire. Although both the

Supreme Lord and the living entities are qualitatively fire, there is yet a distinction. Viṣṇu, the Supreme, is infinite, whereas the living entities, which are but sparks, are infinitesimal. The infinitesimal living entities are emanations from the original infinite spirit. In their constitutional position as infinitesimal spirits, there is no trace of matter.

The living entities are not as great as Nārāyaṇa, Viṣṇu, who is beyond this material creation. Even Śaṅkarācārya accepts Nārāyaṇa to be beyond the material creation. Since neither Viṣṇu nor the living entity are of the material creation, someone may inquire, "Why were the small particles of spirit created at all?" The answer is that the Supreme Absolute Truth is complete in His perfection when He is both infinite and infinitesimal. If He were simply infinite but not infinitesimal, He would not be perfect. The infinite portion is the *viṣṇu-tattva,* or the Supreme Personality of Godhead, and the infinitesimal portion is the living entity.

Due to the infinite desires of the Supreme Personality of Godhead, the spiritual world exists, and due to the infinitesimal desires of the living entity, the material world exists. When the infinitesimal living entities are engaged in trying to fulfill their infinitesimal desires for material enjoyment, they are called *jīva-śakti,* but when they are dovetailed with the infinite, they are called liberated souls. There is no need to ask, therefore, why God created the infinitesimal portions: they are simply the complementary side of the Supreme. It is doubtlessly essential for the infinite to have infinitesimal portions which are inseparable parts and parcels of the Supreme Soul. Because the living entities are infinitesimal parts and parcels of the Supreme, there is a reciprocation of feelings between the infinite and the infinitesimal. Had there been no infinitesimal living entities, the Supreme Lord would have been inactive, and there would not be variegatedness in spiritual life. There would be no meaning to a king if there were no subjects, and there would be no meaning to the Supreme God if there were no infinitesimal living entities. How can there be meaning to the word "lord" if there is no one to rule? The conclusion is that the living entities are expansions of the energy of the Supreme Lord and that the Supreme Lord, the Personality of Godhead, Kṛṣṇa, is the energetic.

In all Vedic literatures, including the *Bhagavad-gītā* and *Viṣṇu Purāṇa,* much evidence is given to distinguish between the energy and the energetic. In the *Bhagavad-gītā* (7.4) it is clearly stated that earth, water, fire, air and ether (the five gross elements of the material world) and mind, intelligence and false ego (the three subtle elements) are the Lord's energies. All material nature is divided into these eight elements, which together comprise His inferior nature, or energy. Another name for this inferior nature is *māyā,* or illusion. Beyond these eight inferior elements is His superior energy, which is called *parā prakṛti.* This *parā prakṛti* comprises the living entities, who are found in great numbers throughout the material world. The purport is that the Supreme Lord is the Absolute Truth, the energetic, and that as such He has energies. When one of His energies is not properly manifested, or when it is covered by some shadow, it is called *māyā-śakti.* The material cosmic manifestation is a product of that *māyā-śakti.*

The living entities are factually beyond this covered, inferior energy. They have their pure spiritual existence, their pure identity and their pure mental activities—all beyond the manifestation of this material cosmos. Although the living entity's mind, intelligence and identity are beyond the range of this material world, when he enters into this material world due to his desire to lord it over matter, his original mind, intelligence and body become covered by the material energy. When he is again free of the covering of this material, inferior energy, he is called liberated. When he is liberated he has no false ego, but his real ego again comes into existence. Foolish mental speculators think that after liberation one's identity is lost, but that is not so. Because the living entity is eternally part and parcel of God, when he is liberated he revives his original, eternal, part-and-parcel identity. The realization of *ahaṁ brahmāsmi* ("I am spirit, not this body") does not mean that the living entity loses his identity. At the present moment a person may consider himself to be matter, but in his liberated state he will understand that he is not matter but spirit soul, part of the infinite. To become Kṛṣṇa conscious, or spiritually conscious, and to engage in the transcendental loving service of Kṛṣṇa are signs of the liberated stage.

In the *Viṣṇu Purāṇa* (6.7.61) it is clearly stated:

viṣṇu-śaktiḥ parā prokta kṣetra-jñākhyā tathā parā
avidyā-karma-saṁjñānyā tṛtīyā śaktir iṣyate

"The energy of the Supreme Lord is divided into three: *parā, kṣetra-jña* and *avidyā*." The *parā* energy is actually the energy of the Supreme Lord Himself, the *kṣetra-jña* energy is the living entity, and the *avidyā* energy is the material world, or *māyā*. It is called *avidyā,* or ignorance, because under the spell of this material energy one forgets his actual position and his relationship with the Supreme Lord. The conclusion is that the living entities represent one of the energies of the Supreme Lord. As infinitesimal parts and parcels of the Supreme, they are called *jīvas*. If the *jīvas* are artificially placed on the same level with the infinite Supreme because both of them are Brahman, or spirit, then bewilderment will certainly be the result.

Generally Māyāvādī philosophers are perplexed before a learned Vaiṣṇava because the Māyāvādīs cannot explain the cause of the bondage of the living entities. They simply say, "It is due to ignorance." But they cannot explain how the living entities can be covered by ignorance if they are supreme. The actual reason is that the living entities, although qualitatively one with the Supreme, are infinitesimal, not infinite. Had they been infinite, there would have been no possibility of their being covered by ignorance. Because the living entity is infinitesimal, he can be covered by an inferior energy. The foolishness and ignorance of the Māyāvādīs are revealed when they try to explain how the infinite can be covered by ignorance. It is offensive to attempt to qualify the infinite by arguing that He is subject to the spell of ignorance.

Although Śaṅkara attempted to cover the Supreme Lord by his Māyāvāda philosophy, he was simply following the order of the Supreme Lord. It should be understood that his teachings were a timely necessity but not a permanent fact. In the *Vedānta-sūtra* the distinction between the energy and the energetic is accepted from the very beginning. The second aphorism of the *Vedānta-sūtra*—*janmādy asya yataḥ*—clearly states that the Supreme Absolute Truth is the source of all emanations. Thus the emanations are the energy of the Supreme, whereas the Supreme Himself is the energetic. Śaṅkara has falsely argued that if the transformation of energy is accepted, the Supreme Absolute Truth cannot remain immutable. But this is not true. Despite the fact that unlimited energies are always being generated, the Supreme Absolute Truth remains always the same. He is not affected by the emanation of unlimited energies. Śaṅkarācārya has therefore incorrectly established his theory of illusion.

Rāmānujācārya has discussed this point very nicely: "One may argue, 'Since there was only one Absolute Truth before the creation of this material world, how is it possible that the living entities emanated from Him? If He were alone, how could He have produced or generated the infinitesimal living entities?' In answer to this question, the *Vedas* state that everything is generated from the Absolute Truth, everything is maintained by the Absolute Truth, and, after annihilation, everything enters into the Absolute Truth. This statement from the *Upaniṣads* makes it clear that when the living entities are liberated they enter into the supreme existence without changing their original constitutional position."

We must always remember that the Supreme Lord has His creative function and that the infinitesimal living entities have their creative functions also. It is not that their creative function is lost when they are liberated and enter into the Supreme after the dissolution of the material body. On the contrary, the creative function of the living entity is properly manifested in the liberated state. If the living entity's activities are manifest even when he is materially conditioned, then how is it possible for his activities to stop when he attains liberation? The living entity's entering the state of liberation may be compared to a bird entering a tree, or an animal entering the forest, or a plane entering the sky. In no case are activities stopped.

When explaining the second aphorism of the *Vedānta-sūtra*, Śaṅkara has most unceremoniously tried to explain that Brahman, or the Supreme Absolute Truth, is impersonal. He has also cunningly tried to switch the doctrine of by-products into the doctrine of change. For the Supreme Absolute Truth, there is no change. It is simply that a by-product results from His inconceivable powers of action. In other words, a relative truth—a by-product—is produced out of the Supreme Truth. For example, when a chair is produced out of crude wood, it is said that a by-product is produced. The Supreme Absolute Truth, Brahman, is immutable, and when we find a by-product—the living entity or this cosmic manifestation—it is a transformation of the Supreme's energies, or a by-product of the Supreme. It is like milk being transformed into yogurt. In this way, if we study the living entities in the cosmic manifestation, it will appear that they are not different from the original Absolute Truth, but from the Vedic literature we understand that the Absolute Truth has varieties of energy and that the living entities and the cosmic manifestation are but a demonstration of His energies. The energies are not separate from the energetic; therefore the living entity and the cosmic manifestation are inseparable truths, part of the Absolute Truth. Such a conclusion regarding the Absolute Truth and the relative truth should be acceptable to any sane man.

The Supreme Absolute Truth has His inconceivable potency, out of which this cosmic manifestation has been produced. In other words, the Supreme Absolute Truth supplies the ingredients, and the living entity and the cosmic manifestation are the by-products. In the *Taittirīya Upaniṣad* it is clearly stated, *yato vā imāni bhūtāni jāyante:* "The Absolute Truth is the original reservoir of all ingredients, and this material world and its living entities are produced from those ingredients."

Less intelligent persons who cannot understand this doctrine of by-products cannot grasp how the cosmic manifestation and the living entity are simultaneously one with and different from the Absolute Truth. Not understanding this, one concludes that the doctrine of by-products implies that the Absolute Truth itself is transformed. Unnecessarily fearing this, one then concludes that this cosmic manifestation and the living entity are false. Śaṅkarācārya gives the example of a rope being mistaken for a snake, and sometimes the example of mistaking an oyster shell for gold is cited, but surely such arguments are ways of cheating. As mentioned in the *Māṇḍūkya Upaniṣad,* the examples of mistaking a rope for a snake and an oyster shell for gold have their proper applications and can be understood as follows. The living entity in his original constitutional position is pure spirit. When a human being identifies himself with the material body, his misidentification is like mistaking a rope for a snake, or an oyster shell for gold. The doctrine of illusory transformation of state is accepted when one thing is mistaken for another. Actually the body is not the living entity, but according to the doctrine of illusory transformation of state one accepts the body as the living entity. Every conditioned soul is undoubtedly contaminated by this doctrine of illusory transformation of state.

The conditioned state of the living entity is his diseased condition. Originally the living entity and the original cause of this cosmic manifestation exist outside the state of transformation. But mistaken thoughts and arguments can overcome a person when he forgets the inconceivable energies of the Supreme Lord. Even in the material world there are many examples of inconceivable energy. The sun has been producing unlimited energy from time immemorial, and so many by-products result from the sun; yet there is no change in the heat and temperature of the sun itself. If the sun, despite being a material product, can maintain its original temperature and yet produce so many by-products, is it difficult to understand that the Supreme Absolute Truth remains unchanged in spite of producing so many by-products by His inconceivable energy? Thus there is no question of transformation as far as the Supreme Absolute Truth is concerned.

In the Vedic literature there is information of a material object called a "touchstone," which, simply by touch, can transform iron into gold. The touchstone can produce an unlimited quantity of gold and yet remain unchanged. Only in the state of ignorance can one accept the Māyāvāda conclusion that this cosmic manifestation and the living entities are false or illusory. No sane man would attempt to impose ignorance and illusion upon the Supreme Absolute Truth, who is absolute in everything. There is no possibility of change, ignorance or illusion in Him. The Supreme Brahman, the Supreme Absolute Truth, is transcendental, completely different from all material conceptions, and full of inconceivable potencies. The *Śvetāśvatara Upaniṣad* confirms that the Supreme Absolute Personality of Godhead is full of inconceivable energies and that no one else possesses such energies.

It is only by misunderstanding the inconceivable energies of the

Supreme that one may conclude that the Supreme Absolute Truth is impersonal. Such a deluded conclusion is experienced by a living being when he is in an acute stage of disease. In *Śrīmad-Bhāgavatam* (3.33.3) there is a clear statement that the supreme *ātmā*, the Lord, has inconceivable and innumerable potencies. It is also stated in the *Brahma-saṁhitā* (5.5) that the Supreme Spirit has many variegated and inconceivable energies. Nor should one think that there is any possibility of ignorance existing in the Absolute Truth. Ignorance and knowledge are conceptions in this world of duality, but in the Absolute there cannot be any ignorance. It is simply foolishness to consider that the Absolute is covered by ignorance. If the Absolute Truth could be covered by ignorance, how could it be said to be Absolute?

Understanding the inconceivable energies of the Absolute is the only solution to the question of duality. This is because duality arises from the inconceivable energies of the Absolute. By His inconceivable energies, the Supreme Absolute Truth can remain unchanged and yet produce this cosmic manifestation with all its living entities, just as a touchstone can produce unlimited quantities of gold and yet remain unchanged. Because the Absolute Truth has such inconceivable energies, the material quality of ignorance cannot pertain to Him. The true variegatedness which exists in the Absolute Truth is a product of His inconceivable energies. Indeed, it can be safely concluded that this cosmic manifestation is but a by-product of His inconceivable energies. Once we accept the inconceivable energies of the Supreme Lord, we will find that there is no duality at all. The expansion of the energies of the Supreme Lord is as true as the Supreme Lord Himself. But despite all the variegated manifestations of the Supreme Lord's energies, there is no question of transformation for the Supreme Lord Himself. Once again the example of the touchstone can be cited: in spite of producing unlimited quantities of gold, the touchstone remains the same. (We therefore hear some sages say that the Supreme is the "ingredient cause" of this cosmic manifestation.)

Also, the example of the rope and the snake is not irregular. When we accept a rope to be a snake, it is to be understood that we have experienced a snake previously. Otherwise, how can the rope be mistaken for a snake? Thus the conception of a snake is not untrue or unreal in itself. It is the false identification that is untrue or unreal. When, by mistake, we consider the rope to be a snake, that is our ignorance. But the very idea of a snake is not in itself ignorance. Similarly, when we accept a mirage in the desert to be water, there is no question of water being a false concept. Water is a fact, but it is a mistake to think that there is water in the desert.

Thus this cosmic manifestation is not false, as Śaṅkarācārya maintains. Actually, there is nothing false here. It is because of ignorance that the Māyāvādīs say this world is false. The conclusion of the Vaiṣṇava philosophy is that this cosmic manifestation is a by-product of the inconceivable energies of the Supreme Lord.

The principal word in the *Vedas—praṇava,* or *oṁkāra*—is the sound representation of the Supreme Lord. Therefore *oṁkāra* should be considered the supreme sound. But Śaṅkarācārya has falsely preached that the phrase *tat tvam asi* is the supreme vibration. *Oṁkāra* is the reservoir of all the energies of the Supreme Lord. Śaṅkara is wrong in maintaining that *tat tvam asi* is the supreme vibration of the *Vedas,* for *tat tvam asi* is only a secondary vibration. *Tat tvam asi* suggests only a partial representation of the *Vedas.* In several verses of the *Bhagavad-gītā* (8.13, 9.17, 17.24) the Lord has given importance to *oṁkāra.* Similarly, *oṁkāra* is given importance in the *Atharva Veda* and the *Māṇḍūkya Upaniṣad.* In his *Bhagavat-sandarbha,* Śrīla Jīva Gosvāmī has given great importance to *oṁkāra:* "*Oṁkāra* is the most confidential sound representation of the Supreme Lord." The sound representation or name of the Supreme Lord is as good as the Supreme Lord Himself. By vibrating such sounds as *oṁkāra* or Hare Kṛṣṇa, Hare Kṛṣṇa, Kṛṣṇa Kṛṣṇa, Hare Hare/ Hare Rāma, Hare Rāma, Rāma Rāma, Hare Hare, one can be delivered from the contamination of this material world. Because such vibrations of transcendental sound can deliver a conditioned soul, they are known as *tāraka-mantras.*

That the sound vibration of the Supreme Lord is identical with the Supreme Lord is confirmed in the *Nārada-pañcarātra:*

vyaktaṁ hi bhagavān eva sākṣān-nārāyaṇaḥ svayam
aṣṭākṣara-svarūpeṇa mukheṣu parivartate

"When the transcendental sound is vibrated by a conditioned soul, the Supreme Lord is present on his tongue." In the *Māṇḍūkya Upaniṣad* it is said that when *oṁkāra* is chanted one attains perfect spiritual vision. In other words, in spiritual vision, or the spiritual world, there is nothing but *oṁkāra*. Unfortunately, Śaṅkara has abandoned this chief word, *oṁkāra,* and has whimsically accepted *tat tvam asi* as the supreme vibration of the *Vedas*. By accepting such a secondary vibration and leaving aside the principal vibration, he has given up the direct interpretation of the scripture in favor of his own indirect interpretation.

Śrīpāda Śaṅkarācārya has unceremoniously obscured the Kṛṣṇa consciousness described in the *puruṣa Vedānta-sūtra* by manufacturing an indirect interpretation and abandoning the direct interpretation. Unless we take all the statements of the *Vedānta-sūtra* as self-evident, there is no point in studying the *Vedānta-sūtra*. Interpreting the aphorisms of the *Vedānta-sūtra* according to one's own whim is the greatest disservice to the self-evident *Vedas*.

As far as *oṁkāra* (*praṇava*) is concerned, it is considered to be the sound incarnation of the Supreme Personality of Godhead. As such, *oṁkāra* is eternal, unlimited, transcendental, supreme and indestructible. He (*oṁkāra*) is the beginning, middle and end, and He is beginningless as well. When one understands *oṁkāra* as such, he becomes immortal. One should thus know *oṁkāra* as a representation of the Supreme situated in everyone's heart. One who understands *oṁkāra* and Viṣṇu as being one and the same and all-pervading never laments in the material world, nor does he remain a *śūdra*.

Although He (*oṁkāra*) has no material form, He is unlimitedly expanded and has unlimited form. By understanding *oṁkāra* one can become free from the duality of the material world and attain absolute knowledge. Therefore *oṁkāra* is the most auspicious representation of the Supreme Lord. Such is the description given by the *Māṇḍūkya Upaniṣad*. One should not foolishly interpret an Upaniṣadic description and say that it is because the Supreme Personality of Godhead cannot appear Himself in this material world in His own form that He sends His sound representation (*oṁkāra*) instead. Due to such a false interpretation, *oṁkāra* has come to be considered something material, and consequently *oṁkāra* is misunderstood and eulogized as being simply an exhibition or symbol of the Lord. Actually *oṁkāra* is as good as any other incarnation of the Supreme Lord.

The Lord has innumerable incarnations, and *oṁkāra* is one of them, in the form of a transcendental syllable. As Kṛṣṇa states in the *Bhagavad-gītā* (9.17): "Among vibrations, I am the syllable *oṁ*." This means that *oṁkāra* is nondifferent from Kṛṣṇa. Impersonalists, however, give more importance to *oṁkāra* than to the Personality of Godhead, Kṛṣṇa. But the fact is that any representational incarnation of the Supreme Lord is nondifferent from Him. Such an incarnation or representation is as good spiritually as the Supreme Lord. *Oṁkāra* is therefore the ultimate representation of all the *Vedas*. Indeed, the Vedic *mantras* or hymns have transcendental value because they are prefixed by the syllable *oṁ*. The Vaiṣṇavas interpret *oṁkāra,* a combination of the letters *a, u* and *m,* as follows: The letter *a* indicates Kṛṣṇa, the Supreme Personality of Godhead, the letter *u* indicates Śrīmatī Rādhārāṇī, Kṛṣṇa's eternal consort, and the letter *m* indicates the living entity, the eternal servitor of the Supreme Lord. Śaṅkara has not given such importance to *oṁkāra*. But such importance is given in the *Vedas,* the *Rāmāyaṇa,* the *Purāṇas* and the *Mahābhārata,* from beginning to end. Thus the glories of the Supreme Lord, the Supreme Personality of Godhead, are declared.

CHAPTER 21

The Māyāvādī Philosophers Are Converted

In this way Lord Caitanya condemned attempts at indirect interpretation of the *Vedānta-sūtra,* and all the *sannyāsīs* present were struck with wonder by His explanation. After hearing the direct interpretation, one of the *sannyāsīs* immediately declared, "O Śrīpāda Caitanya, whatever You have explained in Your condemnation of the indirect interpretation of *oṁkāra* is not at all a useless argument. Still, only a fortunate person can accept Your interpretation as the right one. Actually, every one of us now knows that the interpretations given by Śaṅkara are all artificial and imaginary, but because we belong to his sect, we took it for granted that his interpretation was the right one. We shall be very glad to hear You further explain the *Vedānta-sūtra* by direct interpretation."

Being so requested, Lord Caitanya explained each and every aphorism of the *Vedānta-sūtra* according to the direct interpretation. He began by explaining the word "Brahman," indicating that "Brahman" means "the greatest," the Supreme Personality of Godhead. The word "Brahman" indicates that the greatest is full with six opulences; in other words, the Supreme Personality of Godhead is the reservoir of all wealth, all fame, all strength, all beauty, all knowledge and all renunciation. When Lord Kṛṣṇa was present personally on earth, He exhibited these six opulences in full. No one was richer than Lord Kṛṣṇa, no one was more learned than Kṛṣṇa, no one was more beautiful than Kṛṣṇa, no one was stronger than Kṛṣṇa, no one was more famous than Kṛṣṇa, and no one was more renounced than Kṛṣṇa. Therefore the Supreme Personality of Godhead, Kṛṣṇa, is the Supreme Brahman. This is confirmed by Arjuna in the *Bhagavad-gītā* (10.12): *paraṁ brahma paraṁ dhāma.* "You are the Supreme Brahman, the ultimate, the supreme abode." Therefore "Brahman" indicates the greatest, and the greatest is the Supreme Personality of Godhead, Kṛṣṇa. He is the shelter of the Absolute Truth (*para-tattva*) because He is *paraṁ brahma*. There is nothing material in His opulences of wealth, fame, strength, beauty, knowledge and renunciation. All the Vedic verses and hymns indicate that everything about Kṛṣṇa is spiritual and transcendental. Wherever the word "Brahman" appears in the *Vedas,* it should be understood that Kṛṣṇa, the Supreme Personality of Godhead, is indicated. An intelligent person at once replaces the word "Brahman" with the name Kṛṣṇa.

The Supreme Personality of Godhead is transcendental to the material modes of nature, but He is fully qualified with transcendental attributes. To accept the Supreme as impersonal is to deny the full manifestation of His spiritual energies. Since the Supreme Brahman, the Supreme Personality of Godhead, is full with all varieties of spiritual energy, one who simply accepts the impersonal exhibition of spiritual energy does not accept the Absolute Truth in full. To accept the Supreme in full is to accept spiritual variegatedness, which is transcendental to the material modes of nature. By failing to accept the Supreme Personality of Godhead, the impersonalists are left with an incomplete conception of Brahman.

The approved method for understanding the Supreme Personality of Godhead, Kṛṣṇa, is the path of devotional service, and this is confirmed in every Vedic scripture. The devotional service of the Lord begins with hearing about Him. There are nine different methods of devotional service, of which hearing is the chief. Hearing, chanting, remembering, worshiping—all these are used in the process of attaining the highest perfection, understanding the Supreme Personality of Godhead. This process by which the Supreme

Personality of Godhead is understood is known as *abhidheya,* practice of devotional service within conditioned life.

In practice it is experienced that one who takes to Kṛṣṇa consciousness does not like to deviate to any other consciousness. Kṛṣṇa consciousness is the development of love for Kṛṣṇa, the Supreme Personality of Godhead, and this is the fifth and highest interest of the human being. When one takes to this process of transcendental devotional service leading to love of Godhead, he relishes his relationship with Kṛṣṇa directly, and from this reciprocation of relishing transcendental dealings with Kṛṣṇa, Kṛṣṇa gradually becomes a personal associate of the devotee. Then the devotee eternally enjoys blissful life. Therefore the purpose of the *Vedānta-sūtra* is to reestablish the living entity's lost relationship with the Supreme Lord Kṛṣṇa, to describe the execution of devotional service, and to enable one to ultimately achieve the highest goal of life, love of Godhead. The *Vedānta-sūtra* describes these three principles of transcendental life, and nothing more.

After Lord Caitanya explained the *Vedānta-sūtra* by directly interpreting the aphorisms, the chief disciple of Prakāśānanda Sarasvatī stood up in the assembly and began to praise Lord Caitanya as the Supreme Personality of Godhead, Nārāyaṇa. The chief disciple not only very much appreciated the explanation of the *Vedānta-sūtra* by Lord Caitanya, but he publicly stated, "The direct explanation of the *Upaniṣads* and *Vedānta-sūtra* is so pleasing that we forget ourselves and also forget that we belong to the Māyāvādī sect. We must admit that Śaṅkarācārya's explanations of the *Upaniṣads* and *Vedānta-sūtra* are all imaginary. We may sometimes accept such imaginary explanations for the sake of sectarian feuds, but actually such explanations do not satisfy us. It is not that one becomes free from material entanglements simply by accepting the order of *sannyāsa*. But if we actually understand the explanations given by Lord Caitanya, we will be helped. Indeed, Śrī Kṛṣṇa Caitanya's explanation of the verse beginning *harer nāma harer nāma harer nāmaiva kevalam* is pleasing to all of us.

"There is no alternative to devotional service for one who wants to attain liberation from the material clutches. Especially in this age, one can achieve the highest liberation simply by chanting Hare

Kṛṣṇa, Hare Kṛṣṇa, Kṛṣṇa Kṛṣṇa, Hare Hare/ Hare Rāma, Hare Rāma, Rāma Rāma, Hare Hare. In *Śrīmad-Bhāgavatam* (10.14.4) it is stated that when a person abandons the path of devotional service and simply labors for knowledge, his only profit is the trouble he takes to understand the difference between matter and spirit. His efforts are like the useless labor one undergoes trying to get grains from empty husks. Similarly, *Śrīmad-Bhāgavatam* 10.2.32 states that a person who gives up the transcendental loving service of the Supreme Lord and superficially considers himself liberated never attains actual liberation. Although with great labor, austerity and penance he may be elevated to the liberated platform, for want of shelter at the lotus feet of the Supreme Lord he falls down again into material contamination.

"The Supreme Brahman cannot be accepted as impersonal, for if it is then the six opulences belonging to the Supreme Personality of Godhead cannot be attributed to Brahman. All the *Vedas* and *Purāṇas* affirm that the Supreme Personality of Godhead is full of spiritual energies, but foolish people do not accept this, and therefore they deride His activities. They misinterpret the transcendental body of Kṛṣṇa to be a creation of material nature, and this is considered to be the greatest offense and greatest sin. One should simply accept the words of Lord Caitanya that He spoke in this assembly.

"The individual personality of the Supreme Absolute Truth is explained in *Śrīmad-Bhāgavatam* (3.9.3–4): 'O Supreme Lord, the transcendental form which I am seeing is the embodiment of transcendental pleasure. It is eternal and devoid of the contamination of the material modes. It is the greatest manifestation of the Absolute Truth, and it is full of effulgence. O soul of everyone, You are the creator of this cosmic manifestation, with all its material elements. I surrender unto You in Your transcendental form, O Kṛṣṇa! O most auspicious one in the universe! You advent Yourself in Your original personal form in order to be worshiped by us, and we perceive You either by meditation or by direct worship. Foolish people contaminated by the material nature do not give much importance to Your transcendental form, and consequently they glide down to hell.' This is confirmed in the *Bhagavad-gītā* (9.11):

avajānanti māṁ mūḍhā mānuṣīṁ tanum āśritam
paraṁ bhāvam ajānanto mama bhūta-maheśvaram

"'Foolish persons mock Me when I appear in the form of a human being. They do not know the intrinsic value of this transcendental form—that I am the proprietor, the master and the Lord of all creation.' That such foolish and demoniac persons go to the hellish planets is stated later in the *Bhagavad-gītā* (16.19–20):

tān ahaṁ dviṣataḥ krūrān saṁsāreṣu narādhamān
kṣipāmy ajasram aśubhān āsurīṣv eva yoniṣu

āsurīṁ yonim āpannā mūḍhā janmani janmani
mām aprāpyaiva kaunteya tato yānty adhamāṁ gatim

"'I place those who are envious of Me and My devotees into the most degraded species of life. Thus situated, such demoniac souls have no chance of understanding the Supreme Personality of Godhead.'

"The doctrine of by-products, *pariṇāma-vāda,* is asserted from the very beginning of the *Vedānta-sūtra,* but Śaṅkarācārya has superficially tried to hide it and establish the doctrine of illusory transformation of state, *vivarta-vāda*. He also has the audacity to say that Vyāsa is mistaken. All Vedic literatures, including the *Purāṇas,* confirm that the Supreme Lord is the center of all spiritual energy and variegatedness. The Māyāvādī philosophers, puffed-up and incompetent, cannot understand variegatedness in spiritual energy. They consequently falsely believe that spiritual variegatedness is no different than material variegatedness. Deluded by this false belief, the Māyāvādīs deride the pastimes of the Supreme Personality of Godhead. Such foolish persons, unable to understand the spiritual activities of the Supreme Lord, consider Kṛṣṇa a product of this material nature. This is the greatest offense any human being can commit. Lord Caitanya has conclusively established that Kṛṣṇa is *sac-cid-ānanda-vigraha,* the form of eternity, knowledge and bliss, and that He is always engaged in His transcendental pastimes, in which there is all spiritual variegatedness."

In this way the student of Prakāśānanda summarized the explanations of Lord Caitanya, and then he concluded: "We have given up the actual path of spiritual realization. We simply engage in nonsensical talk. Māyāvādī philosophers who are serious about attaining benediction should engage in the devotional service of Kṛṣṇa, but instead they take pleasure in useless argument only. We hereby admit that the explanation of Śaṅkarācārya hides the actual import of the Vedic literature. Only the explanation given by Caitanya is acceptable. All other interpretations are useless."

After thus explaining his position, the chief student of Prakāśānanda Sarasvatī began to chant Hare Kṛṣṇa, Hare Kṛṣṇa, Kṛṣṇa Kṛṣṇa, Hare Hare/ Hare Rāma, Hare Rāma, Rāma Rāma, Hare Hare. When Prakāśānanda Sarasvatī saw this, he too admitted the fault of Śaṅkarācārya and said, "Because Śaṅkarācārya wanted to establish the doctrine of monism, he had no alternative but to interpret the *Vedānta-sūtra* in a different way. Once one accepts the Supreme Personality of Godhead, the doctrine of monism cannot be established. Therefore by mundane scholarship Śaṅkarācārya has tried to obscure the actual meaning of the *Vedānta-sūtra*. Not only has Śaṅkarācārya done this, but all authors who attempt to give their own views must misinterpret the *Vedānta-sūtra*.

"Thus it is Lord Caitanya who has given the direct meaning of the *Vedānta-sūtra*. No Vedic scripture should be used for indirect speculation. In addition to Śaṅkarācārya, other materialistic philosophers like the atheist Kapila, Gautama, Aṣṭāvakra and Patañjali have put forward philosophical speculations in various ways. Indeed, the philosopher Jaimini and his followers, who are all more or less logicians, have abandoned the real meaning of the *Vedas*—devotional service—and tried to establish that the Absolute Truth is subordinate to the material world. It is their opinion that if there is a God He will be pleased with us and give us all desired results if we simply perform our material activities nicely. Similarly, the atheist Kapila tried to establish that it is not God who created the material world but rather a combination of material elements. Gautama and Kaṇāda have also given stress to the material elements, trying to establish that atomic energy is the origin of creation. Impersonalists and monists like Aṣṭāvakra have tried to establish the impersonal effulgence (*brahmajyoti*) as the Supreme. And Patañjali, one of the greatest authorities on the *yoga* system, has tried to conceive of an imaginary form of the Supreme Lord.

"In summary, it should be understood that all these materialistic philosophers have tried to avoid the Supreme Personality of Godhead by putting forward their own mentally concocted philosophies. But Vyāsadeva, the great sage and incarnation of Godhead, has thoroughly studied all these philosophical speculations and in answer has compiled the *Vedānta-sūtra,* which describes the relationship of everything with the Supreme Personality of Godhead, the execution of devotional service, and the ultimate achievement, love of Godhead. The *Vedānta-sūtra* begins with the aphorism *janmādy asya yataḥ,* which Vyāsadeva explains in the first verse of *Śrīmad-Bhāgavatam*, thus establishing from the very beginning that the supreme source of everything is a cognizant, transcendental person.

"The impersonalist tries to explain that the Supreme Lord's impersonal effulgence (the *brahmajyoti*) is beyond the material modes of nature, but at the same time he tries to establish that the Supreme Personality of Godhead is contaminated by the modes of material nature. In truth, the *Vedānta-sūtra* establishes not only that the Supreme Personality of Godhead is transcendental to the material modes of nature but also that He has innumerable transcendental qualities and energies. All these various speculative philosophers are one in denying the existence of the Supreme Lord Viṣṇu, and they are very enthusiastic to put forward their own theories and be recognized by the people. Unfortunate persons become enamored of these atheistic philosophers and thus can never understand the real nature of the Absolute Truth. It is far better to follow in the footsteps of great souls, or *mahājanas*. According to *Śrīmad-Bhāgavatam,* there are twelve *mahājanas*: (1) Brahmā, (2) Lord Śiva, (3) Nārada, (4) Vaivasvata Manu, (5) Kapila (not the atheist but the original Kapila), (6) the Kumāras, (7) Prahlāda, (8) Bhīṣma, (9) Janaka, (10) Bali, (11) Śukadeva Gosvāmī and (12) Yamarāja. According to the *Mahābhārata,* there is no point in arguing about the Absolute Truth because there are so many different Vedic scriptures and philosophical understandings that no one philosopher can agree with another. Since everyone is trying to present his own point of view and reject others, it is very difficult to understand the prime necessity of life expressed by religious principles. Therefore it is better to follow in the footsteps of the *mahājanas,* great souls; then one can achieve the desired success. Lord Caitanya's teachings are just like nectar, and they hold whatever you need. The best way is to take to this path and follow it."

CHAPTER 22

Śrīmad-Bhāgavatam

After the conversion of the Māyāvādī *sannyāsīs* to the path of Caitanya Mahāprabhu, many scholars and inquisitive people visited the Lord at Benares. Since it was not possible for everyone to see Caitanya Mahāprabhu at His residence, people stood in lines to see Him as He passed on His way to the temples of Viśvanātha and Bindu Mādhava. One day, when the Lord visited the temple of Bindu Mādhava with His associates—Candraśekhara, Paramānanda, Tapana Miśra, Sanātana Gosvāmī and others—He sang:

hari haraye namaḥ kṛṣṇa yādavāya namaḥ
gopāla govinda rāma śrī-madhusūdana

When the Lord sang in this way, chanting and dancing, thousands of people gathered around Him, and when the Lord chanted, they roared. The vibration was so tumultuous that Prakāśānanda Sarasvatī, who was sitting nearby, immediately joined the crowd with his disciples. As soon as he saw the beautiful body of Lord Caitanya and saw how He was dancing with His associates, Prakāśānanda Sarasvatī joined and began to sing: "Hari! Hari!" All the inhabitants of Benares were struck with wonder upon seeing the ecstatic dancing of Lord Caitanya. But Lord Caitanya checked His continuous ecstasy and stopped dancing when He saw the Māyāvādī *sannyāsīs*. As soon as the Lord stopped chanting and dancing, Prakāśānanda Sarasvatī fell at His feet. Trying to stop him, Lord Caitanya said, "Oh, you are the spiritual master of the whole world, *jagad-guru,* and I am not even equal to your disciples. You should therefore not worship an inferior like Me, for actually I am not even equal to the disciple of your disciple. You are exactly like the Supreme Brahman, and if I allow you to fall down at My feet, I will commit a very great offense. Although you have no vision of duality, for the sake of teaching the people in general you should not do this."

"Previously I spoke ill of You many times," Prakāśānanda Sarasvatī replied. "Now in order to free myself from the results of my offense, I fall down at Your feet." He then quoted a verse from the Vedic literature which states that even a liberated soul will again become a victim of material contamination if he commits an offense against the Supreme Lord. Prakāśānanda Sarasvatī then quoted a verse from *Śrīmad-Bhāgavatam* (10.34.9) regarding Nanda Mahārāja's being attacked by a serpent who had previously been a worshipable Vidyādhara. When the serpent was touched by the lotus feet of Kṛṣṇa, he regained his previous body and was freed from the reactions of his sinful activities.

When Lord Caitanya thus heard Himself equated with Kṛṣṇa, He mildly protested. He wanted to warn people in general not to equate the Supreme Lord with any living entity. Although He was the Supreme Lord Himself, He protested against this comparison in order to teach us. Thus He said that it is the greatest offense to equate anyone with the Supreme Lord Kṛṣṇa. Lord Caitanya always maintained that Viṣṇu, the Supreme Personality of Godhead, is infinite and that the living entities, however great they may be, are but infinitesimal. In this connection He quoted a verse from the *Padma Purāṇa* which is found in the Vaiṣṇava *tantra* (*Hari-bhakti-vilāsa* 1.73): "A person who equates the Supreme Lord with even the greatest of demigods, such as Brahmā and Śiva, must be considered a number-one atheist."

"I can understand that You are the Supreme Personality of Godhead, Kṛṣṇa," Prakāśānanda Sarasvatī continued, "and even though You present Yourself as a devotee, You are still worshipable because You are greater than all of us in education and realization. Therefore by blaspheming You, we have committed the greatest offense. Please excuse us."

How a devotee becomes the greatest of all transcendentalists is stated in *Śrīmad-Bhāgavatam* (6.14.5):

muktānām api siddhānāṁ nārāyaṇa-parāyaṇaḥ
su-durlabhaḥ praśāntātmā koṭiṣv api mahāmune

"There are many liberated souls and perfected souls, but out of all of them he who is a devotee of the Supreme Personality of Godhead is best. Such a devotee of the Supreme Lord is always calm and quiet, and his perfection is very rarely seen, even among millions of persons." Prakāśānanda then quoted another verse from *Śrīmad-Bhāgavatam* (10.4.46), in which it is stated that one's duration of life, prosperity, fame, religion and the benediction of higher authorities are all lost when one offends a devotee. Finally Prakāśānanda quoted *Śrīmad-Bhāgavatam* 7.5.32, which says that although all the misgivings of the conditioned soul disappear at the touch of the lotus feet of the Supreme Personality of Godhead, one cannot touch His lotus feet unless one receives the benediction of the dust of the lotus feet of the Lord's pure devotee. In other words, one cannot become a pure devotee of the Supreme Personality of Godhead unless he is favored by another pure devotee of the Lord.

"Now I am taking shelter of Your lotus feet," Prakāśānanda Sarasvatī said, "for I want to be elevated to the position of a devotee of the Supreme Lord."

After talking in this way, Prakāśānanda Sarasvatī and Lord Caitanya sat together. "Whatever You have said concerning discrepancies in the Māyāvāda philosophy is also known by us," Prakāśānanda said. "Indeed, we know that all the commentaries on Vedic scriptures by Māyāvādī philosophers are erroneous, especially those of Śaṅkarācārya. Śaṅkarācārya's interpretations of the *Vedānta-sūtra* are all figments of his imagination. You have not explained the aphorisms of the *Vedānta-sūtra* and verses of the *Upaniṣads* according to Your imagination but have presented them as they are. Thus we are all pleased to have heard Your explanation.

Such explanations of the *Vedānta-sūtra* and *Upaniṣads* cannot be given by anyone but the Supreme Personality of Godhead. Since You have all the potencies of the Supreme Lord, please explain the *Vedānta-sūtra* further so that I may be benefited."

Lord Caitanya protested against being called the Supreme Lord: "My dear sir, I am an ordinary living entity. I cannot know the real meaning of the *Vedānta-sūtra,* but Vyāsadeva, who is an incarnation of Nārāyaṇa, knows its real meaning. No ordinary living entity can interpret the *Vedānta-sūtra* according to his mundane conceptions. In order to curb commentaries on the *Vedānta-sūtra* by unscrupulous persons, the author himself, Vyāsadeva, has already commented upon the *Vedānta-sūtra* by writing *Śrīmad-Bhāgavatam.*" In other words, the best explanation of a book is written by the author himself. No one can understand the author's mind unless the author himself discloses the meaning of his words. Therefore the *Vedānta-sūtra* should be understood through *Śrīmad-Bhāgavatam,* the commentary written by the author of the *Vedānta-sūtra.*

Praṇava, or *oṁkāra,* is the divine substance of all the *Vedas. Oṁkāra* is further explained in the Gāyatrī *mantra,* exactly as it is explained in *Śrīmad-Bhāgavatam.* In the *Bhāgavatam* there are four verses written in this connection, and these were explained to Brahmā by Lord Kṛṣṇa Himself. In his turn, Brahmā explained them to Nārada, and Nārada explained them to Vyāsadeva. In this way the purport of the verses of *Śrīmad-Bhāgavatam* has come down through disciplic succession. It is not that anyone and everyone can make his own foolish commentary on the *Vedānta-sūtra* and mislead his readers. Anyone who wants to understand the *Vedānta-sūtra* must read *Śrīmad-Bhāgavatam* carefully. Under the instructions of Nārada Muni, Vyāsadeva compiled *Śrīmad-Bhāgavatam* with the purpose of explaining the aphorisms of the *Vedānta-sūtra.* In writing *Śrīmad-Bhāgavatam,* Vyāsadeva collected all the essence of the *Upaniṣads,* the purport of which was also explained in the *Vedānta-sūtra. Śrīmad-Bhāgavatam* is thus the essence of all Vedic knowledge. That which is stated in the *Upaniṣads* and restated in the *Vedānta-sūtra* is explained very nicely in *Śrīmad-Bhāgavatam.*

There is a verse in the *Īśopaniṣad* similar to one found in *Śrīmad-Bhāgavatam* (8.1.10), which states that whatever one sees in the cosmic manifestation is but the Supreme Lord's energy and is non-different from Him. Consequently He is the controller, friend and maintainer of all living entities. We should live by the mercy of God and take only those things which are allotted to us according to our particular living condition. In this way, by not encroaching on another's property, one can enjoy life.

In other words, the purport of the *Upaniṣads, Vedānta-sūtra* and *Śrīmad-Bhāgavatam* is one and the same. If one studies *Śrīmad-Bhāgavatam* carefully, he will find that all the *Upaniṣads* and the *Vedānta-sūtra* are nicely explained therein. *Śrīmad-Bhāgavatam* teaches us three subjects: how to reestablish our eternal relationship with the Supreme Lord, how to act in that relationship, and, lastly, how to achieve the highest benefit from it.

The four *Śrīmad-Bhāgavatam* verses beginning with *aham evāsam evāgre* (2.9.33–36) are the gist of the whole *Bhāgavatam*. These are nicely summarized by Lord Caitanya as follows: "I [Kṛṣṇa] am the supreme center for the relationships of all living entities, and knowledge of Me is the supreme knowledge. The process by which a living entity can attain Me is called *abhidheya*. By it, one can attain the highest perfection of life, love of Godhead. When one attains love of Godhead, his life becomes perfect." The explanation of these four verses is given in *Śrīmad-Bhāgavatam*, and Lord Caitanya gave a short description of the principles of these verses. He said that by mental speculation or academic education no one can understand the constitutional position of the Supreme Lord—how He is situated, His transcendental qualities, His transcendental activities and His six opulences. These can be understood only by the mercy of the Lord. As stated in the *Bhagavad-gītā*, one who is fortunate enough to receive the Lord's favor can understand all these explanations by the mercy of the Lord.

The Lord existed before the material creation; therefore the material ingredients, nature and the living entities all emanated from Him, and after dissolution they rest in Him. When the creation is manifest, it is maintained by Him; indeed, whatever manifestation we see is but a transformation of His external energy. When the Supreme Lord withdraws His external energy, everything enters into Him. In the first of the four verses, the word *aham* is given three times to stress that the Supreme Personality of Godhead is full with all opulences. *Aham* is stated three times just to chastise one who cannot understand or believe in the transcendental nature and form of the Supreme Lord.

The Lord possesses His internal energy, His external, marginal and relative energies, and the manifestation of the cosmic world and the living entities. The external energy is manifested by the qualitative modes (*guṇas*) of material nature. One who can understand the nature of the living entity in the spiritual world can actually understand *vedyam,* or perfect knowledge. One cannot understand the Supreme Lord simply by seeing the material energy and the conditioned soul, but when one is in perfect knowledge, he is freed from the influence of the external energy. The moon reflects the light of the sun, and without the sun the moon cannot illuminate anything. Similarly, this material cosmic manifestation is but the reflection of the spiritual world. When one is actually liberated from the spell of the external energy, he can understand the constitutional nature of the Supreme Lord. Devotional service to the Lord is the only means for attaining Him, and this devotional service can be accepted by everyone and anyone in any country and under any circumstance. Devotional service is above the four principles of religion, culminating in liberation. Actually, even the preliminary processes of devotional service are transcendental to liberation, the highest subject of ordinary religion.

Therefore, irrespective of one's caste, creed, color, country, etc., one should approach a bona fide spiritual master and hear from him everything about devotional service. The real purpose of life is to revive our dormant love of God. Indeed, that is our ultimate necessity. How that love of God can be attained is explained in *Śrīmad-Bhāgavatam*. There is theoretical knowledge and specific or realized knowledge, and perfect realized knowledge is attained when one realizes the teachings received from the spiritual master.

CHAPTER 23

Why Study the Vedānta-sūtra?

Knowledge is information gathered from the scriptures, and science is practical realization of that knowledge. Knowledge is scientific when it is gathered from the scriptures through the bona fide spiritual master, but when it is interpreted by speculation, it is mental concoction. By scientifically understanding the scriptural information through the bona fide spiritual master, one learns, by one's own realization, the truths of the Supreme Personality of Godhead. The transcendental form of the Supreme Personality of Godhead is different from material manifestations, and it is above the reactions of matter. Unless one scientifically understands the spiritual form of the Personality of Godhead, one becomes an impersonalist. The example comparing the Lord and the material manifestations to the sun and the sunshine is often given. The sunshine in itself is illumination, but that illumination is different from the sun. Yet the sun and the sunshine are not differently situated, for without the sun there can be no sunshine, and without sunshine there is no meaning to the word *sun*.

Unless one is freed from the influence of the material energy, he cannot understand the Supreme Lord and His different energies. Nor can one who is captivated by the spell of material energy understand the spiritual form of the Supreme Lord. Unless there is realization of the transcendental form of the Supreme Personality of Godhead, there is no question of love of God, and without love of God there is no perfection of human life. Just as the five gross elements of nature—namely earth, water, fire, air and ether—are both within and without all living beings in this world, the Supreme Lord is both inside and outside this existence, and those who are His devotees can realize this.

Pure devotees know very well that they are meant to serve the Supreme Personality of Godhead and that all things that exist constitute the means by which they can serve the Lord. Therefore, because a pure devotee has been blessed by the Supreme Lord from within the core of his heart, wherever he looks he sees the Lord and nothing more. *Śrīmad-Bhāgavatam* 11.2.55 confirms this relationship between the pure devotee and the Supreme Lord as follows:

visṛjati hṛdayaṁ na yasya sākṣād
dharir avaśābhihito 'py aghaugha-nāśaḥ
praṇaya-raśanayā dhṛtāṅghri-padmaḥ
sa bhavati bhāgavata-pradhāna uktaḥ

"If a person's heart is always tied to the lotus feet of the Supreme Lord with the rope of love, the Lord does not leave him, even if his remembrance is not perfect. Such a devotee is to be considered first class." An example of this is described in *Śrīmad-Bhāgavatam* (10.30.4). When the *gopīs* assembled for their *rāsa* dance with Kṛṣṇa, Kṛṣṇa apparently left them. Consequently they began to chant the holy name of Kṛṣṇa and, being overwhelmed with madness, inquired about Kṛṣṇa from the flowers and creepers in the forest. Kṛṣṇa is like the sky: He is situated everywhere.

Therefore, by studying *Śrīmad-Bhāgavatam* we can learn about our eternal relationship with the Supreme Lord, understand the procedure for regaining Him, and attain the ultimate realization, which is love of Godhead.

Next Lord Caitanya explained to Prakāśānanda Sarasvatī how one can achieve the Supreme Personality of Godhead by devotional service. First the Lord quoted a verse from *Śrīmad-Bhāgavatam* (11.14.21) in which Kṛṣṇa says that He can be realized only through devotional service executed with faith and love. Indeed, it is devotional service alone which purifies the heart of the devotee and elevates him to the ultimate realization, by which he serves the Supreme Lord with faith and love. Even if one is born in a low family, like a family of *caṇḍālas* (dog-eaters), one can become filled with transcendental symptoms through realization of the supreme stage of love of Godhead. These transcendental symptoms are mentioned in *Śrīmad-Bhāgavatam* (11.3.31):

> *smarantaḥ smārayantaś ca mitho 'ghaugha-haraṁ harim*
> *bhaktyā sañjātayā bhaktyā bibhraty utpulakāṁ tanum*

"When pure devotees discuss subjects dealing with the Supreme Lord, who can cleanse all kinds of sinful reactions from the heart of His devotee, they become overwhelmed with ecstasy and display different symptoms due to their devotional service." The *Bhāgavatam* (11.2.40) also states: "When pure devotees chant the Lord's holy name, due to their spontaneous attachment for the Lord they sometimes cry, sometimes laugh, sometimes dance, sometimes sing and so on, not caring for any social convention."

We should understand, therefore, that *Śrīmad-Bhāgavatam* is the real explanation of the *Brahma-sūtra,* for it is compiled by the same author, Vyāsadeva himself. In the *Garuḍa Purāṇa* it is said:

> *artho 'yaṁ brahma-sūtrāṇāṁ bhāratārtha-vinirṇayaḥ*
> *gāyatrī-bhāṣya-rūpo 'sau vedārtha-paribṛṁhitaḥ*
> *grantho 'ṣṭādaśa-sāhasraḥ śrīmad-bhāgavatābhidhaḥ*

"*Śrīmad-Bhāgavatam* is the authorized explanation of the *Brahma-sūtra,* and it is a further explanation of the *Mahābhārata.* It is the explanation of the Gāyatrī *mantra* and the essence of all Vedic knowledge. This *Śrīmad-Bhāgavatam,* containing eighteen thousand verses, is known as the explanation of all Vedic literature." In the First Canto of *Śrīmad-Bhāgavatam* the sages of Naimiṣāraṇya asked Sūta Gosvāmī to explain the essence of Vedic literature. In answer, Sūta Gosvāmī presented *Śrīmad-Bhāgavatam* as the essence of all the *Vedas,* histories and other Vedic literatures. Elsewhere in *Śrīmad-Bhāgavatam* (12.13.15) it is clearly stated that

Śrīmad-Bhāgavatam is the essence of all Vedānta knowledge and that one who relishes the knowledge of *Śrīmad-Bhāgavatam* has no taste for studying any other literature. In the very beginning of *Śrīmad-Bhāgavatam,* the purport of the Gāyatrī *mantra* is described: "I offer my obeisances unto the Supreme Truth." Thus from the first verse *Śrīmad-Bhāgavatam* deals with the Supreme Truth, which is described in the *Bhāgavatam* as the source of creation, maintenance and destruction of the cosmic manifestation. Obeisances unto the Personality of Godhead, Vāsudeva (*oṁ namo bhagavate vāsudevāya*), directly indicate Lord Śrī Kṛṣṇa, who is the divine son of Vasudeva and Devakī. That Kṛṣṇa is the Supreme Personality of Godhead is more explicitly presented later in *Śrīmad-Bhāgavatam* (1.3.28), where Vyāsadeva asserts that Śrī Kṛṣṇa is the original Personality of Godhead and that all others are either His direct or indirect plenary portions or portions of those portions. Śrīla Jīva Gosvāmī has still more explicitly developed this subject in his *Kṛṣṇa-sandarbha,* and Brahmā, the original living being, has substantially explained the subject of Śrī Kṛṣṇa in his treatise *Brahma-saṁhitā*. The *Sāma Veda* also verifies the fact that Lord Śrī Kṛṣṇa is the divine son of Devakī.

In his prayer (*Śrīmad-Bhāgavatam* 1.1.1), the author of *Śrīmad-Bhāgavatam* first proposes that Lord Śrī Kṛṣṇa is the primeval Lord, and if any transcendental nomenclature for the absolute Personality of Godhead is to be accepted, it should be the name Kṛṣṇa, meaning "all-attractive." In the *Bhagavad-gītā* the Lord has affirmed in many passages that He is the original Personality of Godhead, and this was confirmed by Arjuna, who cited great sages like Nārada, Vyāsa and many others. Also, in the *Padma Purāṇa* it is stated that of the innumerable names of the Lord, the name Kṛṣṇa is the principal one. Therefore, although the name Vāsudeva indicates the plenary portion of the Personality of Godhead, and although all the different forms of the Lord are identical with Vāsudeva, in this text Vāsudeva principally indicates the divine son of Vasudeva and Devakī. Śrī Kṛṣṇa is always meditated upon by the *paramahaṁsas,* those who are most perfect in the renounced order of life. Vāsudeva, or Lord Śrī Kṛṣṇa, is the cause of all causes, and everything that exists is an emanation from Him. How this is so is explained in later chapters of *Śrīmad-Bhāgavatam.*

Caitanya Mahāprabhu describes *Śrīmad-Bhāgavatam* as the spotless *Purāṇa* because it contains transcendental narrations of the pastimes of the Supreme Personality of Godhead, Śrī Kṛṣṇa. The history of *Śrīmad-Bhāgavatam* is also very glorious. Śrī Vyāsadeva, drawing on his mature experience of transcendental knowledge, compiled it under the instruction of Śrī Nāradajī, his spiritual master. Vyāsadeva had compiled all the Vedic literatures—the four *Vedas*, the *Vedānta-sūtra* (or *Brahma-sūtra*), the *Purāṇas* and the *Mahābhārata*. Yet he was not satisfied. His dissatisfaction was observed by his spiritual master, and thus Nārada advised him to write about the transcendental activities of the Lord, Śrī Kṛṣṇa. Śrī Kṛṣṇa's transcendental activities are specifically described in the Tenth Canto of *Śrīmad-Bhāgavatam,* the canto considered to contain the substance of the whole work. One should not approach the Tenth Canto immediately but should approach it gradually by developing knowledge of the subject matters first presented.

Generally a person with a philosophical mind is inquisitive to learn of the origin of the creation. He sees the night sky and naturally asks, "What are the stars? How are they situated? Who lives there?" and so on. All these inquiries are quite natural for a human being because his consciousness is more developed than the animals'. In answer to such inquiries, the author of *Śrīmad-Bhāgavatam* says that the Lord is the origin of the creation. He is not only the creator but the maintainer and annihilator as well. The manifested cosmic nature is created at a certain period by the will of the Lord, it is maintained for some time, and finally it is annihilated by His will. Thus He is the supreme will behind all activities.

Of course, there are atheists of various categories who do not believe in the creator, but that is due only to their poor fund of knowledge. The modern scientist creates sputniks, and by some arrangement or other they are thrown into outer space to fly for some time under the control of a scientist far away. All the universes and the innumerable planets within them are similar to such sputniks, and they are all controlled by the Personality of Godhead.

In the Vedic literature it is said that the Absolute Truth, the Personality of Godhead, is the chief among all living personalities. All living beings, from the first created being, Brahmā, down to the smallest ant, are individual living entities. And above Brahmā there are many other living beings with individual capacities. The Personality of Godhead Himself is also a living being, as much an individual as other living beings. But the Supreme Lord is the supreme living being, with the greatest mind and the supermost inconceivable energies in great variety. If a man's mind can produce a sputnik, we can very easily imagine that a mind higher than man's can produce wonderful things far superior to man-made sputniks. A reasonable person will accept this argument, but stubborn, obstinate people will not.

Śrīla Vyāsadeva at once accepts the supreme mind as the *parameśvara,* the supreme controller, and offers His respectful obeisances to Him. As stated in the *Bhagavad-gītā* and all other scriptures written by Śrīla Vyāsadeva, that *parameśvara* is Śrī Kṛṣṇa Himself. This is specifically stated in *Śrīmad-Bhāgavatam.* In the *Bhagavad-gītā* the Lord Himself says that there is no *para-tattva* (*summum bonum*) other than Him. Therefore the author at once worships the *para-tattva,* Śrī Kṛṣṇa, whose transcendental activities are described in the Tenth Canto.

Unscrupulous persons go at once to the Tenth Canto, especially to the five chapters in which Śrīla Vyāsadeva has kindly described the Lord's *rāsa* dance. However, this portion of *Śrīmad-Bhāgavatam* is the most confidential part of that great literature. Unless one is thoroughly accomplished in the transcendental knowledge of the Lord, one is sure to misunderstand the Lord's worshipable transcendental pastimes in the *rāsa* dance and His loving dealings with the *gopīs.* This subject matter is highly spiritual and technical, and only liberated personalities who have gradually attained the stage of *paramahaṁsa* can transcendentally relish the worshipable *rāsa* dance.

Therefore Śrīla Vyāsadeva gives the reader a chance to gradually develop in spiritual realization before actually relishing the essence of the pastimes of the Lord. Thus at the beginning Vyāsadeva purposefully invokes the Gāyatrī *mantra* with the word *dhīmahi.* The Gāyatrī *mantra* is especially meant for spiritually advanced people. When one attains success in chanting the Gāyatrī *mantra,* he can enter into the transcendental position of the Lord. But in order to chant the Gāyatrī *mantra* successfully, one must first acquire the brahminical qualities and become perfectly situated in the mode of goodness. From that point one can begin to transcendentally realize the Lord—His name, His fame, His qualities, etc.

Śrīmad-Bhāgavatam is a narration dealing with the *svarūpa* (form) of the Lord, which is manifested by His internal potency. This potency is distinguished from the external potency, which has manifested the cosmic world within our experience. Śrīla Vyāsadeva makes a clear distinction between the internal and external potencies in the very first verse of the First Chapter of *Śrīmad-Bhāgavatam*. In that verse he says that the internal potency is factual reality whereas the external manifested energy in the form of material existence is temporary and illusory, no more real than a mirage in the desert. Water may appear present in a mirage, but real water is somewhere else. Similarly, the manifested cosmic creation appears to be reality, but it is simply a reflection of the true reality, which exists in the spiritual world. In the spiritual world there are no mirages. Absolute Truth is there; it is not here in the material world. Here everything is relative truth, with one apparent truth depending upon another. This cosmic creation results from an interaction of the three modes of material nature. The temporary manifestations are so created as to present an illusion of reality to the bewildered mind of the conditioned soul, who appears in so many species of life, including higher demigods like Brahmā, Indra, Candra, and so on. In fact there is no reality in the manifested world, but there appears to be reality because of the true reality in the spiritual world, where the Personality of Godhead eternally resides with His transcendental paraphernalia.

The chief engineer of a complicated construction does not personally take part in the construction itself, but it is he only who knows every nook and corner of the construction because everything is carried out under his direction only. In other words, he knows everything about the construction, directly and indirectly. Similarly, the Personality of Godhead, who is the supreme engineer of this cosmic creation, knows very well what is happening in every nook and corner of the cosmic creation, although activities appear to be performed by someone else. In actuality, from Brahmā down to the insignificant ant, no one is independent in the material creation; the hand of the Supreme Lord is everywhere. All material elements, as well as all spiritual sparks, are but emanations from Him only. Whatever is created in this material world is a result of the interaction of these two energies, material and spiritual, which emanate from the Absolute Truth, the Personality of Godhead, Śrī Kṛṣṇa (Vāsudeva).

A living entity known as a chemist can manufacture water in the laboratory by mixing hydrogen and oxygen. But in reality the living entity works under the direction of the Supreme Lord, and all the materials he uses are supplied by the Lord. Thus the Lord knows everything directly and indirectly, in minute detail, and He is fully independent as well. He can be compared to a gold mine, and the objects within the cosmic creation can be compared to ornaments made from that gold, such as gold rings, gold necklaces, and so on. The gold ring and necklace are qualitatively one with the gold in the mine, but quantitatively the gold in the mine and the gold in the ring or necklace are different. The complete philosophy of the Absolute Truth, therefore, centers about the fact that the Absolute Truth is simultaneously one with and different from His creation. Nothing is absolutely equal to the Absolute Truth, but at the same time nothing is independent of the Absolute Truth.

Conditioned souls, from Brahmā, the engineer of this particular universe, down to an insignificant ant, are all creating something, but none of them are independent of the Supreme Lord. The materialist wrongly thinks that there is no creator but his own good self, and this misconception is called *māyā,* or illusion. Due to his poor fund of knowledge, the materialist cannot see beyond the purview of his imperfect senses; thus he thinks that matter automatically takes its own shape independent of a conscious background. This is refuted by Śrīla Vyāsadeva in the first verse of *Śrīmad-Bhāgavatam.* As stated before, Vyāsadeva is a liberated soul, and he compiled this book of authority after attaining spiritual perfection. Since the complete whole, or the Absolute Truth, is the source of everything, nothing is independent of Him. In one sense, everything that exists is the body of the Absolute Truth. Any action or reaction of a part of a body becomes a cognizable fact to the embodied soul. Similarly, since the creation is the body of the Absolute Truth, then everything in the creation is known to the Absolute, both directly and indirectly.

In the *śruti-mantra* it is stated that the absolute whole, or Brahman, is the ultimate source of everything. Everything emanates from Him, everything is maintained by Him, and at the end everything enters into Him again. That is the law of nature. This is confirmed in the *smṛti-mantra*. There it is said that at the beginning of Brahmā's millennium the source from which everything emanates is the Absolute Truth, or Brahman, and that at the end of that millennium the reservoir into which everything enters is that same Absolute Truth. Material scientists haphazardly take it for granted that the ultimate source of this planetary system is the sun, but they are unable to explain the source of the sun. In the first verse of *Śrīmad-Bhāgavatam* the ultimate source is explained. According to the Vedic literature, Brahmā is the creator of this universe, but because he had to meditate to receive the inspiration for such creation, he is not the ultimate creator. As stated in the first verse of *Śrīmad-Bhāgavatam,* Brahmā was taught Vedic knowledge by the Personality of Godhead. There it is said that the Supreme Lord inspired Brahmā, the secondary creator, and enabled him to carry out his creative functions. In this way the Supreme Lord is the supervising engineer; the real mind behind all creative agents is the Absolute Personality of Godhead, Śrī Kṛṣṇa. In the *Bhagavad-gītā* (9.10) Śrī Kṛṣṇa Himself states that it is He only who superintends the creative energy (*prakṛti*), the sum total of matter. Thus Śrī Vyāsadeva worships neither Brahmā nor the sun but the Supreme Lord, who guides both Brahmā and the sun in their creative activities.

The Sanskrit words *abhijña* and *svarāṭ,* appearing in the first verse of *Śrīmad-Bhāgavatam,* are significant. These two words distinguish the Lord from all other living entities. No living entity other than the Supreme Being, the Absolute Personality of Godhead, is either *abhijña* or *svarāṭ*—that is, none of them are either fully cognizant or fully independent. Everyone has to receive knowledge from his superior; even Brahmā, who is the first living being within this material world, has to meditate upon the Supreme

Lord and take help from Him in order to create. If neither Brahmā nor the sun can create anything without acquiring knowledge from a superior, then what to speak of the material scientists, who are fully dependent on so many things? Modern scientists like Jagadisha Chandra Bose, Isaac Newton, Albert Einstein, etc., may boast of their respective creative energies, but all were dependent on the Supreme Lord for so many things. After all, the highly intelligent brains of these gentlemen were certainly not products of any human being. The brains were created by another agent. If brains like those of Einstein or Newton could have been manufactured by a human being, then mankind would produce many such brains instead of eulogizing these scientists. If such scientists cannot even manufacture such brains, what to speak of foolish atheists who defy the authority of the Lord?

Even the Māyāvādī impersonalists, who flatter themselves that they have become the Lord, are not *abhijña* or *svarāṭ*, fully cognizant or fully independent. The Māyāvādī monists undergo a severe process of austerity and penance to acquire the knowledge needed for becoming one with the Lord, but ultimately they become dependent on some rich follower, who supplies them with requisite paraphernalia to construct great monasteries and temples. Atheists like Rāvaṇa and Hiraṇyakaśipu had to undergo severe austerities before they could flout the authority of the Lord, but ultimately they were so helpless that they could not save themselves when the Lord appeared before them as cruel death. This is also applicable to the modern atheists who dare flout the authority of the Lord. Such atheists will be dealt the same awards as were given in the past to great atheists like Rāvaṇa and Hiraṇyakaśipu. History repeats itself, and what occurred in the past will recur again and again when there is necessity. Whenever the authority of the Lord is neglected, the penalties dealt by the laws of nature are always there.

That the Supreme Lord, the Personality of Godhead, is all-perfect is confirmed in all *śruti-mantras*. It is said in the *śruti-mantras* that the all-perfect Lord glanced over matter and thus created all living beings. The living beings are parts and parcels of the Lord, and He impregnates the vast material nature with the seeds of the spiritual sparks. Thus the creative energies are set in motion for so many wonderful creations. When one atheist argued that God is no more expert than the manufacturer of a subtle watch that has so many delicate parts, we had to reply that God is a greater mechanic than the watchmaker because He creates one machine in male and female forms that go on producing innumerable similar machines without the further attention of God. If a man could manufacture a set of machines capable of producing other machines without the man giving the matter any further attention, then that man could be said to equal the intelligence of God. But that is not possible. Each and every one of man's imperfect machines has to be handled individually by a mechanic. Because no one can be equal to God in intelligence, another name for God is *asamaurdhva,* which indicates that no one is equal to or greater than Him. Everyone has his intellectual equal and superior, and no one can claim that he has neither. But this is not the case with the Lord. The *śruti-mantras* indicate that before the creation of the material universe there existed the Lord, who is the master of everyone. It was the Lord who instructed Brahmā in Vedic knowledge. That Personality of Godhead has to be obeyed in all respects. Anyone who wants to become freed from material entanglement must surrender unto Him, and this is confirmed in the *Bhagavad-gītā.*

Unless one surrenders unto the lotus feet of the Personality of Godhead, it is sure and certain that one will be bewildered, even if he happens to be a great mind. Only when great minds surrender unto the lotus feet of Vāsudeva and know fully that Vāsudeva is the cause of all causes, as confirmed in the *Bhagavad-gītā* (7.19), can they become *mahātmās,* or the truly broad-minded. But such broad-minded *mahātmās* are rarely seen. Only they, however, can understand that the Supreme Lord, the absolute Personality of Godhead, is the primeval cause of all creations. He is the ultimate (*parama*) truth because all other truths are dependent on Him. And because He is the source of everyone's knowledge, He is omniscient; there is no illusion for Him, as there is for the relative knower.

Some Māyāvādī scholars argue that *Śrīmad-Bhāgavatam* was not compiled by Śrīla Vyāsadeva, and some suggest that the book is a modern creation written by someone named Vopadeva. In order to refute this meaningless argument, Śrīla Śrīdhara Svāmī points out that many of the oldest *Purāṇas* make reference to *Śrīmad-Bhāgavatam*. The first *śloka,* or verse, of *Śrīmad-Bhāgavatam* begins with the Gāyatrī *mantra,* and there is reference to this in the *Matsya Purāṇa* (the oldest *Purāṇa*). In that *Purāṇa* it is said about the *Bhāgavatam* that in it there are many narrations and spiritual instructions, that it begins with the Gāyatrī *mantra,* and that it contains the history of Vṛtrāsura. It is also said that whoever makes a gift of this great work on a full-moon day attains to the highest perfection of life and goes back to Godhead. There is also reference to *Śrīmad-Bhāgavatam* in other *Purāṇas,* which even indicate that the work consists of twelve cantos and eighteen thousand *ślokas*. In the *Padma Purāṇa* there is also a reference to *Śrīmad-Bhāgavatam,* during a conversation between Gautama and Mahārāja Ambarīṣa. The king was advised to read *Śrīmad-Bhāgavatam* regularly if he at all desired liberation from material bondage. Under these circumstances, there is no doubt regarding the authority of *Śrīmad-Bhāgavatam*. For the past five hundred years, since the time of Śrī Caitanya Mahāprabhu, many scholars have made elaborate commentaries upon *Śrīmad-Bhāgavatam* and have displayed unique scholarship. The serious student will do well to attempt to go through these commentaries in order to more happily relish the transcendental messages of the *Bhāgavatam*.

In his commentary on the *Bhāgavatam,* Śrīla Viśvanātha Cakravartī Ṭhākura specifically deals with original and pure sex psychology (*ādi-rasa*), devoid of all mundane inebriety. The entire material world turns due to the basic principle of sex life. In modern human civilization, sex is the central point of all activities; indeed, wherever we turn our face we see sex life prominent. Thus sex life is not unreal, but its true reality is experienced in the spiritual world. Material sex is but a perverted reflection of the original; the original is found in the Absolute Truth. This validates the fact that the Absolute Truth is personal, for the Absolute Truth cannot be impersonal and have a sense of pure sex life. The impersonal, monist philosophy has given an indirect impetus to abominable mundane sex because it overly stresses the impersonality of the ultimate truth. The result is that men who lack knowledge have accepted perverted material sex life as all in all because they have no information of the actual spiritual form of sex. There is a distinction between sex in the diseased condition of material life and sex in the spiritual existence. *Śrīmad-Bhāgavatam* gradually elevates the unbiased reader to the highest perfectional stage of transcendence, above the three kinds of material activities, namely fruitive actions, speculative philosophy and worship of functional deities indicated in the *Vedas*. *Śrīmad-Bhāgavatam* is the embodiment of devotional service to the Supreme Personality of Godhead, Kṛṣṇa, and is therefore situated in a position superior to other Vedic literatures.

Religion includes four primary subjects: (1) pious activities, (2) economic development, (3) satisfaction of the senses, and (4) liberation from material bondage. Religious life is distinguished from the irreligious life of barbarism. Indeed, it may be said that human life actually begins with religion. The four principles of animal life—eating, sleeping, defending and mating—are common to both the animals and human beings, but religion is the special concern of human beings. Since human life without religion is no better than animal life, in real human society there is some form of religion aiming at self-realization and referring to one's eternal relationship with God.

In the lower stage of human civilization there is always competition between men in their attempt to dominate material nature. In other words, there is continuous rivalry in an attempt to satisfy the senses. Thus driven by sense gratificatory consciousness, men perform religious rituals and pious activities with the aim of acquiring some material gain. But if such material gain is obtainable in another way, this so-called religion is neglected. This can be seen in modern human civilization. Since the economic desires of the people appear to be fulfilled in another way, no one is interested in religion now. The churches, mosques and temples are practically vacant, for people are more interested in factories, shops and cinemas than in the religious places erected by their forefathers. This definitely proves that religious rituals are generally performed for the sake of economic development, which is needed for sense gratification. And when one is baffled in his attempt to attain sense gratification, he takes to the cause of salvation in order to become one with the supreme whole. All these activities arise with the same aim in view—sense gratification.

In the *Vedas,* the four primary subjects mentioned above are prescribed in a regulative way so that there will not be undue competition for sense gratification. But *Śrīmad-Bhāgavatam* is transcendental to all these sense-gratifying activities of the material world. It is a purely transcendental literature, understandable by the devotees of the Lord, who are above the competition for sense gratification. In the material world there is keen competition between animals, between men, between communities and even between nations in an attempt to gratify the senses. But the devotees of the Lord are above all this. Devotees have no need to compete with materialists because they are on the path back to Godhead, back home, where everything is eternal and fully blissful. Such transcendentalists are a hundred percent nonenvious and are therefore pure in heart. Because everyone in the material world is envious, there is competition. But the transcendentalists, or devotees of the Lord, are not only free from all material envy but are also kind to everyone in an attempt to establish a competitionless society with God in the center. The socialist's idea of a society devoid of competition is artificial because even in the socialist states there is competition for the post of dictator.

It is a fact, therefore, that sense gratification is the central principle of materialistic life, whether based on the *Vedas* or simply on common human activities. There are three divisions of the *Vedas.* The first division (the *karma-kāṇḍa*) recommends fruitive activities by which people can advance to higher planets. Above this is the *upāsanā-kāṇḍa,* which recommends worship of the various demigods for the purpose of attaining their planets. Finally there is the *jñāna-kāṇḍa,* which recommends activities that enable one to reach the Absolute Truth and realize His impersonal feature in order to become one with Him. But the impersonal aspect of the Absolute Truth is not the last word. Above the impersonal feature is the Paramātmā, or Supersoul, and above that is the personal aspect of the Absolute Truth. *Śrīmad-Bhāgavatam* gives information about the personal qualities of the Absolute Truth, beyond the impersonal aspect. Topics concerning these qualities are greater than topics of impersonal philosophical speculation; consequently *Śrīmad-Bhāgavatam* is given higher status than the *jñāna-kāṇḍa* division of the *Vedas*. *Śrīmad-Bhāgavatam* is also greater than the *karma-kāṇḍa* and *upāsanā-kāṇḍa* divisions because it recommends the worship of the Supreme Personality of Godhead, Śrī Kṛṣṇa, the divine son of Vasudeva. The *karma-kāṇḍa* division of the *Vedas* is fraught with competition to reach heavenly planets for better sense gratification, and this competition is also seen in the *jñāna-kāṇḍa* and *upāsanā-kāṇḍa* divisions. *Śrīmad-Bhāgavatam* is above all of these because it aims only at the Supreme Truth, the substance or root of all categories.

In other words, from *Śrīmad-Bhāgavatam* we can know the substance as well as the relativities in their true sense and perspective. The substance is the Absolute Truth, the Supreme Personality of Godhead, and the relativities are the different forms of energy which emanate from Him. Since the living entities are also His energies, there is nothing really different from the substance. At the same time, the energies *are* different from the substance. This conception is not self-contradictory. *Śrīmad-Bhāgavatam* explicitly deals with this simultaneously-one-and-different philosophy—a philosophy also found in the *Vedānta-sūtra,* which begins with the *janmādy asya sūtra*.

Knowledge of the simultaneously-one-and-different nature of the Absolute Truth has been imparted for the well-being of everyone. Mental speculators mislead people by trying to establish the energy of the Lord as absolute, but when the truth of simultaneous oneness and difference is understood, that truth is more pleasing than the imperfect concepts of monism and dualism. By understanding the Lord's simultaneous oneness with and difference from His creation, one can immediately attain freedom from the threefold miseries—miseries inflicted by the body and mind, by other living entities, and by acts of nature, over which we have no control.

Śrīmad-Bhāgavatam begins with the surrender of the living entity unto the Absolute Person. This surrender is made with full awareness of the devotee's oneness with the Absolute Person and, at the same time, his eternal position of servitorship toward Him. In the material conception one falsely thinks himself the Lord of all he surveys; consequently he is always troubled by the threefold miseries of life. But as soon as one comes to know his real position in transcendental service, he at once becomes freed from all the above-mentioned threefold miseries. The position of servitor is wasted in the material conception of life. In an attempt to dominate material nature, the living entity is forced to offer his service to the relative material energy. When this service is transferred to the Lord in pure consciousness of spiritual identity, the living entity at once becomes free from the encumbrances of material affliction.

Over and above this, *Śrīmad-Bhāgavatam* is the personal commentary on the *Vedānta-sūtra* by Vyāsadeva after he had attained maturity in spiritual realization. He was able to write it by the mercy of Nārada. Śrīla Vyāsadeva is an incarnation of Nārāyaṇa, the Personality of Godhead; therefore there is no question about his authority. Although he is the author of all Vedic literature, he specifically recommends the study of *Śrīmad-Bhāgavatam* above all other books. In other *Purāṇas* various methods for worshiping demigods are mentioned, but in *Śrīmad-Bhāgavatam* only worship of the Supreme Personality of Godhead is mentioned. The Supreme Lord is the whole body, and the demigods are different parts of that body. Thus one who worships the Supreme Lord need not worship the demigods, for the Supreme Lord is at once fixed in one's heart. Lord Caitanya Mahāprabhu distinguished *Śrīmad-Bhāgavatam* from all other *Purāṇas* by recommending it as the spotless *Purāṇa*.

The transcendental message is received through the ears, by the method of submissive hearing. A challenging attitude cannot help one receive or realize the transcendental message; therefore in the second verse of *Śrīmad-Bhāgavatam* the word *śuśrūṣu* is used. This word indicates that one should be eager to hear the transcendental message. The desire to hear with interest is the primary qualification for assimilating transcendental knowledge.

Unfortunately, few people are interested in patiently hearing the message of *Śrīmad-Bhāgavatam*. The process is simple, but the application is difficult. Those who are unfortunate will find time to hear ordinary social and political topics and all sorts of idle talks, but when they are invited to join an assembly of devotees to hear *Śrīmad-Bhāgavatam,* they are reluctant to attend. Or they will indulge in hearing portions of *Śrīmad-Bhāgavatam* they are unfit to hear. Professional reciters of the *Bhāgavatam* indulge in reciting the portions dealing with the confidential pastimes of the Supreme Lord. These portions appear to be sex literature. *Śrīmad-Bhāgavatam* is meant to be heard from the beginning, and those who are fit to assimilate the messages of the *Bhāgavatam* are mentioned in the very beginning (SB 1.1.2): The bona fide audience fit to hear *Śrīmad-Bhāgavatam* consists of those who have performed many pious deeds. But any intelligent person, by thoughtful discretion, can come to believe in the assurances of the great sage Vyāsadeva and patiently hear the messages of *Śrīmad-Bhāgavatam* in order to realize the Supreme Personality of Godhead directly. One need not struggle through the different Vedic stages of realization, for one can quickly be lifted to the position of *paramahaṁsa* simply by agreeing to patiently hear the message of *Śrīmad-Bhāgavatam*. The sages of Naimiṣāraṇya told Sūta Gosvāmī that they intensely desired to understand *Śrīmad-Bhāgavatam*. They were hearing from Sūta Gosvāmī about Kṛṣṇa, the Supreme Personality of Godhead, and they were never satiated by these discussions. People who are really attached to Kṛṣṇa never stop wanting to hear more and more about Him.

Lord Caitanya therefore advised Prakāśānanda Sarasvatī: "Always read *Śrīmad-Bhāgavatam* and try to understand each and every verse. Then you will actually understand the *Brahma-sūtra*. You say that you are very eager to study the *Vedānta-sūtra,* but you cannot understand the *Vedānta-sūtra* without understanding *Śrīmad-Bhāgavatam*." He also advised Prakāśānanda Sarasvatī to always chant Hare Kṛṣṇa, Hare Kṛṣṇa, Kṛṣṇa Kṛṣṇa, Hare Hare/ Hare Rāma, Hare Rāma, Rāma Rāma, Hare Hare. "By doing this you will very easily be liberated. After liberation you will be eligible to achieve the highest goal of life, love of Godhead."

The Lord then recited many verses from authoritative scriptures like *Śrīmad-Bhāgavatam,* the *Bhagavad-gītā* and the *Nṛsiṁha-tāpanī Upaniṣad*. First He quoted this verse from the *Bhagavad-gītā* (18.54):

brahma-bhūtaḥ prasannātmā na śocati na kāṅkṣati
samaḥ sarveṣu bhūteṣu mad-bhaktiṁ labhate parām

"When one actually becomes self-realized, knowing that he is Brahman, he becomes happy and joyful, and he no longer feels any lamentation or hankering. Such a person sees all living entities on an equal level, and he becomes a pure devotee of the Supreme Personality of Godhead." Next He quoted a statement from Śaṅkarācārya's commentary on the *Nṛsiṁha-tāpanī Upaniṣad* (2.5.16); this statement says that when a person is actually liberated he can understand the transcendental pastimes of the Supreme Lord and thus engage in His devotional service. Lord Caitanya also quoted a verse from the Second Canto of *Śrīmad-Bhāgavatam* (2.1.9), in which Śukadeva Gosvāmī states that although he was elevated to the liberated stage and free from the clutches of *māyā,* he was still attracted by the transcendental pastimes of Kṛṣṇa. Consequently he studied *Śrīmad-Bhāgavatam* from his great father, Vyāsadeva.

Next Lord Caitanya quoted another *śloka* from *Śrīmad-Bhāgavatam* (3.15.43), which deals with the Kumāras. When the Kumāras entered the temple of the Lord, they were attracted by the aroma of the flowers and *tulasī* leaves offered to the lotus feet of the Lord with pulp of sandalwood. Simply by the Kumāras' smelling the aroma of these offerings, their minds turned to the service of the Supreme Lord, although the Kumāras were already liberated souls. It is stated elsewhere in *Bhāgavatam* (1.7.10) that even if one is a liberated soul and is actually free from material contamination, he can still become attracted to rendering the Supreme Lord devotional service that is causeless and unhampered by any material propensity. This is because God is so attractive. And because He is so attractive, He is called Kṛṣṇa.

In this way Lord Caitanya began to discuss the *ātmārāma* verse from *Śrīmad-Bhāgavatam* with Prakāśānanda Sarasvatī. Lord Caitanya's admirer, the Maharashtriyan *brāhmaṇa,* related that the Lord had earlier explained this verse in sixty-one different ways. Everyone assembled was very eager to hear the different versions of the Lord's explanation of the *ātmārāma śloka,* and since they were so eager, Lord Caitanya again explained the *śloka* in the same way that He had explained it to Sanātana Gosvāmī. Everyone who heard the explanations of the *ātmārāma śloka* was amazed. Indeed, everyone considered Lord Caitanya to be none other than Śrī Kṛṣṇa Himself.

CHAPTER 24

Talks with Sārvabhauma Bhaṭṭācārya

When Lord Caitanya met Sārvabhauma Bhaṭṭācārya at Jagannātha Purī, the Bhaṭṭācārya, being the greatest logician of the day, wanted to teach the Lord Vedānta philosophy. Since the Bhaṭṭācārya was an elderly man, the age of Lord Caitanya's father, He took compassion on the young *sannyāsī* and requested Him to learn the *Vedānta-sūtra* from him. Otherwise, the Bhaṭṭācārya maintained, it would be difficult for the youthful Lord Caitanya to continue as a *sannyāsī*. When the Lord agreed, the Bhaṭṭācārya began to teach Him in the temple of Jagannātha. The Bhaṭṭācārya spoke to the Lord about the *Vedānta-sūtra* continually for seven days, and the Lord heard him without speaking a word. On the eighth day the Bhaṭṭācārya said, "You have been hearing the *Vedānta-sūtra* from me for the past week, but You have not asked any questions, nor have You indicated whether I am explaining it nicely. So I cannot tell whether You are understanding me or not."

"I am a fool," the Lord replied. "I have no capacity to study the *Vedānta-sūtra*, but since you asked Me to hear you, I am trying to listen. I am simply listening to you because you said that it is the duty of every *sannyāsī* to hear the *Vedānta-sūtra*. But as far as your explanation is concerned—that I cannot understand." Thus the

Lord indicated that in the Māyāvādī *sampradāya* there are many so-called *sannyāsīs* who, even though illiterate and unintelligent, hear the *Vedānta-sūtra* from their spiritual master just as a matter of formality. Although they listen, they do not understand anything. As far as Lord Caitanya was concerned, the reason He said He did not understand the explanation of the Bhaṭṭācārya was not because it was too difficult for Him to understand but because He did not approve of the Māyāvādī interpretation.

When the Lord said that He was an uneducated fool and could not follow the expositions, the Bhaṭṭācārya replied: "If You do not follow what I am saying, why don't You inquire? Why do You simply sit silently? It appears that You do have something to say about my explanations."

"My dear sir," the Lord replied, "as far as the *Vedānta-sūtra* itself is concerned, I can understand the meaning quite well. But I cannot understand your explanations. There is nothing difficult about understanding the meaning of the original aphorisms of the *Vedānta-sūtra,* but the way you explain them obscures the real meaning. You do not elucidate the direct meaning but imagine something and thus obscure the true meaning. I think that you have a particular doctrine you are trying to expound through the aphorisms of the *Vedānta-sūtra.*"

According to the *Muktikā Upaniṣad,* there are 108 *Upaniṣads.* Among these are the (1) *Īśa,* (2) *Kena,* (3) *Kaṭha,* (4) *Praśna,* (5) *Muṇḍaka,* (6) *Māṇḍūkya,* (7) *Taittirīya,* (8) *Aitareya,* (9) *Chāndogya,* (10) *Bṛhad-āraṇyaka,* (11) *Brahma,* (12) *Kaivalya,* (13) *Jābāla,* (14) *Śvetāśvatara,* (15) *Haṁsa,* (16) *Āruṇeya,* (17) *Garbha* and (18) *Nārāyaṇa Upaniṣad.* The 108 *Upaniṣads* contain all knowledge about the Absolute Truth. Sometimes people ask why Vaiṣṇavas use 108 prayer beads for chanting the holy names. We think it is because there are 108 *Upaniṣads* containing full knowledge of the Absolute Truth. On the other hand, some Vaiṣṇava transcendentalists think that the 108 beads represent the 108 companions of Lord Kṛṣṇa in His *rāsa* dance.

Lord Caitanya protested against misinterpretations of the *Upaniṣads,* rejecting any explanation which did not give their direct meaning. The direct interpretation is called *abhidhā-vṛtti,* whereas the indirect interpretation is called *lakṣaṇā-vṛtti.* The indirect interpretation serves no purpose. There are four kinds of understanding: (1) direct understanding (*pratyakṣa*), (2) hypothetical understanding (*anumāna*), (3) historical understanding (*aitihya*) and (4) understanding through sound (*śabda*). Of these four, understanding from the Vedic scriptures, the sound representations of the Absolute Truth, is the best method. Traditional Vedic students accept understanding through sound to be the best.

The stool and bone of any living entity are considered to be impure according to the Vedic literature, yet the same Vedic literature asserts that cow dung and conch shells are very pure. Apparently these statements are contradictory, but because cow dung and conch shells are considered pure by the *Vedas,* they are accepted as pure by the followers of the *Vedas,* without argument. If we try to understand the statements by indirect interpretation, creating some hypothesis, then we challenge the evidential authority of the Vedic statements. In other words, Vedic statements cannot be accepted according to our imperfect interpretations; they must be accepted as they are. If they are not accepted in this way, there is no authority in the Vedic statements.

According to Lord Caitanya, those who try to give some personal interpretation of Vedic statements are not at all intelligent. They mislead their followers by inventing their own interpretations. In India there is a class of men known as Ārya-samājists, who say that they accept the original *Vedas* only and reject all other Vedic literature. The motive of these people, however, is to give their own interpretation. According to Lord Caitanya, such interpretations are not to be accepted. They are simply not Vedic. Lord Caitanya said that the Vedic statements of the *Upaniṣads* are like sunlight. Everything is clear and very distinct when it is seen in the sunlight; the statements of the *Vedas* are similarly clear and distinct. The Māyāvādī philosophers simply cover the sunlight with the cloud of their misinterpretation.

Lord Caitanya then said that all the Vedic statements of the *Upaniṣads* aim at the ultimate truth, known as Brahman. The word Brahman means "the greatest," and "the greatest" should immediately be understood to refer to the Supreme Personality of Godhead, the source of all emanations. Unless the greatest possesses six opulences in full, he cannot be called the greatest. The greatest is therefore the Supreme Personality of Godhead. In other words, the

Supreme Brahman is the Supreme Personality of Godhead. In the *Bhagavad-gītā* (10.12), the Supreme Personality of Godhead, Kṛṣṇa, is accepted by Arjuna as the Supreme Brahman. The conceptions of the impersonal Brahman and the localized Supersoul are contained within the understanding of the Supreme Personality of Godhead.

Whenever we speak of the Supreme Personality of Godhead, we add the word *śrī,* indicating that He is full with six opulences. This means that He is eternally a person; if He were not a person, the six opulences could not be present in fullness. Therefore, whenever it is said that the Supreme Absolute Truth is impersonal, what is meant is that His personality is not material. To distinguish His transcendental body from material bodies, some philosophers have explained Him as having no material personality. In other words, His material personality is denied and His spiritual personality is established. In the *Śvetāśvatara Upaniṣad* (3.19) this is clearly explained:

apāṇi-pādo javano grahītā
paśyaty acakṣuḥ sa śṛṇoty akarṇaḥ
sa vetti vedyaṁ na ca tasyāsti vettā
tam āhur agryaṁ puruṣaṁ mahāntam

"The Absolute Truth has no material legs and hands, but He has spiritual hands by which He accepts everything offered to Him. He has no material eyes, but He has spiritual eyes by which He can see everything and anything. He has no material ears, but He can hear everything and anything with His spiritual ears. Having perfect senses, He knows past, future and present. Indeed, He knows everything, but no one can understand Him, for by material senses He cannot be understood. Being the origin of all emanations, He is the supreme, the greatest, the Personality of Godhead."

There are many similar Vedic hymns which definitely establish that the Supreme Absolute Truth is a person who is not of this material world. The *Hayaśīrṣa-pañcarātra* explains that although in each and every *Upaniṣad* the Supreme Brahman is first viewed as impersonal, at the end the personal form of the Supreme Lord is accepted. Another example is *Śrī Īśopaniṣad,* the fifteenth *mantra* of which runs as follows:

hiraṇmayena pātreṇa satyasyāpihitaṁ mukham
tat tvaṁ pūṣann apāvṛṇu satya-dharmāya dṛṣṭaye

"O my Lord, O Supreme Personality of Godhead, You are the maintainer of the whole universe. Everyone is sustained by Your mercy. Therefore devotional service unto You is the true religion of life. I am engaged in such devotional service, and so I request You to please maintain me and ever-increasingly engage me in Your transcendental service. You are the eternal form of *sac-cid-ānanda,* and Your effulgence is spread all over the creation, just like the sunshine. As the sun disc is covered by the glaring sunshine, so Your transcendental form is covered by the *brahmajyoti.* I desire to find You within that *brahmajyoti.* Therefore please remove this glaring effulgence."

In this verse it is clearly stated that the eternal, blissful, cognizant form of the Supreme Lord is to be found within the glaring effulgence of the *brahmajyoti*, which emanates from the body of the Supreme Lord. Thus the personal body of the Lord is the source of the *brahmajyoti,* as confirmed in the *Bhagavad-gītā* (14.27). That the impersonal Brahman is dependent on the Supreme Personality is also stated in the *Hayaśīrṣa-pañcarātra.* In every other Vedic scripture, such as the *Upaniṣads,* whenever there is talk of the impersonal Brahman in the beginning, the Supreme Personality is finally established at the end. The *Īśopaniṣad mantra* we quoted above indicates that the Supreme Absolute Truth is both impersonal and personal eternally, but His personal aspect is more important than the impersonal one.

According to a *mantra* in the *Taittirīya Upaniṣad—yato vā imāni bhūtāni jāyante*—this cosmic manifestation is an emanation from the Supreme Absolute Truth and it rests in the Supreme Absolute Truth. Thus the Absolute Truth has been called the ablative, causative and locative performer, and as such He must be the Supreme Personality of Godhead, for these are symptoms of personality. As the ablative performer, He is the source of all thinking, feeling and willing in this cosmic manifestation. Without thinking, feeling and willing, there is no possibility of the arrangement and design of the cosmic manifestation. Then again, He is causative, for He is the original designer of the cosmos. And He is also locative: that is, everything is resting in His energy. These attributes are all clearly attributes of His personality.

In the *Chāndogya Upaniṣad* (6.2.3), it is said that when the Supreme Personality of Godhead desires to become many, He glances over material nature. This is confirmed in the *Aitareya Upaniṣad* (1.1.1) with the words *sa aikṣata:* "The Lord glanced at material nature." The cosmic manifestation did not exist before His glance; therefore His glance is not materially contaminated. His seeing power existed before the material creation; therefore His body is not material. His thinking, feeling and acting are all transcendental. In other words, it should be concluded that the mind by which the Lord thinks, feels and wills is transcendental, and that the eyes by which He glances over material nature are also transcendental. Since His transcendental body and all His senses existed before the material creation, the Lord also has a transcendental mind and transcendental thinking, feeling and willing. This is the conclusion of all Vedic literature.

The word Brahman is found everywhere throughout the *Upaniṣads.* In *Śrīmad-Bhāgavatam,* Brahman, Paramātmā and Bhagavān, the Supreme Personality of Godhead, are all taken together as the Absolute Truth. Brahman and Paramātmā realization are considered stages toward the ultimate realization, which is realization of the Supreme Personality of Godhead. This is the real conclusion of all Vedic literature.

Thus according to the evidences afforded by various Vedic scriptures, the Supreme Lord Kṛṣṇa is accepted as the ultimate goal of Brahman realization. The *Bhagavad-gītā* (7.7) confirms that there is nothing superior to Kṛṣṇa. Madhvācārya, one of the greatest *ācāryas* in Brahmā's disciplic succession, has stated in his explanation of the *Vedānta-sūtra* that everything can be seen through the authorities of the scriptures. He has quoted a verse from the *Bhaviṣya Purāṇa* in which it is stated that the *Ṛg Veda, Yajur Veda, Sāma Veda, Atharva Veda, Mahābhārata, Pañcarātra* and the original *Rāmāyaṇa* are actually Vedic evidence. The *Purāṇas* accepted by the Vaiṣṇavas are also considered Vedic evidence. Indeed, whatever is contained in that literature should be taken without argument as the ultimate conclusion, and all these literatures proclaim Kṛṣṇa to be the Supreme Personality of Godhead.

CHAPTER 25

Personal and Impersonal Realization

The *Purāṇas* are supplementary Vedic literatures. Because sometimes in the original *Vedas* the subject matter is too difficult for the common man to understand, the *Purāṇas* explain matters by the use of stories and historical incidents. In *Śrīmad-Bhāgavatam* (10.14.32) it is stated, "Mahārāja Nanda and the cowherd men and the other inhabitants of Vṛndāvana are very fortunate because the Supreme Brahman, the Personality of Godhead, full of bliss, is now engaged there in His eternal pastimes as their friend."

According to the verse beginning *apāṇi-pādo javano grahītā* (*Śvetāśvatara Upaniṣad* 3.19), although Brahman has no material hands and legs, He nonetheless walks in a very stately way and accepts everything that is offered to Him. This suggests that He has transcendental limbs and is therefore not impersonal. One who does not understand the Vedic principles simply stresses the impersonal, material features of the Supreme Absolute Truth and thus unceremoniously calls the Absolute Truth impersonal. The impersonalist, Māyāvādī philosophers want to establish the Absolute Truth as impersonal, but this contradicts the Vedic literature. Although the Vedic literature confirms the fact that the Supreme Absolute Truth has multiple energies, the Māyāvādī impersonalists still try to establish that the Absolute Truth has no energy. The fact remains, however, that the Absolute Truth is full of energy and is a person as well. It is not possible to establish Him as impersonal.

According to the *Viṣṇu Purāṇa* (6.7.61–63), the living entities are considered *kṣetra-jña* energy. Although the living entity is part and parcel of the Supreme Lord and is fully cognizant, he still becomes entrapped by material contamination and thus suffers all the miseries of material life. Such living entities live in different ways according to the degree of their entanglement in material nature. The original energy of the Supreme Lord is spiritual and nondifferent from the Supreme Absolute Personality of Godhead. The living entity is called the marginal energy of the Supreme Lord, and the material energy is called the inferior energy. On account of his inert, material inebriety, the living entity in the marginal position becomes entangled with the inferior energy, matter. At that time he forgets his spiritual significance, identifies himself with the material energy and thereby becomes subjected to the threefold miseries. Only when he is free from such material contamination can he be situated in his proper position.

According to Vedic instructions, one should understand the constitutional position of the living entity, the position of the Lord, the position of material energy, and their interrelations. First of all, one should try to understand the constitutional position of the Supreme Lord, the Personality of Godhead. The Supreme Personality of Godhead has an eternal, cognizant, blissful body, and His spiritual energy is distributed as eternity, knowledge and bliss. In His blissful identity can be found His pleasure potency, in His eternal identity He is the cause of everything, and in His cognizant identity He is the supreme knowledge. Indeed, the word *kṛṣṇa* indicates that supreme knowledge. In other words, the Supreme Personality, Kṛṣṇa, is the reservoir of all knowledge, all pleasure and all eternity. The supreme knowledge of Kṛṣṇa is exhibited in three different energies—internal, marginal and external. By virtue of His internal energy He exists in Himself with His spiritual paraphernalia, by means of His marginal energy He exhibits Himself as the living entities, and by means of His external energy He exhibits Himself as the material world. Behind each and every exhibition of energy there is the background of eternity, His pleasure potency and His cognizance potency.

The conditioned soul is the marginal potency overpowered by the external potency. However, when the marginal potency comes under the influence of the spiritual potency, it becomes eligible for love of Godhead. The Supreme Lord enjoys six kinds of opulences, and no one can establish that He is formless or that He is without energy. If someone claims so, his contention is completely opposed to the Vedic instructions. Actually, the Supreme Personality of Godhead is the master of all energies. The living entity, however, being His infinitesimal part and parcel, can be overpowered by the material energy.

In the *Muṇḍaka Upaniṣad* it is stated that two birds are sitting on the same tree. One of them is eating the fruit of the tree, while the other is not eating but simply witnessing the activities of the first bird. Only when the bird eating the fruit looks toward the other bird does he become free from all anxieties. This is the position of the infinitesimal living entity. As long as he is forgetful of the Supreme Personality of Godhead, he is subjected to the threefold miseries. But when he looks toward the Supreme Lord and becomes the Lord's devotee, he becomes free from all anxieties and miseries of material existence. The living entity is eternally subordinate to the Supreme Lord: the Supreme Lord is always the master of all energies, whereas the living entity is always under the control of the Lord's energies. Being qualitatively one with the Supreme Lord, the living entity has the tendency to try to lord it over the material nature; however, being infinitesimal, he is then controlled by the material nature. Thus the living entity is called the marginal potency of the Lord.

Because the living entity can be controlled by the material nature, he cannot at any stage become one with the Supreme Lord. If the living entity were equal to the Supreme Lord, there would be no possibility of his being controlled by the material energy. In the *Bhagavad-gītā* (7.5) the living entity is described as one of the energies of the Supreme Lord. Although inseparable from the energetic, energy is still energy, and it cannot be equal with the energetic. In other words, the living entity is simultaneously one with and different from the Supreme Lord. The *Bhagavad-gītā* (7.4–5) clearly states that earth, water, fire, air, ether, mind, intelligence and false ego are the eight elementary energies of the Supreme Lord and are of inferior quality, whereas the living entity is an energy of superior quality.

The Vedic instructions confirm that the transcendental form of the Supreme Lord is eternal, blissful and full of knowledge. The impersonalists' conception of the Lord's form, however, is just the opposite, for they say that it is a transformation of the material modes of nature. Actually, the form of the Supreme Lord is beyond the modes of material nature and thus is not like the forms of this material world. His form is fully spiritual and cannot be compared with any material form. Anyone who does not accept the spiritual form of the Supreme Lord is counted among the atheists. Because Lord Buddha did not accept these Vedic principles, the Vedic teachers consider him an atheist. Although Māyāvādī philosophers pretend to accept the Vedic principles, because they do not accept the Supreme Personality of Godhead they indirectly preach Buddhist philosophy, or atheistic philosophy. Māyāvāda philosophy is inferior to Buddhist philosophy, which directly denies Vedic authority. Because Māyāvāda philosophy is disguised as Vedānta philosophy, it is more dangerous than Buddhism or atheism.

The only reason Vyāsadeva compiled the *Vedānta-sūtra* was so that all living entities could benefit from it by understanding the philosophy of *bhakti-yoga*. Unfortunately, the Māyāvādī commentary, the *Śārīraka-bhāṣya,* has practically defeated the purpose of the *Vedānta-sūtra*. In the Māyāvādī commentary the spiritual, transcendental form of the Supreme Personality of Godhead has been denied and the Supreme Brahman has been dragged down to the level of the individual Brahman, the living entity. Both the Supreme Brahman and the individual Brahman have been denied spiritual form and individuality, although it is clearly stated that the Supreme Lord is the one supreme living entity and the other living entities are the many subordinate living entities. Thus reading the Māyāvādī commentaries on the *Vedānta-sūtra* is always dangerous. The danger is that through these commentaries one may come to falsely equate the living entity with the Supreme Lord. In this way a conditioned living entity can be falsely directed, and then he can never come to his actual position of eternal activity in *bhakti-yoga*. In other words, the Māyāvādī philosophers have rendered the greatest disservice to humanity by promoting the impersonal view of the Supreme Lord and thus depriving human society of the real message of the *Vedānta-sūtra*.

From the very beginning of the *Vedānta-sūtra* it is accepted that the cosmic manifestation is a display of the Supreme Lord's energies. The aphorism *janmādy asya yataḥ* (*Vedānta-sūtra* 1.1.2) describes the Supreme Brahman as He from whom everything emanates, He by whom everything is maintained, and He into whom everything is dissolved. Thus the Absolute Truth is the cause of creation, maintenance and dissolution. The cause of a fruit is the tree, but when a tree produces a fruit one cannot say that the tree is impersonal or that it vanishes. The tree may produce hundreds and thousands of fruits, but it remains as it is. The fruit is produced, and then it develops, stays for some time, dwindles and finally vanishes. This does not mean that the tree also vanishes. Thus from the very beginning the *Vedānta-sūtra* explains the doctrine of by-products. The activities of production, maintenance and dissolution are carried out by the inconceivable energy of the Supreme Lord. Thus the cosmic manifestation is a transformation of the energy of the Supreme Lord, although the energy of the Supreme Lord and the Supreme Lord Himself are nondifferent and inseparable. A touchstone may produce great quantities of gold in contact with iron, but still the touchstone remains as it is. Similarly the Supreme Lord, despite His producing the huge material cosmic manifestation, always remains in His transcendental form.

The Māyāvādī philosophers have the audacity to reject the purport of what Vyāsadeva explained in the *Vedānta-sūtra* and to say he attempted to establish a doctrine of transformation of the Supreme, which is totally imaginary. According to the Māyāvāda philosophy, the cosmic manifestation is an illusory transformation of the Absolute Truth and has no separate existence outside the Absolute Truth. This is not the message of the *Vedānta-sūtra*. The cosmic manifestation has been explained by Māyāvādī philosophers as false, but it is not false—it is temporary. The Māyāvādī philosophers maintain that the Absolute Truth is the only truth and that this material manifestation known as the world is false. Actually, this is not so. The material manifestation is not false; it is truth, but because it is relative truth it is temporary.

Praṇava, or *oṁkāra,* is the chief sound vibration found in the Vedic hymns, and it is considered to be the sound form of the Supreme Lord. From *oṁkāra* all Vedic hymns have emanated, and the world itself has also emanated from this *oṁkāra* sound. The vibration *tat tvam asi,* also found in the Vedic hymns, is not the chief vibration but is an explanation of the constitutional position of the living entity. *Tat tvam asi* means that the living entity is a spiritual particle of the supreme spirit, but this is not the chief motif of the *Vedānta-sūtra* or the Vedic literature. The chief sound representation of the Supreme is *oṁkāra.*

All these faulty explanations of the *Vedānta-sūtra* are considered atheistic. Because the Māyāvādī philosophers do not accept the eternal transcendental form of the Supreme Lord, they are unable to engage in real devotional service. Thus the Māyāvādī philosopher is forever bereft of Kṛṣṇa consciousness and Kṛṣṇa's devotional service. The pure devotee of the Personality of Godhead never accepts the Māyāvāda philosophy as an actual path to transcendental realization. The Māyāvādī philosophers hover in the moral and immoral material atmosphere of the cosmic world and are thus always engaged in rejecting and accepting material enjoyment. They have falsely accepted the nonspiritual as the spiritual, and as a result they have forgotten the eternal spiritual form of the Supreme Personality of Godhead, as well as His name, qualities and entourage. They consider the transcendental pastimes, name, form and qualities of the Supreme to be products of material nature. Because of their acceptance and rejection of material pleasure and misery, the Māyāvādī philosophers are eternally subjected to material misery.

The actual devotees of the Lord are always in disagreement with the Māyāvādī philosophers. Impersonalism cannot possibly represent eternity, bliss and knowledge. Being situated in imperfect knowledge of liberation, the Māyāvādīs decry the eternity, knowledge and bliss of the devotees as materialism. Because they reject devotional service, they are unintelligent and unable to understand the effects of devotional service. The word jugglery they use in an attempt to amalgamate knowledge, the knowable and the knower simply proves that they are unintelligent. The doctrine of by-products is the real purport of the beginning of the *Vedānta-sūtra*. The Lord possesses innumerable unlimited energies, and He displays the by-products of these energies in different ways. Everything is under His control. The Supreme Personality of Godhead is also the supreme controller, and He is manifested in innumerable energies and expansions.

CHAPTER 26

The Bhaṭṭācārya Is Converted

For the impersonalist and voidist philosophers, the next world is a world of senseless eternity and bliss. The voidist philosophers want to establish that ultimately everything is senseless, and the impersonalists want to establish that in the next world there is simply knowledge without any activities. Thus less intelligent salvationists try to carry imperfect knowledge into the sphere of perfect spiritual activity. Because the impersonalist experiences material activity as miserable, he wants to establish spiritual life without activity. He cannot understand the activities of devotional service. Indeed, spiritual activity in devotional service is unintelligible to the voidist philosophers and impersonalists. The Vaiṣṇava philosophers know perfectly well that the Absolute Truth, the Supreme Personality of Godhead, can never be impersonal or void, because He possesses innumerable potencies. Through His innumerable energies, He can present Himself in multiple forms and still remain the Absolute Supreme Personality of Godhead. Thus despite expanding Himself in multiple forms and diffusing His innumerable energies, He can maintain His transcendental position.

Thus Lord Caitanya exposed many defects in the Māyāvāda philosophy, and although the Bhaṭṭācārya tried to establish himself by logic and word jugglery, Lord Caitanya was able to defend Himself from his attacks. The Lord established that the Vedic literature is meant for three things: understanding our relationship with the Absolute Supreme Personality of Godhead, acting according to that understanding, and achieving the highest perfection of life, love of Godhead. Anyone who tries to prove that the Vedic literature aims at anything else must be a victim of his own imagination.

The Lord then quoted some verses from the *Purāṇas* by which He established that Śaṅkarācārya was ordered to teach Māyāvāda philosophy by the Supreme Personality of Godhead. He quoted a verse from the *Padma Purāṇa* (*Uttara-khaṇḍa* 62.31) in which it is stated that the Lord ordered Mahādeva, Lord Śiva, to present some imaginary interpretation of the Vedic literature to divert people from the actual purpose of the *Vedas*. "In this way try to make them atheists," the Lord said. "After that, they can be engaged in producing more population." It is also stated in the *Padma Purāṇa* (*Uttara-khaṇḍa* 25.7) that Lord Śiva explained to his wife Pārvatī that in the Age of Kali he would come in the form of a *brāhmaṇa* to preach an imperfect interpretation of the *Vedas* known as Māyāvāda, which in actuality is but a second edition of atheistic Buddhist philosophy.

The Bhaṭṭācārya was overwhelmed by these explanations of Lord Caitanya. After hearing Māyāvāda philosophy explained by Lord Caitanya, he could not speak. After he had remained silent for some time, Lord Caitanya said to him, "My dear Bhaṭṭācārya, don't be astonished by this explanation. Please take it from Me that the devotional service of the Supreme Lord is the highest perfectional stage of human understanding. Indeed, it is so attractive that even those who are already liberated become devotees by the inconceivable potency of the Supreme Personality of Godhead." There are many such conversions in the Vedic literature. For instance, in *Śrīmad-Bhāgavatam* (1.7.10) the famous *ātmārāma* verse describes how impersonalist sages who are absorbed in self-realization and liberated from all material attachments become attracted to devotional service by the various activities of Lord Kṛṣṇa. Such are the transcendental qualities of the Supreme Personality of Godhead.

Actually, in pure consciousness the living entity understands himself as the eternal servant of the Supreme Lord. Under the spell of illusion, a person accepts the gross and subtle bodies as his self;

such a conception is the basis of the doctrine of transference from spirit to matter. But the part and parcel of the Supreme is not eternally subjected to gross and subtle bodily life. The gross and subtle coverings do not comprise the living entity's eternal form; they can be changed, or the living entity can be freed entirely from material existence. While the living entity is under the illusion that he is the body and mind, however, he has certainly transferred his position from spirit to matter. Māyāvādī philosophers, taking advantage of this doctrine of transference, say that the living entity is under the wrong impression when he thinks himself to be part and parcel of the Supreme. They maintain that the living entity is the Supreme Himself. This doctrine cannot be tenable.

The Bhaṭṭācārya then asked Lord Caitanya to explain the famous *ātmārāma* verse, for he desired to hear it from the Lord Himself. Lord Caitanya replied that first of all the Bhaṭṭācārya should explain the verse according to his own understanding, and then Lord Caitanya would explain it. The Bhaṭṭācārya then began to explain the *ātmārāma śloka,* using his methods of logic and grammar. Thus he explained the *ātmārāma śloka* in nine different ways. The Lord appreciated his erudite scholarship in explaining the verse and said, "My dear Bhaṭṭācārya, I know that you are a personal manifestation of the learned scholar Bṛhaspati and can explain any portion of the *śāstras* nicely. Yet your explanation is more or less based on academic education only. But there is another explanation beside the academic, scholarly one."

Then, at the request of the Bhaṭṭācārya, Lord Caitanya explained the *ātmārāma śloka*. The words of the verse were analyzed thus: (1) *ātmārāmāḥ,* (2) *ca,* (3) *munayaḥ,* (4) *nirgranthāḥ,* (5) *api,* (6) *urukrame,* (7) *kurvanti,* (8) *ahaitukīm,* (9) *bhaktim,* (10) *ittham-bhūta-guṇaḥ,* (11) *hariḥ*. (This verse has already been explained in connection with the Lord's teachings to Sanātana Gosvāmī.) Without mentioning the nine explanations of the Bhaṭṭācārya, Lord Caitanya explained the verse by analyzing these eleven words. In this way He expounded eighteen different explanations of the verse. In summary, He said that the Supreme Personality of Godhead is full of innumerable potencies; no one can estimate how many transcendental qualities He possesses. His qualities are always inconceivable, and all processes of self-realization inquire in a general way into the potencies and qualities of the Supreme Personality of Godhead. But the devotees of the Lord immediately accept the inconceivable position of the Lord. Lord Caitanya explained that even great liberated souls like the Kumāras and Śukadeva Gosvāmī were also attracted to the transcendental qualities of the Supreme Lord.

The Bhaṭṭācārya appreciated Lord Caitanya's explanation, and he concluded that Lord Caitanya was none other than Kṛṣṇa Himself. The Bhaṭṭācārya then began to deprecate his own position, relating that he had at first considered Lord Caitanya to be an ordinary human being and therefore committed a great offense. He then fell down at the lotus feet of Lord Caitanya, deprecating himself, and requested the Lord to show His causeless mercy to him. Lord Caitanya appreciated the humility of this great scholar and therefore exhibited His own form, first with four hands, and then with six hands (*ṣaḍ-bhuja*). Sārvabhauma Bhaṭṭācārya then repeatedly fell down at the Lord's lotus feet and composed various prayers to Him. He was undoubtedly a great scholar, and after receiving the causeless mercy of the Lord, he was empowered to explain the Lord's activities in different ways. For instance, he was able to express the benefit of chanting Hare Kṛṣṇa, Hare Kṛṣṇa, Kṛṣṇa Kṛṣṇa, Hare Hare/ Hare Rāma, Hare Rāma, Rāma Rāma, Hare Hare.

It is said that at this time Sārvabhauma Bhaṭṭācārya composed a hundred verses in appreciation of the Lord's activities, and that those verses were so great that they could not be surpassed even by Bṛhaspati, the greatest learned scholar in the heavenly planets. The Lord was very much pleased to hear these hundred verses, and He embraced the Bhaṭṭācārya. The Bhaṭṭācārya became overwhelmed with ecstasy by the Lord's touch, and he practically fell unconscious. He cried, trembled, shivered and perspired, and sometimes he danced and sang and fell at the lotus feet of Lord Caitanya. The Bhaṭṭācārya's brother-in-law, Gopīnātha Ācārya, and the devotees of the Lord were surprised to see the Bhaṭṭācārya transformed into a great devotee.

Gopīnātha Ācārya then began to thank the Lord: "It is by Your grace only that the Bhaṭṭācārya has been transformed from his stonelike position into such a devotee." Lord Caitanya replied to Gopīnātha Ācārya that it was due to a devotee's favor that a stonelike man could be transformed into a mild, flowerlike devotee. Actually, Gopīnātha Ācārya had sincerely wished that his brother-in-law, the Bhaṭṭācārya, would become a devotee of the Lord. He had sincerely desired that the Lord favor the Bhaṭṭācārya, and he was glad to see that his desire had been fulfilled by Lord Caitanya. In other words, a devotee of the Lord is more merciful than the Lord Himself. When a devotee desires to show his mercy to a person, the Lord accepts him, and by the Lord's grace he becomes a devotee.

Lord Caitanya pacified the Bhaṭṭācārya and asked him to go home. The Bhaṭṭācārya again began to praise the Lord and said, "You have descended to deliver all the fallen souls of this material world. That project is not so difficult for You. But You have turned a stonehearted man like me into a devotee, and that is very wonderful indeed. Although I was very expert at logical arguments and grammatical explanations of the *Vedas,* I was as hard as a lump of iron. But Your influence and temperature were so great that You could melt even a hard piece of iron like me."

Lord Caitanya then returned to His place, and the Bhaṭṭācārya sent Gopīnātha Ācārya to Him with various kinds of *prasādam* from the Jagannātha temple. The next day the Lord went to the temple of Jagannātha early in the morning to attend *maṅgala-ārati*. The priests in the temple brought Him a garland from the Deity and also offered Him various kinds of *prasādam*. The Lord was very much pleased to receive them, and He at once went to the house of the Bhaṭṭācārya, taking the *prasādam* and flower garland to present to him. Although it was early in the morning, the Bhaṭṭācārya understood that the Lord had come and was knocking on his door. He at once rose from his bed and began to say, "Kṛṣṇa! Kṛṣṇa!" This was heard by Lord Caitanya. When the Bhaṭṭācārya opened the door, he saw the Lord standing there, and he was very much pleased to see Him early in the morning. Receiving Him with all care, the Bhaṭṭācārya offered Him a nice seat, and both of them sat there. Lord Caitanya then offered him the *prasādam* He had received in the temple of Jagannātha, and the Bhaṭṭācārya was very glad to receive this *prasādam* from the hands of Lord Caitanya Himself. Indeed, without taking his bath and without performing his daily duties or even cleansing his teeth, he immediately began to eat the *prasādam*. In this way he was freed from all material contamination and attachment.

As the Bhaṭṭācārya began to eat the *prasādam*, he recited a verse from the *Padma Purāṇa*. There it is stated that when *prasādam* is received it must be eaten immediately, even if it has become very dry or old, or even if it is brought from a distant place, or even if one has not completed executing his daily duties. Since it is enjoined in the *śāstras* that *prasādam* should immediately be taken, there is no restriction of time, place or atmosphere; the order of the Supreme Personality of Godhead must be followed. There are restrictions one must follow before accepting food from various people, but there are no restrictions on accepting *prasādam* from all kinds of people. *Prasādam* is always transcendental and can be taken under any condition.

Lord Caitanya was very much pleased to see that the Bhaṭṭācārya, who had always obeyed the rules and regulations strictly, accepted *prasādam* without following any rules and regulations. Being so pleased, Lord Caitanya embraced the Bhaṭṭācārya, and they both began to dance in transcendental ecstasy. In that ecstasy Lord Caitanya exclaimed, "My mission in Jagannātha Purī is now fulfilled! I have converted a person like Sārvabhauma Bhaṭṭācārya. I shall now be able to attain Vaikuṇṭha without fail."

The missionary goal of a devotee is to convert simply one person into a pure devotee. Then the devotee's admission to the spiritual kingdom is guaranteed. The Lord was so much pleased with the Bhaṭṭācārya that He began to bless him repeatedly: "Dear Bhaṭṭācārya, now you are a completely pure devotee of Lord Kṛṣṇa, and Kṛṣṇa is now very much pleased with you. From today you are free from the contamination of this material body and the entanglement under the spell of the material energy. You are now fit to go back to Godhead, back home." The Lord then cited a verse from *Śrīmad-Bhāgavatam* (2.7.42):

yeṣāṁ sa eṣa bhagavān dayayed anantaḥ
sarvātmanāśrita-pado yadi nirvyalīkam
te dustarām atitaranti ca deva-māyāṁ
naiṣāṁ mamāham iti dhīḥ śva-śṛgāla-bhakṣye

"Whoever takes complete shelter of the lotus feet of the Supreme Lord is favored by the Supreme Lord, who is known to be unlimited. Such a person also receives permission to cross the ocean of nescience. However, one who is under the misconception that his material body is himself cannot receive the causeless mercy of the Supreme Personality of Godhead."

After this incident, Lord Caitanya returned to His place, and the Bhaṭṭācārya became a pure and faultless devotee. Since he had formerly been a great academic scholar, the Bhaṭṭācārya could only have been converted by the causeless mercy of Caitanya Mahāprabhu. From that day forward the Bhaṭṭācārya never explained any Vedic literature without explaining devotional service. Gopīnātha Ācārya, his brother-in-law, was very much pleased to see the Bhaṭṭācārya's condition, and he began to dance in ecstasy and vibrate the transcendental sound Hare Kṛṣṇa, Hare Kṛṣṇa, Kṛṣṇa Kṛṣṇa, Hare Hare/ Hare Rāma, Hare Rāma, Rāma Rāma, Hare Hare.

The next day, after visiting the Jagannātha temple early in the morning, the Bhaṭṭācārya went to see Lord Caitanya, and he offered his respects by falling down before the Lord. He then began to explain his past undesirable behavior. When he asked the Lord to speak something about devotional service, the Lord began to elaborately explain the verse in the *Bṛhan-nāradīya Purāṇa* beginning *harer nāma harer nāma*. While hearing this explanation, the Bhaṭṭācārya became more and more ecstatic. Seeing the condition of his brother-in-law, Gopīnātha Ācārya said, "My dear Bhaṭṭācārya, previously I had said that when one is favored by the Supreme Lord he will understand the techniques of devotional service. Today I am seeing this fulfilled."

The Bhaṭṭācārya offered him his due respect and replied, "My dear Gopīnātha Ācārya, it is through your mercy that I have received the mercy of the Supreme Lord." The mercy of the Supreme Personality of Godhead can be obtained by the mercy of a pure devotee. Lord Caitanya's mercy was bestowed upon the Bhaṭṭācārya because of Gopīnātha Ācārya's endeavor. "You are a great devotee of the Lord," the Bhaṭṭācārya continued, "and I was simply blinded by my academic education. So it is only through your agency that I have obtained the mercy of the Lord." Lord Caitanya was greatly pleased to hear the Bhaṭṭācārya say that a man can achieve the mercy of the Lord through the agency of a devotee. Lord Caitanya appreciated his words and embraced the Bhaṭṭācārya, confirming his statement.

The Lord then requested the Bhaṭṭācārya to go see Jagannātha in the temple, and the Bhaṭṭācārya started out for the temple accompanied by Jagadānanda and Dāmodara, two principal associates of Lord Caitanya. After seeing Jagannātha the Bhaṭṭācārya returned home, bringing with him much *prasādam* purchased from the temple. He sent all this *prasādam* to Lord Caitanya through his *brāhmaṇa* servant.

The Bhaṭṭācārya also dispatched two verses written on a palm-tree leaf and requested Jagadānanda to do him a favor by delivering them to the Lord. Thus Lord Caitanya was offered the *prasādam* and the verses on the palm leaf. But before reaching the Lord, Mukunda Datta, who had also undertaken the delivery of the verses, had copied the verses into his book. When Lord Caitanya read the verses on the palm leaf, He tore it to pieces, for He never liked to be praised by anyone. The verses only survive because they had been copied by Mukunda Datta.

The verses praised Lord Caitanya as the Supreme Original Personality of Godhead, declaring that He had descended as Lord Caitanya to preach to the people in general about detachment, transcendental knowledge and devotional service. Comparing Lord Caitanya to an ocean of mercy, the Bhaṭṭācārya wrote, "Let me surrender unto that Lord Caitanya Mahāprabhu. The Lord, seeing that devotional service was absent, descended in the form of Caitanya Mahāprabhu to preach devotional service. Let us all surrender unto His lotus feet and learn from Him what devotional service actually is." These two important verses are considered the most valuable jewels by the devotees of the Lord in disciplic succession, and by virtue of these famous verses Sārvabhauma Bhaṭṭācārya has become known as the highest of devotees.

Thus Sārvabhauma Bhaṭṭācārya was converted into one of the most important devotees of the Lord, and he had no other interest than to serve the Lord. His only concern was to think of Lord

Caitanya constantly, and this meditation, along with chanting, became the main purpose of his life.

One day Sārvabhauma Bhaṭṭācārya came before the Lord, offered his respects and began to recite one of Lord Brahmā's prayers from *Śrīmad-Bhāgavatam* (10.14.8). The Bhaṭṭācārya recited as follows:

tat te 'nukampāṁ su-samīkṣamāṇo
bhuñjāna evātma-kṛtaṁ vipākam
hṛd-vāg-vapurbhir vidadhan namas te
jīveta yo bhakti-pade sa dāya-bhāk

In reciting the verse the Bhaṭṭācārya changed the original word *mukti* (liberation) to *bhakti* (devotional service) in the last line. The meaning of the original verse is "A person who devotes his mind, body and speech to the service of the Lord, even though in the midst of a miserable life caused by his past misdeeds, is assured of liberation."

"Why have you changed the original verse?" the Lord asked the Bhaṭṭācārya. "The word is *mukti,* and you have changed it to *bhakti.*" The Bhaṭṭācārya replied that *mukti* is not as valuable as *bhakti* and that *mukti* is actually a sort of punishment for the pure devotee. For this reason he changed the word *mukti* to *bhakti.* The Bhaṭṭācārya then began to explain his realization of *bhakti.* "Anyone who does not accept the transcendental Personality of Godhead and His transcendental form cannot know the Absolute Truth. One who does not understand the transcendental nature of the body of Kṛṣṇa becomes His enemy and decries Him or fights with Him. The destination of such enemies is to merge into the Lord's Brahman effulgence. Such *mukti,* or liberation, is never desired by the Lord's devotees. There are five kinds of liberation: (1) gaining admission to the planet where the Lord resides, (2) being able to associate with the Lord, (3) attaining a transcendental body like the Lord's, (4) attaining opulence like the Lord's, and (5) merging into the existence of the Lord. A devotee has no particular interest in any of these types of liberation. He is satisfied simply by being engaged in the transcendental loving service of the Lord. A devotee is especially averse to merging into the existence of the Lord and losing his individual identity. Indeed, a devotee considers oneness with the Lord to be worse than hell. But he will accept one of the four other kinds of liberation if it enables him to be engaged in the service of the Lord. Out of the two possibilities of merging in transcendence—namely becoming one with the impersonal Brahman effulgence and becoming one with the Personality of Godhead—the latter is more abominable to the devotee. The devotee has no aspiration other than engaging in the transcendental loving service of the Lord."

On hearing this, Lord Caitanya informed the Bhaṭṭācārya that there is another meaning to the word *mukti-pade*. The word *mukti-pade* directly indicates the Personality of Godhead. The Personality of Godhead has innumerable liberated souls engaged in His transcendental loving service, and He is the ultimate resort of liberation. In either case, Kṛṣṇa is the ultimate shelter.

"Despite this reading," Sārvabhauma Bhaṭṭācārya replied, "I prefer *bhakti-pade* to *mukti-pade*. Although according to You there are two meanings to the word *mukti-pade*, still, because this word is ambiguous, I prefer *bhakti-pade* to *mukti-pade* because when one hears the word *mukti* he immediately thinks of becoming one with the Supreme. I therefore even hate to utter the word *mukti*. But I am very enthusiastic to speak of *bhakti*."

At this, Lord Caitanya laughed very loudly and embraced the Bhaṭṭācārya with great love.

Thus the Bhaṭṭācārya, who had taken pleasure in explaining Māyāvāda philosophy, became such a staunch devotee that he hated even to utter the word *mukti*. This is possible only by the causeless mercy of Lord Śrī Caitanya. The Lord is like a touchstone, for by His grace He can turn iron into gold. After the Bhaṭṭācārya's conversion, everyone marked a great change in him, and they concluded that this change was made possible only by the inconceivable power of Lord Caitanya. Thus they took it for granted that Lord Caitanya was none other than Lord Kṛṣṇa Himself.

CHAPTER 27

Lord Caitanya and Rāmānanda Rāya

The author of the *Caitanya-caritāmṛta* has described Lord Caitanya Mahāprabhu as the ocean of transcendental knowledge, and Śrī Rāmānanda Rāya as the cloud which is produced from that ocean. Rāmānanda Rāya was a greatly advanced scholar in devotional service, and by the grace of Lord Caitanya he gathered all transcendental conclusions just as a cloud gathers water from the ocean. As clouds appear from the ocean and then go all over the world to distribute water, which then returns to the ocean, so by the grace of Lord Caitanya, Rāmānanda Rāya attained his higher knowledge of devotional service and again, after retiring from service, went to join Lord Caitanya in Purī.

When Lord Caitanya visited the southern part of India, He first went to the great temple known as Jiyaḍa-nṛsiṁha. This temple is situated in a place known as Siṁhācala, five miles from Visakhapatnam. The temple is situated on the top of a hill. There are many temples in that area, but the Jiyaḍa-nṛsiṁha temple is the largest of all. This temple is filled with beautiful sculpture, of interest to many students, and due to its popularity it is a very rich temple. An inscription in the temple states that the King of Vijayanagara formerly decorated this temple with gold and even covered the body of the Deity with gold plate. To facilitate attendance at the temple, there are free apartments for visitors. The temple is managed by priests of the Rāmānujācārya sect.

When Lord Caitanya visited this temple, He praised the Deity and quoted a verse from Śrīdhara Svāmī's commentary on *Śrīmad-Bhāgavatam* (7.9.1):

ugro 'py anugra evāyaṁ sva-bhaktānāṁ nṛ-keśarī
keśarīva sva-potānām anyeṣām ugra-vikramaḥ

"Although Lord Nṛsiṁha is very severe to demons and nondevotees, He is very kind to His submissive devotees like Prahlāda." Lord Nṛsiṁha appeared as a half-man, half-lion incarnation of Kṛṣṇa when Prahlāda, a boy devotee of the Lord, was harassed by his demoniac father Hiraṇyakaśipu. Just as a lion is very ferocious to other animals but very kind and submissive to his cubs, so Lord Nṛsiṁha appeared ferocious to Hiraṇyakaśipu and very kind to His devotee Prahlāda.

After visiting the temple of Jiyaḍa-nṛsiṁha, the Lord proceeded further into south India and ultimately reached Vidyānagara, on the bank of the Godāvarī. While on the bank of this river, the Lord remembered the Yamunā River in Vṛndāvana, and He considered the trees on the bank to be the forest of Vṛndāvana. Thus He was in ecstasy there. After taking a bath in the Godāvarī, the Lord sat near the bank and began chanting Hare Kṛṣṇa, Hare Kṛṣṇa, Kṛṣṇa Kṛṣṇa, Hare Hare/ Hare Rāma, Hare Rāma, Rāma Rāma, Hare Hare. While sitting and chanting, the Lord saw that the governor of the province, Śrī Rāmānanda Rāya, had reached the banks of the river accompanied by his associates, which included a musical band and many *brāhmaṇas.* Previously the Lord had been asked by Sārvabhauma Bhaṭṭācārya to visit the great devotee Rāmānanda Rāya at Kabur. The Lord could understand that the man approaching the riverbank was Rāmānanda Rāya, and He desired to see him immediately. But because He was in the renounced order of life, He restrained Himself from going to see a person involved in political affairs. Being a great devotee, Rāmānanda Rāya was attracted by the features of Lord Caitanya, who appeared as a *sannyāsī,* and he himself came to see the

Rāmānanda Rāya discusses the highest level of Kṛṣṇa consciousness with Lord Caitanya.

Lord. Upon reaching Caitanya Mahāprabhu, Rāmānanda Rāya prostrated himself to offer his obeisances and respects. Lord Caitanya received him by vibrating Hare Kṛṣṇa, Hare Kṛṣṇa, Kṛṣṇa Kṛṣṇa, Hare Hare/ Hare Rāma, Hare Rāma, Rāma Rāma, Hare Hare.

When Rāmānanda Rāya presented his credentials, Lord Caitanya embraced him, and both of them were overwhelmed with ecstasy. The *brāhmaṇas* who accompanied Rāmānanda Rāya were surprised to see them embracing in transcendental ecstasy. The *brāhmaṇas* were all stalwart followers of the rituals, and they could not understand the meaning of such devotional symptoms. Indeed, they were rather surprised to see such a great *sannyāsī* touch a *śūdra,* and they were also surprised to see Rāmānanda Rāya, who was a great governor and practically king of that province, crying simply by touching a *sannyāsī.* Lord Caitanya understood the *brāhmaṇas'* thoughts, and, considering the unfavorable situation, He pacified Himself.

After this, Lord Caitanya and Rāmānanda Rāya sat down together. "Sārvabhauma Bhaṭṭācārya has spoken very highly of you," Lord Caitanya informed him. "So I have come to see you."

"Sārvabhauma Bhaṭṭācārya considers me one of his devotees," Rāmānanda Rāya replied. "Therefore he has kindly recommended that You see me."

Rāmānanda Rāya very much appreciated the Lord's touching a man of wealth. Generally a king, governor or any politician is always absorbed in thoughts of political affairs and pounds-shillings-pence; therefore such persons are avoided by *sannyāsīs.* Lord Caitanya, however, knew Rāmānanda Rāya to be a great devotee, and so He did not hesitate to touch and embrace him. Rāmānanda Rāya was surprised by Lord Caitanya's behavior, and he cited a verse from *Śrīmad-Bhāgavatam* (10.8.4): "Great personalities and sages appear in the homes of worldly men just to show them mercy."

Lord Caitanya's special treatment of Rāmānanda Rāya indicated that although Rāmānanda Rāya was born in a nonbrahminical family he was far, far advanced in spiritual knowledge and activity. Therefore he was more respectable than one who simply happens to be born in a brahminical family. Although Rāmānanda, out of his meek and gentle nature, considered himself to be born in a lower, *śūdra* family, Lord Caitanya nonetheless considered him to be situated in the highest transcendental stage of devotion. Devotees never advertise themselves as great, but the Lord is very eager to advertise the glory of His devotees. After meeting for the first time that morning on the bank of the Godāvarī, Rāmānanda Rāya and Lord Caitanya separated with the understanding that Rāmānanda Rāya would come in the evening to see the Lord.

That evening, after the Lord had taken His bath and seated Himself, Rāmānanda Rāya came to see Him with a servant. He offered his respects and sat down before the Lord. Before Rāmānanda Rāya could even ask the Lord a question about the advancement of spiritual knowledge, the Lord said, "Please quote some verses from scripture about the ultimate goal of human life."

Śrī Rāmānanda Rāya at once replied: "A person who is sincere in performing his occupational duty will gradually develop a sense of God consciousness." In this connection he quoted a verse from the *Viṣṇu Purāṇa* (3.8.9) which states that one worships the Supreme Lord by following the principles of one's occupational duty and that there is no alternative for satisfying Him. The purport is that human life is meant for understanding one's relationship with the Supreme Lord and acting in that relationship. Any human being can do this by dovetailing himself in the service of the Lord while discharging his prescribed duties. For this purpose human society is divided into four classes: the intellectuals (*brāhmaṇas*), the administrators (*kṣatriyas*), the merchants (*vaiśyas*), and the laborers (*śūdras*). For each class there are prescribed rules and regulations, as well as occupational functions. The prescribed duties and qualities of the four classes are described in the *Bhagavad-gītā* (18.41–44). A civilized society should be organized so that people follow the prescribed rules and regulations for their particular class. At the same time, for spiritual advancement they should follow the four stages of *āśrama*, namely student life (*brahmacarya*), householder life (*gṛhastha*), retired life (*vānaprastha*) and renounced life (*sannyāsa*).

Rāmānanda Rāya stated that those who strictly follow the rules and regulations of these eight social divisions can actually satisfy the Supreme Lord, and one who does not follow them certainly spoils his human form of life and glides down toward hell. One can peacefully achieve the goal of human life simply by following the rules and regulations which apply to oneself. The character of a particular person develops when he follows the regulative principles in accordance with his work, association and education. The divisions of society are so designed that many people with different characteristics can be regulated under those divisions for the peaceful administration of society and for spiritual advancement as well. The social classes can be further characterized as follows: (1) One whose aim is to understand the Supreme Lord, the Personality of Godhead, and who has thus devoted himself to learning the *Vedas* and similar literatures is called a *brāhmaṇa*. (2) A person whose occupation involves displaying force and administering the government is called a *kṣatriya*. (3) One who is engaged in agriculture, herding cows and doing business is called a *vaiśya*. (4) One who has no special knowledge but is satisfied by serving the other three classes is called a *śūdra*. If one faithfully discharges his prescribed duties, he is sure to advance toward perfection. Thus regulated life is the source of perfection for everyone. One who leads a regulated life centered around devotional service to the Lord attains perfection. Otherwise such a regulated life is simply a useless waste of time.

After hearing Rāmānanda Rāya expound upon the proper execution of a regulated life, Lord Caitanya said that such a life is simply external. Indirectly He asked Rāmānanda to describe something superior to such an external exhibition. Formal execution of rituals and religion is useless unless aimed at attaining the perfection of devotional service. Lord Viṣṇu is not satisfied simply by a ritualistic adherence to Vedic instructions; He is actually pleased when one attains the stage of devotional service.

According to the verse cited by Rāmānanda Rāya, one can rise to the point of devotional service by ritualistic performance. In the *Bhagavad-gītā* (18.45–46), Śrī Kṛṣṇa, who appeared in order to deliver all classes of people, states:

sve sve karmaṇy abhirataḥ saṁsiddhiṁ labhate naraḥ
sva-karma-nirataḥ siddhiṁ yathā vindati tac chṛṇu

yataḥ pravṛttir bhūtānāṁ yena sarvam idaṁ tatam
sva-karmaṇā tam abhyarcya siddhiṁ vindati mānavaḥ

"A human being can attain the highest perfectional stage of life by worshiping the Supreme Lord, from whom everything has emanated, through his occupational duties." This perfectional process was followed by great devotees like Bodhāyana, Ṭaṅka, Dramiḍa, Guhadeva, Kapardi and Bhāruci. All these great personalities followed this particular path of perfection. The Vedic injunctions also aim in this direction. Rāmānanda Rāya wanted to present these facts before the Lord, but apparently mere discharge of ritualistic duties is not perfection. Therefore Lord Caitanya said that it was external, indicating that if a man has a material conception of life he cannot attain the highest perfection, even if he follows all the ritualistic regulations.

CHAPTER 28

Relationship with the Supreme Lord

Lord Caitanya rejected the statement cited by Rāmānanda Rāya from the *Viṣṇu Purāṇa* because the Lord wished to reject a class of philosophers known as Mīmāṁsakas. The followers of Karma-mīmāṁsā philosophy teach that God is subject to one's work. Their conclusion is that if one works nicely God is bound to give good results. Thus from the statement of the *Viṣṇu Purāṇa* cited by Rāmānanda Rāya one might conclude that Viṣṇu, the Supreme Lord, has no independence but is bound to award a certain kind of result to the worker. Such a dependent God becomes subject to the worshiper, who accepts the Supreme Lord as both impersonal and personal, as he wishes. Actually, the Karma-mīmāṁsā philosophy stresses the impersonal feature of the Supreme Absolute Truth. Because Lord Caitanya did not like such impersonalism, He rejected it.

"Tell Me if you know something beyond this conception of the Supreme Absolute Truth," Lord Caitanya said.

Rāmānanda Rāya understood the purpose of Lord Caitanya, and, after stating that it is better to give Kṛṣṇa the results of fruitive activities, he quoted a verse from the *Bhagavad-gītā* (9.27):

yat karoṣi yad aśnāsi yaj juhoṣi dadāsi yat
yat tapasyasi kaunteya tat kuruṣva mad-arpaṇam

"O son of Kuntī, whatever you do, whatever you eat, whatever you sacrifice, whatever you give away, and whatever austerity you undergo to achieve some goal, everything should be dedicated to My service." There is a similar passage in *Śrīmad-Bhāgavatam* (11.2.36), which states that one should submit everything—all the results of the fruitive activities one performs with body, speech, mind, senses, intelligence, soul and modes of nature—to the Supreme Personality of Godhead, Nārāyaṇa.

Lord Caitanya, however, also rejected this second statement, saying, "If you know of something higher, state it."

Offering everything to the Supreme Personality of Godhead, as enjoined by the *Bhagavad-gītā* and *Śrīmad-Bhāgavatam,* is better than impersonally making the Supreme Lord subject to our work, but it is still short of surrendering to the Supreme Lord. A worker's identification with material existence cannot be changed without proper guidance. Such fruitive activity will continue one's material existence. A worker is simply instructed here to offer the results of his work to the Supreme Lord, but there is no information given to enable one to get out of the material entanglement. Therefore Lord Caitanya rejected his proposal.

After having his suggestions rejected twice, Rāmānanda proposed that one should forsake his occupational activities altogether and by such detachment rise to the transcendental plane. In other words, he recommended complete renunciation of worldly life. To support this proposal he cited evidence from *Śrīmad-Bhāgavatam* (11.11.32) wherein the Lord says, "In the scriptures I have described the ritualistic principles and the way one can become situated in devotional service by giving them up. That is the highest perfection of religion." Rāmānanda also quoted Lord Kṛṣṇa's similar statement in the *Bhagavad-gītā* (18.66):

sarva-dharmān parityajya māṁ ekaṁ śaraṇaṁ vraja
ahaṁ tvāṁ sarva-pāpebhyo mokṣayiṣyāmi mā śucaḥ

"Give up all kinds of religiousness and just surrender unto Me, the Supreme Personality of Godhead. I shall protect you from all sinful reactions, and you will have nothing to be aggrieved over."

Lord Caitanya also rejected this third proposal from Rāmānanda Rāya, for He wanted to demonstrate that renunciation in itself is not sufficient. There must be positive engagement. Without positive engagement, the highest perfectional stage cannot be attained. Generally there are two kinds of philosophers in the renounced order of life. The goal of one is *nirvāṇa,* and the goal of the other is the impersonal Brahman effulgence. Such philosophers cannot imagine that they can reach beyond *nirvāṇa* and the Brahman effulgence to the Vaikuṇṭha planets of the spiritual sky. Because in simple renunciation there is no conception of spiritual planets and spiritual activities, Lord Caitanya rejected this third proposal.

Rāmānanda Rāya then cited more evidence from the *Bhagavad-gītā* (18.54):

brahma-bhūtaḥ prasannātmā na śocati na kāṅkṣati
samaḥ sarveṣu bhūteṣu mad-bhaktiṁ labhate parām

"When by cultivation of knowledge a person realizes himself to be nondifferent from the Supreme Absolute Truth, he becomes joyful and is freed from all kinds of lamentation and material desires. At that time he perfects his Brahman realization by seeing everyone on the same spiritual level. Such Brahman realization can elevate one to the transcendental stage of devotional service." Rāmānanda Rāya first suggested devotional service with renunciation of the fruits of one's work, but here he suggests that devotional service with full knowledge and spiritual realization is superior.

Lord Caitanya, however, also rejected this proposal because simply by renouncing material results in Brahman realization one does not realize the spiritual world and spiritual activities. Although there is no material contamination when one attains the stage of Brahman realization, in that stage one is still not perfectly pure because there is no positive engagement in spiritual activity. Because it is still on the mental plane, it is external. The pure living entity is not liberated unless he is completely engaged in spiritual activity. As long as one is absorbed in impersonal thoughts or in thoughts of the void, one's entrance into an eternal, blissful life of knowledge is not complete. When spiritual knowledge is not complete, one will be hindered in his attempt to cleanse the mind of all material variegatedness. Thus impersonalists are frustrated in their attempts to make the mind void by artificial meditation. It is very difficult to void the mind of all material conceptions. In the *Bhagavad-gītā* (12.5) it is stated that those who indulge in such impersonal meditation find it very difficult to make spiritual advancement. In addition, whatever state they do attain is not complete liberation. Therefore Lord Caitanya rejected it.

After his fourth proposal was rejected, Rāmānanda Rāya said that devotional service rendered without any attempt at mental speculation or cultivation of knowledge is the highest stage of perfection. To support this view he gave evidence from *Śrīmad-Bhāgavatam* (10.14.3), wherein Lord Brahmā tells the Supreme Personality of Godhead:

jñāne prayāsam udapāsya namanta eva
jīvanti san-mukharitāṁ bhavadīya-vārtām
sthāne sthitāḥ śruti-gatāṁ tanu-vāṅ-manobhir
ye prāyaśo 'jita jito 'py asi tais tri-lokyām

"My dear Lord, one should give up monistic speculation and the cultivation of knowledge altogether. He should begin his spiritual life in devotional service by receiving information of Your activities from a realized devotee of the Lord. If one cultivates his spiritual life by adhering to these principles and keeping himself on the honest path in life, then although Your Lordship is never conquered, You become conquered by the devotee following such a process."

When Rāmānanda Rāya presented this proposal, Lord Caitanya at once said, "Yes, this is right." In other words, Lord Caitanya agreed that this process conforms to His mission. In this age there is no possibility of acquiring spiritual knowledge by discharging one's duties in the *varṇāśrama-dharma* system, by devotional service mixed with fruitive activity, by renunciation, or by devotional service mixed with the culture of knowledge. Because most people are fallen and because there is no time to elevate them by a gradual process, the best course, according to Lord Caitanya, is to let them remain in whatever condition they are in but to engage them in hearing of the activities of the Supreme Lord as those activities are explained in the *Bhagavad-gītā* and *Śrīmad-Bhāgavatam*. The transcendental messages of the scriptures should be heard from the lips of realized souls. In this way a person may continue to live in whatever condition he is in and still make spiritual progress. Thus one can surely advance and fully realize the Supreme Personality of Godhead.

Although Lord Caitanya accepted these principles, He still requested Rāmānanda Rāya to further explain advanced devotional service. Thus Lord Caitanya gave Rāmānanda Rāya a chance to discuss gradual advancement from the principles of *varṇāśrama-dharma* (the four castes and the four orders of spiritual life), through the offering of the results of fruitive activity, and through the speculative discussion of spiritual knowledge. Lord Caitanya rejected all these because in the field of executing pure devotional service there is very little use for such principles. Without self-realization, such artificial methods of devotional service cannot be accepted as pure devotional service. Self-realized, pure devotional service is completely different from all other kinds of transcendental activity. The highest stage of transcendental activity is always free from all material desires, fruitive efforts and speculative attempts at knowledge. In the highest stage one concentrates on the simple, favorable execution of pure devotional service.

Rāmānanda Rāya could understand the motive of Lord Caitanya, and therefore he stated that attainment of pure love of Godhead is the highest perfectional stage. In the *Padyāvalī* there is a very nice verse which is said to be composed by Rāmānanda Rāya himself. The meaning of the verse is: "As long as there is hunger in the belly and one feels like eating and drinking, one can become happy by taking various eatables. Similarly, there may be much paraphernalia for worshiping the Supreme Lord, but only when that worship is mixed with pure love of Godhead does it become an actual source of transcendental happiness." Another verse composed by Rāmānanda Rāya states, "Even after millions and millions of births of pious activities, one cannot achieve a sense of devotional service, but if somehow or other one desires to attain devotional service, the association of a pure devotee will make it possible. Thus from any available source one should try to acquire a strong desire to engage in devotional service." In these two verses, Rāmānanda Rāya has described the regulative principles and developed love of Godhead, respectively. Lord Caitanya wanted to bring him to the stage of developed love of Godhead, and He wanted him to speak from that platform. Thus the discussion between Rāmānanda Rāya and Lord Caitanya will now proceed on the basis of love of Godhead.

If love of Godhead is elevated to personal affinity, it is called *prema-bhakti*. In the beginning of *prema-bhakti* a particular relationship between the Supreme Lord and the devotee is not established, but when *prema-bhakti* develops, a relationship with the Supreme Lord is manifested in different transcendental flavors. The first stage is servitude, wherein the Supreme Lord is accepted as the master and the devotee as His eternal servitor. When Lord Caitanya accepted this process, Rāmānanda Rāya described the relationship between the servitor and the master. He cited a verse from *Śrīmad-Bhāgavatam* (9.5.16) spoken by Durvāsā Muni, a great mystic *yogī* who considered himself very elevated and envied Mahārāja Ambarīṣa, who was known as the greatest devotee of the time. In an attempt to harass Mahārāja Ambarīṣa, Durvāsā Muni had met with a great catastrophe and been defeated by the Sudarśana *cakra* of the Lord. Durvāsā Muni admitted his fault and said, "For pure devotees who are always engaged in the transcendental loving service of the Lord, whose very name is sufficient for liberation, nothing is considered impossible."

In the *Stotra-ratna* (43), Yāmunācārya writes: "My Lord, those who keep themselves independent of Your service are helpless. They work on their own account and thus receive no support from superior authority. Therefore I long for the time when I shall engage fully in Your transcendental loving service without any desire for material satisfaction and without hovering on the mental plane. Only when I engage in such unalloyed devotional service will I enjoy actual spiritual life."

Upon hearing this statement, the Lord requested Rāmānanda Rāya to go still further.

CHAPTER 29

Pure Love for Kṛṣṇa

Encouraged by Lord Caitanya to proceed further, Rāmānanda Rāya said that the fraternal relationship with Lord Kṛṣṇa is a still higher transcendental position. The reason Rāmānanda Rāya said this is because when the relationship with Kṛṣṇa increases in affection, the mood of fear and the consciousness of the superiority of the Supreme Lord diminish. At this point the mood of faithfulness increases, and this faithfulness is called friendship. In this friendly relationship, there is a sense of equality between Lord Kṛṣṇa and His friends.

In this regard Rāmānanda Rāya quoted a nice verse from *Śrīmad-Bhāgavatam* (10.12.11), which Śukadeva Gosvāmī spoke while describing Lord Kṛṣṇa's lunch with His friends in the forest. Lord Kṛṣṇa and His friends had gone to the forest with the cows to play, and it is said in this verse that the boys who accompanied Kṛṣṇa enjoyed transcendental friendship with the Supreme Personality of Godhead, who is considered to be the impersonal Brahman by great sages, the Supreme Personality of Godhead by devotees in the mood of servitude, and an ordinary human being by common men.

Lord Caitanya appreciated this statement very much, yet still He said, "You can go even further." Being so requested, Rāmānanda Rāya then stated that the parental relationship with Kṛṣṇa is a still higher transcendental position. When the friendly attitude toward

Kṛṣṇa increases in affection, it develops into the relationship found between parents and their son. Regarding this, Rāmānanda Rāya quoted a verse from *Śrīmad-Bhāgavatam* (10.8.46) wherein Mahārāja Parīkṣit inquired from Śukadeva Gosvāmī about the magnitude of righteous activity performed by Yaśodā, the mother of Kṛṣṇa, enabling her to be called "Mother" by the Supreme Personality of Godhead and to have Him suck her breasts. Then Rāmānanda quoted another verse from *Śrīmad-Bhāgavatam* (10.9.20), in which it is stated that Yaśodā, the wife of the cowherd Nanda, received such mercy from the Supreme Personality of Godhead that it is beyond comparison even to the mercy received by Brahmā, the first created living being, or by Lord Śiva, or even by the goddess of fortune, Lakṣmī, who is always situated on the chest of Lord Viṣṇu.

Lord Caitanya then asked Rāmānanda Rāya to proceed further in order to come to the point of conjugal love. Understanding the mind of Lord Caitanya, Rāmānanda Rāya immediately answered that it was indeed conjugal love with Kṛṣṇa that constituted the highest relationship. In other words, one's intimate relationship with Kṛṣṇa develops from an ordinary conception of the Supreme Personality of Godhead, to the conception of master and servant, and, when this becomes confidential, it develops into a friendly relationship, and when this relationship further develops, it becomes parental, and when this develops to the highest point of complete love and affection, it is known as conjugal love with the Supreme Personality of Godhead. Rāmānanda Rāya then quoted another verse from *Śrīmad-Bhāgavatam* (10.47.60), which states that the transcendental mode of ecstasy exhibited during the *rāsa* dance between the *gopīs* and Kṛṣṇa was never relished even by the goddess of fortune, who is always situated on the chest of the Lord in the spiritual kingdom. And what to speak of the experience of ordinary women?

Rāmānanda Rāya then explained the gradual process by which pure love for Kṛṣṇa is developed. He pointed out that the relationship a living entity has with the Supreme Personality of Godhead in any of the modes of affection is just suitable for him. Still, there are higher and lower relationships. A relationship with the Supreme

Lord begins with the master-and-servant relationship and further develops into friendship, parental love and conjugal love. One who is situated in his particular relationship with the Supreme Personality of Godhead is in the best relationship for him. But when we study these different flavors of transcendental taste in relationship with the Supreme Lord, we can see that the neutral stage of realization (*brahma-bhūta*) is the first stage, that the stage of accepting the Lord as master and oneself as His servant is better, that the conception of oneself as the Lord's friend is even more developed, that a parental relationship with the Lord is of a still superior quality, and that conjugal love is the supreme relationship with the Lord.

In other words, self-realization with a sense of servitude for the Lord is certainly transcendental, but when a sense of fraternity is added the relationship develops, and as affection increases, this relationship develops into parenthood and conjugal love. Rāmānanda Rāya then quoted a verse from the *Bhakti-rasāmṛta-sindhu* (2.5.38) stating that spiritual affection for the Supreme Lord is transcendental in all cases, but that the individual devotee has a specific aptitude for a particular relationship, which is more relishable for him than the others.

Such transcendental relationships with the Supreme Lord cannot be manufactured by the mental concoctions of pseudo-devotees. In this connection, Rūpa Gosvāmī has stated in his *Bhakti-rasāmṛta-sindhu* (1.2.101) that devotional service which makes no reference to the Vedic scriptures and which does not follow the principles set forth therein can never be approved. Śrīla Bhaktisiddhānta Sarasvatī Gosvāmī Mahārāja has also remarked that professional spiritual masters, professional *Bhāgavatam* reciters, professional *kīrtana* performers and those engaged in devotional service according to their own mental concoctions cannot be accepted. In India there are various professional communities known as *āula, bāula, kartābhajā, neḍā, daraveśa, sāṅi, ativāḍī, cūḍādhārī* and *gaurāṅga-nāgarī*. A member of the Ventor Gosvāmī Society, or the caste called *gosvāmī,* cannot be accepted as a descendant of the six original *gosvāmīs*. Nor can so-called devotees who manufacture songs about Lord Caitanya, nor those who are professional priests or paid reciters, be accepted. One who does not follow the principles of the *Pañcarātra,* or one who is an impersonalist or addicted to sex life, cannot be compared with those who have dedicated their lives to the service of Kṛṣṇa. A pure devotee who is always engaged in Kṛṣṇa consciousness can sacrifice everything for the service of the Lord. Whether following the principles of householder life or those of the renounced life in the line of Caitanya Mahāprabhu, such a pure devotee who has dedicated his life to the service of Lord Caitanya, Kṛṣṇa and the spiritual master cannot be compared with professional men.

When one is freed from all material contaminations, any one of the relationships with Kṛṣṇa is transcendentally relishable. Unfortunately, those who are inexperienced in the transcendental science cannot appreciate the different relationships with the Supreme Lord. They think that all such relationships arise from *māyā*. The author of the *Caitanya-caritāmṛta* has given a nice example concerning these relationships. He points out that earth, water, fire, air and ether (the five gross elements) develop from subtle forms to grosser forms. For example, sound is found in ether, but in air there is both sound and touch. In fire there is sound, touch and form as well, and in water there is sound, touch, form and taste. Finally, in earth there is sound, touch, form, taste and smell. Just as the various characteristics increase in the progression from ether to earth, so the five characteristics of devotion increase with each relationship, until all five are found in the relationship of conjugal love. Thus the relationship with Kṛṣṇa in conjugal love is accepted as the highest perfectional stage of love of God.

In this connection, Lord Kṛṣṇa says to the damsels of Vraja in *Śrīmad-Bhāgavatam* (10.82.44): "Devotional service to Me is the life of every living entity. Indeed, your love for Me is the only cause of achieving My association." It is said that Lord Kṛṣṇa, in His relationship with His devotees, accepts all kinds of devotional service and then reciprocates according to the devotee's attitude. If one wants a relationship with Kṛṣṇa as master and servant, Kṛṣṇa plays the part of the perfect master. For one who wants Kṛṣṇa as a son in the parental relationship, Kṛṣṇa plays the part of a perfect son. Similarly, if a devotee wants to worship Kṛṣṇa in conjugal love, Kṛṣṇa perfectly plays the part of a husband or paramour.

However, Kṛṣṇa has admitted that His loving relationship with the damsels of Vraja in conjugal love is the highest perfectional stage. In *Śrīmad-Bhāgavatam* (10.32.22) Kṛṣṇa told the *gopīs:*

na pāraye 'haṁ niravadya-saṁyujāṁ
sva-sādhu-kṛtyaṁ vibudhāyuṣāpi vaḥ
yā mābhajan durjaya-geha-śṛṅkhalāḥ
saṁvṛścya tad vaḥ pratiyātu sādhunā

"My dear *gopīs,* your relationship with Me is completely transcendental, and it is not possible for Me to offer anything in exchange for your love, even after many births. You have given up all attachment for material enjoyment, and you have searched after Me. Since I am unable to repay your love, kindly be pleased with your own activities."

Śrīla Bhaktisiddhānta Sarasvatī Gosvāmī Mahārāja has remarked that there is a class of common men who claim that anyone and everyone can worship the Supreme Lord according to his own invented mode of worship and still attain the Supreme Personality of Godhead. They claim that one can approach the Supreme Lord either through fruitive activities, speculative knowledge, meditation or austerity and that any one of these methods will enable one to reach the perfectional stage. They generally give the example that just as a place may be reached by one of many different paths, so the Supreme Absolute Truth may be worshiped either as Goddess Kālī, or Goddess Durgā, or Lord Śiva, Gaṇeśa, Rāma, Hari or Brahmā. In short, they maintain that it does not matter how the Absolute Truth is addressed, for all names are one and the same. They give the example of a man with many names: if he is called by any of those names, he will answer.

Such mentally concocted views may be very pleasing to an ordinary person, but they are full of misconceptions concerning transcendental life. One who worships the demigods out of material lust cannot attain the Supreme Personality of Godhead, although the external energy of the Lord may award such a worshiper some material results. Kṛṣṇa discourages demigod worship in the *Bhagavad-gītā* (7.23):

antavat tu phalaṁ teṣāṁ tad bhavaty alpa-medhasām
devān deva-yajo yānti mad-bhaktā yānti mām api

"Men of small intelligence worship the demigods, and their fruits are limited and temporary. Those who worship the demigods go to the planets of the demigods, but My devotees ultimately reach My supreme planet." Thus the Supreme Lord awards the benediction of His association only to those who worship Him, and not to those who worship the demigods. It is not a fact that everyone and anyone can reach the Supreme Personality of Godhead by worshiping the material demigods. It is therefore surprising that a man can imagine that he will become perfect by worshiping the demigods. The results of devotional service rendered in full Kṛṣṇa consciousness cannot be compared to the results of demigod worship, fruitive activity or mental speculation. The result of fruitive activity is that one can go to the heavenly planets, or one can go to hell.

CHAPTER 30

The Transcendental Pastimes of Rādhā and Kṛṣṇa

The difference between ordinary religious activities and devotional service is very great. By executing religious rituals one can achieve economic development, sense gratification or liberation (merging into the existence of the Supreme), but the results of transcendental devotional service are completely different from such temporary benefits. Devotional service of the Lord is ever green, and it is increasingly transcendentally pleasing. Thus there is a gulf of difference between the results derived from devotional service and those derived from religious rituals. The great divine energy known as Jaḍādhiṣṭhātrī, or Mahāmāyā, the superintendent of the material world, and the material departmental directors, the demigods, as well as the products of the external energy of the Supreme Lord, are but perverted reflections of the opulence of the Supreme Lord. The demigods are actually order carriers of the Supreme Lord, and they help manage the material creation. In the *Brahma-saṁhitā* (5.44, 52, 49) it is stated that the workings of the supremely powerful superintendent, Durgā, are but shadows of the workings of the Supreme Lord, that the sun works just like the eye of the Supreme Lord, and that Brahmā works just like a jewel reflecting the light of the Supreme Lord. Thus in the material world all the demigods, as well as the external energy herself, Durgādevī, and all the different departmental directors are but servants of the Supreme Lord.

In the spiritual world there is another energy: the superior, spiritual energy, or internal energy, known as Yogamāyā. She also works under the Lord's direction, but in the spiritual world. When the living entity puts himself under the direction of Yogamāyā instead of Mahāmāyā, he gradually becomes a devotee of Kṛṣṇa. On the other hand, those who are after material opulence and material happiness place themselves under the care of the material energy, Mahāmāyā, or under the care of material demigods like Lord Śiva. In *Śrīmad-Bhāgavatam* it is found that when the *gopīs* of Vṛndāvana desired Kṛṣṇa as their husband, they prayed to the spiritual energy, Yogamāyā, for the fulfillment of their desire. In the *Saptaśatī* it is found that King Suratha and a merchant named Samādhi, being under the modes of material nature, worshiped Mahāmāyā for material opulence. Thus one should not mistakenly equate Yogamāyā with Mahāmāyā.

Because the Lord is on the absolute platform, there is no difference between the holy name of the Lord and the Supreme Lord Himself. There are many different names for the Supreme Lord, such as Paramātmā (the Supersoul), Brahman (the Supreme Absolute), Sṛṣṭikartā (the creator), Nārāyaṇa (the transcendental Lord), Rukmiṇī-ramaṇa (the husband of Rukmiṇī), Gopīnātha (the enjoyer of the *gopīs*) and Kṛṣṇa. In this way the Lord has different names, and these names indicate different functions. The aspect of the Supreme Lord as the creator is different from His aspect as Nārāyaṇa. Some of the names of the Lord as the creator are conceived by materialistic men. One cannot fully realize the essence of the Supreme Personality of Godhead by understanding His name as the creator because this material creation is a function of the external energy of the Supreme Lord. Thus the conception of God as the creator includes only the external feature. Similarly, when we call the Supreme Lord Brahman, we cannot have any understanding of His six opulences. In Brahman realization, the six opulences are not realized in full, nor is there recognition of eternity, bliss and knowledge. Therefore Brahman realization is also not a complete understanding of the Supreme Lord. Nor is Paramātmā realization,

realization of the Supersoul, full realization of the Supreme Personality of Godhead, for the all-pervading nature of the Supreme Lord is but a partial representation of His opulence.

Even the transcendental relationship experienced by a devotee of Nārāyaṇa in Vaikuṇṭha is incomplete because devotees in that relationship cannot realize the relationship between Kṛṣṇa and His devotees in Goloka Vṛndāvana. The devotees of Kṛṣṇa do not relish devotional service to Nārāyaṇa because devotional service to Kṛṣṇa is so attractive that Kṛṣṇa's devotees do not desire to worship any other form. Thus the *gopīs* of Vṛndāvana do not like to see Kṛṣṇa as Rukmiṇī-ramaṇa, the husband of Rukmiṇī, nor do they address Him by that name. In Vṛndāvana Kṛṣṇa is addressed as Rādhā-Kṛṣṇa—Kṛṣṇa, the property of Rādhārāṇī. Although the names Rukmiṇī-ramaṇa and Rādhā-Kṛṣṇa are on the same level in the ordinary sense, still, in the spiritual world these names indicate different understandings of various aspects of Kṛṣṇa's transcendental personality. If one equates the names Rādhā-ramaṇa or Rādhā-Kṛṣṇa with Rukmiṇī-ramaṇa, Nārāyaṇa or any other name of the Supreme Lord, he commits the fault of overlapping tastes, which is technically called *rasābhāsa*. Those who are expert, discriminating devotees do not accept such amalgamations, which are against the conclusions of pure devotional service. Less intelligent men think such discrimination is bigotry.

Although Śrī Kṛṣṇa, the Supreme Personality of Godhead, embodies all superexcellence and beauty, when He is among the damsels of Vraja, where He is known as Gopījana-vallabha, devotees feel that His superexcellence and beauty have reached the highest perfectional stage. The devotees cannot relish the beauty of the Supreme Lord more than this. In *Śrīmad-Bhāgavatam* (10.33.6) it is confirmed that although Kṛṣṇa, the son of Devakī, is the last word in superexcellence and beauty, when He is among the *gopīs* He appears even more beautiful—like a sublime jewel set among divine golden craftsmanship. Although Lord Caitanya accepted this as the highest realization of the Supreme Lord as conjugal lover, He nonetheless requested Rāmānanda Rāya to proceed further.

Upon hearing this request, Rāmānanda Rāya remarked that this was the first time he had been asked to go further than the *gopīs'* relationship with Kṛṣṇa in the matter of understanding Kṛṣṇa. Rāmānanda went on to say that although there is certainly transcendental intimacy between the damsels of Vraja and Kṛṣṇa, out of all the relationships, the relationship between Rādhārāṇī and Kṛṣṇa in conjugal love is the most perfect. No common man can understand the transcendental flavor of the transcendental love between Kṛṣṇa and the *gopīs,* what to speak of the ecstasy of transcendental love between Kṛṣṇa and Rādhārāṇī. But if one tries to follow in the footsteps of the *gopīs*, he may become situated in the highest stage of transcendental love. Thus one who wants to be elevated to this transcendental stage of perfection should follow in the footsteps of the damsels of Vraja as an assistant maidservant of the *gopīs.*

Lord Caitanya exhibited the mood of Śrīmatī Rādhārāṇī when She contacted Kṛṣṇa at Kurukṣetra after He had come from Dvārakā. Such transcendental love is not possible for any common man; therefore one should not imitate this highest perfectional stage exhibited by Caitanya Mahāprabhu. But if one desires to be in that association, he may follow in the footsteps of the *gopīs*. In the *Padma Purāṇa* it is stated that just as Rādhārāṇī is dear to Kṛṣṇa, similarly the pond known as Rādhā-kuṇḍa is also very dear to Him, and that Rādhārāṇī is dearer to Kṛṣṇa than all the other *gopīs*. In *Śrīmad-Bhāgavatam* (10.30.28) it is also stated that Rādhārāṇī and the *gopīs* render the highest perfectional loving service to the Lord and that the Lord is so pleased with them that He does not wish to leave the company of Śrīmatī Rādhārāṇī.

When Lord Caitanya heard Rāmānanda Rāya speak of the loving affairs between Kṛṣṇa and Rādhārāṇī, He said, "Please go further. Go on and on." The Lord also said that He was enjoying with great relish the descriptions of the loving affairs between Kṛṣṇa and the *gopīs*. "It is as if a river of nectar is flowing from your lips," He said. Rāmānanda Rāya continued by saying that when Kṛṣṇa danced among the *gopīs* He thought, "I am not giving any special attention to Rādhārāṇī." Because among the other *gopīs* Rādhārāṇī was not so much an object of special love, Kṛṣṇa stole Her away from the arena of the *rāsa* dance and showed Her special favor.

After explaining this to Lord Caitanya, Rāmānanda Rāya said,

"Now let us relish the transcendental loving affairs between Kṛṣṇa and Rādhā. These have no comparison in this material world." Thus Rāmānanda Rāya continued by saying that during the *rāsa* dance Rādhārāṇī suddenly left the arena, as if She were angry that no special favor was being shown Her. Kṛṣṇa was desirous of seeing Rādhārāṇī in order to fulfill the purpose of the *rāsa* dance, but not seeing Rādhārāṇī there, He became very sorrowful and went to search Her out. In the *Gīta-govinda* there is a nice verse which states that Kṛṣṇa, the enemy of Kaṁsa, wanted to be entangled in loving affairs with women and thus simply took Rādhārāṇī into His heart and left the company of the other damsels of Vraja. The next verse describes how Kṛṣṇa was very much afflicted by Rādhārāṇī's absence and, being thus distressed in mind, began to search Her out along the banks of the Yamunā. Failing to find Her, He entered the bushes of Vṛndāvana and began to lament. Rāmānanda Rāya pointed out that one who discusses the purport of these two special verses of the *Gīta-govinda* (3.1–2) can relish the highest nectar of Rādhā and Kṛṣṇa's loving affairs. Although there were many *gopīs* to dance with, Kṛṣṇa especially wanted to dance with Rādhārāṇī. In the *rāsa* dance Kṛṣṇa expanded Himself and placed Himself between every two *gopīs,* but He was especially present with Rādhārāṇī. However, Rādhārāṇī was not pleased with Kṛṣṇa's behavior. As described in the *Ujjvala-nīlamaṇi:* "The path of loving affairs is just like the movement of a snake. Among young lovers, there are two kinds of mentality—causeless and causal." Thus when Rādhārāṇī left the arena of the *rāsa* dance out of anger at not receiving special treatment, Kṛṣṇa became very sad because He could not see Her among the other *gopīs*. The perfection of the *rāsa* dance was considered complete due to Rādhārāṇī's presence, and in Her absence Kṛṣṇa considered the dance to be disrupted. Therefore He left the arena to search Her out. When He could not find Rādhārāṇī after wandering in several places, He became very distressed. Thus it is understood that Kṛṣṇa could not enjoy His pleasure potency even in the midst of all the other *gopīs,* but that in the presence of Rādhārāṇī He was satisfied.

When this transcendental love between Rādhārāṇī and Kṛṣṇa was described by Rāmānanda Rāya, Lord Caitanya said, "I came to you to understand the transcendental loving affairs between Kṛṣṇa and Rādhā, and now I am very satisfied that you have described them so nicely. I can understand from your version that the highest loving state is that between Kṛṣṇa and Rādhā." Yet Lord Caitanya still requested Rāmānanda Rāya to explain something more: "What are the transcendental features of Kṛṣṇa and Rādhārāṇī, and what are the transcendental features of the reciprocation of Their feelings, and what is the love between Them? If you kindly describe all this to Me, I will be very much obliged. Except for you, no one can describe such things."

"I do not know anything," Rāmānanda Rāya replied in all humility. "I am simply saying what You are causing me to say. I know that You are Kṛṣṇa Himself, yet still You are relishing hearing about Kṛṣṇa from me. Therefore please excuse me for my faulty expression. I am just trying to express whatever You are causing me to express."

"I am a Māyāvādī *sannyāsī,*" Lord Caitanya protested. "I have no knowledge of the transcendental features of devotional service. By the greatness of Sārvabhauma Bhaṭṭācārya My mind has become clear, and I am now trying to understand the nature of devotional service to Lord Kṛṣṇa. The Bhaṭṭācārya recommended that I see you in order to understand Kṛṣṇa. Indeed, he said that you are the only person who knows something about love of Kṛṣṇa. Therefore I have come to you upon the recommendation of Sārvabhauma Bhaṭṭācārya. Please, then, do not hesitate to relate to Me all the confidential affairs between Rādhā and Kṛṣṇa."

In this way Lord Caitanya actually took the subordinate position before Rāmānanda Rāya. This has very great significance. One who is serious about understanding the transcendental nature of Kṛṣṇa should approach a person who is actually enriched with Kṛṣṇa consciousness. One should not be proud of his material birth, material opulence, material education and material beauty and with these things try to conquer the mind of an advanced student of Kṛṣṇa consciousness. One who thus goes to a Kṛṣṇa conscious person, thinking that he would be favorably induced, is under a misconception about this science. One should approach a Kṛṣṇa conscious person with all humility, put relevant questions to him and not challenge him. If one were to challenge him, such a highly elevated Kṛṣṇa conscious person would not be available to receive any tangible service. A challenging, puffed-up person cannot gain anything from a Kṛṣṇa conscious man; he simply remains in material consciousness. Although Lord Caitanya was born in a high *brāhmaṇa* family and was situated in the highest perfectional stage of *sannyāsa,* He nonetheless showed by His behavior that even an elevated person would not hesitate to take lessons from Rāmānanda Rāya, although Rāmānanda appeared as a householder situated in a social status beneath that of a *brāhmaṇa.*

Thus Lord Caitanya clearly showed that a sincere student never cares whether his spiritual master is born in a high *brāhmaṇa* family or *kṣatriya* family, or whether he is a high-grade *sannyāsī,* a *brahmacārī* or whatever. Whoever can teach one about the science of Kṛṣṇa is to be accepted as a *guru.*

CHAPTER 31

The Supreme Perfection

Whatever position one may have, if he is fully conversant with the science of Kṛṣṇa, Kṛṣṇa consciousness, he can become a bona fide spiritual master—an initiator or a teacher of the science. In other words, one can become a bona fide spiritual master if he has sufficient knowledge of the science of Kṛṣṇa, Kṛṣṇa consciousness. Becoming such a spiritual master does not depend on a particular position in society or on birth. This is the conclusion of Lord Caitanya Mahāprabhu, and it is in accordance with the Vedic injunctions. On the strength of this conclusion, Lord Caitanya, previously known as Viśvambhara, accepted a spiritual master, Īśvara Purī, who was a *sannyāsī*. Similarly, Lord Nityānanda Prabhu and Śrī Advaita Ācārya also accepted a *sannyāsī* as their spiritual master, namely Mādhavendra Purī, who was a disciple of Lakṣmīpati Tīrtha. Similarly, another great *ācārya*, Śrī Rasikānanda, accepted Śrī Śyāmānanda as his spiritual master, although Śyāmānanda was not born in a *brāhmaṇa* family. So also did Gaṅgānārāyaṇa Cakravartī accept Narottama Dāsa Ṭhākura as his spiritual master. In ancient days there was even a hunter named Dharma who became a spiritual master for many people. There are clear instructions in the *Mahābhārata* and *Śrīmad-Bhāgavatam* (7.11.35) stating that a person should be accepted as a *brāhmaṇa, kṣatriya, vaiśya* or *śūdra* according to his personal qualifications and not his birth. For example, if a man is born in a *brāhmaṇa* family but his personal qualifications are those of a *śūdra,* he should be accepted as a *śūdra*. Similarly, if a person is born in a *śūdra* family but has the qualifications of a *brāhmaṇa,* he should be accepted as a *brāhmaṇa*. All śāstric injunctions, as well as the versions of great sages and authorities, establish that a bona fide spiritual master is not necessarily a *brāhmaṇa* by caste. The only qualification is that he be conversant with the science of Kṛṣṇa, Kṛṣṇa consciousness. That alone makes one perfectly eligible to become a spiritual master. This is the conclusion of Śrī Caitanya Mahāprabhu in His discussions with Rāmānanda Rāya.

In the *Hari-bhakti-vilāsa* it is stated that if one bona fide spiritual master is born in a *brāhmaṇa* family and another qualified spiritual master is born in a *śūdra* family, one should accept the one who is born in a *brāhmaṇa* family. This statement serves as a social compromise, but it has nothing to do with spiritual understanding. This injunction is applicable only for those who consider social status more important than spiritual status. It is not for people who are spiritually serious. A serious person would accept Caitanya Mahāprabhu's instruction that anyone conversant with the science of Kṛṣṇa must be accepted as a spiritual master, regardless of his social position. There is an injunction in the *Padma Purāṇa* which states that though a highly elevated, spiritually advanced devotee of the Lord may have been born in a family of dog-eaters, he can be a spiritual master, but that a highly elevated person born in a *brāhmaṇa* family cannot be a spiritual master unless he is a devotee of the Lord. A person born in a *brāhmaṇa* family may be conversant with all of the rituals of the Vedic scriptures, but if he is not a pure devotee he cannot be a spiritual master. In all *śāstras* the chief qualification of a bona fide spiritual master is that he be conversant with the science of Kṛṣṇa.

Lord Caitanya therefore requested Rāmānanda Rāya to go on teaching Him without hesitation, not considering Lord Caitanya's position as a *sannyāsī*. Thus Lord Caitanya urged him to continue speaking on the pastimes of Rādhā and Kṛṣṇa.

"Because You are asking me to speak of the pastimes of Rādhā and Kṛṣṇa," Rāmānanda Rāya humbly submitted, "I will obey

Your order. I will speak in whatever way You like." Thus Rāmānanda Rāya humbly submitted himself as a puppet before Lord Caitanya, the puppet master. He only wanted to dance according to the will of Caitanya Mahāprabhu. He compared his tongue to a stringed instrument, saying, "You are the player of that instrument." Thus as Lord Caitanya would play, Rāmānanda Rāya would vibrate the sound.

Rāmānanda Rāya said that Lord Kṛṣṇa is the Supreme Personality of Godhead—the source of all incarnations and the cause of all causes. There are innumerable Vaikuṇṭha planets, innumerable incarnations and expansions of the Supreme Lord, and innumerable universes also, and of all these existences the Supreme Lord Kṛṣṇa is the only source. His transcendental body is composed of eternity, bliss and knowledge, and He is known as the son of Mahārāja Nanda and the inhabitant of Goloka Vṛndāvana. He is full with six opulences—all wealth, strength, fame, beauty, knowledge and renunciation. In the *Brahma-saṁhitā* (5.1) it is confirmed that Kṛṣṇa is the Supreme Lord, the Lord of all lords, and that His transcendental body is *sac-cid-ānanda*. No one is the source of Kṛṣṇa, but Kṛṣṇa is the source of everyone. He is the supreme cause of all causes and a resident of Vṛndāvana. He is also very attractive, just like Cupid. One can worship Him by the Kāma-gāyatrī *mantra*.

In the *Brahma-saṁhitā* the transcendental land of Vṛndāvana is described as being always spiritual. That spiritual land is populated by goddesses of fortune who are known as *gopīs*. These are all beloved of Kṛṣṇa, and Kṛṣṇa is the only lover of all those *gopīs*. The trees of that land are all desire trees: you can have anything you want from any tree. The land is made of touchstone and the water is nectar. In that land all speech is song, all walking is dancing, and the constant companion is the flute. Everything is self-illuminated, just like the sun and moon in this material world. The human form of life is meant for understanding this transcendental land of Vṛndāvana, and one who is fortunate should cultivate knowledge of Vṛndāvana and its residents. In that supreme abode of Kṛṣṇa are *surabhi* cows who overflood the land with milk. Since not even a moment there is misused, there is no past, present or future. An expansion of that Vṛndāvana is present on this earth, and superior devotees worship the earthly Vṛndāvana as nondifferent from the supreme abode. No one can appreciate Vṛndāvana without being highly elevated in spiritual knowledge, Kṛṣṇa consciousness. According to ordinary experience, Vṛndāvana appears to be just like an ordinary tract of land, but in the eyes of a highly elevated devotee, it is as good as the original Vṛndāvana. A great saintly *ācārya* has sung: "When will my mind be cleared of all dirty things so I will be able to see Vṛndāvana as it is? And when will I be able to understand the literature left by the Six Gosvāmīs so that I will be able to understand the transcendental pastimes of Rādhā and Kṛṣṇa?"

The loving affairs between Kṛṣṇa and the *gopīs* in Vṛndāvana are also transcendental. Such affairs appear like the ordinary lusty affairs of this material world, but there is a gulf of difference between the moods of Vṛndāvana and those of this material world. In the material world there may be the temporary awakening of lust, but it disappears after so-called satisfaction. In the spiritual world the love between the *gopīs* and Kṛṣṇa is constantly increasing. That is the difference between the love in the transcendental world and the lust in the material world. The lust, or so-called love, arising out of this body is as temporary as the body itself, but the love arising from the eternal soul in the spiritual world is on the spiritual platform, and since the spirit soul is eternal, that love is also eternal. Therefore Kṛṣṇa is addressed as the ever green Cupid.

Lord Kṛṣṇa is worshiped by the Gāyatrī *mantra,* and the specific *mantra* by which He is worshiped is called Kāma-gāyatrī. The Vedic literature explains that that sound vibration which can elevate one from mental concoction is called Gāyatrī. The Kāma-gāyatrī *mantra* is composed of 24½ syllables thus: *klīṁ kāma-devāya vidmahe puṣpa-bāṇāya dhīmahi tan no 'naṅgaḥ pracodayāt.* This Kāma-gāyatrī is received from the spiritual master when the disciple is advanced in chanting Hare Kṛṣṇa, Hare Kṛṣṇa, Kṛṣṇa Kṛṣṇa, Hare Hare/ Hare Rāma, Hare Rāma, Rāma Rāma, Hare Hare. In other words, this Kāma-gāyatrī *mantra* and *saṁskāra,* or reformation of a perfect *brāhmaṇa,* are offered by the spiritual master when he sees that his disciple is advanced in spiritual knowledge. Even then, the Kāma-gāyatrī is not uttered under certain circumstances. In any case, the chanting of Hare Kṛṣṇa is sufficient to elevate one to the highest spiritual platform.

In the *Brahma-saṁhitā* a nice description of the sound of Kṛṣṇa's flute is given: "When Kṛṣṇa began to play on His flute, the sound vibration entered into the ear of Brahmā as the Vedic *mantra oṁ.*" This *oṁ* is composed of three letters—A, U, and M—and it describes our relationship with the Supreme Lord, our activities by which we can achieve the highest perfection of love and the actual position of love on the spiritual platform. When the sound vibration of Kṛṣṇa's flute is expressed through the mouth of Brahmā, it becomes Gāyatrī. Thus by being influenced by the sound vibration of Kṛṣṇa's flute, Brahmā, the supreme creature and first living entity of this material world, was initiated as a *brāhmaṇa*. That Brahmā was initiated as a *brāhmaṇa* by the flute of Kṛṣṇa is confirmed by Śrīla Jīva Gosvāmī. When Brahmā was enlightened by the Gāyatrī *mantra* through Kṛṣṇa's flute, he attained all Vedic knowledge. Acknowledging the benediction offered to him by Kṛṣṇa, he became the original spiritual master of all living entities.

The word *klīm* added to the Gāyatrī *mantra* is explained in the *Brahma-saṁhitā* as the transcendental seed of love of Godhead, or the seed of the Kāma-gāyatrī. The object is Kṛṣṇa, who is the ever green Cupid, and by utterance of *klīm* Kṛṣṇa is worshiped. It is also stated in the *Gopāla-tāpanī Upaniṣad* that when Kṛṣṇa is spoken of as Cupid one should not think of Him as the Cupid of this material world. As already explained, Vṛndāvana is the spiritual abode of Kṛṣṇa, and thus the word Cupid is also spiritual and transcendental when applied to Kṛṣṇa. One should not take the material Cupid and Kṛṣṇa to be on the same level. The material Cupid increases the attraction of the external flesh and body, but the spiritual Cupid increases the attraction the Supersoul exerts upon the individual soul. Actually, lust and the sex urge are there in spiritual life, but when the spirit soul is embodied in material elements, that spiritual urge is expressed through the material body and is therefore pervertedly reflected. One who actually becomes conversant with the science of Kṛṣṇa consciousness can understand that his material desire for sex is abominable whereas spiritual sex is desirable.

Spiritual sex is of two kinds: one in accordance with the constitutional position of the self, and the other in accordance with the object. When one understands the truth about this life but is not completely cleansed of material contamination, he is not factually situated in the transcendental abode, Vṛndāvana, although he may understand spiritual life. In this stage he can utter the Kāma-gāyatrī with the *kāma-bīja*. When, however, he becomes free from all bodily sex urges, he can actually attain the supreme abode of Vṛndāvana.

Rāmānanda Rāya then explained that Kṛṣṇa is attractive for both men and women, for the moving and the nonmoving—indeed, for all living entities. For this reason He is called the transcendental Cupid. Rāmānanda Rāya then quoted a verse from *Śrīmad-Bhāgavatam* (10.32.2) stating that when the Lord appeared before the damsels of Vraja smiling and playing on His flute, He appeared just like Cupid.

The different kinds of devotees of the Supreme Lord have different aptitudes and relationships with Him. Any relationship with the Lord is as good as any other because the central point is Kṛṣṇa. In this connection there is a nice verse in the *Bhakti-rasāmṛta-sindhu* (1.1.1) that states: "Kṛṣṇa is the reservoir of all pleasures, and He is always attracting the *gopīs* by the spiritual luster of His body. He especially attracts Tārakā, Pāli, Śyāmā and Lalitā. Kṛṣṇa is very dear to Rādhārāṇī, the foremost *gopī*." Like Kṛṣṇa, the *gopīs* are glorified by Kṛṣṇa's pastimes. There are different kinds of relationships with Kṛṣṇa, and anyone who is attracted to Kṛṣṇa in a particular mellow is glorious.

Kṛṣṇa is so beautiful, transcendental and attractive that He sometimes attracts even Himself. The following verse appears in the *Gīta-govinda* (1.11):

viśveṣām anurañjanena janayann ānandam indīvara-
śreṇī-śyāmala-komalair upanayann aṅgair anaṅgotsavam
svacchandaṁ vraja-sundarībhir abhitaḥ praty-aṅgam āliṅgitaḥ
śṛṅgāraḥ sakhi mūrtimān iva madhau mugdho hariḥ krīḍati

"My dear friend, just see how Kṛṣṇa is enjoying His transcendental pastimes in the spring by expanding the beauty of His personal body. His soft legs and hands, just like the most beautiful moon, are used on the bodies of the *gopīs*. When He embraces different parts of their bodies, He is so beautiful!" Kṛṣṇa is so beautiful that He attracts even Nārāyaṇa, as well as the goddess of fortune, who associates with Nārāyaṇa.

In *Śrīmad-Bhāgavatam* (10.89.58) the Bhūmā-puruṣa (Mahā-Viṣṇu) told Kṛṣṇa and Arjuna, "My dear Kṛṣṇa and Arjuna, I have taken the *brāhmaṇa's* sons just to see you." Arjuna had attempted to save some youths who had died untimely at Dvārakā, and when he failed to save them, Kṛṣṇa took him to the Bhūmā-puruṣa. When the Bhūmā-puruṣa brought forth those dead youths as living entities, He said, "Both of you appeared in order to preserve religious principles in the world and to annihilate the demons." In other words, the Bhūmā-puruṣa, being also attracted by the beauty of Kṛṣṇa, concocted this pastime just as a pretext to see Him. It is recorded in *Śrīmad-Bhāgavatam* (10.16.36) that after the serpent Kāliya was punished by Kṛṣṇa, one of Kāliya's wives told Kṛṣṇa, "Dear Lord, we cannot understand how this fallen serpent got the opportunity of being kicked by Your lotus feet when even the goddess of fortune underwent austerities for many years just to see You."

How Kṛṣṇa is attracted by His own beauty is described in the *Lalita-mādhava* (8.34). Upon seeing His own picture, Kṛṣṇa lamented, "How glorious this picture is! It is attracting Me just as it attracts Rādhārāṇī."

After giving a summary description of Kṛṣṇa's beauty, Rāmānanda Rāya began to speak of His spiritual energies, headed by Śrīmatī Rādhārāṇī. Kṛṣṇa has immense energetic expansions, of which three are predominant: the internal energy, the external energy and the marginal energy, comprising the living entities. This threefold division of energies is confirmed in the *Viṣṇu Purāṇa* (6.7.61), where it is said that Viṣṇu has one spiritual energy, which is manifested in three ways. When the spiritual energy is overwhelmed by ignorance, it is called the marginal energy. As far as the spiritual energy itself is concerned, it is exhibited in three forms because Kṛṣṇa is a combination of eternity, bliss and knowledge. As far as His bliss and peacefulness are concerned, His spiritual energy is manifested as the pleasure-giving potency. His eternity is a manifesting energy, and His knowledge is manifested as spiritual perfection. As confirmed in the *Viṣṇu Purāṇa* (1.12.69): "The pleasure potency of Kṛṣṇa gives Kṛṣṇa transcendental pleasure and bliss." Thus when Kṛṣṇa wants to enjoy pleasure, He exhibits His own spiritual potency known as *āhlādinī*.

In His spiritual form, Kṛṣṇa enjoys His spiritual energy, and that is the sum and substance of the Rādhā-Kṛṣṇa pastimes. These pastimes can be understood only by elevated devotees. One should not try to understand the Rādhā-Kṛṣṇa potencies and pastimes from the mundane platform. Generally people misunderstand these as being material.

When the pleasure potency is further condensed, it is called *mahābhāva*. Śrīmatī Rādhārāṇī, the eternal consort of Kṛṣṇa, is the personification of that *mahābhāva*. In this regard, in the *Ujjvala-nīlamaṇi* (4.3) Rūpa Gosvāmī states that there are two competitors in loving Kṛṣṇa, Rādhārāṇī and Candrāvalī. When they are compared, it appears that Rādhārāṇī is superior, for She is *mahābhāva-svarūpa*. The term *mahābhāva-svarūpa*, "the personification of *mahābhāva*," is applicable to Rādhārāṇī only, and no one else. *Mahābhāva* is full of the pleasure potency, and it is an exhibition of the highest love for Kṛṣṇa. Rādhārāṇī is therefore known throughout the world as the most beloved of Kṛṣṇa, and Her name is always associated with Kṛṣṇa as Rādhā-Kṛṣṇa.

The *Brahma-saṁhitā* (5.37) also confirms that Kṛṣṇa expands Himself by His pleasure potency in the spiritual world and that these potencies are all nondifferent from Him, the Absolute Truth. Although Kṛṣṇa is always enjoying the company of His pleasure-potency expansions, He is all-pervading. Therefore Brahmā offers his respectful obeisances to Govinda, the cause of all causes.

As Kṛṣṇa is the highest emblem of spiritual perfection, so Rādhārāṇī is the highest emblem of the spiritual pleasure potency meant for satisfying Kṛṣṇa. Kṛṣṇa is unlimited, and Rādhārāṇī is also unlimited in Her ability to satisfy Him. Kṛṣṇa is satisfied just by seeing Rādhārāṇī, but Rādhārāṇī expands Herself in such a way that Kṛṣṇa desires to enjoy Her more. Because Kṛṣṇa was unable to estimate the pleasure potency of Rādhārāṇī, He decided to accept the role of Rādhārāṇī, and that combination of Kṛṣṇa and Rādhārāṇī is Śrī Caitanya Mahāprabhu.

Rāmānanda Rāya then began to explain how Rādhārāṇī is the supreme emblem of Kṛṣṇa's pleasure potency. Rādhārāṇī expands Herself in different forms, known as Lalitā, Viśākhā and Her other confidential associates. In his *Ujjvala-nīlamaṇi,* Rūpa Gosvāmī explains that one of the characteristics of Śrīmatī Rādhārāṇī is that Her body is an evolution of transcendental pleasure. That body is decorated with flowers and fragrant aromas and is complete with transcendental love for Kṛṣṇa. Indeed, that body is the personification of His pleasure potency. Rādhārāṇī bathes Her transcendental body three times: first in the water of mercy, second in the water of youthful beauty, and third in the water of youthful luster. After She bathes three times in that way, Her body is covered with shining garments and decorated with Her personal beauty, which is compared to cosmetics. Thus Her beauty constitutes the highest artistry. Her body is also decorated with the ornaments of spiritual ecstasy—trembling, shedding of tears, perspiring, choking of the voice, cessation of all bodily functions due to transcendental pleasure, standing up of the bodily hairs, changing of bodily color, and madness.

The decorative transcendental pleasure potency manifests nine symptoms. Five of these are manifested by the expansion of Rādhārāṇī's personal beauty, which is adorned with garlands of flowers. Her patient calmness is compared to a covering of cloths which have been cleansed by camphor. Her confidential agony for Kṛṣṇa is the knot in Her hair, and the mark of *tilaka* on Her forehead is Her good fortune. Rādhārāṇī's sense of hearing is eternally fixed on Kṛṣṇa's name and fame. Chewing betel nuts makes one's lips reddish. Similarly, Rādhārāṇī's complete attachment to Kṛṣṇa has blackened the borders of Her eyes. This darkness might be compared to ointment produced by Rādhā's joking with Kṛṣṇa. Rādhārāṇī's smile is just like the taste of camphor. The garland of separation moves on Her body when She lies down on the bed of pride within the room of aroma. Her breasts are covered by the blouse of anger born of Her ecstatic affection for Kṛṣṇa. Her reputation as the best of all Kṛṣṇa's girlfriends is the stringed instrument She plays. When Kṛṣṇa stands in His youthful posture, She puts Her hand on His shoulder. Although She possesses so many transcendental qualities, She is still always engaged in the service of Kṛṣṇa.

Śrīmatī Rādhārāṇī is decorated with *sūddīpta-sāttvika* emotions, which sometimes include jubilation and sometimes pacification. All the transcendental ecstasies are manifested in the body of Śrīmatī Rādhārāṇī. *Sūddīpta-sāttvika* emotions are manifest when a lover is overwhelmed with certain feelings which he or she cannot check. Rādhārāṇī has another emotion called *kilakiñcita,* which is manifest in twenty different ways. These emotions are manifested partly due to one's body, partly due to one's mind, and partly due to habit. As far as the bodily emotions are concerned, they are manifested in posture and movement. As far as the emotions of the mind are concerned, they are manifested as beauty, luster, complexion, sweetness, talking, magnanimity and patience. As far as habitual emotions are concerned, they are manifested as pastimes, enjoyment, preparing for separation, and forgetfulness.

The *tilaka* of good fortune is on the forehead of Śrīmatī Rādhārāṇī, and She also has a locket of *prema-vaicittya. Prema-vaicittya* is manifest when a lover and beloved meet and fear separation.

Śrīmatī Rādhārāṇī is fifteen days younger than Kṛṣṇa. She always keeps Her hand on the shoulder of one of Her friends, and She always talks and thinks of pastimes with Kṛṣṇa. She always offers Kṛṣṇa a kind of intoxicant by Her sweet talks, and She is always prepared to fulfill all His desires. In other words, She supplies everything needed to meet all the demands of Śrī Kṛṣṇa, and She possesses unique and uncommon qualities for Kṛṣṇa's satisfaction.

A nice verse in the *Govinda-līlāmṛta* (11.122) states: "Who is the breeding ground of affection for Kṛṣṇa? The answer is that it is only Śrīmatī Rādhikā. Who is Kṛṣṇa's dearmost lovable object? The answer is that it is only Śrīmatī Rādhikā and no one else. Sheen in the hair, moisture in the eyes, firmness in the breasts—all these qualities are present in Śrīmatī Rādhikā. Therefore only Śrīmatī Rādhikā is able to fulfill all the desires of Kṛṣṇa. No one else can do so."

Satyabhāmā is a competitor of Śrīmatī Rādhārāṇī's, but she always desires to come to the standard of Śrīmatī Rādhārāṇī. Rādhārāṇī is so expert in all affairs that all the damsels of Vraja come to learn arts from Her. She is so extraordinarily beautiful that even the goddess of fortune and Pārvatī, the wife of Lord Śiva, desire elevation to Her standard of beauty. Arundhatī, who is known as the most chaste lady in the universe, desires to learn the standard of chastity from Śrīmatī Rādhārāṇī. Since even Lord Kṛṣṇa cannot estimate Rādhārāṇī's highly transcendental qualities, it is not possible for an ordinary man to estimate them.

After hearing Rāmānanda Rāya speak of the qualities of Śrīmatī Rādhārāṇī and Kṛṣṇa, Lord Caitanya desired to hear from him about the reciprocal exchange of love between Them. Rāmānanda Rāya described Kṛṣṇa as *dhīra-lalita,* a word indicating a person who is very cunning and youthful, who is always expert in joking, who is without anxiety, and who is always subservient to his girlfriend. Kṛṣṇa is always engaged in loving affairs with Rādhārāṇī, and He takes to the bushes of Vṛndāvana to enjoy His lusty activities with Her. Thus He successfully carries out His lusty instincts. In the *Bhakti-rasāmṛta-sindhu* it is stated: "By His impudent and daring talks about sex indulgence, Kṛṣṇa obliged Śrīmatī Rādhārāṇī to close Her eyes, and taking advantage of this, Kṛṣṇa painted many pictures on Her breasts. These pictures served as subject matter for Rādhārāṇī's friends to joke about. Kṛṣṇa was always engaged in such lusty activities, and thus He made His youthful life successful."

Upon hearing of these transcendental activities, Lord Caitanya said, "My dear Rāmānanda, what you have explained regarding the transcendental pastimes of Śrī Rādhā and Kṛṣṇa is perfectly correct, yet there is something more I would like to hear from you."

"It is very difficult for me to express anything beyond this," Rāmānanda Rāya replied. "I can only say that there is an emotional activity called *prema-vilāsa-vivarta,* which I may try to explain. But I do not know whether You will be happy to hear of it." In *prema-vilāsa* there are two kinds of emotional activities—meeting and separation. This transcendental separation is so acute that it is actually more ecstatic than meeting. Rāmānanda Rāya was expert in understanding these highly elevated dealings between Rādhā and Kṛṣṇa, and in this regard he had composed a nice song, which he narrated to the Lord. The purport of the song is that the lover and the beloved, before meeting, generate a kind of emotion by the exchange of their transcendental activities. That emotion is called *rāga*, or attraction. Śrīmatī Rādhārāṇī noted that "this attraction and affection between Us has risen to the highest extent," but the cause of this attraction is Rādhārāṇī Herself. "Whatever the cause may be," Rādhārāṇī said, "that affection between You and Me has mixed Us in oneness. Now that it is the time of separation, I cannot see the history of the evolution of this love. There was no cause or mediator in Our love save Our meeting itself and the exchange of feelings through Our glances."

This exchange of feelings between Kṛṣṇa and Rādhārāṇī is very difficult to understand unless one is elevated to the platform of pure goodness. Such transcendental reciprocation is not possible to understand even from the platform of material goodness. One has to transcend even material goodness in order to understand. This is because the exchange of feelings between Rādhā and Kṛṣṇa is not a subject matter of this material world. Even the greatest mental speculators cannot understand this, directly or indirectly. Material activities are manifested for either the gross body or the subtle mind, but this exchange of feelings between Rādhā and Kṛṣṇa is beyond such manifestations and beyond intellectual mental speculation. It can be understood only with purified senses freed from all the designations of the material world.

Those who have purified senses can understand these transcendental features and exchanges, but those who are impersonalists and who have no knowledge of spiritual senses can only discriminate within the scope of the material senses and thus cannot understand spiritual exchanges or spiritual-sensual activities. Those who are elevated by virtue of experimental knowledge can only satisfy their blunt material senses, either by gross bodily activities or by mental speculation. Everything generated from the body or the mind is always imperfect and perishable, but transcendental spiritual activities are always bright and wonderful. Pure love on the transcendental platform is the paragon of purity because it is devoid of material affection and is completely spiritual. Affection for matter is perishable, as indicated by the inebriety of sex in the material world. But there is no such inebriety in the spiritual world. Hindrances on the path of sense satisfaction cause material distress, but one cannot compare that with the spiritual distress of separation from Kṛṣṇa. In such spiritual separation there is neither inebriety nor ineffectiveness, as one finds with material separation.

Lord Caitanya said that this is the highest position of transcendental loving reciprocation, and He told Rāmānanda Rāya, "By your grace only have I been able to understand such a high transcendental position. Such a position cannot be attained without the performance of transcendental activities. So will you kindly explain to Me how I can raise Myself to this platform?"

"It is similarly difficult for me to make You understand," Rāmānanda replied. "As far as I am concerned, I can only speak what You wish me to, for no one can escape Your supreme will. Indeed, there is no one in the world who can surpass Your supreme will, and although I appear to be speaking, I am actually not the speaker. You are. Therefore You are both the speaker and the audience. Thus let me speak only as You will me to speak about the activities required to attain this highest transcendental position."

Rāmānanda Rāya then began his explanation, saying that the transcendental activities of Rādhā and Kṛṣṇa are very confidential. These activities cannot be understood by one who has an emotional relationship with the Supreme Lord as servant to master, friend to friend, or parent to son. This confidential subject matter can be understood only in the association of the damsels of Vraja, for these confidential activities have arisen from the feelings and emotions of those damsels. Without the association of the damsels of Vraja, one cannot nourish or cherish such a transcendental understanding. In other words, because these confidential pastimes of Rādhā and Kṛṣṇa have expanded through the mercy of the damsels of Vraja, without their mercy one cannot understand them. One has to follow in the footsteps of the damsels of Vraja in order to understand.

When one is actually situated in that understanding, he becomes eligible to enter into the confidential pastimes of Rādhā and Kṛṣṇa. For one who wants to understand these confidential pastimes, there is no alternative to following in the footsteps of the damsels of Vraja. This is confirmed in the *Govinda-līlāmṛta* (10.17): "Although manifest, happy, expanded and unlimited, the emotional exchanges between Rādhā and Kṛṣṇa can be understood only by the damsels of Vraja or their followers. Just as no one can understand the expansion of the spiritual energy of the Supreme Lord without His causeless mercy, no one can understand the transcendental sex life between Rādhā and Kṛṣṇa without following in the footsteps of the damsels of Vraja."

The associates of Rādhārāṇī include Her personal associates, called *sakhīs,* and Her near assistants, called *mañjarīs.* It is very difficult to express the dealings of Rādhārāṇī's associates with Kṛṣṇa because they have no desire to mix with Him or enjoy with Him personally. Rather, they are always ready to help Rādhārāṇī associate with Kṛṣṇa. Their affection for Kṛṣṇa and Rādhārāṇī is so pure that they are simply satisfied when Rādhā and Kṛṣṇa are together. Indeed, their transcendental pleasure is in seeing Rādhā and Kṛṣṇa united. The actual form of Rādhārāṇī is just like a creeper embracing the tree of Kṛṣṇa, and the damsels of Vraja, the associates of Rādhārāṇī, are just like the leaves and flowers of that creeper. When a creeper embraces a tree, the leaves and flowers of the creeper automatically embrace it. The *Govinda-līlāmṛta* (10.16) describes the pleasure of Rādhārāṇī's associates as follows: "Rādhārāṇī, the expansion of the pleasure potency of Kṛṣṇa, is compared to a creeper, and Her associates, the damsels of Vraja, are compared to the flowers and leaves of that creeper. When Rādhārāṇī and Kṛṣṇa enjoy Themselves, the damsels of Vraja relish the pleasure more than Rādhārāṇī Herself."

Although the associates of Rādhārāṇī do not expect any personal attention from Kṛṣṇa, Rādhārāṇī is so pleased with them that She arranges individual meetings between Kṛṣṇa and the damsels of Vraja. Indeed, Rādhārāṇī tries to unite Her associates with Kṛṣṇa by many transcendental maneuvers, and She takes more pleasure in these meetings than in Her own meetings with Him. When Kṛṣṇa sees that both Rādhārāṇī and Her associates are pleased by His association, He becomes more satisfied. Such loving reciprocation has nothing to do with material lust, although it resembles the material union between man and woman. Because of that similarity, such reciprocation is sometimes called, in transcendental language, transcendental lust, as confirmed in the *Gautamīya-tantra.* Lust means attachment to one's personal sense gratification. But as far as Rādhārāṇī and Her associates are concerned, they have no desire for personal sense gratification. They only want to satisfy Kṛṣṇa. This is confirmed in *Śrīmad-Bhāgavatam* (10.31.19), in a verse spoken by the *gopīs* among themselves:

yat te sujāta-caraṇāmburuhaṁ staneṣu
bhītāḥ śanaiḥ priya dadhīmahi karkaśeṣu
tenāṭavīm aṭasi tad vyathate na kiṁ svit
kūrpādibhir bhramati dhīr bhavad-āyuṣāṁ naḥ

"My dear friend Kṛṣṇa, You are now roaming in the forest with Your bare feet, which You sometimes keep on our breasts. When Your feet are on our breasts, we think that our breasts are too hard for Your soft feet. Now You are wandering in the forest and walking over rough stones, and we do not know how You are feeling. Since You are our life and soul, the displeasure You are undergoing in traveling over the rough stones is giving us great distress."

Such feelings expressed by the damsels of Vraja constitute the highest Kṛṣṇa conscious emotions. Anyone who actually becomes captivated by Kṛṣṇa consciousness approaches this level of the *gopīs*. There are sixty-four categories of regulated devotional service, the performance of which helps one rise to the *gopīs'* stage of unconditional devotion. Affection for Kṛṣṇa on the level of the *gopīs* is called *rāgātmikā,* spontaneous love. When one enters into a spontaneous loving affair with Kṛṣṇa, there is no need to follow the Vedic rules and regulations.

There are various kinds of personal devotees of Lord Kṛṣṇa in the transcendental abode. For example, there are servants of Kṛṣṇa, like Raktaka and Patraka, and friends of Kṛṣṇa, like Śrīdāmā and Subala. There are also Kṛṣṇa's parents, Nanda and Yaśodā. All these personal devotees are engaged in His service according to their respective transcendental emotions. One who desires to enter into the supreme abode of Kṛṣṇa can take shelter of one of such transcendental servitors. Then, through the execution of loving service one can ultimately attain transcendental affection for Kṛṣṇa, the highest goal. In other words, the devotee in this material world who executes loving service in pursuance of the activities of the eternal associates of Kṛṣṇa attains the same post when he is perfected.

The sages known as the *śrutis,* the personified *Upaniṣads,* also desired the post of the *gopīs,* and they also followed in the footsteps of the *gopīs* in order to attain that highest goal of life. This is confirmed in *Śrīmad-Bhāgavatam* (10.87.23), where it is said that in general sages control their mind and senses by practicing *prāṇāyāma* (control of the breathing process) and mystic *yoga.* Thus they try to merge into the Supreme Brahman. But this same goal is attained by atheists, who deny the existence of God, if they are killed by an incarnation of the Supreme Personality of Godhead. They also merge into the Brahman existence of the Supreme Lord. But the damsels of Vṛndāvana worship Śrī Kṛṣṇa, having been bitten by Him just as a person is bitten by a snake, for Kṛṣṇa's body is compared with the body of a snake. A snake's body is never straight; it is always curved. Similarly, Kṛṣṇa often stands in a three-curved posture, and He has bitten the *gopīs* with transcendental love. The *gopīs* are certainly better situated than all mystic *yogīs* and others who desire to merge into the Supreme Brahman. Therefore the sages known as the *śrutis* followed in the footsteps of the damsels of Vraja in order to attain a similar position. One cannot attain that position simply by following the regulative principles. Rather, one must seriously follow the principles of the *gopīs.* This is confirmed in *Śrīmad-Bhāgavatam* (10.9.21), wherein it is stated that Lord Śrī Kṛṣṇa, the son of Śrīmatī Yaśodā, is not easily available to those following the principles of mental speculation but is very easily available to all kinds of living beings who follow the path of spontaneous devotional service.

There are many pseudo-devotees, claiming to belong to Lord Caitanya Mahāprabhu's sect, who artificially dress themselves as the damsels of Vraja. This is not approved by advanced spiritualists, or advanced students of devotional service. Such people dress the outward material body because they foolishly confuse the body with the soul. They are mistaken when they think that the spiritual bodies of Kṛṣṇa, Rādhārāṇī and Their associates, the damsels of Vraja, are composed of material nature. One should know perfectly well that all such manifestations are expansions of the eternal bliss and knowledge in the transcendental world. They have nothing to do with these material bodies; thus the bodies, dresses, decorations and activities of the damsels of Vṛndāvana do not belong to this material cosmic manifestation. The damsels of Vṛndāvana are not a subject for the attraction of those in the material world; they are the transcendental attractions for the all-attractive Kṛṣṇa. Because the Lord is all-attractive, He is called Kṛṣṇa, but the damsels of Vṛndāvana are attractive even to Kṛṣṇa. Therefore they are not of this material world.

If one wrongly thinks that the material body is as perfect as the spiritual body and thus begins to worship Kṛṣṇa by imitating the damsels of Vṛndāvana, he becomes infested with Māyāvāda (impersonal) philosophy. The impersonalists recommend a process of *ahaṅgrahopāsanā,* by which one worships his own body as the Supreme. Thinking in this way, such pseudo-transcendentalists dress themselves as the damsels of Vraja. Such activities are not acceptable in devotional service. Śrīla Jīva Gosvāmī, the most authoritative *ācārya* in the Gauḍīya-sampradāya, has condemned these imitators. The process of transcendental realization is to follow in the footsteps of the associates of the Supreme Lord; therefore to think oneself a direct associate of the Supreme Lord is condemned. According to authorized Vaiṣṇava principles, one should follow a particular devotee and not think of himself as Kṛṣṇa's associate.

In this way Rāmānanda Rāya explained that one should accept the mood of the damsels of Vraja. In the *Caitanya-caritāmṛta* it is clearly said that one should accept the emotional activities of the associates of Kṛṣṇa, not imitate their dress. One should also always meditate upon the dealings between Rādhā and Kṛṣṇa in the transcendental world. One should think of Rādhā and Kṛṣṇa twenty-four hours a day and engage in Their service within one's mind, not externally change one's dress. By adopting the mood of the associates and friends of Rādhārāṇī and following in their footsteps, one can ultimately achieve the perfectional stage of being transferred to Goloka Vṛndāvana, the transcendental abode of Kṛṣṇa.

By adopting this emotional mood of following in the footsteps of the *gopīs,* one attains his *siddha-deha.* This word indicates the pure spiritual body, which is beyond the senses, mind and intelligence. The *siddha-deha* is the purified soul who is just suitable to serve the Supreme Lord. No one can serve the Supreme Lord as His associate without being situated in his perfectly pure spiritual identity. That identity is completely free from all material contamination. As stated in the *Bhagavad-gītā*, a materially contaminated person transmigrates to another material body by material consciousness. At the time of death he thinks materially and is therefore transferred to another material body. Similarly, one who at the time of death is situated in his pure spiritual identity thinks of the spiritual loving service rendered to the Supreme Lord and is transferred to the spiritual kingdom, to enter into the association of Kṛṣṇa. In other words, the qualification for being transferred to the spiritual kingdom at the time of death is to think, in one's spiritual identity, of Kṛṣṇa and His associates. No one can contemplate the activities of the spiritual kingdom without being situated in his pure, spiritual identity (*siddha-deha*). Thus Rāmānanda Rāya said that without attaining one's *siddha-deha* one can neither become an associate of the damsels of Vraja nor render service directly to the Personality of Godhead, Kṛṣṇa, and His eternal consort, Rādhārāṇī. In this regard, Rāmānanda quoted a nice verse from *Śrīmad-Bhāgavatam* (10.47.60):

nāyaṁ śriyo 'ṅga u nitānta-rateḥ prasādaḥ
svar-yoṣitāṁ nalina-gandha-rucāṁ kuto 'nyāḥ
rāsotsave 'sya bhuja-daṇḍa-gṛhīta-kaṇṭha-
labdhāśiṣāṁ ya udagād vraja-vallabhīnām

"Neither the goddess of fortune, Lakṣmī, nor the damsels of the heavenly kingdom can attain the facilities of the damsels of Vraja-bhūmi—and what to speak of others?"

Lord Caitanya was very satisfied to hear these statements from Rāmānanda Rāya, and He embraced him. Then both of them began to cry in the ecstasy of transcendental realization. Thus the Lord and Rāmānanda Rāya discussed the transcendental pastimes of Rādhā and Kṛṣṇa throughout the night, and in the morning they separated. Rāmānanda left to go to his place, and the Lord went to take His bath.

At the time of separation, Rāmānanda fell at the feet of Lord Caitanya and prayed, "My dear Lord, You have come just to deliver me from this mire of nescience. Therefore I request that You remain here for at least ten days to purify my mind of material contamination. There is no one else who can deliver such transcendental love of God."

The Lord replied, "I have come to you to purify Myself by hearing from you the transcendental pastimes of Rādhā and Kṛṣṇa. I am so fortunate, for you are the only teacher of such transcendental pastimes. I can find no one else in the world who has realized the transcendental loving reciprocation between Rādhā and Kṛṣṇa. You are asking Me to stay here for ten days, but I wish to remain with you for the rest of My life. Please come to Jagannātha Purī, My headquarters, and we will remain together for the rest of our lives. Thus I can pass My remaining days in understanding Kṛṣṇa and Rādhā by your association."

CHAPTER 32

Conclusion

The next day Śrīman Rāmānanda Rāya again came to see the Lord in the evening, and there were further discourses on transcendental subject matter.

"What is the highest standard of education?" Lord Caitanya began His inquiry, and Rāmānanda Rāya immediately replied that the highest standard of education is knowledge of the science of Kṛṣṇa. The standard of material education is sense gratification, but the highest standard of spiritual education is knowledge of the science of Kṛṣṇa. *Śrīmad-Bhāgavatam* (4.29.49) states: "That work which pleases the Supreme Personality of Godhead is the highest work, and that science or knowledge which places one in full Kṛṣṇa consciousness is the highest knowledge." Similarly, Prahlāda Mahārāja, while instructing his childhood friends at school, stated that hearing of the Lord, chanting about Him, remembering Him, worshiping Him, praying to Him, serving Him, making friends with Him and offering everything to Him constitute the highest spiritual knowledge.

Then Lord Caitanya asked Rāmānanda Rāya, "What is the greatest reputation one can have?" Rāmānanda immediately replied that a person reputed to be Kṛṣṇa conscious should be considered the most famous man in the world. One who is famous as a Kṛṣṇa conscious man has eternal fame. In the material world, everyone is striving for three things: he wants his name to be perpetuated, he wants his fame to be broadcast all over the world, and he wants some profit from his material activities. But no one knows that all this material name, fame and profit belong to the temporary material body and that as soon as the body is finished, all name, fame and profit are finished also. It is only due to ignorance that everyone is striving after the name, fame and profit connected with the body. But actually it is deplorable to become famous on the basis of the body or to become known as a man of spiritually developed consciousness without knowing the supreme spirit, Viṣṇu. Real fame belongs to one who attains Kṛṣṇa consciousness in this very life.

According to *Śrīmad-Bhāgavatam* (6.3.20–21), there are twelve authorities, and they are all famous because they are all great devotees of the Lord. These authorities are Brahmā, Nārada, Lord Śiva, Manu, Kapila, Prahlāda, Janaka, Bhīṣma, Śukadeva Gosvāmī, Bali, Yamarāja and the Kumāras. These personalities are still remembered because they are all great stalwart devotees of the Lord. In the *Garuḍa Purāṇa* it is said that in the Age of Kali it is very rare to find a famous devotee of the Supreme Lord, a position better than that of such demigods as Brahmā or Lord Śiva. Concerning talks between Nārada and Puṇḍarīka, Yudhiṣṭhira said, "He is most famous and can deliver all others who, after many, many births, comes to understand that he is the servant of Vāsudeva." Similarly, in the *Bhagavad-gītā* (7.19) Kṛṣṇa tells Arjuna:

bahūnāṁ janmanām ante jñānavān māṁ prapadyate
vāsudevaḥ sarvam iti sa mahātmā su-durlabhaḥ

"After many births and deaths, he who is actually in knowledge surrenders unto Me, knowing Me to be the cause of all causes and all that is. Such a great soul is very rare." In the *Ādi Purāṇa* it is said that liberation and transcendental life follow all the devotees of God. In the *Bṛhan-nāradīya Purāṇa* it is stated that even personalities like Brahmā and the other demigods do not know the value of a devotee of the Supreme Personality of Godhead. The *Garuḍa Purāṇa* points out that out of many thousands of *brāhmaṇas* the one who is expert in performing sacrifices is famous, out of thousands of such expert *brāhmaṇas* the one who is expert in the knowledge of the *Vedānta-sūtra* is more famous, and out of many, many thousands of such Vedāntists the one who is a devotee of Lord Viṣṇu is most famous. There are many devotees of Viṣṇu, and out of them, he who is unflinching in his devotion is most famous and is eligible to enter into the kingdom of God. In *Śrīmad-Bhāgavatam* (3.13.4) it is also stated that there are many famous students of the *Vedas,* but that one who is always thinking of the Supreme Personality of Godhead within his heart is the best student of all. In the *Nārāyaṇa-vyūha-stava* prayers it is said that if the great Brahmā is not a devotee of the Lord he is most insignificant, whereas if a microbe is a devotee of the Lord he is most famous.

Lord Caitanya next asked Rāmānanda Rāya, "Who possesses the most valuable thing in the world?" Rāmānanda Rāya replied that he who has love for Rādhā-Kṛṣṇa possesses the most valuable jewel and the greatest riches. One who is addicted to material sense gratification or material wealth is not really wealthy. When one comes to the spiritual platform of Kṛṣṇa consciousness, he can understand that there are no riches more valuable than love of Rādhā-Kṛṣṇa. It is recorded in *Śrīmad-Bhāgavatam* that Mahārāja Dhruva sought out the Supreme Lord because he wanted to get some land, but that when he finally saw Kṛṣṇa he said, "I am so pleased, I don't want anything." In the *Bhagavad-gītā* it is also stated that if one takes shelter of the Supreme Personality of Godhead, or in other words is elevated to the supreme state of love of Godhead, he has nothing more to aspire to. Although such devotees can attain whatever they desire from the Lord, they do not ask anything from Him.

When Lord Caitanya asked Rāmānanda Rāya what is the most painful experience in human society, Rāmānanda Rāya replied that separation from a pure devotee is the most painful experience. In other words, when there is no devotee of the Lord present, there is great suffering in society, and association with other people becomes painful. In *Śrīmad-Bhāgavatam* (3.30.6–7) it is stated that if one who is bereft of the association of a pure devotee tries to become happy through society, friendship and love devoid of Kṛṣṇa consciousness, he is to be considered in the most distressed condition. In the *Bṛhad-bhāgavatāmṛta* (1.5.54) it is stated that the association of a pure devotee is more desirable than life itself and that in separation from him one cannot pass even a second happily.

Lord Caitanya then asked Rāmānanda Rāya, "Out of many so-called liberated souls, who is actually liberated?" Rāmānanda replied that one who is completely saturated with devotional love for Rādhā and Kṛṣṇa is to be considered the best of all liberated persons. Similarly, it is stated in *Śrīmad-Bhāgavatam* (6.14.5) that a devotee of Nārāyaṇa is so rare that only one can be found among millions and millions of liberated people.

"And out of all songs, what song do you think is the best?" Caitanya Mahāprabhu asked. Rāmānanda replied that any song which describes the pastimes of Rādhā and Kṛṣṇa is the best song. The conditioned soul is captivated by sex. All literary works of fiction—dramas, novels and so on—describe love between men and women. Since people are so attracted to this kind of literature, Kṛṣṇa appeared in this material world and displayed His transcendental loving affairs with the *gopīs*. There is an immense literature dealing with the loving exchanges between the *gopīs* and Kṛṣṇa, and anyone who takes shelter of this literature, or of the stories about Rādhā and Kṛṣṇa, can enjoy actual happiness. In *Śrīmad-Bhāgavatam* (10.33.36) it is said that the Lord displayed His pastimes in Vṛndāvana in order to reveal His actual life. Any intelligent person who tries to understand the pastimes of Rādhā and Kṛṣṇa is most fortunate. The songs that tell of those pastimes are the greatest songs in the world.

Lord Caitanya then inquired, "What is the most profitable thing in the world, the essence of all auspicious events?" Rāmānanda Rāya replied that there is nothing as profitable as the association of pure devotees.

"And what do you recommend a person should think of?" Lord Caitanya asked. Rāmānanda replied that one should always think of the pastimes of Kṛṣṇa. This is Kṛṣṇa consciousness. Kṛṣṇa has multiple activities, and they are described in many Vedic scriptures. One should always think of those pastimes; that is the best meditation and the highest ecstasy. In *Śrīmad-Bhāgavatam* (2.2.36) Śukadeva Gosvāmī confirms that one should always think of the Supreme Personality of Godhead. Indeed, one should not only think of Him but also hear and chant His name, fame and glories.

"And what is the best type of meditation?" Lord Caitanya inquired.

"He who always meditates on the lotus feet of Rādhā and Kṛṣṇa is the best meditator," Rāmānanda Rāya answered. This is confirmed in *Śrīmad-Bhāgavatam* (1.2.14): "It is the Supreme Personality of Godhead alone—He who is the master of all devotees—whose name one should always chant and who should always be meditated upon and worshiped regularly."

"Where should a person live, giving up all other places?" Lord Caitanya next inquired. Rāmānanda replied that one should give up all other places and live in Vṛndāvana, where Lord Kṛṣṇa had so many pastimes. In *Śrīmad-Bhāgavatam* (10.47.61) Uddhava says that it is best to live in Vṛndāvana, even as a plant or creeper. It was in Vṛndāvana that the Supreme Lord lived, and it was there that the *gopīs* worshiped Him, the ultimate goal of all Vedic knowledge.

"And what is the best subject to hear of?" Caitanya Mahāprabhu next asked.

"The pastimes of Rādhā and Kṛṣṇa," Rāmānanda replied. Actually, when the pastimes of Rādhā and Kṛṣṇa are heard from the right source, one at once attains liberation. Unfortunately, sometimes people are misguided because they do not hear these pastimes from a realized soul. It is stated in *Śrīmad-Bhāgavatam* (10.33.39) that one who hears the pastimes of Kṛṣṇa with the *gopīs* will attain the highest platform of devotional service and be freed from material lust, which overwhelms everyone's heart in the material world. In other words, the actual result of hearing the pastimes of Rādhā and Kṛṣṇa is to get rid of all material lust. One who does not become freed from material lust in this way should not indulge in hearing of the pastimes of Rādhā and Kṛṣṇa. Unless we hear from the right source, we will misinterpret the pastimes of Rādhā and Kṛṣṇa and think they are ordinary affairs between a man and a woman. In this way we shall be misguided.

"Who is the most worshipable Deity?" Caitanya Mahāprabhu next inquired. Rāmānanda Rāya immediately replied that the transcendental couple, Śrī Rādhā and Kṛṣṇa, is the ultimate object of worship. There are many worshipable objects. For example, the impersonalists worship the *brahmajyoti,* but by such worship one becomes bereft of life's symptoms and becomes just like a tree or other nonmoving living entity. Those who worship the so-called void also attain such results. Those who are after material enjoyment (*bhukti*) worship the demigods and achieve their planets and thus enjoy material happiness. Lord Caitanya next inquired about those who are after material happiness and those who are after liberation from material bondage. "Where do they ultimately go?" He asked. Rāmānanda Rāya replied that those who aspire for liberation ultimately turn into trees, and that the others attain the heavenly planets, where they enjoy material happiness.

Rāmānanda Rāya went on to say that those who have no taste for Kṛṣṇa consciousness or spiritual life are just like crows who take pleasure in eating the bitter *nimba* fruit. It is the poetic cuckoo that eats the buds of the mango tree. The unfortunate transcendentalists simply speculate on dry philosophy, whereas the transcendentalists who are in love with Rādhā and Kṛṣṇa are just like cuckoos enjoying the buds of the mango tree of love of Godhead. Thus those who are devotees of Rādhā and Kṛṣṇa are most fortunate. The bitter *nimba* fruit is not at all eatable; it is simply full of dry speculation and is fit only for crowlike philosophers. Mango buds, however, are very relishable, and those in the devotional service of Rādhā and Kṛṣṇa enjoy them.

Thus Rāmānanda Rāya and Caitanya Mahāprabhu talked for the entire night. They sometimes danced, sometimes sang and sometimes cried. After they had passed the night in this way, at dawn Rāmānanda Rāya returned to his place. The next evening he returned to see Caitanya Mahāprabhu. After discussing Kṛṣṇa for some time, Rāmānanda Rāya fell at the feet of the Lord and said, "My dear Lord, You are so kind to me that You have taught me about the science of Kṛṣṇa, the science of Rādhārāṇī, the science of Their loving affairs, the science of Their *rāsa* dance, and the science of Their pastimes. I never thought that I should be able to speak on these subject matters. You have taught me as You formerly taught the *Vedas* to Brahmā."

This is the system of receiving instructions from the Supersoul. Externally He is not to be seen, but internally He speaks to the devotee. That is confirmed in the *Bhagavad-gītā* (10.10): the Lord dictates from within to anyone who is sincerely engaged in His service, and the Lord acts in such a way that such a person can ultimately attain the supreme goal of life. When Brahmā was born, there was no one to instruct him; therefore the Supreme Lord Himself instructed Brahmā in Vedic knowledge through Brahmā's heart. In *Śrīmad-Bhāgavatam* (2.4.22) Śukadeva Gosvāmī confirms that the Gāyatrī *mantra* was first imparted within the heart of Brahmā by the Supreme Lord. Śukadeva Gosvāmī then prays to the Lord to similarly help him speak *Śrīmad-Bhāgavatam* before Mahārāja Parīkṣit.

The first verse of the First Canto of *Śrīmad-Bhāgavatam* describes the Supreme Absolute Truth as He who instructed Brahmā through the heart. In that verse Śrīla Vyāsadeva, the author of *Śrīmad-Bhāgavatam,* states: "Let me offer my respectful obeisances to Śrī Kṛṣṇa, the Supreme Personality of Godhead, who is the cause of the cosmic manifestation and its maintenance and dissolution as well. If we scrutinizingly try to understand the Supreme Truth, we can understand that He knows everything directly and indirectly. He is the only Supreme Personality, and it is He only who is fully independent. He alone instructed Brahmā as the Supersoul within. Even the greatest scholars become bewildered in trying to understand the Supreme Truth because the entire perceivable cosmic manifestation is situated within Him. This material manifestation, a by-product of fire, water, air and earth, only appears to be factual. It is in Him alone that the spiritual and material manifestations, as well as the living entities, rest. Therefore He is the Supreme Truth."

Rāmānanda Rāya continued speaking to Lord Caitanya: "First I saw You as a *sannyāsī,* and then I saw You as a cowherd boy. Now I see before You a golden doll, and due to its presence Your complexion has become golden. Yet I also see You as a dark-complexioned cowherd boy. Will You kindly explain why I am seeing You in this way? Please tell me without reservation."

"It is the nature of highly elevated devotees to see Kṛṣṇa in everything," Lord Caitanya replied. "Whenever they see anything, they do not see the form of that particular thing. They see Kṛṣṇa. This is confirmed in *Śrīmad-Bhāgavatam* [11.2.45]:

sarva-bhūteṣu yaḥ paśyed bhagavad-bhāvam ātmanaḥ
bhūtāni bhagavaty ātmany eṣa bhāgavatottamaḥ

"'One who is highly elevated in devotional service sees the Supersoul, Kṛṣṇa, who is the Soul of all individual souls.' A similar passage is found in the Tenth Canto [10.35.9], where it is stated that when Kṛṣṇa came before the creepers, plants and trees of Vṛndāvana, which were laden with flowers and fruits, because He was the Soul of their soul they all bent down in the ecstasy of love for Him and became thorny.

"Because You have the highest conception of the pastimes of Rādhā and Kṛṣṇa," Lord Caitanya concluded, "you are seeing Rādhā-Kṛṣṇa everywhere."

Rāmānanda Rāya replied, "Sir, I request that You not try to hide Yourself. I understand that You have accepted the complexion and mode of thinking of Śrīmatī Rādhārāṇī and that You are trying to understand Yourself from Her viewpoint. You have advented Yourself to take this point of view. Although You have incarnated mainly to understand Your own Self, You are at the same time distributing love of Kṛṣṇa to the world. Now You have personally come here to deliver me. I request You not to try to deceive me. It is not good for You."

Being very satisfied, Lord Caitanya smiled and showed Rāmānanda His real form as the combination of Śrī Rādhā and Kṛṣṇa—a form He had never before shown anyone else. Thus Lord Caitanya was Śrī Kṛṣṇa Himself with the external features of Śrīmatī Rādhārāṇī. His transcendental ability to become two and then to become one again was revealed to Rāmānanda Rāya. Those who are fortunate enough to understand Lord Caitanya as well as the pastimes of Rādhā and Kṛṣṇa in Vṛndāvana are able, by the mercy of Śrī Rūpa Gosvāmī, to know the real identity of Śrī Kṛṣṇa Caitanya Mahāprabhu.

Upon seeing this unique feature of Lord Caitanya, Rāmānanda Rāya fainted and fell to the floor. Lord Caitanya then touched him, and he came to his senses. Rāmānanda Rāya was surprised to see Lord Caitanya in His mendicant dress again. Lord Caitanya embraced him and pacified him and said that Rāmānanda was the only one to have seen this form. "Because you have understood the purpose of My incarnation, you are privileged to have seen this particular feature of My personality," the Lord said. "My dear Rāmānanda, I am not a different person with a fair complexion, a *gaura-puruṣa*. I am the selfsame Kṛṣṇa, the son of Mahārāja Nanda, and due to contact with the body of Śrīmatī Rādhārāṇī I have now assumed this form. Śrīmatī Rādhārāṇī does not touch anyone but Kṛṣṇa; therefore She has influenced Me with Her complexion, mind and words. In this way I am just trying to understand the transcendental flavor of Her relationship with Kṛṣṇa."

The fact is that both Kṛṣṇa and Lord Caitanya are the original Personality of Godhead. Therefore no one should try to separate Lord Caitanya from Śrī Kṛṣṇa. In His form of Śrī Kṛṣṇa, He is the supreme enjoyer, and in His form of Lord Caitanya, He is the supreme enjoyed. No one can be more superexcellently attractive than Śrī Kṛṣṇa, and no one but Śrī Kṛṣṇa can enjoy the supreme form of devotion, Śrīmatī Rādhārāṇī. All Viṣṇu forms but Śrī Kṛṣṇa lack this ability. In *Caitanya-caritāmṛta* (*Ādi-līlā* 4.82) it is said that Śrīmatī Rādhārāṇī is the only personality who can infuse Govinda with transcendental pleasure. Thus Śrīmatī Rādhārāṇī is the chief of all the damsels of Vraja who love Govinda, the Supreme Personality of Godhead, Śrī Kṛṣṇa.

"Please rest assured that I have nothing to hide from you," Lord Caitanya told Rāmānanda. "Even if I do try to hide something from you, you are such an advanced devotee that you can understand all My secrets. I request that you please keep them secret and do not disclose them to anyone. If they were revealed, everyone would consider Me a madman. The facts I have disclosed to you cannot be understood by materialistic people. Were they to hear of them, they would simply laugh at Me. But you can understand these secrets; please keep them to yourself. From a materialistic point of view, a devotee in the ecstasy of love for Kṛṣṇa is mad. Both you and I are thus just like madmen. So please don't disclose these facts to ordinary men. If you do, they will surely laugh at Me."

Lord Caitanya passed ten nights with Rāmānanda Rāya, enjoying his company by discussing the pastimes of Kṛṣṇa and Rādhā. The discussions between them were on the highest level of love for Kṛṣṇa. Some of these talks are described, but most of them could not be described. In the *Caitanya-caritāmṛta* their talks have been compared to a metallurgic examination. The metals are studied in the following sequence: first copper, then bronze, then silver, then gold and at last touchstone. The preliminary discussions between Lord Caitanya and Rāmānanda Rāya are considered to be like copper, and the higher discussions are considered to be like gold. The fifth and highest dimension of their discussions, however, is considered to be like touchstone. If one is very eager to progress higher and higher to the position of the highest metallurgist, one must begin with an inquiry into the qualities of copper, then progress to bronze, then to silver, to gold, and so on.

The next day Lord Caitanya asked Rāmānanda Rāya to allow Him to return to Jagannātha Purī. "For the rest of our lives we can remain together at Jagannātha Purī and pass our time in discussing Kṛṣṇa." Lord Caitanya then embraced Rāmānanda Rāya and sent him to his own place. In the morning the Lord prepared to start on His journey south. He had met Rāmānanda Rāya on the riverbank, near a temple of Hanumān. After visiting that temple, He left. As long as Caitanya Mahāprabhu remained at Vidyānagara, all kinds of people met Him, and by His grace everyone became a devotee of the Supreme Lord.

After Lord Caitanya's departure, Rāmānanda Rāya became overwhelmed due to his separation from the Lord, and he immediately decided to retire from service so he could meet the Lord again at Jagannātha Purī.

The discussions between Rāmānanda Rāya and Lord Caitanya deal with the most concentrated form of devotional service. By hearing these discussions one can understand the pastimes of Śrī Rādhā and Kṛṣṇa, as well as the confidential role played by Lord Caitanya. One who is fortunate enough to have faith in these discussions can enter into the transcendental association of Rādhā and Kṛṣṇa.

APPENDIXES

A Note About this Edition

Śrīla Prabhupāda completed *Teachings of Lord Caitanya* in 1967, and his Bhaktivedanta Book Trust (then known as ISKCON Press) published it in 1968. In 1974 the BBT published an extensively revised edition with Sanskrit diacritical marks and selected verses from *Śrī Caitanya-caritāmṛta,* the source book for *Teachings of Lord Caitanya.*

For the present edition, the editors compared the two previous editions (the original manuscript is lost) and restored some of the flavor of the original. In addition, they found that, perhaps owing to Śrīla Prabhupāda's heavily accented English, the uneven quality of his dictated tapes, or the difficult philosophical concepts in some passages of *Teachings of Lord Caitanya,* the original transcribers and editors had occasionally erred. These errors, constituting less than three percent of the total text, have now been corrected, so that an already perfect book has become even more perfect for its increased fidelity to Śrīla Prabhupāda's original words and intended meaning.

The Author

His Divine Grace A. C. Bhaktivedanta Swami Prabhupāda appeared in this world in 1896 in Calcutta, India. He first met his spiritual master, Śrīla Bhaktisiddhānta Sarasvatī Gosvāmī, in Calcutta in 1922. Bhaktisiddhānta Sarasvatī, a prominent religious scholar and the founder of sixty-four Gauḍīya Maṭhas (Vedic institutes), liked this educated young man and convinced him to dedicate his life to teaching Vedic knowledge. Śrīla Prabhupāda became his student and, in 1933, his formally initiated disciple.

At their first meeting, in 1922, Śrīla Bhaktisiddhānta Sarasvatī requested Śrīla Prabhupāda to broadcast Vedic knowledge in English. In the years that followed, Śrīla Prabhupāda wrote a commentary on the *Bhagavad-gītā,* assisted the Gauḍīya Maṭha in its work and, in 1944, started *Back to Godhead,* an English fortnightly magazine. Single-handedly, Śrīla Prabhupāda edited it, typed the manuscripts, checked the galley proofs and even distributed the individual copies. The magazine is now being continued by his followers.

In 1950 Śrīla Prabhupāda retired from married life, adopting the *vānaprastha* (retired) order to devote more time to his studies and writing. He traveled to the holy city of Vṛndāvana, where he lived in humble circumstances in the historic temple of Rādhā-Dāmodara. There he engaged for several years in deep study and writing. He accepted the renounced order of life (*sannyāsa*) in 1959. At Rādhā-Dāmodara, Śrīla Prabhupāda began work on his life's masterpiece: a multivolume commentated translation of the eighteen-thousand-verse *Śrīmad-Bhāgavatam* (*Bhāgavata Purāṇa*). He also wrote *Easy Journey to Other Planets.*

After publishing three volumes of the *Śrīmad-Bhāgavatam,* Śrīla Prabhupāda came to the United States, in September 1965, to fulfill the mission of his spiritual master. Subsequently, His Divine Grace wrote more than fifty volumes of authoritative commentated translations and summary studies of the philosophical and religious classics of India.

When he first arrived by freighter in New York City, Śrīla Prabhupāda was practically penniless. Only after almost a year of great difficulty did he establish the International Society for Krishna Consciousness, in July of 1966. Before he passed away on November 14, 1977, he had guided the Society and seen it grow to a worldwide confederation of more than one hundred *āśramas,* schools, temples, institutes, and farm communities.

In 1972 His Divine Grace introduced the Vedic system of primary and secondary education in the West by founding the *gurukula* school in Dallas, Texas. Since then his disciples have established similar schools throughout the United States and the rest of the world.

Śrīla Prabhupāda also inspired the construction of several large international cultural centers in India. At Śrīdhāma Māyāpur, in West Bengal, devotees are building a spiritual city centered on a magnificent temple—an ambitious project for which construction will extend over many years to come. In Vṛndāvana are the Kṛṣṇa-Balarāma Temple and International Guesthouse, *gurukula* school and Śrīla Prabhupāda Memorial and Museum. There are also major temples and cultural centers in Mumbai, New Delhi, Ahmedabad, Siliguri and Ujjain. Other centers are planned in many important locations on the Indian subcontinent.

Śrīla Prabhupāda's most significant contribution, however, is his books. Highly respected by scholars for their authority, depth and clarity, they are used as textbooks in numerous college courses. His writings have been translated into over fifty languages. The Bhaktivedanta Book Trust, established in 1972 to publish the works of His Divine Grace, has thus become the world's largest publisher of books in the field of Indian religion and philosophy.

In just twelve years, despite his advanced age, Śrīla Prabhupāda circled the globe fourteen times on lecture tours that took him to six continents. In spite of such a vigorous schedule, Śrīla Prabhupāda continued to write prolifically. His writings constitute a veritable library of Vedic philosophy, religion, literature and culture.

References

The following authentic scriptures are cited in *Teachings of Lord Caitanya*. For specific page references, consult the general index.

Ādi Purāna
Agni Purāna
Aitareya Upaniṣad
Atharva Veda
Bhagavad-gītā
Bhagavad-sandarbha
Bhakti-rasāmṛta-sindhu
Brahma-saṁhitā
Bṛhan-nāradīya Purāṇa
Caitanya-candrodaya
Caitanya-caritāmṛta
Dāna-keli-kaumudī
Cāndogya Upaniṣad
Gautamīya-tantra
Gīta-govinda
Gopāla-tāpanī Upaniṣad
Govinda-līlāmṛta
Hari-bhakti-sudhodaya
Hari-bhakti-vilāsa
Harivaṁśa
Hayaśīrṣa-pañcarātra
Īśopaniṣad
Kalisantaraṇa Upaniṣad
Kaṭha Upaniṣad
Kātyāyana-saṁhitā
Kṛṣṇa-karṇāmṛta
Kṛṣṇa-sandarbha
Laghu-bhāgavatāmṛta
Lalita-mādhava
Mahābhārata
Māṇḍūkya Upaniṣad
Mārkaṇḍeya Purāṇa
Mātsya Purāṇa
Muktika Upaniṣad
Muṇḍaka Upaniṣad
Nārada-pañcarātra
Nṛsiṁha-tāpanī
Padma Purāṇa
Pādmottara-khaṇḍa
Padyāvalī
Praśna Upaniṣad
Rāmāyaṇa
Ṛg Veda
Sāma Veda
Siddhārtha-saṁhitā
Śiva Purāṇa
Smṛti-mantras
Śrī Caitanya-candrāmṛta
Śrīmad-Bhāgavatam
Śruti-mantras
Stotraratna
Śvetāśvatara Upaniṣad
Taittirīya Upaniṣad
Ujjvala-nīlamaṇi
Vāyu Purāṇa
Vedāntra-sūtra
Viśvaprakāśa dictionary

Glossary

A

Abhidhā-vrtti—direct interpretation of the scriptures.
Abhidheya—practice of devotional service within conditioned life.
Ācārya—a spiritual master who teaches by example.
Acintya—inconceivable.
Acyuta—He who never falls down; a name of Kṛṣṇa.
Ādhibhautika—miseries inflicted by other living beings.
Ādhidaivika—natural disasters that originate with the demigods of the higher planets.
Adhirūḍha—the pure, intense conjugal love for Kṛṣṇa exhibited by the damsels of Vraja.
Ādhyātmika—miseries caused by the mind or body.
Ādi-rasa—original and pure sex psychology.
Advaita—nondual.
Ahaṁ brahmāsmi—realization that "I am not this body."
Ahaṅgrahopāsanā—the process of worshiping one's own body as the Supreme.
Akāma—the absence of material desires.
Amṛta—immortal.
Anubhāva—bodily symptoms manifested by a devotee in ecstatic love for Kṛṣṇa.
Ārurukṣu yoga—the beginning stage of mystic *yoga,* in which one practices various sitting postures and concentrates the mind.
Ārya—those who believe in advancing in spiritual life.
Ārya-samājists—a class of men who accept the original *Vedas* and reject other Vedic literatures.
Asamaurdhva—unequalled and unsurpassed.
Āśraya-tattva—the Absolute Truth, the shelter of all manifestations.
Avatāra—one who descends from the spiritual sky.
Āveśa-avatāras—living beings invested with a specific opulence of the Supreme Lord.
Āveśa-rupa—see *Śaktyāveśa-avatāra.*

Avidyā energy—the material world, where ignorance prevails.
Avyakta—unmanifested.

B

Bālya—the childhood aspect of Kṛṣṇa.
Bhakti-rasāmṛta-sindhu—a book by Rūpa Gosvāmī setting forth the science of devotional service in detail.
Bhāva—devotional ecstasy, the condition immediately preceding love of God.
Bhukti—material enjoyment.
Brahmacāri—a celibate student.
Brahmajyoti—the personal effulgence of Kṛṣṇa's body.
Brahmānda—a universe.

C

Caitanya—the living force.
Caṇḍāla—dog-eater.
Caraṇāmṛta—water that has washed the Deity.
Catur-vyūha—the original four-handed forms of Kṛṣṇa.

D

Dāmodara—(1) a name given to Kṛṣṇa when His mother bound Him with ropes. (2) the Vaiṣṇava month of October-November.
Daṇḍa—stick carried by *sannyāsis*.
Dāsya-rasa—eternal relation of servitorship with the Supreme Lord.
Dhīra—pacified stage when one is never disturbed by urges of tongue and genitals.
Dhṛti—ability to control urges of the tongue and genitals.

E

Ekādaśī—fast day occurring on eleventh day after full moon and eleventh day after new moon.

G

Gaurāṅga—Lord Caitanya, the golden one.

Goloka Vṛndāvana—Kṛṣṇa's abode in spiritual sky.
Gopīnātha—Kṛṣṇa, the beloved master of the *gopīs.*
Gopīs—cowherd girls of Vṛndāvana.
Gosvāmīs—principle disciples of Lord Caitanya.
Govinda—Vaiṣṇava month equivalent to February.
Gṛhastha—householder.
Guṇa-avatāras—incarnations who control the three modes of nature.
Guṇas—modes of nature.
Guru—spiritual master.

H

Hlādinī potency—Kṛṣṇa's pleasure potency.
Hṛṣikeśa—Vaiṣṇava month equivalent to August.
Jagad-guru—spiritual master of the whole world.
Jaṅgama—moving entities.
Jīva-śakti—living beings engaged in desires for material enjoyment.
Jñāna—the cultivation of knowledge.
Jñānīs—empiric philosophers.

K

Kalpa-vṛkṣa—wish-fulfilling trees in the spiritual world.
Kamaṇḍalu—hermit's water pot.
Karma-kāṇḍa—purely ritualistic activities.
Karma-mīmāṁsā—philosophy of accepting God to be subject to one's work.
Keśava—Vaiṣṇava month equivalent to late November.
Kīrtana—glorification of the Supreme Lord.
Kṛpā—grace.
Kṛṣṇa-bhaktas—liberated souls fully engaged in devotional service.
Kṛṣṇa-bhakti-rasa—exchange in loving reciprocation between Kṛṣṇa and His devotee.
Kṛṣṇaloka—the planet in the spiritual world where Kṛṣṇa resides.
Kṣatriyas—administrators of society.
Kṣetrajña—the living being as the knower of the field of activities.

L

Lakṣanā-vṛtti—indirect interpretation of scriptures.
Līlā-avatāras—incarnations who descend to display spiritual pastimes in the material world.

M

Mādana—meeting in conjugal love.
Madana-mohana—Kṛṣṇa, the attracter of Cupid.
Mādhava—Vaiṣṇava month equivalent to January.
Madhura-rasa—relation of conjugal love with the Supreme Lord.
Madhusūdana—Vaiṣṇava month equivalent to April.
Mahābhāva—highest perfectional stage of love of God.
Mahāraurava—hell meant for animal killers.
Mahātmā—great soul.
Mahat-tattva—the total material energy.
Mañjarīs—near assistants of Rādhārāṇī.
Manvantara-avatāras—the Manu incarnations
Mārgaśīrṣa—Vaiṣṇava month equivalent to late October and early November.
Mauṣala-līlā—last phase of Kṛṣṇa's pastimes in material world.
Māyā—forgetfulness of one's relationship with Kṛṣṇa.
Māyā-śakti—the covered energy of Absolute Truth.
Mohana—separation in conjugal love.
Mokṣa-kāma—one who seeks liberation.
Mukta—liberated soul.
Munis—great thinkers and learned scholars.

N

Nārāyaṇa—Vaiṣṇava month equivalent to December.
Nirguṇa—without material qualities; Kṛṣṇa described as.
Nirvāṇa—the end of the process of materialistic life.

P

Padmanābha—Vaiṣṇava month equivalent to September.
Parameśvara—the supreme controller, Kṛṣṇa.
Paramparā—the chain of disciplic succession beginning with Kṛṣṇa Himself.

Parā-prakṛti—superior energy.
Para-tattva—Absolute Truth.
Pariṇāma-vāda—doctrine of by-products.
Patitapāvana—Lord Caitanya, the deliverer of the most fallen conditioned souls.
Pauganḍa—Kṛṣṇa's age from the sixth to the tenth year.
Prābhava-prakāśa—the four-handed form of Kṛṣṇa.
Pradhāna—elements of the material manifestation.
Prākṛta-sahajiyā—pseudo-devotees with a mundane conception of Kṛṣṇa's pastimes.
Prasāda—food offered to Kṛṣṇa, the remnants of which are taken by devotees.
Prasthāna-traya—three divisions of knowledge in transcendental realization.
Premā—love of God without any expectation of exchange or return.
Puruṣa-avatāras—Viṣṇu expansions who create, maintain and wind up the cosmos.

R

Rāga-mārga-bhakti—devotional service in attachment to the Lord.
Rāgānuga—spontaneous love of God.
Rāgātmikā—deep attachment with deep absorption in the object of love.
Rasa—relationship between the Lord and the living beings.
Rasābhāsa—overlapping tastes in devotional service.
Rati—attachment.
Rūḍha—conjugal love exhibited by queens at Dvārakā.
Rukmiṇīramaṇa—Kṛṣṇa, the husband of Rukmiṇī.

S

Śabda—transcendental sound.
Sac-cid-ānanda-vigraha— Kṛṣṇa's form of eternity, knowledge and bliss.
Śacīnandana—Caitanya Mahāprabhu, the son of mother Śacī.

Ṣaḍbhuja—six-handed form of Lord Caitanya.
Sādhana-bhakti—occupational devotional service.
Sakhīs—personal associates of Rādhārāṇī.
Sakhya-rasa—eternal relation of friendship with the Supreme Lord.
Śaktyāveśa-avatāra—a suitable living being empowered by Kṛṣṇa to represent Him.
Śama—controlling the mind by fixing it on the Supreme Lord.
Saṁskāra—purificatory ceremonies for twice-born castes.
Sankīrtana—congregational chanting of the Lord's glories.
Sannyāsa—the renounced order of life.
Sannyāsī—person in the renounced life.
Śānta-rasa—initial stage of love of God wherein one who is liberated from material contamination appreciates the greatness of the Lord.
Sarva-kāma—one who has material desire to enjoy.
Siddha-deha—purified soul suitable to serve Kṛṣṇa.
Smṛti-prasthāna—authoritative books indicating the ultimate goal and written by liberated souls.
Śrīdhara—Vaiṣṇava month equivalent to July.
Sṛṣṭikartā—Kṛṣṇa, the creator.
Śruti-prasthāna—department of knowledge which is proved by Vedic instruction.
Sudarśana-cakra—the disc weapon of Lord Viṣṇu.
Śūdras—laborers in society.
Surabhi cows—cows in the spiritual sky who give unlimited milk.
Sūtra—a condensed work which carries meaning and import of immeasurable strength without mistake or fault.
Svarūpa-śakti—Kṛṣṇa's internal potency.
Svayaṁ-rūpa—Kṛṣṇa's personal form.

T

Tadekātma-rūpa—form most resembling Kṛṣṇa's personal form but with some differences in bodily features.
Tilaka—sacred clay used to sanctify the body of a devotee.
Titikṣā—readiness to tolerate suffering to control senses and keep mind steady.
Trivikrama—Vaiṣṇava month equivalent to May.

Tryadhīśvara—Kṛṣṇa as master of Gokula, Mathurā and Dvārakā.

U

Udbhāsvara—external features exhibited on bodies of devotees.

V

Vaibhava-prakāśa—"emotional" forms of Kṛṣṇa.
Vaibhava-vilāsa—twenty-four principal four-handed forms of Kṛṣṇa.
Vaiṣṇavāparādha—offense to pure devotee of the Lord.
Vaiṣṇavas—devotees of the Supreme Lord.
Vaiśyas—businessmen and farmers in society.
Vāmana—Vaiṣṇava month equivalent to June.
Vānaprastha—retired order of life.
Varṇāśrama-dharma—four castes and four orders of spiritual life.
Vātsalya-rasa—eternal relation of parenthood with the Supreme Lord.
Vibhāva—that which increases one's love of Kṛṣṇa.
Vibhūti—the special favor of the Supreme Lord upon a living being.
Vidhi-bhakti—devotional service with regulative principles.
Viṣṇu—Vaiṣṇava month equivalent to March.
Viṣṇu-tattva—innumerable primary expansions of Kṛṣṇa.
Viśrambha—Loving confidence in the Lord with no sense of awe and veneration.
Viśuddha-sattva-pradhāna—Māyāvādī term for collective ignorance.
Viśvambhara—one who maintains the entire universe and who leads all living entities.
Vivartavāda—doctrine of transformation.
Vrajavāsīs—inhabitants of Vṛndāvana.

Y

Yajña—sacrifice.
Yajñeśvara—Viṣṇu, Lord of sacrifices.
Yuga-avatāras—incarnations who prescribe form of spiritual realization for each millennium.

Sanskrit Pronunciation Guide

The system of transliteration used in this book conforms to a system that scholars have accepted to indicate the pronunciation of each sound in the Sanskrit language.

The short vowel **a** is pronounced like the **u** in b**u**t, long **ā** like the **a** in f**a**r. Short **i** is pronounced as in p**i**n, long **ī** as in p**i**que, short **u** as in p**u**ll, and long **ū** as in r**u**le. The vowel **ṛ** is pronounced like the **ri** in **ri**m, **e** like the **ey** in th**ey**, **o** like the **o** in g**o**, **ai** like the **ai** in **ai**sle, and **au** like the **ow** in h**ow**. The *anusvāra* (**ṁ**) is pronounced like the **n** in the French word *bo***n**, and *visarga* (**ḥ**) is pronounced as a final **h** sound. At the end of a couplet, **aḥ** is pronounced **aha**, and **iḥ** is pronounced **ihi**.

The guttural consonants—**k, kh, g, gh,** and **ṅ**—are pronounced from the throat in much the same manner as in English. **K** is pronounced as in **k**ite, **kh** as in Ec**kh**art, **g** as in **g**ive, **gh** as in di**g h**ard, and **ṅ** as in si**ng**.

The palatal consonants—**c, ch, j, jh,** and **ñ**—are pronounced with the tongue touching the firm ridge behind the teeth. **C** is pronounced as in **ch**air, **ch** as in staun**ch-h**eart, **j** as in **j**oy, **jh** as in he**dgeh**og, and **ñ** as in ca**ny**on.

The cerebral consonants—**ṭ, ṭh, ḍ, ḍh,** and **ṇ**—are pronounced with the tip of the tongue turned up and drawn back against the dome of the palate. **Ṭ** is pronounced as in **t**ub, **ṭh** as in ligh**t-h**eart, **ḍ** as in **d**ove, **ḍh** as in re**d-h**ot, and **ṇ** as in **n**ut. The dental consonants—**t, th, d, dh,** and **n**—are pronounced in the same manner as the cerebrals, but with the forepart of the tongue against the teeth.

The labial consonants—**p, ph, b, bh,** and **m**—are pronounced with the lips. **P** is pronounced as in **p**ine, **ph** as in u**ph**ill, **b** as in **b**ird, **bh** as in ru**b-h**ard, and **m** as in **m**other.

The semivowels—**y, r, l,** and **v**—are pronounced as in **y**es, **r**un, **l**ight, and **v**ine respectively. The sibilants—**ś, ṣ,** and **s**—are pronounced, respectively, as in the German word *s***prechen** and the English words **sh**ine and **s**un. The letter **h** is pronounced as in **h**ome.

Index

N

Q

The International Society for Krishna Consciousness

CENTERS AROUND THE WORLD

Founder-*Ācārya:* His Divine Grace A. C. Bhaktivedanta Swami Prabhupada

Partial List*

CANADA

Brampton-Mississauga, Ontario — 6 George Street South, 2nd Floor, L6Y 1P3/ Tel. (416) 648-3312/ iskconbrampton@gmail.com
Calgary, Alberta — 313 Fourth St. N.E., T2E 3S3/ Tel. (403) 265-3302/ vamanstones@shaw.ca
Edmonton, Alberta — 9353 35th Ave. NW, T6E 5R5/ Tel. (780) 439-9999/ edmonton@harekrishnatemple.com
Montreal, Quebec — 1626 Pie IX Blvd., H1V 2C5/ Tel. & fax: (514) 521-1301/ iskconmontreal@gmail.com
◆ **Ottawa, Ontario** — 212 Somerset St. E., K1N 6V4/ Tel. (613) 565-6544/ radha_damodara@yahoo.com
Regina, Saskatchewan — 1279 Retallack St., S4T 2H8/ Tel. (306) 525-0002 or -6461/ jagadishadas@yahoo.com
Scarborough, Ontario — 3500 McNicoll Avenue, Unit #3, M1V 4C7/ Tel. (416) 300 7101/ iskconscarborough@hotmail.com
◆ **Toronto, Ontario** — 243 Avenue Rd., M5R 2J6/ Tel. (416) 922-5415/ toronto@iskcon.net
Vancouver, B.C. — 5462 S.E. Marine Dr., Burnaby V5J 3G8/ Tel. (604) 433-9728/ akrura@krishna.com; Govinda's Bookstore & Cafe/ Tel. (604) 433-7100 or (888) 433-8722

RURAL COMMUNITY

Ashcroft, B.C. — Saranagati Dhama (mail: P.O. Box 99, VOK 1A0)/ Tel. (250) 457-7438/ iskconsaranagati@hotmail.com

U.S.A.

Atlanta, Georgia — 1287 South Ponce de Leon Ave. N.E., 30306/ Tel. & fax: (404) 377-8680/ admin@atlantaharekrishnas.com
Austin, Texas — 10700 Jonwood Way, 78753/ Tel. (512) 835-2121/ sda@backtohome.com
Baltimore, Maryland —200 Bloomsbury Ave., Catonsville, 21228/ Tel. (410) 744-1624/ contact@iskconbaltimore.org
Berkeley, California — 2334 Stuart Street, 94705/ Tel. (510) 540-9215/ info@iskconberkeley.net
Boise, Idaho — 1615 Martha St., 83706/ Tel. (208) 344-4274/ boise_temple@yahoo.com
Boston, Massachusetts — 72 Commonwealth Ave., 02116/ Tel. (617) 247-8611/ info@iskconboston.org
◆ **Chicago, Illinois** — 1716 W. Lunt Ave., 60626/ Tel. (773) 973-0900/ chicagoiskcon@yahoo.com
Columbus, Ohio — 379 W. Eighth Ave., 43201/ Tel. (614) 421-1661/ premvilasdas.rns@gmail.com
◆ **Dallas, Texas** — 5430 Gurley Ave., 75223/ Tel. (214) 827-6330/ info@radhakalachandji.com
◆ **Denver, Colorado** — 1400 Cherry St., 80220/ Tel. (303) 333-5461/ info@krishnadenver.com
Detroit, Michigan — 383 Lenox Ave., 48215/ Tel. (313) 824-6000/ gaurangi108@hotmail.com
Gainesville, Florida — 214 N.W. 14th St., 32603/ Tel. (352) 336-4183/ kalakantha.acbsp@pamho.net
Hartford, Connecticut — 1683 Main St., E. Hartford, 06108/ Tel. (860) 289-7252/ pyari108@gmail.com
Hillsboro, Oregon — 612 North 1st Ave., Hillsboro 97124/ Tel. (503) 567-7363/ info@iskconportland.com
◆ **Honolulu, Hawaii** — 51 Coelho Way, 96817/ Tel. (808) 595-4913/ hawaii.iskcon@gmail.com
Houston, Texas — 1320 W. 34th St., 77018/ Tel. (713) 686-4482/ management@iskconhouston.org
Kansas City, Missouri — Rupanuga Vedic College, 5201 Paseo Blvd., 64110/ Tel. (816) 924-5619/ rvc@rvc.edu
Laguna Beach, California — 285 Legion St., 92651/ Tel. (949) 494-7029/ info@lagunatemple.com
Las Vegas, Nevada — Govinda's Center of Vedic India, 7181 Dean Martin Dr., 89118/ Tel. (702) 434-8332/ info@govindascenter.com
◆ **Los Angeles, California** — 3764 Watseka Ave., 90034/ Tel. (310) 836-2676/ membership@harekrishnala.com
◆ **Miami, Florida** — 3220 Virginia St., 33133 (mail: 3109 Grand Ave., #491, Coconut Grove, FL 33133)/ Tel. (305) 461-1348/ devotionalservice@iskcon-miami.org
Mountain View, California — 1965 Latham St., 94040/ Tel. (650) 336 7993 / isvconnect@gmail.com
New Orleans, Louisiana — 2936 Esplanade Ave., 70119/ Tel. (504) 304-0032 (office) or (504) 638-1944 (temple)/ gopal211@aol.com
New York, New York — 305 Schermerhorn St., Brooklyn, 11217/ Tel. (718) 855-6714/ ramabhadra@aol.com
New York, New York — The Bhakti Center, 25 First Ave., 10003/ Tel. (920) 624-2584/ info@bhakticenter.org
Orlando, Florida — 2651 Rouse Rd., 32817/ Tel. (407) 257-3865/ info@iskconorlando.com
Philadelphia, Pennsylvania — 41 West Allens Lane, 19119/ Tel. (215) 247-4600/ info@iskconphiladelphia.com
Phoenix, Arizona — 100 S. Weber Dr., Chandler, 85226/ Tel. (480) 705-4900/ premadhatridd@gmail.com
Plainfield, New Jersey — 1020 W. 7th St., 07063/ Tel. (973) 519-3374/ harekrsna@iskconnj.com
◆ **St. Louis, Missouri** — 3926 Lindell Blvd., 63108/ Tel. (314) 535-8085 or 255-2207/ iskconstl@pamho.net
Salt Lake City, Utah — 965 E. 3370 South, 84106/ Tel. (801) 487-4005/ utahkrishnas@gmail.com
San Antonio, Texas — 103 Bernice, 78228/ Tel. (210) 570 7571/ Krishnatemplesatx@gmail.com
San Diego, California — 1030 Grand Ave., Pacific Beach, 92109/ Tel. (858) 429-9375/ krishna.sandiego@gmail.com
Seattle, Washington — 1420 228th Ave. S.E., Sammamish, 98075/ Tel. (425) 246-8436/ info@vedicculturalcenter.org
◆ **Spanish Fork, Utah** — Krishna Temple Project & KHQN Radio, 8628 S. State Road, 84660/ Tel. (801) 798-3559/ utahkrishnas@gmail.com
Tallahassee, Florida — 4601 Crawfordville Rd., 32305/ Tel. (850) 727-5785/ tallahassee.iskcon@gmail.com
Towaco, New Jersey — 100 Jacksonville Rd., 07082/ Tel. (973) 299-0970/ madhupati.jas@pamho.net
◆ **Tucson, Arizona** — 711 E. Blacklidge Dr., 85719/ Tel. (520) 792-0630/ sandaminidd@cs.com
Washington, D.C. — 10310 Oaklyn Dr., Potomac, Maryland 20854/ Tel. (301) 299-2100/ info@iskconofdc.org

RURAL COMMUNITIES

Alachua, Florida (New Raman Reti) — 17306 N.W. 112th Blvd., 32615/ Tel. (386) 462-2017/ alachuatemple@gmail.com
Carriere, Mississippi (New Talavan) — 31492 Anner Road, 39426/ Tel. (601) 213-3586/ newtalavan@gmail.com

To save space, we've skipped the codes for North America (1) and India (91).
◆ Temples with restaurants or dining
*The full list is always available at Krishna.com, where it also includes Krishna conscious gatherings.

Gurabo, Puerto Rico (New Govardhana Hill) — Carr. 181, Km. 16.3, Bo. Santa Rita, Gurabo (mail: HC-01, Box 8440, Gurabo, PR 00778)/ Tel. & fax: (787) 767-3530 or 737-1722/ manonatha@gmail.com
Hillsborough, North Carolina (New Goloka) — 1032 Dimmocks Mill Rd., 27278/ Tel. (919) 732-6492/ bkgoswami@earthlink.net
• **Moundsville, West Virginia (New Vrindaban)** — 3759 McCrearys Ridge Rd., 26041/ Tel. (304) 843-1600/ mail@newvrindaban.com
Mulberry, Tennessee (Murari-sevaka) — 532 Murari Lane, 37359 Tel. (931) 759-6888/ murari_sevaka@yahoo.com
Port Royal, Pennsylvania (Gita Nagari) — 534 Gita Nagari Rd., 17082/ Tel. (717) 527-4101/ dhruva.bts@pamho.net
Sandy Ridge, North Carolina (Prabhupada Village) — 1283 Prabhupada Rd., 27046/ Tel. (336) 593-2322/ prabhupadavillage@gmail.com

ADDITIONAL RESTAURANT

Hato Rey, Puerto Rico — Tamal Krishna's Veggie Garden, 131 Eleanor Roosevelt, 00918/ Tel. (787) 754-6959/ tkveggiegarden@aol.com

UNITED KINGDOM AND IRELAND

Belfast, Northern Ireland — Brooklands, 140 Upper Dunmurray Lane, BT17 OHE/ Tel. +44 (028) 9062 0530/ hk.temple108@gmail.com
Birmingham, England — 84 Stanmore Rd., Edgbaston B16 9TB/ Tel. +44 (121) 420 4999/ iskconbirmingham@gmail.com
Cardiff, Wales — The Soul Centre, 116 Cowbridge Rd., Canton/ Tel. +44 (29) 2039 0391/ the.soul.centre@pamho.net
Coventry, England — Kingfield Rd., Coventry (mail: 19 Gloucester St., Coventry CV1 3BZ)/ Tel. +44 (24) 7655 2822 or 5420/ haridas.kds@pamho.net
Dublin, Ireland — 83 Middle Abbey St., Dublin 1/ Tel. +353 (1) 661 5095/ dublin@krishna.ie; Govinda's: info@govindas.ie
Leicester, England — 31 Granby Street, LE1 6EP/ Tel. +44 (0) 7597 786 676/ pradyumna.jas@pamho.net
Lesmahagow, Scotland — Karuna Bhavan, Bankhouse Rd., Lesmahagow, Lanarkshire, ML11 0ES/ Tel. +44 (1555) 894790/ karunabhavan@aol.com
• **London, England (city)** — 10 Soho St., W1D 3DL/ Tel. +44 (20) 7437-3662; residential /pujaris, 7439-3606; shop, 7287-0269; Govinda's Restaurant, 7437-4928/ london@pamho.net
• **London, England (country)** — Bhaktivedanta Manor, Dharam Marg, Hilfield Lane, Watford, Herts, WD25 8EZ/ Tel. +44 (1923) 851000/ info@krishnatemple.com; (for accommodations:) bmguesthouse@krishna.com
London, England (south) — 42 Enmore Road, South Norwood, SE25 5NG/ Tel. +44 7988857530/ krishnaprema89@hotmail.com
London, England (Kings Cross) — 102 Caledonian Rd., Kings Cross, Islington, N1 9DN/ Tel. +44 (20) 7168 5732/ foodforalluk@aol.com
Manchester, England — 20 Mayfield Rd., Whalley Range, M16 8FT/ Tel. +44 (161) 226-4416/ contact@iskconmanchester.com
Newcastle-upon-Tyne, England — 304 Westgate Rd., NE4 6AR/ Tel. +44 (191) 272 1911
• **Swansea, Wales** — 8 Craddock St., SA1 3EN/ Tel. +44 (1792) 468469/ iskcon.swansea@pamho.net; restaurant: govin-das@hotmail.com

RURAL COMMUNITIES

London, England — (contact Bhaktivedanta Manor)
Upper Lough Erne, Northern Ireland — Govindadwipa Dhama, Inisrath Island, Derrylin, Co. Fermanagh, BT92 9GN/ Tel. +44 (28) 6772 1512/ iskconbirmingham@gmail.com

ADDITIONAL RESTAURANTS

Dublin, Ireland — Govinda's, 4 Aungier St., Dublin 2/ Tel. +353 (1) 475 0309/ info@govindas.ie
Dublin, Ireland — Govinda's, 83 Middle Abbey St., Dublin 1/ Tel. +353 (1) 661 5095/ info@govindas.ie
Nottingham, England — Govinda's Nottingham, 7–9 Thurland Street, NG1 3DR/ Tel. +44 115 985 9639/ govindasnottingham@gmail.com

AUSTRALASIA

AUSTRALIA

Adelaide — 25 Le Hunte St. (mail: P.O. Box 114, Kilburn, SA 5084)/ Tel. & fax: +61 (8) 8359-5120/ iskconsa@tpg.com.au
Brisbane — 32 Jennifer St., Seventeen Mile Rocks, QLD 4073 (mail: PO Box 525, Sherwood, QLD 4075)/ Tel. +61 (7) 3376 2388/ info@iskcon.org.au
Canberra — 44 Limestone Ave., Ainslie, ACT 2602 (mail: P.O. Box 1411, Canberra, ACT 2601)/ Tel. & fax: +61 (2) 6262-6208
Melbourne — 197 Danks St. (mail: P.O. Box 125), Albert Park , VIC 3206/ Tel. +61 (3) 9699-5122/ melbourne@pamho.net
Perth — 155–159 Canning Rd., Kalamunda (mail: P.O. Box 201 Kalamunda 6076)/ Tel. +61 (8) 6293-1519/ perth@pamho.net
Sydney — 180 Falcon St., North Sydney, NSW 2060 (mail: P.O. Box 459, Cammeray, NSW 2062)/ Tel. +61 (2) 9959-4558/ admin@iskcon.com.au
Sydney — Govinda's Yoga and Meditation Centre, 112 Darlinghurst Rd., Darlinghurst NSW 2010 (mail: P.O. Box 174, Kings Cross 1340)/ Tel. +61 (2) 9380-5162/ sita@govindas.com.au

RURAL COMMUNITIES

Bambra, VIC (New Nandagram) — 50 Seaches Outlet, off 1265 Winchelsea Deans Marsh Rd., Bambra VIC 3241/ Tel. +61 (3) 5288-7383
Cessnock, NSW (New Gokula) — Lewis Lane (off Mount View Rd., Millfield, near Cessnock (mail: P.O. Box 399, Cessnock, NSW 2325)/ Tel. +61 (2) 4998-1800/
Murwillumbah, NSW (New Govardhana) — Tyalgum Rd., Eungella (mail: P.O. Box 687), NSW 2484/ Tel. +61 (2) 6672-6579/ ajita@in.com.au

RESTAURANTS

Brisbane — Govinda's, 358 George St , QLD 4000/ Tel. +61 (7) 3210-0255
Brisbane — Krishna's Cafe, 1st Floor, 82 Vulture St., West End, QLD 4101/ Tel. +61 (7) 3844-2316/ brisbane@iskcon.org.au
Burleigh Heads — Govindas, 20 James St., Burleigh Heads, QLD 4220/ Tel. +61 (7) 5607-0782/ ajita@in.com.au
Maroochydore — Govinda's Vegetarian Cafe, 2/7 First Avenue, QLD 4558/ Tel. +61 (7) 5451-0299
Melbourne — Crossways, 1st Floor, 123 Swanston St., VIC 3000/ Tel. +61 (3) 9650-2939
Melbourne — Gopal's, 139 Swanston St., VIC 3000/ Tel. +61 (3) 9650-1578
Newcastle — 110 King Street, NSW 2300/ Tel. +61 (02) 4929-6900/ info@govindascafe.com.au
Perth — Govinda's Restaurant, 194 William St., Northbridge, W.A. 6003/ Tel. +61 (8) 9227-1648/ perth@pamho.net
Perth — Hare Krishna Food for Life, NSW 2300/ Tel. +61 (02) 4929-6900/ info@govindascafe.com.au

NEW ZEALAND AND FIJI

Christchurch, NZ — 83 Bealey Ave. (mail: P.O. Box 25-190)/ Tel. +64 (3) 366-5174/ iskconchch@clear.net.nz
Dunedin, NZ — 133 London Street, Dunedin 9016/ Tel. +64 (2) 749-1369/ jambavati85@hotmail.com
Hamilton, NZ — 188 Maui St., RD 8, Te Rapa/ Tel. +64 (7) 850-5108/ rmaster@wave.co.nz
Labasa, Fiji — Delailabasa (mail: P.O. Box 133)/ Tel. +679 812912
Lautoka, Fiji — 5 Tavewa Ave. (mail: P.O. Box 125)/ Tel. +679 6664112/ regprakash@excite.com
Nausori, Fiji — Hare Krishna Cultural Centre, 2nd Floor, Shop &

Save Building, 11 Gulam Nadi St., Nausori Town (mail: P.O. Box 2183, Govt. Bldgs., Suva)/ Tel. +679 9969748 or 3475097/ vdas@frca.org.fj
Rakiraki, Fiji — Rewasa (mail: P.O. Box 204)/ Tel. +679 694243
Sigatoka, Fiji — Sri Sri Radha Damodar Temple, Off Mission St., Sigatoka Town/ Tel. +679 9373703/ drgsmarna@connect.com.fj
Suva, Fiji — 166 Brewster St. (mail: P.O. Box 4299, Samabula)/ Tel. +679 3318441/ iskconsuva@connect.com.fj
Wellington, NZ — 105 Newlands Rd., Newlands/ Tel. +64 (4) 478-4108/ info@iskconwellington.org.nz
Wellington, NZ — Bhakti Lounge, 1st Floor, 175 Vivian St., Te Aro/ Tel. +64 (4) 801-5500/ yoga@bhaktilounge.org.nz/ www.bhaktilounge.org.nz

RURAL COMMUNITY

Auckland, NZ (New Varshan) — Hwy. 28, Riverhead, next to Huapai Golf Course (mail: R.D. 2, Kumeu)/ Tel. +64 (9) 412-8075/

RESTAURANT

Wellington, NZ — Higher Taste Hare Krishna Restaurant, Old Bank Arcade, Ground Flr., Corner Customhouse, Quay & Hunter St., Wellington/ Tel. +64 (4) 472-2233

EUROPE (partial list)*

Amsterdam — Van Hilligaertstraat 17, 1072 JX/ Tel. +31 (020) 675-1404 or -1694/ Fax: +31 (020) 675-1405/ amsterdam@pamho.net
Barcelona — Plaza Reial 12, Entlo 2, 08002/ Tel. +34 93 302-5194/ templobcn@hotmail.com
Bergamo, Italy — Villaggio Hare Krishna (da Medolago strada per Terno d'Isola), 24040 Chignolo d'Isola (BG)/ Tel. +39 (035) 4940706
Budapest — Lehel Street 15–17, 1039 Budapest/ Tel. +36 (01) 391-0435/ Fax: (01) 397-5219/ nai@pamho.net
Copenhagen — Skjulhoj Alle 44, 2720 Vanlose, Copenhagen/ Tel. +45 4828 6446/ Fax: +45 4828 7331/ iskcon.denmark@pamho.net
Grödinge, Sweden — Radha-Krishna Temple, Korsnäs Gård, 14792 Grödinge, Tel.+46 (08) 53029800/ Fax: +46 (08) 53025062 / bmd@pamho.net
Helsinki — Ruoholahdenkatu 24 D (III krs) 00180/ Tel. +358 (9) 694-9879 or -9837
• **Lisbon** — Rua Dona Estefânia, 91 R/C 1000 Lisboa/ Tel. & fax: +351(01) 314-0314 or 352-0038
Madrid — Espíritu Santo 19, 28004 Madrid/ Tel. +34 91 521-3096
Paris — 35 Rue Docteur Jean Vaquier, 93160 Noisy le Grand/ Tel. & fax: +33 (01) 4303-0951/ param.gati.swami@pamho.net
Prague — Jilova 290, Prague 5 - Zlicin 155 21/ Tel. +42 (02) 5795-0391/ info@harekrsna.cz
• **Radhadesh, Belgium** — Chateau de Petite Somme, 6940 Septon-Durbuy/ Tel. +32 (086) 322926 (restaurant: 321421)/ Fax: +32 (086) 322929/ radhadesh@pamho.net
• **Rome** — Govinda Centro Hare Krsna, via di Santa Maria del Pianto 16, 00186/ Tel. +39 (06) 68891540/ govinda.roma@harekrsna.it
• **Stockholm** — Fridhemsgatan 22, 11240/ Tel. +46 (08) 654-9002/ Fax: +46 (08) 650-881; Restaurant: Tel. & fax: +46 (08) 654-9004/ lokanatha@hotmail.com
Warsaw — Mysiadlo k. Warszawy, 05-500 Piaseczno, ul. Zakret 11/ Tel. +48 (022) 750-7797 or -8247/ Fax: +48 (022) 750-8249/ kryszna@post.pl
Zürich — Bergstrasse 54, 8030/ Tel. +41 (01) 262-3388/ Fax: +41 (01) 262-3114/ kgs@pamho.net

RURAL COMMUNITIES

France (La Nouvelle Mayapura) — Domaine d'Oublaisse, 36360, Lucay le Mâle/ Tel. +33 (02) 5440-2395/ Fax: +33 (02) 5440-2823/ oublaise@free.fr
Germany (Simhachalam) — Zielberg 20, 94118 Jandelsbrunn/ Tel. +49 (08583) 316/ info@simhachalam.de
Hungary (New Vraja-dhama) — Krisna-völgy, 8699 Somogyvamos, Fö u, 38/ Tel. & fax: +36 (085) 540-002 or 340-185/ info@krisnavolgy.hu
Italy (Villa Vrindavan) — Via Scopeti 108, 50026 San Casciano in Val di Pesa (FL)/ Tel. +39 (055) 820054/ Fax: +39 (055) 828470/ isvaripriya@libero.it
Spain (New Vraja Mandala) — (Santa Clara) Brihuega, Guadalajara/ Tel. +34 949 280436

ADDITIONAL RESTAURANTS

Barcelona — Restaurante Govinda, Plaza de la Villa de Madrid 4–5, 08002/ Tel. +34 (93) 318-7729
Copenhagen — Govinda's, Nørre Farimagsgade 82, DK-1364 Kbh K/ Tel. +45 3333 7444
Milan — Govinda's, Via Valpetrosa 5, 20123/ Tel. +39 (02) 862417
Oslo — Krishna's Cuisine, Kirkeveien 59B, 0364/ Tel. +47 (02) 260-6250
Zürich — Govinda Veda-Kultur, Preyergrasse 16, 8001/ Tel. & fax: +41 (01) 251-8859/ info@govinda-shop.ch

AFRICA (partial list)*

Accra, Ghana — Samsam Rd., Off Accra-Nsawam Hwy., Medie, Accra North (mail: P.O. Box 11686)/ Tel. & fax +233 (021) 229988/ srivas_bts@yahoo.co.in
Cape Town, South Africa — 17 St. Andrews Rd., Rondebosch 7700/ Tel. +27 (021) 6861179/ Fax: +27 (021) 686-8233/ cape.town@pamho.net
• **Durban, South Africa** — 50 Bhaktivedanta Swami Circle, Unit 5 (mail: P.O. Box 56003), Chatsworth, 4030/ Tel. +27 (031) 403-3328/ Fax: +27 (031) 403-4429/ iskcon.durban@pamho.net
Johannesburg, South Africa — 7971 Capricorn Ave. (entrance on Nirvana Drive East), Ext. 9, Lenasia (mail: P.O. Box 926, Lenasia 1820)/ Tel. +27 (011) 854-1975 or 7969/ iskconjh@iafrica.com
Lagos, Nigeria — 12, Gani Williams Close, off Osolo Way, Ajao Estate, International Airport Rd. (mail: P.O. Box 8793, Marina)/ Tel. +234 (01) 7744926 or 7928906/ bdds.bts@pamho.net
Mombasa, Kenya — Hare Krishna House, Sauti Ya Kenya and Kisumu Rds. (mail: P.O. Box 82224, Mombasa)/ Tel. +254 (011) 312248
Nairobi, Kenya — Muhuroni Close, off West Nagara Rd. (mail: P.O. Box 28946)/ Tel. +254 (203) 744365/ Fax: +254 (203) 740957/ iskcon_nairobi@yahoo.com
• **Phoenix, Mauritius** — Hare Krishna Land, Pont Fer (mail: P.O. Box 108, Quartre Bornes)/ Tel. +230 696-5804/ Fax: +230 696-8576/ iskcon.hkl@intnet.mu
Port Harcourt, Nigeria — Umuebule 11, 2nd tarred road, Etche (mail: P.O. Box 4429, Trans Amadi)/ Tel. +234 08033215096/ canakyaus@yahoo.com
Pretoria, South Africa — 1189 Church St., Hatfield, 0083 (mail: P.O. Box 14077, Hatfield, 0028)/ Tel. & fax: +27 (12) 342-6216/ iskconpt@global.co.za

RURAL COMMUNITY

Mauritius (ISKCON Vedic Farm) — Hare Krishna Rd., Vrindaban/ Tel. +230 418-3185 or 418-3955/ Fax: +230 418-6470

Far from a Center?
Call us at 1-800-927-4152
Or write us at
bbt.usa@krishna.com